Dixie Emporium

Dixie Emporium

Tourism, Foodways, and Consumer Culture in the American South

edited by
ANTHONY J. STANONIS

The University of Georgia Press   Athens and London

This volume is published with support from the Institute for
Southern Studies at the University of South Carolina.
© 2008 by the University of Georgia Press
Athens, Georgia 30602
www.ugapress.org
All rights reserved
Set in Sabon by Graphic Composition, Inc.

Printed digitally in the United States of America

Library of Congress Cataloging-in-Publication Data
Dixie emporium : tourism, foodways, and consumer culture
in the American South / edited by Anthony J. Stanonis.
ix, 296 p. : ill. ; 25 cm.
Includes bibliographical references and index.
ISBN-13: 978-0-8203-2951-2 (hardcover : alk. paper)
ISBN-10: 0-8203-2951-7 (hardcover : alk. paper)
ISBN-13: 978-0-8203-3169-0 (pbk. : alk. paper)
ISBN-10: 0-8203-3169-4 (pbk. : alk. paper)
1. Culture and tourism—Southern States.
2. Popular culture—Southern States.
3. Souvenirs (Keepsakes)—Southern States.
4. Southern States—Civilization.
I. Stanonis, Anthony J. (Anthony Joseph)
F209.D59 2008
306.4'8190975—dc22   2008007308

British Library Cataloging-in-Publication Data available

Contents

Part III. Consuming the South: Foodways and the Performance of Southern Culture

Illustrations

Acknowledgments

It seems appropriate to remember debts accumulated over the course of compiling an essay collection about consumerism and memory. And there are certainly many creditors to repay.

All of the contributors extend a big thanks to Tad Brown of the Watson-Brown Foundation. Working with the Institute for Southern Studies at the University of South Carolina, the foundation graciously funded a post-doctoral fellowship that allowed me time during the 2004–5 academic year not only to refine my dissertation into a book but also to organize a symposium that eventually led to the creation of this essay collection. Tad embraced our rather unconventional papers and encouraged us to put our ideas into print. Without his hospitality, generosity, and support, this collection could never have been completed. We also thank Michelle Zupan and the rest of the staff at the Watson-Brown Foundation for helping make the symposium enjoyable as well as insightful.

The contributors likewise thank Tom Brown, Walter Edgar, and Bob Ellis at the Institute for Southern Studies. Each made my all-too-brief stay at the University of South Carolina a wonderful experience. They are a credit to the university and to the field of southern studies, and their constant support for this project has kept us diligent.

I thank all the contributors for their willingness to share their work (and for their patience). I also thank Ellen Furlough at the University of Kentucky and Charles Reagan Wilson at the University of Mississippi for their thoughts on various aspects of this collection. Finally, we thank the anonymous reviewers and the staff at the University of Georgia Press who have shepherded these essays through the rigors of the publication process.

Dixie Emporium

Selling Dixies

Anthony J. Stanonis

The past is our only real possession in life. It is the one piece of property of which time cannot deprive us; it is our own in a way that nothing else in life is. —Grace King, *Memories of a Southern Woman of Letters*

We spent the night on the edge of Mississippi and in the morning followed Interstate 20 and 59 into the state of Alabama, working ourselves into the proper state of mind by turning up loud our tape recording of "Sweet Home Alabama." —Dale Peterson, *Storyville USA*

My mind preserves several childhood memories of trips to the small Louisiana town of Laplace. The road west from New Orleans on U.S. 61 cut through swamps on which urban sprawl now encroaches. The highway, paved muck dredged from the marsh, served as the main artery for traffic between New Orleans and Baton Rouge before the construction of Interstate 10 during the 1960s. Alone in the isolation of the swamp was what locals called the "snake farm." Signs along the highway beckoned tourists by promising them must-see "Jungle Killers!" Far from just a home for snakes, the farm offered passersby an eclectic gathering of insects, spiders, and other creatures, most of them contained inside a pastel-painted building constructed of cinder blocks. Outside, a labyrinth of paths guided tourists past cement ponds populated with alligators. The farm, opened in 1949 by a carny named Mac McKlung, had long since passed its heyday by the time my parents discovered the site in the late 1970s. The exterior was faded. The interior was dark and musty. Yet the so-called farm thrilled me. One of my most vivid memories involved looking down into the snake pit filled with cottonmouths and copperheads, an unsettling experience for a kid raised in suburbia. But no visit was complete without some time spent watching the lone chimp contained inside a cage of glass and concrete. Visitors could feed the animal by dropping peanuts or candy down a chute. My dad, always the prankster, gifted tablets of Pepto-Bismol. The appreciative, pink-mouthed primate thanked us just as he did other guests—by snatching the treats and then mooning all present.[1]

The snake farm of my memory provides but one example of ways by which entrepreneurial southerners packaged their region to harvest the financial rewards of an increasingly consumer- and tourism-oriented nation. As a staple attraction on the road between New Orleans and Baton Rouge, the snake farm thrived by window-dressing local wildlife and a few imported novelties. In the process, the owner created memories for tourists seeking exotic sights seemingly worth their time and money. Avenues to prosperity such as the farm, however, did not exist in a vacuum. In 1967, McKlung took his idea to Texas, where he opened a second snake farm in New Braunfels to capitalize on the HemisFair hosted by San Antonio the next year. Unsubstantiated rumors swirled that McKlung's animal kingdoms of kitsch merely fronted for his true enterprise, prostitution. The bright-colored buildings and gaudy highway signage shocked staid neighbors. Southerners thus engaged in conversations— and in many cases arguments—about the resources and imagery used to sell the region. Locals sneered at the outlandish gimmickry celebrated by both the Louisiana and Texas farms. To some neighbors, such outlandishness had to be related to outlawry and the whoring of southern culture.[2]

As the former Confederacy came to terms with defeat during the nineteenth century and as agriculture waned over the course of the twentieth, tourism and consumerism emerged as social and economic crutches as well as facilitators of positive publicity.[3] Dave Morine, an environmentalist from the National Conservancy who worked to preserve Mississippi's Pascagoula Swamp during the late 1970s, commented on the anxiety he witnessed among the state's political leaders—anxiety that made Morine's task easier. The lethal civil rights battles of the previous two decades had cast a dark shadow over the state. Morine explained, "I come from Boston, where we were always told that Mississippi was a backwards state. Backwards was a nice way of saying that Mississippi was full of ignorant redneck farmers, dissipated plantation owners, and corrupt cigar smoking politicians who spent all of their time harassing blacks and any 'foreigner' who dared set foot in the state. This image was strongly reinforced by the media and Hollywood." To counteract the negative impression, Mississippi governor Bill Waller distributed buttons bearing the phrase "Rethink Mississippi." Morine received one the first time he met Waller. Morine chuckled, "I am sure that a similar button was given to everyone the Governor met from north of Memphis." A catchy slogan and a souvenir button converted Mississippi into a nicely packaged consumer product ripe for investment, nothing new in a region still devoted to the message of famed booster Henry Grady, who used the editor's desk of the *Atlanta Constitution* during the 1880s to call for southern industrialization and agricultural diversification—in other words, the creation of a modern economy similar to that in the North. Waller's button represented a twentieth-century twist, however, on the old Gradyesque refrains. The button targeted public opinion in the same manner as state tourism departments, which disseminated thousands of maps and pamphlets showcasing the magnificence of state attractions and the friendliness of southern people. The strategy elaborated on Grady's vision of an economically diverse New South, a vision that a century earlier inspired southern urbanites to showcase their resurrected cities with touristic expositions, including ones in Atlanta (1881, 1887, and 1895), New Orleans (1884), and Nashville (1897). Furthermore, forest preservation during the late twentieth century not only fostered an image of progressivism (much as the expositions had) but also, by marking areas as pristine and therefore worthy of visitation, created profitable tourist attractions little different from manicured battlefields or neon-framed resorts. As Anthony Wilson notes in his study of southern swamps, "The wetlands have become not only national parks but theme parks—a kind of simulacral 'Natureworld' built on paradox."[4]

Tourism, foodways, consumerism, and memory are tightly interwoven—indeed, oftentimes inseparable. Frederick Skiff crisscrossed the country gathering antiques and then turned his experiences into *Adventures in Americana: Recollections of Forty Years Collecting Books, Furniture, China, Guns, and Glass* (1935). His chapter on the South provides particular insight into the ways Skiff's travels, hobby, and conception of the region intertwined. He began, "Crowded memories press forward as I recall the many delightful visits that I have made to the southern states." Skiff's journeys carried him to various estates, where he rummaged through attics in search of treasure. He also stopped at tourist meccas, such as Beauvoir, Jefferson Davis's late-life retreat on the Mississippi Gulf Coast. Trips to New Orleans included obligatory sojourns on Bourbon Street and in French Quarter antique shops. His adventures, which "radiate[d] in memory's channels," became inseparable from locations and material goods, both in terms of durables and edibles. He fondly remembered the "days of sport, fishing and hunting, or motoring on glorious drives while hunting books and antiques, or seeking waters for fishing, or marshes and uplands for shooting." Fresh quail, largemouth black bass, and sea trout came to mind, as did visits to orchards, where he and his companions "cut delicious ripe oranges and grapefruit for our own use." Southern flavors were not entirely centered on the tongue, however; like other sensual experiences, flavors were also culturally constructed. After all, travel involved enduring foreign climes, entering foreign terrains, and engaging foreign customs. And each adventure into strangeness pressed tourists to make sense of their surroundings by relating experiences to familiar cultural signposts. A visit to one Louisiana plantation stunned Skiff: "I was somewhat depressed by the barren and bleak appearance of this plantation home. Perhaps it was that I had a mental picture of some old-time houses that I had visited in Connecticut, Massachusetts or Vermont, or I may have had a vision of the old-time plantations so graphically described by Thomas Nelson Page in his writings of 'Ole Virginia.'" On a sporting trip in Florida, Skiff remembered shooting "a pair of 'possums,' that southern delicacy, of which Joel Chandler Harris has told us in his writings of the Southland." Literary references were not all that shaped Skiff's understanding of the region. When he crossed the Suwannee River in Florida, his "mind reverted to that dear, honored song with the refrain, 'Way Down Upon the Swanee River,' and [to] its author, Stephen Foster, and his ill-fated life, and [to] the monumental work he left behind him of genius and untiring industry—monuments that will live forever in the hearts of his countrymen."[5]

Sights, sounds, scents, tastes, and touches—combined with cultural templates (in this case, literary and musical)—molded Skiff's understanding of a unique "Southland," to borrow his term. Travel, sensations, and material purchases anchored memories of the region. But personal experiences could fray conceptions of a singular South. Even as Skiff spoke of visiting "every section of our country" as if regions were indivisible, he reminded readers that when set against the imagination, travel exposed regional incongruities. Skiff explained, "As one journey after another is taken through the passing years, the traveler's appreciation grows more and more profound, as he marvels at our country's greatness—the diversity of our people, the geographic range in magnitude and scenic attraction, is an education that cannot help adding to one's fuller and more profound knowledge." Memory, like region, remained an individual's construction, although shared experiences could manifest synonymous memories.[6]

What, however, is southern about the multiple Souths forged through individual experiences such as that of Frederick Skiff and artistic visions such as those popularized by Stephen Foster and Thomas Nelson Page? What imagery and characteristics grant a semblance of unity to the region? As cultural historian Helen Taylor notes, the South lacks an "authentic 'southernness.'" Although "steeped in a singular social and especially racial history" that provides a basis for a powerful "cultural memory," the region harbors southern cultures rooted in localities fertilized by a "hybrid, performative mixture" incorporating "European, African, and Protestant American" elements. Defining a singular South's geographic boundaries is therefore less fruitful than identifying spaces, services, and products that construct various Souths at different times that exaggerate, refute, or self-consciously safeguard elements of southernness. As sociologist John Shelton Reed's research on the appearance of the words *southern* and *Dixie* in phone book business listings demonstrates, perceptions and meanings of region can shift geographically over time given cultural understandings—*Dixie*, for example, has lost ground to *southern* since the 1960s because of its association with the antebellum South and antiquated ideas supportive of white supremacy.[7] The essays in this volume reveal how intertwining questions of race, religious conviction, economic transformation, and social upheaval serve vital roles in defining southern history and discourse. Each of these issues contributes to a cultural vocabulary through which southerners have debated among themselves and with outsiders the meanings that ground their society.[8]

In a region populated by people who have so long struggled with—and even obsessed about—defining themselves to themselves as well as to the rest of the nation, the role of image creation has become crucial. Even as some secessionists strove to inspire southern nationalism on the eve of the Civil War, numerous southerners, like one white Virginian in 1860, chuckled at the prospect of independence: "They don't know what they are talking about. You can not find two men in the country, who can tell where to draw the dividing line."[9] Sectional tensions invigorated efforts to strengthen regional unity just as the institution of slavery and later Jim Crow attempted to unite whites as the master class while uniting blacks through a shared subjugation. Southerners' exposure to tourists and investors, both of whom often bore preconceived notions about the region, further stimulated efforts at self-definition.[10]

The South is filled with ironies and contradictions resulting from the way the region has addressed anxieties about consumerism and the preservation (or distortion) of historical memory. As mass-produced goods and travelers unfamiliar with local customs increasingly penetrated the region beginning in the antebellum period, the South became as much an evolving set of images as an actual place. Transformed into such symbols as a stately plantation or a mammy, the South could easily be marketed, a process that accelerated with the rise of advertising agencies, consumer branding, and railroad (and subsequently automobile) travel during the late nineteenth and early twentieth centuries. By the mid-twentieth century, Mississippi writer James Street quipped, "Florida's Ponce de Leon, the South's first pitchman, used a Fountain of Youth commercial and Virginia's John Smith used a 'faire meadows and goodly Tall trees' routine, but now folks can't agree if ours is a land of moonlight or moonshine, Tobacco Road or tobacco factories, Texas Cadillacs or oxcarts, Uncle Remus or George Washington Carver, Hugo Black or Claghorn, hydrogen plants or hot air, R.F.D. or TVA, hospitality or hostility, violence or tranquility, Miami or mud, fagots or fish fries, Li'l Abner, Prince Valiant or Pogo."[11] Some southerners responded by carefully using the market to salvage their cultural identities; other southerners chose to exploit their identities—or those of others—for a quick buck. Southerners fought the resulting cultural civil war in mail-order catalogs, tourist traps, themed eateries, and store shelves. This war, however, was not about property in slaves but, as Grace King suggests, about ownership of regional identity. But claims of ownership required preservation efforts to justify and sustain possession. Nonownership, conversely, spurred attempts to contest the possessors. As columnist Paul Greenberg asks, "Is there any symbol of the South—from 'Dixie' to the Southern belle—that has not been commercialized, burlesqued, exploited, debunked?"[12]

Preservation, whether of personal memories of a journey or of physical places and cultural practices through souvenirs and tourist sites, aims to halt time, thereby keeping alive traces of the past. Moreover, preservation movements responded to a capitalist impulse to profit from rapid changes in land use and technology as well as to the emergence of leisure travel as a marker of class status. Colonel James Creecy, for example, begged readers in 1851 to rescue George Washington's Mount Vernon from investors intent on converting the estate into a hotel: "Let it be purchased at any price; make it the domain of the nation—the model farm for Americans. Let not the home of our Hero and our Father fall into the hands of unprincipled gambling speculators, who would pollute the sacred soil, desecrate his burial place, and make his residence the dwelling of vagabonds and 'money-changers.'"[13] Just as the pious undertook lengthy pilgrimages to the sacred sites of Medieval Europe, Americans in the early nineteenth century increasingly pursued communion with their supposedly God-blessed countryside and heritage.[14] By the twentieth century, the still largely agrarian (and therefore apparently backward) South emerged as a massive museum for pursuers of Americana. Many contemporary scholars claimed that the region retained authentic traces of English and African traditions.[15] In such a region during the 1920s, oil tycoon John Rockefeller planted Colonial Williamsburg, where Americans witnessed re-creations of life in early Virginia. In such a region during the 1940s, Pearce Lewis shamelessly promoted the Lewis Plantation and Turpentine Still in Brooksville, Florida, by promising tourists that his plantation contained nearly two hundred blacks who lived in much the same way as their ancestors under slavery. In such a region during the 1990s, boosters in South Carolina proposed construction of an African American community named Freewoods Farm to give travelers a glimpse of agrarian life like that endured by freedmen shortly after the Civil War.[16]

The negotiation of needs and desires, whether of locals or outsiders, created the (post)modern South, where time and space collapsed. To draw on the words of theorist Fredric Jameson, the rapidity of change in today's South—a flux facilitated by sophisticated transportation and communication networks—makes "it impossible to distinguish space from time, or object from subject." Consequently, the South not only celebrates sites that keep the past alive in the present but also (though less frequently) revels in examples of the future, whether by emphasizing space travel at Mississippi's Stennis Space Center or future lifestyles at Disney's Epcot Center in Orlando, Florida. Combining love for the past with futuristic comforts creates odd southern experiences. Italian novelist and scholar Umberto Eco comments on the "hyperreality" fostered by attractions in the United States, including the South, during the late twentieth century: "When, in the space of twenty-four hours, you go (as I did deliberately) from the fake New Orleans of Disneyland to the real one, and from the wild river of Adventureland to a trip on the Mississippi, where the captain of the paddle-wheel steamer says it is possible to see alligators on the banks of the river, and then you don't see any, you risk feeling homesick for Disneyland, where the wild animals don't have to be coaxed." Eco laments, "Disneyland tells us that technology can give us more reality than nature can." The difficulty of marketing a history-rich region thus becomes obvious. Tourists seeking contact with the past demand instant gratification of their expectations, a sentiment fostered by the current consumer market. Likewise, tourists seeking exposure to the future nevertheless want to return home again. As the South pursued tourist dollars and greater access to the consumer market, traditional mores bent to customers' desires to know quickly both history and cultures. Symbolic representations of reality, such as a souvenir gray kepi emblazoned with a Confederate flag to mark a trip to the South, are the result. To quote Eco again regarding the sites and material culture of tourism industries, "Knowledge can only be iconic, and iconism can only be absolute."[17]

By entering the tourist and consumer markets, the South certainly has openly engaged the national and even international trade in travel and goods. How else can one explain the popularity of the northern Georgia town of Helen, with its buildings modeled after those of Alpine villages? How else can one explain why the road to Helen leads past Babyland General Hospital in Cleveland, Georgia, where tourists witness "nurses" plucking Cabbage Patch Kids from a faux cabbage patch? The South has left behind sharecropper shacks and handpicked cotton. But even a postmodern South seeded with themed chain restaurants and tacky amusement parks remains tied to its location and history. Helen, redesigned after a brainstorming session by three local businessmen in 1968, thrives not just from window-dressing as a German village but also by hawking Dixie Limited T-shirts adorned with Confederate flags, celebrating the area's 1829 gold rush, and exploiting the mild climate that allows a golf course to besiege the town. A year before introducing their version of Oktoberfest (stretched from September to November to coincide with tourist pilgrimages to see Georgia's fall foliage), Helenites organized the Chattahoochee Trout Festival and Alpine Hoedown. By the 1990s, the town of three hundred residents located in the foothills of the Appalachian Mountains hosted more than three million tourists annually, including thirty thousand celebrants on peak days during the community's Oktoberfest. In contrast, the Cabbage Patch Kids toy phenomenon has roots in the handicraft style celebrated as uniquely Appalachian. The originator of Cabbage Patch Kids, Georgia native Xavier Roberts, incorporated his business as sales boomed in the late 1970s, naming it Original Appalachian Artworks. He and five friends soon thereafter converted a Progressive Era medical clinic into the doll makers' maternity ward to provide the public a first look at each doll's birth. By the 1990s, Cleveland, a town with only two traffic lights, received three hundred thousand visitors a year. Digging beneath the kitsch reveals the deep roots that places as commercialized as Helen or Babyland General Hospital have within southern culture and history. Gaudy hot spots such as Branson, Missouri, and Myrtle Beach, South Carolina, as well as less prominent sites such as Georgia's Helen and Cleveland, could thrive only in relation to the picturesque landscapes nearby and the lifestyle, whether real or imagined, associated with those southern locations.[18]

The tension over displays of the Confederate flag or the construction of memorials to lynching victims illustrates history's and imagery's importance among southerners. Western towns such as Dodge City, Deadwood, and Cripple Creek celebrate a lawless Wild West kitsch of gambling and gunfights while towns around Salem, Massachusetts, profit from the infamous executions of alleged witches in 1692. But reenacting lawlessness or a judicial system gone awry in the South (without projecting it on the Wild West or on a few stereotyped hillbillies like the Hatfields and McCoys) is a very different matter. Southerners annually stage the fictional stand against racial bigotry of lawyer Atticus Finch in Harper Lee's hometown of Monroeville, Alabama, and boosters in Dayton, Tennessee, annually reenact the debate over evolution conducted by William Jennings Bryan and Clarence Darrow during the 1925 Scopes trial. However, allowing audience participation, as in Salem, where tourists can pay to sit on juries that determine the guilt or innocence of accused witches, remains taboo. The ugliness of southern history is too distasteful and too recent to host reminders of such traumatic injustices as the trials of Leo Frank and the Scottsboro Boys. Too many white hoods are tucked away in closets guarded by family skeletons. Instead, many white southerners shoulder arms to restore life to former Confederate regiments, which, according to the Lost Cause mythology, defended southern homes from invaders rather than defended slavery. Black communities regularly recall emancipation at Juneteenth Day gatherings. Only in the 1990s did slavery emerge—with much controversy and in somewhat sanitized fashion—in living history displays at Colonial Williamsburg. The tensions spawned by white supremacy, the maintenance of moral rectitude in the face of an indulgent consumer culture, and the meaning of civil war haunt the southern countryside littered with family memories and historical markers.[19]

Musical recordings, plastic souvenirs, food items, and an enormous variety of other products offered by vendors serve as markers of local identity as well as purchasable mementos of Dixie. In Gatlinburg, Tennessee, nestled on the outskirts of the Great Smoky Mountains, consumer items sold at glitzy stores give tourists an unforgettable visual experience of "southern" culture compressed into a few blocks. In *The Lost Continent: Travels in Small-Town America* (1989), travel writer Bill Bryson may sneer at the kitsch of Gatlinburg, but the eclectic collection of attractions says much about tourism and consumerism in the South. Bryson observes, "There was not much more to it than a single milelong main street, but it was packed from end to end with the most dazzling profusion of tourist clutter—the Elvis Presley Hall of Fame, Stars Over Gatlinburg Wax Museum, two haunted houses, the National Bible Museum, Hillbilly Village, Ripley's Believe It or Not Museum, the American Historical Wax Museum, Gatlinburg Space Needle, something called Paradise Island, something called World of Illusions, the Bonnie Lou and Buster Country Music Show, Carbo's Police Museum ('See "Walking Tall" Sheriff Buford Pusser's Death Car!'), Guinness Book of World Records Exhibition Center and, not least, the Irene Mandrell Hall of Stars Museum and Shopping Mall." Yet Bryson also noted his pleasure at visiting the montage of sites gathered in the Appalachian shadows. Bryson felt "like a priest let loose in Las Vegas with a sockful of quarters." The street lined with kitsch sold experiences and souvenirs that allowed Bryson to capture (and later remember) his encounter with such elements of southern culture as Elvis, powerful county sheriffs, evangelical Christianity, hillbillies, and country music.[20]

Given white southerners' long-held hegemony over southern culture, most of the material in this volume addresses the whiteness stamped onto images of southernness. Slavery initially guaranteed white supremacy. With emancipation, white southerners discovered that the expanding consumer market of the late nineteenth and early twentieth centuries provided a willing ally in affirming racial divisions. Confederate soldiers had barely returned to their families before merchants tempted them to reverse their real-life defeat by marshaling victorious armies in board games. Reflecting the racial tensions of Reconstruction, merchants in Nashville, Tennessee, advertised—the week before Christmas in 1870—a jigsaw puzzle called "Chopped Up Niggers" in which children figuratively pieced together and then dismembered blacks. During the ensuing decades, national companies stamped blacks, to quote historian Grace Elizabeth Hale, "as entertainment, labor, and product" by using black imagery, such as the Gold Dust Twins and Uncle Ben, on a wide range of goods. Objectifying blacks buttressed white southerners' efforts to strip former slaves and their descendants of political, economic, and social power through Jim Crow laws, which survived into the 1960s. Yet a number of essays in this collection also reveal how tourism, memory, and consumerism offered opportunities to challenge white supremacy.[21]

The essays gathered here exhibit the evolution of the consumer-tourist market in the South since the antebellum period. To borrow a line from anthropologist Celeste Ray, the collection examines "what is 'of' the South, rather than what is 'in' it." The essays analyze significant moments and shifts in the cultural history of the region. Moving through time and focusing on different parts of the South exposes the complexity of the region while revealing how individuals and communities manipulated regional imagery to forge different versions of southern identity. The essays thereby abide by intellectual historian Michael O'Brien's definition of the South as "a relationship, not a thing." The essays examine relationships, whether between southerner and market, between southerner and nonsoutherner, or among southerners. Furthermore, the essays offer varied perspectives on tourism (broadly defined as leisure travel) and consumerism (broadly defined as commercial exchange).[22]

Part I examines the interplay of souvenirs and memory in the South. As historian Laurel Thatcher Ulrich notes, "Objects tell stories." Souvenirs, however, tell many stories and often shift meanings with buyers' experiences. Whether leaves tucked in a scrapbook or a tacky plastic figurine purchased at a roadside stand, souvenirs serve as pocket-sized pieces of history as well as personal mementoes of places in time. Eric W. Plaag demonstrates how, even before the advent of mass-produced souvenirs, antebellum northern travelers pursued items to commemorate their southern journeys. These tourists arrived with well-honed preconceptions about what they would find to explain assumed differences between their free-soil society and the proslavery regime in the South. According to Karen L. Cox, white southerners, wounded by the triumph of the North and negative northern perceptions of the South, not only constructed a mythology of the Lost Cause through books and statues that celebrated the Confederacy's failed attempt at nationhood but also encouraged the proliferation of Confederate imagery on consumer goods. Marketers responded to white southerners' need to own a piece of the glorified past and in the process contributed to the mass production of regional identity. As the racial regime represented by the Confederacy fell into disrepute during the civil rights movement, icons of the Confederacy grew less dignified, thereby becoming subversive symbols that function simultaneously as means of ridiculing the past and of celebrating that discredited past. Patrick Huber unravels the riddle of the Horny Hillbilly, a small plastic figurine with a protruding penis manufactured in China and sold at tacky tourist traps throughout the South. The Horny Hillbilly, with its intriguing association of sexuality, politics, and memory, reflects important facets of southern tourism, masculinity and sexuality, representations of poor white southerners, the place of the American South in the national experience, and the region's collective historical memory.[23]

Part II of this collection focuses on the relationship between southerners' identity and marketplaces. Sites of consumerism show how outsiders perceived southerners and how southerners perceived themselves. In *The Ellis Island Snow Globe*, Erica Rand simply states the reason for studying places embedded in consumerism: "Representation is political. What gets represented, and when, where, and how it does, depends on and affects relations of power."[24] Denied much power after Reconstruction, black Christians in the Arkansas and Mississippi Delta, as John M. Giggie argues, turned inward as a means of maintaining their dignity. Home decorations and beautified churches symbolically countered white stereotypes of blacks as uncivilized while strengthening blacks' determination to undermine white supremacy. For some white southerners, empowerment meant celebrating the purity—racial and religious—of isolated mountain folk. Aaron K. Ketchell, examining post–Civil War tourism in the Ozarks, demonstrates how tourist sites around Branson, Missouri, played on popular hillbilly stereotypes to appeal to predominantly white visitors. Accentuating Christian virtues and whiteness washed Ozark mountaineers clean of some of the harshest negative imagery associated with them—that is, images of hillbillies as drunkards and sexual deviants. Such emphasis on whiteness bred opposition, however. Nicole

King shows how Alan Schafer, a Jewish South Carolinian, chafed at local whites' social conservatism and political might after the Second World War. Just as blacks used their churches to physically mark their piety and humanity under Jim Crow, Schafer used his tourist trap—the sprawling, gaudy South of the Border complex—to undermine romantic notions of southern gentility. The growth of his business granted Schafer the ability economically and politically to challenge Jim Crow restrictions, making him popular with area blacks and Native Americans. Finally, Glenn T. Eskew examines civil rights movement tourism in Montgomery, Alabama, since the 1960s. Rather than promoting continued activism, local whites have profited from the movement and its message by constructing museums and tourist sites while demolishing historic neighborhoods.

Part III of this collection explores the often overlooked connection of foodways and the performance of southern identity. A basic function of daily life, foodways harbor deep cultural meanings within the South, as in other regions and nations, reinforcing social barriers and defining regional ambitions. To paraphrase an old saying, southerners are what and how they eat. For example, when restaurant critic Pascale Le Draoulec traveled southward to hunt recipes for her *American Pie: Slices of Life (and Pie) from America's Back Roads* (2002), residents of Natchez, Mississippi, pointed her in the direction of Mammy's Cupboard, a restaurant "shaped like a slim-waisted Aunt Jemima" in which diners enjoyed a "slice of remember when" under the figure's hoop skirt. Le Draoulec also received suggestions that she visit a black woman, Sophronia Dyson, who hawked pies to passing steamboat passengers. In his analysis, Anthony J. Stanonis surveys the evolving meanings of southern foods and eating practices since the Civil War. Foodways identified by commentators as southern have long reinforced (and in many ways continue to reinforce) white racial and patriarchal views. Carolyn de la Peña focuses her argument more narrowly by tracing the history of Krispy Kreme since its appearance during the Great Depression to better understand southerners' relationship to industrialization and technology. In contrast, Mary Rizzo considers how southerners have adapted to deindustrialization and life in the post–civil rights movement South by studying Baltimore's Hon Fest, a festival sponsored by the Café Hon since 1994. The Hon, a white feminine icon, erases the city's minority working-class residents from popular memory. While Baltimore remains a racially diverse city struggling to survive in a postindustrial economy, Hon Fest offers a romanticized past where community rests on racial and class homogeneity as well as traditional gender roles.[25]

The journey undertaken in the following pages began at a weekend symposium graciously hosted by the Watson-Brown Foundation in October 2005. In the restored home of populist politician Tom Watson, now also a tourist site in Thomson, Georgia, we read papers and bantered over our interpretations of southern culture. We left with souvenirs (including caps from a nearby fox hunting club), a few extra pounds gained from the southern cooking enjoyed on the veranda, and an enthusiasm to share our research with a wider audience. The essays in this volume open conversation about southern culture in a field of study that too frequently sticks to the well-worn paths of scholarly debate. As is common for essay collections, the episodic pieces presented here seek to reveal fresh insights into a much-studied region—scholarly pit stops meant to give various views of southern culture from different geographical and temporal perspectives. Welcome to the Dixie Emporium.

NOTES

1. "Snake Farm Razed, Ends Quirky Era," *New Orleans Times-Picayune,* 10 February 1996.

2. "A Slither on the Scaley Side," *Austin Daily Texan,* 22 June 2005.

3. A growing yet still small number of scholarly works, especially those focused on southern memory, have assessed southern culture and history in light of tourism and consumerism. See Jane Becker, *Selling Tradition: Appalachia and the Construction of an American Folk* (Chapel Hill: University of North Carolina Press, 1998), esp. chapter 7; Thomas Bremer, *Blessed with Tourists: The Borderlands of Religion and Tourism in San Antonio* (Chapel Hill: University of North Carolina Press, 2004); W. Fitzhugh Brundage, *The Southern Past: A Clash of Race and Memory* (Cambridge: Harvard University Press, 2006); W. Fitzhugh Brundage, ed., *Where These Memories Grow: History, Memory, and Southern Identity* (Chapel Hill: University of North Carolina Press, 2000), esp. part 4; Thomas Clark, *Pills, Petticoats, and Plows: The Southern Country Store* (1944; Norman: University of Oklahoma Press, 1989); Jack Davis, *Race against Time: Culture and Separation in Natchez since 1930* (Baton Rouge: Louisiana State University Press, 2001), esp. chapter 2; Melissa Fay Greene, *Praying for Sheetrock* (Reading, Mass.: Addison-Wesley, 1991), 14–19, 55–74; Elizabeth Grace Hale, *Making Whiteness: The Culture of Segregation in the South, 1890–1940* (New York: Pantheon, 1998); Lu Ann Jones, "Gender, Race, and Itinerant Commerce in the Rural New South," *Journal of Southern History* 66 (May 2000): 297–320; Ted Ownby, *American Dreams in Mississippi: Consumers, Poverty, and Culture, 1830–1998* (Chapel Hill: University of North Carolina Press, 1999); Richard Starnes, ed., *Southern Journeys: Tourism, History, and Culture in the Modern South* (Tuscaloosa: University of Alabama Press, 2003); Anthony Stanonis, *Creating the Big Easy: New Orleans and the Emergence of Modern Tourism, 1918–1945* (Athens: University of Georgia Press, 2006); Helen Taylor, *Circling Dixie: Contemporary Southern Culture through a Transatlantic Lens* (New Brunswick: Rutgers University Press, 2001); Stephanie Yuhl, *A Golden Haze of Memory: The Making of Historic Charleston* (Chapel Hill: University of North Carolina Press, 2005).

4. Donald Schueler, *Preserving the Pascagoula* (Jackson: University Press of Mississippi, 1980), vii; Anthony Wilson, *Shadow and Shelter: The Swamp in Southern Culture* (Jackson: University Press of Mississippi, 2006), 175. For information on Henry Grady and New South boosterism, see C. Vann Woodward, *Origins of the New South, 1877–1913* (Baton Rouge: Louisiana State University Press, 1951), 124–25, 144–50; Edward Ayers, *The Promise of the New South: Life after Reconstruction* (New York: Oxford University Press, 1992), 87, 322, 336; Paul Gaston, *The New South Creed: A Study in Southern Mythmaking* (Baton Rouge: Louisiana University Press, 1970), 48–56; Don Doyle, *New Men, New Cities, New South: Atlanta, Nashville, Charleston, Mobile, 1860–1910* (Chapel Hill: University of North Carolina Press, 1990), 151–58, 206–7; James Cobb, *The Selling of the South: The Southern Crusade for Industrial Development, 1936–1980* (Baton Rouge: Louisiana State University Press, 1982), 1–4, 64–97, 184–88. Atlanta also hosted the International Cotton Exposition in 1881 and the Piedmont Exposition in 1887.

5. Frederick Woodward Skiff, *Adventures in Americana: Recollections of Forty Years Collecting Books, Furniture, China, Guns, and Glass* (Portland, Ore.: Metropolitan, 1935), 259, 261–63.

6. Skiff, *Adventures in Americana*, 268–69. For insight into the role of the senses within southern culture, see Mark Smith, *How Race Is Made: Slavery, Segregation, and the Senses* (Chapel Hill: University of North Carolina Press, 2006), 3–9, 50–63, 98–110.

7. Taylor, *Circling Dixie*, 23, 25; John Shelton Reed, *Surveying the South: Studies in Regional Sociology* (Columbia: University of Missouri Press, 1993), 51–65; Lothar Hönnighausen, "The Southern Heritage and the Semiotics of Consumer Culture," in *The Southern State of Mind*, ed. Jan Nordby Gretlund (Columbia: University of South Carolina Press, 1999), 80–94.

8. C. Vann Woodward, *The Burden of Southern History*, rev. ed. (Baton Rouge: Louisiana State University Press, 1968), 12–25. For an insightful discussion of southern imagery in a British advertising campaign for the alcoholic beverage Southern Comfort, see Taylor, *Circling Dixie*, 121–28.

9. John S. C. Abbott, *South and North; or, Impressions Received during a Trip to Cuba and the South* (New York: Abbey and Abbott, 1860), 306.

10. Anne Sarah Rubin, *A Shattered Nation: The Rise and Fall of the Confederacy, 1861–1868* (Chapel Hill: University of North Carolina Press, 2005), esp. chapters 1, 6; John Shelton Reed, *Southerners: The Social Psychology of Sectionalism* (Chapel Hill: University of North Carolina Press, 1983), 38. Reed writes, "In short, exposure to non-Southerners can heighten Southerners' regional consciousness through a reactive process. Southerners can observe that non-Southerners use regional concepts to structure *their* experience."

11. James Street, *James Street's South*, ed. James Street Jr. (Garden City, N.Y.: Doubleday, 1955), 13.

12. Paul Greenberg, "Lee and the Lingering South," *Arkansas Democrat-Gazette*, 19 January 2006. For consideration of how literal killing fields become touristic battlegrounds of identity, see Jim Weeks, *Gettysburg: Memory, Market, and an American Shrine* (Princeton: Princeton University Press,

2003); Sarah Farmer, *Martyred Village: Commemorating the 1944 Massacre at Oradour-sur-Glade* (Berkeley: University of California Press, 1999).

13. James Creecy, *Scenes in the South and Other Miscellaneous Pieces* (Washington, D.C.: McGill, 1860), 271. For background on the controversy over preserving Mount Vernon, see Mike Wallace, *Mickey Mouse History and Other Essays on American Memory* (Philadelphia: Temple University Press, 1996), 4–6.

14. For background on the emergence of tourism and historic preservation, see Colin Campbell, *The Romantic Ethic and the Spirit of Modern Consumerism* (Oxford: Blackwell, 1987), 179–201; Orvar Löfgren, *On Holiday: A History of Vacationing* (Berkeley: University pf California Press, 1999), 19–68, 172–73, 216–20; John Sears, *Sacred Places: American Tourist Attractions in the Nineteenth Century* (New York: Oxford University Press, 1989), 49–71; Carol Sheriff, *The Artificial River: The Erie Canal and the Paradox of Progress, 1817–1862* (New York: Hill and Wang, 1996), 27–62; Wallace, *Mickey Mouse History*, 4–27, 179–207; Lynne Withey, *Grand Tours and Cook's Tours: A History of Leisure Travel, 1750–1915* (New York: Morrow, 1997), 7, 33–45, 105–32, 299–336.

15. Robert Dorman, *Revolt of the Provinces: The Regionalist Movement in America, 1920–1945* (Chapel Hill: University of North Carolina Press, 1993); David Whisnant, *All That Is Native and Fine: The Politics of Culture in an American Region* (Chapel Hill: University of North Carolina Press, 1983), esp. chapter 2.

16. John Margolies, *Fun along the Road: American Tourist Attractions* (Boston: Little, Brown, 1998), 18–19; *Freewoods: Where History Is Fun* (n.p.: Freewoods Foundation, circa 1990), South Caroliniana Library, University of South Carolina, Columbia.

17. Fredric Jameson, *The Seeds of Time* (New York: Columbia University Press, 1994), 9; Umberto Eco, *Travels in Hyperreality* (San Diego: Harcourt Brace Jovanovich, 1986), 44, 53. For a discussion of postmodernity, see Perry Anderson, *The Origins of Postmodernity* (New York: Verso, 1998), 3–46, 63, 80–92; J. David Hoeveler Jr., *The Postmodernist Turn: American Thought and Culture in the 1970s* (New York: Twayne, 1996), 13–14, 54–99; Alison Landsberg, *Prosthetic Memory: The Transformation of American Remembrance in the Age of Mass Culture* (New York: Columbia University Press, 2004), 1–24, 32–34.

18. Caroline Swope, "Redesigning Downtown: The Fabrication of German-Themed Villages in Small-Town America" (Ph.D. diss., University of Washington, 2003), 113–63; "Helen: Georgia's Alpine Village," *Atlanta Journal-Constitution,* 31 January 1993; "Silver Celebration of Oktoberfest Begins Thursday," *Chattanooga News–Free Press,* 3 September 1995; "Revived Mountain Town Has Popular Fall Festival," *Memphis Commercial Appeal,* 10 September 1995; "A Swiss Alpine Village in Georgia," *Arkansas Democrat-Gazette,* 12 November 1995; "Not Your Average Nursery," *Chattanooga News–Free Press,* 27 September 1998; "That Ain't Slaw: At 16, Cabbage Patch Still Grows Greenbacks," *Atlanta Journal-Constitution,* 20 December 1999.

19. Kevin Britz, "Long May Their Legend Survive: Memory and Authenticity in Deadwood, South Dakota; Tombstone, Arizona; and Dodge City, Kansas" (Ph.D. diss., University of Arizona, 1999), 129–30, 152–84, 239–40, 322–25;

Robin DeRosa, "Specters, Scholars, and Sightseers: The Salem Witch Trials and American Memory" (Ph.D. diss., Tufts University, 2002), 181–84, 188–193, 207–21. For information on the festivals in Monroeville, Alabama, and Dayton, Tennessee, see http://www.monroecountyal.com/heritage.html (accessed 15 June 2006) and http://www.southeasttennessee.com/www/events/9.1271/scopes_trial_rhea_county.html (accessed 15 June 2006).

20. Bill Bryson, *The Lost Continent: Travels in Small-Town America* (New York: Harper Collins, 1989), 95–96.

21. William Gilmore Simms, ed., *War Poetry of the South* (New York: Richardson, 1867), 486; "Chopped Up Niggers," *Nashville Republican Banner,* 18 December 1870; Hale, *Making Whiteness,* 151. For information on racial imagery in consumer goods, see Hale, *Making Whiteness,* 151–68; Patricia Turner, *Ceramic Uncles and Celluloid Mammies: Black Images and Their Influence on Culture* (New York: Anchor, 1994), 3–61.

22. Celeste Ray, introduction to *Southern Heritage on Display: Public Ritual and Ethnic Diversity within Southern Regionalism,* ed. Celeste Ray (Tuscaloosa: University of Alabama Press, 2003), 3; Michael O'Brien, *Rethinking the South: Essays in Intellectual History* (Baltimore: Johns Hopkins University Press, 1988), 218.

23. Laurel Thatcher Ulrich, *The Age of Homespun: Objects and Stories in the Creation of an American Myth* (New York: Knopf, 2005), 6; Michael Hitchcock, introduction to *Souvenirs: The Material Culture of Tourism,* ed. Michael Hitchcock and Ken Teague (Burlington, Vt.: Ashgate, 2000), 1–14; Werner Muensterberger, *Collecting: An Unruly Passion* (Princeton: Princeton University Press, 1994), 4, 45; Susan Stewart, *On Longing: Narratives of the Miniature, the Gigantic, the Souvenir, the Collection* (Durham, N.C.: Duke University Press, 1993), 132–69.

24. Erica Rand, *The Ellis Island Snow Globe* (Durham, N.C.: Duke University Press, 2005), 98.

25. Pascale Le Draoulec, *American Pie: Slices of Life (and Pie) from America's Back Roads* (New York: Perennial, 2002), 82, 85.

PART I

Buying Memory

Souvenirs of the American South

Thoughtful Souvenirs

Ted Ownby

Are souvenirs important? It may seem harsh or at least impolite to burden the following chapters by questioning the significance of their topic, but souvenirs often seem so ephemeral, odd, or whimsical that the question deserves attention. Usually picked up to commemorate a moment and place outside of people's ordinary experiences, souvenirs seem important mostly for marking what the person choosing the souvenir sees as extraordinary. Thus, souvenirs are about both the subject and the object as well as the potentially complicated relationship between the two.

Above all, the subject of souvenirs raises questions about how to study identity—in this case, southern identity. What are the components of southern identity, and who gets to decide? Do people within the South decide, and if so, which people? Or do people who see themselves as essentially different from people in the South help decide what makes a set of places and people and practices recognizably southern? Or does the real question depend on particular and maybe temporary issues, so that the question of southern identity becomes a tool used in some larger issue? Is a souvenir of the American South part of an ongoing construction of regional identity, or does it reaffirm some preestablished ideas about that identity?

The study of souvenirs lies at the intersection of the study of identity, the study of memory, and usually the study of consumer culture. Some of these essays confront a basic conundrum in consumer culture. On one hand, commercially produced tourist items often rely on a familiarity with what tourists expect to find and commemorate. In that way, tourist items reflect something old, familiar, and maybe by some definitions genuine. On the other hand, consumer culture relies on novelty, with sellers wanting to attract people through their appeal to some new style or new usefulness. Consumer scholar Colin Campbell argues in *The Romantic Ethic and the Spirit of Modern Consumerism* that consumers look forward to the next consumer experience with a kind of unsatisfiable long-ing that has become key to modernity.[1] Thus, souvenirs, more than most consumer products, hold out the two-sided potential to offer something new to address that longing while also offering something familiar to satisfy the fears that everything passes too quickly. Searching for items that are old, authentic, genuine, and lasting goes hand in hand with fears that consumer culture turns experience into something new, passing, and perhaps fraudulent cooked up by manipulating manufacturers and advertisers. As the three authors of the chapters in this section show, associating things with the South has often offered some kind of claim to authenticity to people who want to own something they can define as authentic.

Eric W. Plaag's thorough essay uses the diaries, letters, and travel accounts of antebellum northerners to detail the items they picked up or bought while traveling in the South. Plaag divides souvenirs into ephemeral and physical categories and further divides the latter into representative, historical, and commercial items. With creative and impressive use of those sources, he shows how northern travelers took home moss, leaves, and branches; sketches and engravings; Indian-made baskets and moccasins; and bullets and other items from historically significant sites. Most of the souvenirs, he shows, were not produced for the purpose of commemoration for sale. However, the growing late-antebellum interest in engravings and even the increasing willingness to sell items to recall Mount Vernon and battle sites showed an escalating awareness of the commercial possibilities of the tourist trade. In the minds of these souvenir collectors, the South had natural beauty or at least exotic forms of natural life; it had big houses, homes of presidents, and battlefields—and it had slavery.

The author suggests that the sense of difference that generated northern travelers' desire for souvenirs and the choices they made about what constituted souvenirs embodied a regional identity that helped prepare the way for a much broader sense of difference "that made sectional antagonisms seem irreconcilable in the years before the Civil War." That may be true, but I wonder if difference might have had as much to do with desire or even fascination as with conflict or a sense of superiority. In his classic *Cavalier and Yankee: The Old South and American National Character,* William R. Taylor argues that much of the antebellum South's Cavalier identity came from anxious northerners who were concerned that northern capitalism was creating a culture without leisure, manners, or respect for and connection to any past.[2] To return to my opening question, are these souvenirs important? Along with occasionally displaying the travelers' concerns about slavery, the products Plaag describes strike me as important in showing the variety of regional identifications the travelers made as they thought about the South. Their sense of regional identity does not seem fixed; instead, the travelers were open to a range of things to preserve, think of as southern, and take home on their trips north. Perhaps above all, they wanted things that seemed old and, in the language of Plaag's title, genuine.

Karen L. Cox's essay moves to the period after the Civil War, when mass production and a developing advertising industry made considerable use of the concept of the South. Cox usefully distinguishes between southern manufacturers, who emphasized martial or at least specifically Confederate images, and northern manufacturers, who emphasized a wider range of issues they associated with southern lifestyles. The Confederate South seems in this essay a bit like a home sports team, with supporters trying to associate every item they can with images that marked them as fans. What parts of life hardly seemed to matter. With a few exceptions involving portrayals of African Americans, Cox does not mention advertisements from southern sources that displayed anything but the Confederate military. These items mattered to their purchasers, but they did not dramatize particular parts of life. Instead, for white southerners wrapped up in the Lost Cause, the items simply represented some connection to memories of people at their perceived best. For them, associating goods with the Confederacy seemed to make those goods important.

By contrast, northern manufacturers and advertisers connected the South to leisure, warm weather, tasty and intriguing food, interesting plants and trees, and funny people—especially African Americans—who knew how to enjoy life. People making and selling the goods Cox discusses had a wider range of associations with the South than the traveling collectors of ephemera and other souvenirs Plaag examines. And if a few of Plaag's souvenir seekers disliked slavery, none of Cox's manufacturers seem to have had any problems with postbellum southern race relations. National advertisements tended to reassure all possible consumers that human beings were basically happy and that life—South, North, and in all other regions—was pretty good, especially for people who bought certain products. The breadth of northern images of the South was substantial, but what of the depth? The conclusion of Cox's chapter, in which songwriters—many of them fairly recent immigrants to the United States—portrayed the South as a place full of smiles and place-names suitable for rhyming suggests that many people perceived Dixie as interesting but not really mattering much. In an intriguing way, Cox's essay supports David Blight's argument that white northerners literally bought into the romance of reunion at the expense of any concern for the injustices African Americans faced.[3]

Patrick Huber's engaging discussion of the Horny Hillbilly offers an extraordinary point of view for thinking about souvenirs in a postmodern world. The rebellious hillbilly with an oversized erection is a multilayered symbol, with no clear maker and no clear buyer and open to interpretation by everyone. Huber circles around the small statue, considering its several layers of meaning—Appalachia and the world beyond it, tourists' search for the exotic, the bravado of the Confederate Lost Cause, and worries about defeated masculinity or perhaps a celebration of triumphant masculinity. Emphasizing that southern mountain people have been the victims or recipients of especially extreme images—either romanticized innocence or projected depravity—he argues that the hillbilly is no longer the contemporary ancestor, pure in his separation from the corruptions of modernity. Rather, the hillbilly has become much more the outlandish figure isolated from modern standards and marked only by his rebelliousness and his body.

A question worth asking and perhaps part of what Huber calls the riddle is why so many mass-produced souvenirs seem so funny. Scholars who discuss why things are funny often take the fun out of things, and Huber's amusing essay itself offers an antidote to that tendency. Scholars who have written about black collectibles have argued that selling pieces both intentionally insulting and intentionally amusing is a way of making horror more human,[4] and Huber usefully examines the fact that Americans continue to buy silly hillbilly items long after most have stopped buying items demeaning to African Americans. Perhaps caricaturing is itself part of the conundrum of representing the old and familiar in a new way that consumers will buy. The hillbilly is old and may be genuine. The cantankerous Confederate is old. So perhaps the combination and his horniness offer enough surprise to serve the purposes of making a consumer want to buy (and display?) a new representation of something more or less familiar.

The transition from the antebellum souvenirs to the postbellum consumer items to the recent statue of the Horny Hillbilly suggests something about the relationship between consumer culture and southern identity. A standard question in thinking about regionalism concerns whether mass production, mass distribution, and mass consumption may work against regional identification. At least from these three essays, the answer to that question would be no. The collectors Plaag discusses seem relatively unconscious of or uninterested in the particularly "southern" qualities of those goods. By the time the manufacturers and advertisers in Cox's paper became involved, labeling things "southern" mattered a great deal, although the meanings of southernness (and the depth of people's interest) varied significantly by region. And in the recent period, when images more than ever dominate life, "southernness" can mean all sorts of things, and part of the experience of consumer culture is trying to figure out the riddles of those meanings. Perhaps the silly things sold in souvenir stores ultimately may not matter a great deal, but the question of identity—who creates it, who rejects it, who buys and sells it—seems to have become more important or at least more complex than ever.

NOTES

1. Colin Campbell, *The Romantic Ethic and the Spirit of Modern Consumerism* (Oxford: Blackwell, 1987).

2. William R. Taylor, *Cavalier and Yankee: The Old South and American National Character* (1957; New York: Oxford University Press, 1993).

3. David W. Blight, *Race and Reunion: The Civil War in American Memory* (Cambridge: Belknap Press of Harvard University Press, 2001).

4. See, for example, Kenneth W. Goings, *Mammy and Uncle Mose: Black Collectibles and American Stereotyping* (Bloomington: Indiana University Press, 1994).

"There Is an Abundance of Those Which Are Genuine"

Northern Travelers and Souvenirs of the Antebellum South

Eric W. Plaag

A dominant impulse on encountering beauty is to wish to hold on to it, to possess it and give it weight in one's life. There is an urge to say, "I was here, I saw this and it mattered to me." But beauty is fugitive, being frequently found in places to which we may never return. . . . How then to possess it . . . ? The camera provides one option. . . . Or else we can try to imprint ourselves physically on a place of beauty, perhaps hoping to render it more present in us by making *ourselves* more present in *it*. . . . A more modest step might be to buy something . . . as a reminder of what we have lost, like a lock of hair cut from a departing lover's mane.
—Alain de Botton, *The Art of Travel*

As Joseph Holt Ingraham's early 1830s visit to New Orleans began to wind down, he took a short trip along what locals called the Levée to visit the battlefield at Chalmette, where Andrew Jackson's defensive forces had decimated British general Edward Pakenham's troops at the end of the War of 1812. Like many antebellum visitors to the site, he was surprised to find few commemorative indicators of the battle. So remote and undeveloped was the location—at least in terms of any effort to preserve its historical significance—that Ingraham and his companion needed to inquire at a nearby steam sawmill for help in finding the battle-field. When finally pointed toward their destination, Ingraham skepti-cally concluded that "this field . . . could not be the battlefield—so quiet and farm-like it reposed."[1]

Their guide, however, apparently had led tourists to the battlefield in the past. As they walked over the fields, he identified the houses that had served as Jackson's and Pakenham's headquarters. Leading Ingra-ham a little farther, the guide stopped and with a sweeping gesture again pointed out the field of battle. Ingraham's subsequent description of the location bordered on the sublime, with his imaginings of the "wild and terrible scenes" that had transpired there prompting him to look over the field "wrapped in silence." As his imagination raced, he envisioned the significance of his standing on this spot, noting not only that he stood on hallowed ground but that "every footfall disturbed human ashes! Human dust gathered upon our shoes as the dust of the plain!" When his guide led them to the oak tree under which many of Pakenham's men had both died and been buried, Ingraham waxed poetic about the "many last looks" and "manly sighs" that must have entwined in its branches on the day of battle. Then his guide pointed out the spots where various other key English officers had fallen, exhibiting a completeness of knowledge about the site that "rendered our visit both more satisfactory and agreeable than it otherwise would have been."[2]

Although very impressed by the tour, Ingraham was most intrigued by an exchange at the end of his stroll across the grounds. "Here gentil-hommes, j'ai findé some bullet for you to buy," a mulatto boy shouted at Ingraham, turning out his pockets to reveal a complete traveling souvenir "stock in trade" of "grape shot, bullets, and fragments of lead." When Ingraham questioned the items' origin, the guide assured him of their authenticity, stating that such objects were "found in great numbers by the ploughmen, and disposed of to curious visiters." But the mulatto boy had more than mere "disposal" in mind. Accordingly, Ingraham offered the boy a "piccaiune" for the grapeshot before asking again about the possibility of fakes being substituted in such transactions. "No," the guide replied, "there is no need of that—there is an abundance of those which are genuine."[3]

As darkness encroached, his "pockets heavy with metal," Ingraham stumbled over an object sticking out of the earth. He lifted it and wiped off the dirt, revealing the butt of a musket. "As this was the most valuable relic which the field afforded," Ingraham entrusted the artifact to the care of his traveling companion, a fellow northerner, "for the purpose of placing it in the museum . . . for the benefit of the curious, when he returns to that land of curious bipeds, where such kind of mementos are duly estimated."[4] Such souveniring, it seemed, was the province of northerners gifted with the curiosity necessary to recognize the value in such objects. Southerners—including Ingraham's helpful guide but excluding children and perhaps slaves—apparently saw little need to preserve or profit from such objects, given their abundance.

Ingraham's assumptions about southerners—and their differences from northerners—were by no means unusual in the raft of travel accounts, both private and written for publication, penned by northerners who wandered south between 1815 and 1860. Nor was Ingraham the only northern traveler to the antebellum South to bring back objects representative of his journey. While pinpointing exact numbers is difficult, evidence suggests that by 1835, tens of thousands of northerners traveled to the South each year.[5] Like Ingraham, most of these northern travelers journeyed to the South with well-honed preconceptions about the differences between northerners and southerners as well as about the items that symbolized those differences. Early travel accounts of the South by foreigners, later travel accounts from fellow northerners, and even a spate of popular novels reinforced a northern national narrative generated in large part by the northern press. As tensions over slavery intensified after 1830, the northern national narrative was reified through the lens of slavery, so that by 1850 an entrenched national myth of a simplistic sectional binary emerged, depicting a solid South whose inferior social structures and cultural ideals contrasted sharply with those of a homogenous culturally and socially superior North.[6]

Defining the Antebellum Souvenir

As some historians, sociologists, and anthropologists have demonstrated, formal souvenir practices date at least to the eighteenth century, and some early travelers in the United States engaged in both gift exchange and commercial transactions that allowed those travelers to return home with objects that functioned as souvenirs.[7] For the most part, however, references to an incipient antebellum American souvenir trade have been fleeting. Almost no scholarship exists on the material culture of antebellum southern travel, and no scholar has yet connected that material culture with the development and perpetuation of the perceived sectional differences. No one, in fact, has comprehensively probed the link between antebellum travel memorabilia and the formation of southern identity.

At first glance, a discussion of "souvenirs" from the antebellum period seems patently absurd. For example, commemorative postcards, which many observers see as the first commercial souvenir in the United States, did not emerge until 1893, perhaps as an outgrowth of the *carte de visite*–sized advertising trade cards popularized during the 1860s.[8] Further, the modern commercialized souvenir trade, focusing on mass-produced tchotchkes and knickknacks with images representative of the places visited (such as miniature Mount Vernons), also did not emerge in the United States until the very late nineteenth century. However, a substantial difference exists between the development of a commercialized souvenir trade per se and the use of commercially produced and appropriated objects as souvenirs.

Eric J. Leed, in his philosophical exploration of travel sensibility, notes that the "experience of travel . . . engenders a collective self-consciousness as it acquaints travelers with the precise nature of their sameness and difference with respect to a world of others. As an experience of contrastive ethnic groups, travel entails the generation of a cultural self-image, and this is cultural change."[9] The "contrastive groups" of northerners and southerners were every bit as Othered by one another as the ethnic groups of which Leed writes. A more accurate interpretation of the progressive antagonism of sectional relations during the antebellum period requires considering the informal emissaries of the North, those travelers who went to the South for a myriad of reasons.[10] One explanation for the development of a northern (as distinct from southern) "cultural self-image" lies in understanding what northerners sought in their journeys through the South. Another explanation rests in the ways northern travelers distinguished southern places from their northern parallels (or interpreted southern places as unique). Yet another explanation, however, is the way in which northerners used the material culture of travel in the antebellum South to commemorate and mark southern identity. Comprehending the interplay between the material culture of antebellum travel in the South and the northern perception of southern difference requires outlining the kinds of objects that served as commemorative place markers of the South—what are today called souvenirs—and distinguishing them from other objects purchased or collected along the journey for either their intrinsic value or their importance as but one more contribution to a collection.[11]

Recognizing that northerners ventured south to experience aspects of perceived southern culture and identity (slavery, hospitality, and good climate, for example) provides only half of an understanding of the role and importance of material culture in the construction of memory about the South. Discussing the construction of the image of Jerusalem in the minds of Christians who had never visited the city, Maurice Halbwachs notes, "Whenever a collective remembrance has a double focus—a physical object, a material reality such as a statue, a monument, a place in space, and also a symbol, or something of spiritual significance, something shared by the group that adheres to and is superimposed on this physical reality," then an "image" emerges that the "universal community . . . slowly construe[s]."[12] For many northerners, the "collective remembrances" of southern identity included not only the sounds of slavery but the tastes of southern food and the exotic elements of southern climate and landscape. Thus, if a unified northern view of the South existed and was transmitted repeatedly through the travel accounts of northern visitors (whether professional writers or private travelers), then the material culture associated with such journeys—the objects those travelers chose as signifiers of southern difference—should have amplified those collective memories or at least more solidly rooted notions of southern difference in the collective consciousness of all antebellum northerners, whether or not they had personally traveled to the South.

Celia Lury hints that traveling objects (souvenirs, postcards, and photographs) serve not merely as "adjunct[s] of the movement of tourists" or "little more than the traveller's extended baggage" but also as integral aspects of the tourist experience, thus implying that these objects of travel are just as important in shaping travel experience and meaning as the events of travel.[13] Likewise, Dean MacCannell concludes that while the original "attraction is the more authentic, the memories and other souvenirs are more important in establishing society in consciousness." Because "tourists return home carrying souvenirs and talking of their experiences, spreading, wherever they go, a vicarious experience of the sight," souvenirs contribute to a collective memory about the original attraction that never can trump the authentic experience of a place or sight but nevertheless shapes meaning even as it drives other members of the society toward their own authentic experiences of the sight in question.[14] In this sense, the souvenirs of southern experience function as both markers and motivators of experience, helping to mark southern identity in the minds of northern travelers who visited, verifying the vicarious experiences of those who heard about these trips, and encouraging vicarious travelers to see/experience the South for themselves.

Some scholars of tourism and material culture choose to distinguish between souvenirs and mementos, using the commercial transaction as the distinction between these two classes of commemorative object. Such a division is not particularly useful, since souvenirs and mementos "on a structural or associative level . . . serve the same concretizing function."[15] My analysis therefore uses a much more inclusive definition of the term *souvenir* but nevertheless excludes certain types of objects. Objects collected for their use value are different from those collected specifically for the more symbolic purpose of establishing, sustaining, or reifying conceptions of southern difference. Understanding this distinction requires fully appreciating the souvenir object's function in commemorating experience. As Susan Stewart writes, "We do not need or desire souvenirs of events that are repeatable. Rather we need and desire souvenirs of events that are reportable, events whose materiality has escaped us, events that thereby exist only through the invention of narrative."[16] Stewart's interpretation of souvenirs appropriately excludes two types of objects commonly mentioned in antebellum travel narratives. First, any object associated with the southern travel experience that did not in some way represent regional distinctiveness falls outside the souvenir category—for example, a guidebook that covered all the rail lines in the country and thus assisted travelers in both the North and the South. If the book in no other way commemorated a southern journey per se (as a place for recording observations about the South, for example) and thus failed to distinguish itself from its nominal use value, it failed to function as a souvenir. Likewise, for naturalists collecting specimens of species particular to the South, their use value lies in their function within the larger meaning of a scientific collection rather than as a souvenir of the southern travel experience per se.[17]

I thus divide souvenir objects into two distinct categories. The first consists of objects that function as physical markers of memory, accessible to the traveler at some future time to hold and handle as reminders of "southern experience," a group hereafter called _retained souvenirs_. This category can be further subdivided into representative, historical, and commercially (re)produced items. The second type, a more symbolic category of objects nevertheless representative of the "southern experience" when their form is recalled, is the class of objects hereafter called _ephemeral souvenirs_.[18] Regardless of their precise nature and function, however, both groups of objects served the same purpose in the antebellum period as that collective group of objects—mass-produced tchotchkes, postcards, and "pieces of the real"—that modern travelers call _souvenirs_.

Collecting the Antebellum South

More than twenty years after Ingraham's visit to New Orleans, while on a family sightseeing journey through the South, Mary S. Lamson carefully recorded in her journal entry for 28 March 1855 the particulars of her trip to the battleground at Chalmette. Commenting on the gorgeous weather and the lavish gardens and weary slaves she saw, Lamson suddenly stalled her narrative when she reached the field where Pakenham had been cut down. Like Ingraham, she was shown the field at no charge, "the whole place . . . owned by Mr. J. A. Livandais [who] is improving it very much now with a view to making some profit out of it." A pile of munitions lay nearby, as he "had recently ploughed up a field." She expressed particular delight in seeing the oaks under which Pakenham and other officers had been buried, many of the trees still embedded with shot and cannonballs, and she marveled at the live oaks and the Spanish moss hanging from them, so much so that she felt compelled to grab some as a souvenir. "Enclosed in these sheets are some clover leaves gathered beneath the trees & some of the moss hanging from the branches," she noted, adding that she saw similar moss proffered in the city market houses for use in "very comfortable mattresses for which it is used almost entirely at the South . . . selling at four \$s a pound."[19]

Lamson's activities could easily be dismissed as just one more example of naturalist collecting—picking a leaf or other specimen as evidence of the varieties of natural life in an unfamiliar region. But Lamson was no naturalist. Before the development of the modern souvenir trade, Lamson pursued the easiest means available to commemorate her journey. By collecting the clover from beneath the natural and symbolic monuments of British defeat and the moss that draped itself across those monuments as nature's mournful bunting, Lamson instinctively nodded to the well-honed romantic sensibilities of her period. At the same time, she displayed a keen awareness of the value of what she gathered, alert not only to its symbolic historical significance but also to its value as a marker of a distinctively southern way of life and, by pejorative extension, southern backwardness. Like Ingraham, Lamson interpreted these fragile markers of national memory through the lens of their southern associations. Noting with precision the high price for more ordinary moss in the southern markets, Lamson believed she had discovered a bargain, and she pressed those objects into her journal to preserve them, to keep them not only as permanent reminders of her personal encounter with America's patriotic history but also as relics of the distinctively southern culture that so disturbed and bewildered her during her long journey.

Lamson's items—representing the first class of antebellum souvenir objects, retained souvenirs—are, of course, the type of souvenir most familiar to modern readers. This class of antebellum souvenir objects included three distinct types. The first category is representative souvenirs—objects that carried symbolic significance in their ability to encapsulate the meaning and memory of a particular southern destination or experience despite their sometimes loose associations with the southern experience in question. The second category is historical souvenirs—those objects selected to commemorate historically significant locations, people, and events that often had no sectional association per se but that were sometimes interpreted through the lens of sectional difference. The third category is commercial souvenirs—those objects not simply collected by antebellum travelers but available for purchase, either directly as a souvenir object or as a standard commodity appropriated for the souvenir purpose. All three categories of souvenirs included both three-dimensional objects (often in miniature) and two-dimensional representations.[20]

Historical evidence suggests that northern travelers most commonly collected representative souvenirs, perhaps because of their ubiquitous nature, the ease with which travelers could impute private symbolic meaning to such objects independent of culturally predetermined symbolism (as with commercial souvenirs), and the ease with which such objects could be transported. Visiting Midway, Georgia, in 1818, for example, Ebenezer Kellogg found a way to take the rice plantations of the South back home to satisfy friends and family: "I here for the first time see the manner in which rice is prepared for market. I have taken from the rice stack specimens of the several kinds of rice, the gold rice, the white the volunteer rice, and a blasted stalk. These Mrs. Stevens has kindly sewed up in a linen rag. I hope to bring them to you in such preservation as to satisfy in some measure your curiosity."[21] John Frey sent some St. Augustine oranges to a relative in New York City in 1829, aiming not just to deliver oranges but to send a piece of the South in the midst of winter for novelty's sake.[22] Similarly, an anonymous travel writer in Florida criticized invalids who spent their days in the sun at St. Augustine whittling canes, thus unwittingly underscoring the multivalence of some representative souvenirs: "Every one intends to carry home canes enough to present one to each of his friends, as an everlasting memorial of the far-off and never-to-be-forgotten city of St. Augustine, where orange trees will grow in spite of frost."[23] Likewise, when antislavery advocate Bartholomew Van Dame, eager to learn firsthand about the evils of slavery, traveled to Virginia in 1848, he purchased a pair of slave shackles. He "thereupon returned to New Hampshire fortified with eye-witness material," later employing them at the climax of his "frequent subsequent talks about slavery [with] a melodramatic shaking of the chains before the eyes of his listeners in the villages and towns of the eastern part of the State"—his own creative method for symbolically conveying the meaning of "the South" (and his experience of it) to the folks back home and thus motivating his audience to action.[24]

Often, though, representative souvenirs were small items picked up or snipped from the natural landscape of a particularly impressive southern scene. Writing from New Orleans to her sister in 1851, Anna Whitney linked the "southern day" to the object she enclosed with her letter: "I am sitting by the open window, the air is sweet, heavenly. I send you a bit of the fig banana leaf from the garden. The leave from wh. we cut it is 3 yds. long & a yard wide. Notice the beauty of its texture. . . . I took a long walk this a.m. & another this Evng. & I wish I cd. send you a breath & a beam of this beautiful southern day."[25] Natural Bridge, Virginia, was closely associated with Thomas Jefferson and remained throughout the antebellum period the South's chief sublime landscape competitor with Niagara Falls. One anonymous visitor to Natural Bridge symbolically secured the memory of this distinctively southern destination: "For our parts, we contented ourselves with bearing away a hawthorn stick and a cypress bough as our memorials of a visit so full of impressive associations."[26] Such practices were common. Displaying a remarkably well-developed sense of traveler entitlement, George Cheyne Shattuck, also at Natural Bridge, boasted of taking "as relics a piece of limestone, & some twigs of a cedar growing on the bridge," having come "160 miles to see this object." A few days later, at Weyer's Cave, he "brought away several specimens," having "paid a dollar for my entertainment."[27] Perhaps regarding his descriptive talents as insufficient to convey the power of what he saw, Henry D. Gilpin took a relic of nature from Harper's Ferry, Virginia, to convey his experience of the southern sublime to others: "I immediately made my way to the top of Jefferson's rock, which rises directly above the village to an immense height, and affords you a varied & magnificent prospect of the great features I have described. I tore a branch from a tree near its summit which I shall take home for the girls, as a memento of the greatest natural wonder I have seen, with the exception of the Falls of Niagara."[28] Encounters with exotic southern wildlife offered equally meaningful souvenir opportunities. James Kirke Paulding gloated over the fourteen rattles he collected from a rattlesnake he killed one morning, prizes he intended to "keep as trophies" since "these fellows are by no means common; though they tell stories of places in the mountains, where nobody but hunters ever go, where there are thousands."[29]

Sometimes the simplest object functioned rather creatively as a representative souvenir of assorted tropes of southern difference. Some natural objects were so full of associations with the South that they operated in and of themselves as markers of southern experience—as pieces of the real—which is surely what New Hampshire native Walter D. Smith intended when he noted in his diary that he had enclosed mistletoe and Spanish moss in a letter mailed home to a friend.[30] Likewise, Charles Clinton reported that when his train stopped midway through North Carolina in fields of cotton "new to most of the travellers," several passengers disembarked and returned with "several stalks [that] were much admired by those who had never seen cotton growing before."[31] Where the real was not accessible or transportable, its representation sufficed. After having "seen a good deal of Southern life," Levi Lincoln Newton described sturgeon as a distinctive Richmond dish that he "dare[d] not taste." He also observed "other very strange fish caught in" the James River, whose waters he described as the color of "yellow saffrons." Tucked into his letter was a clipped quarter-sheet of paper, apparently a portion of the bill of fare from a Richmond hotel, on which Newton had scrawled, "This paper is the exact color of the James River."[32]

Two-dimensional representative souvenirs abounded during the antebellum period, particularly as sketches drawn neatly into the margins of letters and journals, sometimes suggesting other souvenir items that might have been brought back if not for their cumbersome nature. Joseph Wharton offered one variety in his letters home, carefully sketching a broom commonly sold in Savannah and made from the split stem of a yucca plant. He included sketches of southern people, noting what he regarded as their distinctive physical features—beards, moustaches, and a "large proportion of aquiline and roman noses and of hawk eyes" and comparing them to the "knights of a few centuries back."[33] Gilpin also drew a handful of southern sights, including Harper's Ferry, but "regretted very much as I have done on several other occasions that I had not a sketch book with me, as no language can at all give you an idea of the scene."[34] A few days later, he inserted another sketch into his letter home: "To this map of the country I will add a plan of Weyer's cave," he wrote, "sketched from one hanging in the inn at Staunton, said to have been made from actual survey soon after its discovery; though I confess it appears to me to be incorrect in some particulars."[35]

Others drew architecture, landscape, and people, visually depicting what seemed unusual and unique about their experience of the region. Jeremiah Evarts, traveling only thirty miles west of Charleston, South Carolina, in 1826, was so struck by the vast distances between homes that he mapped the intervals in his journal.[36] In 1857, Ledyard Lincklaen sketched nearly anything that struck him as particularly representative of southern backwardness and ruin—slaves carrying cornstalks on their heads in Virginia ("I thought Old Virginny seemed thoroughly tired out"); slaves operating turpentine distilleries in North Carolina ("The negroes through the pine woods have a very stupid, slovenly look, and no wonder, as they drudge at peeling and dipping and scraping and boiling in little isolated gangs in this dismal region, without seeing anything with life or motion"); and Spanish moss in a South Carolina swamp ("The whole swamp was the most repulsive and desolate of objects, and looked literally a hiding place for dragons").[37] As he added sketches to the journal, Lincklaen increasingly yearned for access to the newest technology to produce a superior form of two-dimensional representation. On one occasion he noted, "I am constantly wishing that I could photograph the objects of this country, trees, buildings, and especially negros," and several days later he complained that "nothing but photographic pictures would give a perfect representation of the buildings or population of [Charleston], and I have been wishing for the means of taking such pictures ever since landing on the southern side of the Potomac."[38]

Northern travelers also frequently collected historical souvenirs while journeying through the South. These items often were commonplace objects, not necessarily a piece of the real but nevertheless associated with the historical location in question. In many cases, the souvenirs ostensibly were not chosen to represent southern distinctiveness, except perhaps by loose association.[39] Pressed leaves regularly served as souvenirs, as in Lamson's case, where the clover acted strictly as a miniature for the "tree marker" of British casualties, while the Spanish moss embodied southern distinctiveness. Travelers also gathered various other natural objects. Traveling to Washington's tomb at Mount Vernon in 1834, Benjamin French "plucked a sprig of evergreen & a weed" to help him remember "how many illustrious individuals had passed in the very footpaths I was traversing & had stood where I then was, & paid to the shade of the mighty man whose remains were there deposited the tribute of gratitude for a Free & Independent Country."[40]

But some northern travelers selected historic souvenirs that also functioned as symbolic markers of southern distinction. One northern traveler introduced his neatly arranged journal of southern travels by weaving into the flyleaf "a slip of evergreen trimming from the tomb of John C. Calhoun Charleston SC," a rather intriguing choice for the one distinct southern experience most emblematic of his journey.[41] Similarly, when visiting General Francis Marion's tomb near Pineville, South Carolina, Smith snipped a palmetto leaf to commemorate not only the historical significance of the place but also "one of the most beautiful places I have seen in S.C."[42] Shattuck, who seemed to pluck souvenirs everywhere along his journey, spent a long day with the aging James Madison at Montpelier, conversing about southern slavery, the possibility of Virginians shifting their attentions to "factory investments," and southern mismanagement of timber resources. At the end of the visit, Shattuck "rode slowly off gazing at the house as I went & . . . stopped to break some evergreens from the trees as mementoes."[43]

If pieces of the real or at least natural objects representative of historical places and persons could be removed without a second thought, the possibility of buying such objects horrified some northern travelers. While visiting Mount Vernon in 1839, one New Jersey man expressed disdain for the burgeoning souvenir trade he encountered. Mount Vernon's gardener was busily selling clippings of Washington's flowers and shrubs to visitors, ostensibly to finance the care of the house and gardens. The traveler nevertheless deemed the practice "unseemly," concluding that the gardener could only be engaged in such business "to supply him with tobacco and pipe money." The traveler continued, "Relics from such a source are surely invested with too much dignity and value to be bartered for a few shillings. . . . It surely can't be done with consent and by authority; for every one must see the revulsion it must cause in a visitor's feelings. What would a foreigner think of us, if, on going to Mount Vernon, he were offered for some paltry sum a flower to dry in his notebook to the memory of Washington, and were told that the heirs and assigns of this great man eked out their living by the sale of such relics[?]"[44]

Such discomfort with selling pieces of Mount Vernon to curious travelers does not seem to have halted the practice, given the image engraved on the cover of the sheet music for T. P. Coulston's "Washington's Tomb: Ballad" (1850). The illustration depicts a black man, possibly a slave, leaning against the wall of the tomb with an assortment of walking sticks for sale while three white visitors turn their attention in his

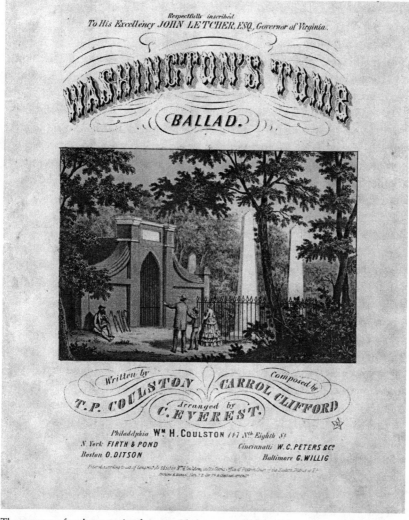

The cover art for sheet music often provided a means for travelers to memorialize their southern journeys. This cover for "Washington's Tomb: Ballad" (1850) depicts the first president's grave at Mount Vernon, a popular tourist site, as well as a black man, possibly a slave, selling souvenir canes. (Virginia Historical Society, Richmond, Virginia)

direction.[45] Nine years later, even some members of the patriotic and unionist Knights Templars of Massachusetts and Rhode Island showed no misgivings about owning a piece of the "holy ground" on which rested "the precious deposit of Washington's dust." After exploring the house and the grounds, the touring party "purchas[ed] a few of the canes which the negroes furnish so plentifully to all comers."[46]

In less sacred places, however, purchasing a piece of the real was commonplace and expected.[47] This variety of commercial souvenir repeatedly appears in accounts of northerners' experiences in the South. Northern travelers converted locally produced goods into fashionable souvenirs of southern distinctiveness—for example, the "work basket, very beautiful though small, made of the Palmetto leaf," that Connecticut native John Pierpont Jr. purchased in Savannah for a female relative. Such baskets, Pierpont told his father, "are quite the rage here among those returning to their friends at the North."[48] Writing from Charleston in 1851, Almira Coffin told Mattie Osgood of Hollis, Maine, that the box she sent back with other returning northerners contained a basket obtained at a church fair, where "mats, lamp-lighter cases," and a variety of other souvenirs, "equally curious and southern," were also available.[49]

Native American exchange, prompted by trips through Indian country (particularly in Georgia and Alabama), was also a common component of the travels through the South before 1840. Visitors to Indian country in the southern states often used their experiences to underscore the notion that the South remained both dangerous and somehow historically, culturally, and socially behind the North, in part because the presence of "uncivilized" Native Americans contributed to the portrayal of the southern backcountry as still untamed. James D. Davidson, for example, bought "two pair of Indian Mocasins for my little boys, ornamented with beads," immediately noting the "bones of the dead men and the horses" he had seen the preceding night as he passed the scene of a Creek attack on a stagecoach the previous year. Prized by him for their display of both artisanal skill and beauty, the moccasins also functioned as physical props for the narrative of his Indian encounter, an experience no longer possible in many northern regions of the United States and thus foreign. In short, like most souvenirs, the moccasins came with a built-in story.[50]

Commercial transactions, however, were not always part of an established trade. Enterprising children sometimes sought to profit from selling a piece of southern culture, as Ingraham's purchase of grapeshot suggests. Simri Rose, a northern transplant who maintained a thorough disdain for anything southern outside of his new hometown, Macon, Georgia, found an even more informal trade in southern "fine art" just a few counties away in 1830. He purchased a child's drawing that in his eyes epitomized southern backwardness and deplorable educational opportunities.[51]

Commercially produced two-dimensional representations, however, took on greater significance as the antebellum period progressed. This variety of souvenir revealed the commercialization and standardization of northern conceptions of the South, thus wedding commercially produced images to the northern national narrative of southern difference.[52] Prior to 1850, the commercial images collected by northern travelers to commemorate their southern journeys were limited largely to engravings of noteworthy landscapes or buildings, primarily located in or near the cities of Savannah, Charleston, Wilmington, Mobile, and New Orleans. Later in the antebellum period, some travelers likely purchased both northern and southern periodicals containing low-quality versions of similar engravings and tore them out to serve as representational images of what the travelers had seen on their visits.[53] Some travelers compiled lengthy albums of these engraved images, not unlike modern photo albums, to use as props while describing their journeys to family and friends at home.[54]

After 1850, the widespread availability of multiple forms of engraved and lithographic images made visual commemoration of the South much easier. In early 1856, Edward Beyer began accepting subscriptions from Richmond for his *Album of Virginia,* a collection of forty colored plates depicting various Virginia springs; natural wonders such as the Peaks of Otter, Weyer's Cave, and Natural Bridge; and railroad scenes.[55] Visitors to Richmond three years later could purchase "views of Hotels, Springs, Factories, Machine Shops, &c.[,] DESCRIPTIVE VIEWS OF SCENERY" from L. F. Citti's Lithographic Establishment. A year later, competitors not only opened a shop just around the corner but also copied Citti's 1859 advertisement word for word.[56]

Sheet music produced in the South typically featured images to accompany songs about southern places and people, emphasizing the pastoral beauty of the region and its significant tourist destinations. As discussed earlier, the cover of "Washington's Tomb: Ballad" portrayed a scene of the first president's final resting place. Francis Buck's "Blue Ridge Quick Step" showed troops marching off to the Mexican War through an imposing, heaven-bound gap through the Blue Ridge Mountains. J. E. Magruder's "Berkeley Springs Schottisch" featured an engraving of visitors cavorting on horseback in front of the buildings at the popular Virginia resort. F. Seibert's "Natural Bridge Schottisch" showed a lone tourist glancing up at the arch in sublime bewilderment. The cover of G. George's "Richmond Schottisch" displayed a view of the city from across the James River. All were available to northern travelers passing through Richmond and Baltimore.[57] Northern publishers of music about the South, such as Bernard Covert's "The Dismal Swamp" and the minstrel tune "Floating Scow of Old Virginia" (better known today as "Carry Me Back to Ole Virginny"), conversely, produced often image-less sheet music that nevertheless commemorated southern tropes or stereotypes.[58] The covers of some northern song sheets, however, included stereotypical images of "happy" or "dandy" blacks in southern settings. A. F. Winnemore's "Farewell to Georgia" and his "Away to de Sugar Cane Field" featured the same image of two black musicians performing with glee. B. Williams's "Dandy Jim, from Carolina" portrayed a well-dressed black man showing off in front of a mirror.[59]

By 1850, though, the daguerreotype had revolutionized image making, and itinerant daguerreotypists scattered across the South, settling in cities for a few months before moving on.[60] Residents often used such services, but judging by city directories, travelers were also prized as patrons. Carvalho's Grand Sky-Light Daguerrean Gallery, advertising in the 1852 Charleston directory, invited "strangers visiting Charleston . . . to visit this Gallery, whether they wish Pictures or not." Sensitive to the demands on travelers' time, the ad noted that "persons arriving at night, and about to leave in the morning train of cars, can have their pictures taken and finished in the space of a quarter of an hour." Starting at only $1.50, a daguerreotype was not an unreasonable purchase for most travelers, especially those seeking to commemorate a visit to one of the South's grandest cities. For those seeking souvenirs of the "famous personages" they might have encountered along their journey (or simply associated with the places they had visited), Carvalho's offered "many specimens of paintings, engravings, and daguerreotypes of distinguished individuals." Smith, for example, visited several daguerreotype establishments while on a day trip to Charleston in early 1847 and was especially intrigued by an image of John C. Calhoun.[61] By 1860, Charleston's photographic artists had improved their art, taking their cameras outdoors to offer travelers "stereoscopes" and "views." Such images, it seemed, had become the perfect commercial souvenir for every aspect of southern travel.[62]

Collecting the Uncollectible

The variety of retained souvenirs steadily expanded during the antebellum period, supplying northern travelers many opportunities to collect objects that represented the idiosyncracies of southern difference by which so many northerners defined and commemorated their journeys. For all of these opportunities, however, travelers' direct experiences with objects that could not be removed (or might not survive the journey)

As S.N. Carvalho's ad in the 1852 Charleston, South Carolina, city directory illustrates, antebellum photographers sought to exploit travelers' desire for mementos. (South Caroliniana Library, University of South Carolina, Columbia) offered the most intriguing—and perhaps the most lasting—memories of southern difference. These ephemeral souvenirs constituted a separate class of objects that retained associative memories of southern experiences and helped reinforce the northern national narrative in the minds of travelers and those they told about their journeys. These ephemeral souvenirs are the most difficult to uncover in the historical record because they survive only through written accounts of southern travels (a category of objects that includes letters, diaries, and journals and that is often overlooked as a separate form of souvenir when considering the material culture of travel).

For example, Pierpont, who ventured to Georgia in 1852, did not mean to suggest that blackberries were intrinsically and distinctively southern when he wrote to his father, "I ate blackberries which [I] picked on the old fort at St. Augustine. Think of that in March!"[63] They possessed, of course, a use value as something to eat. But the experience of consuming them in March was distinctively southern. While he retained no physical object in a collection of souvenirs (in the modern sense) that could be pulled out and viewed or handled at some future date, Pierpont nevertheless recognized the category of objects he knew as "St. Augustine blackberries consumed in March" that indicated to him a southern difference from life in Connecticut. This symbolic attachment to the ephemeral object associated with southern distinctiveness explains Samuel Thorne's letter of disappointment to his mother from Charleston in April 1848: "Father cannot send thee on any peas yet a while as they are to[o] dear, being $1 a peck. Strawberries were also very scarce and of quite a high price."[64] Young Samuel had hoped to share a bit of the South—fresh produce at the end of winter—with his mother but could not do so because of the expense of these markers of life in the South (and because they would probably have rotted before completing their journey north).

Thus, the experience of these ephemeral markers of memory supplied the narrative that substituted for the actual object described in letters, journals, and diaries. Such writings provided a vital means of commemorating the southern travel experience through objects considered emblematic of southern difference. If, as Stewart suggests, "oral traditions were [previously] seen as the abstract equivalent to material culture,"[65] it does not seem unreasonable to propose that materially constructed narratives, conveying the same memories of objects as oral traditions and in the process reconstituting ephemeral objects of experience, became in fact carrying cases for ephemeral souvenirs.

To qualify as an ephemeral souvenir of the antebellum South, the object in question had to possess certain intrinsic qualities.[66] First, it had to be both nonfixed and at least temporarily possessable by the traveler in a way that objects of pilgrimage or historical sites could not be without diminishing the value of the whole (Washington's tomb, for example, or Washington's bed inside Mount Vernon). Thus, when Abiel Abbot wrote about handling the whip used to punish slaves at Charleston's Sugar House, he in essence described an object that thereafter conveyed powerful associations and triggers of memory about southern difference, even though he could not own or possess the whip. The particular whip displayed at the Sugar House was not special (had Abbot stolen the item, it could certainly have been replaced by a similar whip without diminishing its symbolic value to Charlestonians, Sugar House slaves, or future visitors) except in its symbolic significance to Abbot as a visitor who had held the instrument in a slave state.[67] Similarly, when Sophia Dreer, writing from Richmond in 1841 to her brother, Henry Dreer, suggested that he should "excuse the bad writing for the little negro brought me such a stick of a pen, I should have put him in the letter and sent him on to Ferdinand but he was rather large," she did not intend, of course, to mail off the slave. Nevertheless, her commentary expressed not only her disappointment with the services offered by the Exchange Hotel's servants but also her adjustment to the distinctly southern notion of blacks as things to be owned and traded. The slave was *her* servant—at least as long as she rented a room—and her quip that size alone prevented his transport suggested her (possibly humorous) recognition that she had possessed him, albeit temporarily.[68]

A second characteristic defined ephemeral souvenirs: possession by the traveler had to be fleeting. As Abbot's experience suggested, travelers lacked the ability to separate the ephemeral object from its environment. But the nature of such a souvenir—its tendency to escape preservation as a tangible object to be placed permanently on a shelf at home—could also be related to its physical properties. Not surprisingly, many of these kinds of ephemeral souvenirs were tied directly to proximate sensory experiences of perceived southern difference, emphasizing olfactory, haptic, and gustatory events in particular, because such instances proved most difficult to commemorate through representative objects. Thus, the narration about the taste of St. Augustine blackberries and Charleston strawberries became the repository of memory about southern climatic and agricultural difference, even though the blackberries and strawberries had already been consumed. Likewise, Coffin's wish to send "one of the beautiful gardens, with which I am surrounded, just as it lies before me now with an atmosphere balmy enough to keep it in all its glory!" highlighted the perishability of those Charleston gardens outside of their southern climatic context and the elusiveness of the balmy atmosphere as an item to mail home.[69]

Fleeting possession came in other forms besides perishability. Writing from Columbus, Georgia, in 1845, Cyprian P. Willcox lamented that he could neither send the air home to family nor take it with him for himself. Instead, by recording his thoughts about southern air, he effectively made a souvenir of the air by permanently preserving its symbolic significance in his journal.[70] A month later, he acknowledged his journal's function as a collection of such ephemera, imagining it as the receptacle he needed to preserve the beautiful southern days if only he could make it work correctly: "I must appease conscience in these days with simple jottings in my Journal, for it does seem as if I had a distinct duty for every sand of time. I must stick a pin through these beautiful days for future comparison and reference." He continued, "I wish I could transcribe the luscious softness of this air that it might puff an emollient exhalation into my face when I hereafter open to this page or perhaps—capital! why did I not think of it instinctively—of a morning after shaving! To lean out the window and feel said softness fairly melting through every [pore] of your body—if it don't dry up the foul humors and drive the devil out of you what will?"[71]

Whether ephemeral or retained, the souvenirs northern travelers selected on their journeys through the South both commemorated their experiences and underscored the essential southern characteristics on which the northern national narrative of southern difference so frequently harped. These differences at times resided in the objects themselves, as in the slave whip Abbot briefly held or the slave shackles Van Dame shook in the faces of his fellow abolitionists. On other occasions, difference was constructed at the margins, as when Ingraham saw southern indolence and backwardness in New Orleans farmers' failure to profit from the historical value of the battlefield lands and artifacts they continued to plow up.

In any event, northern travelers found difference everywhere in the South, and they consistently used a burgeoning souvenir mentality to commemorate that difference in an era when the ubiquitous commercial souvenir trade with which modern travelers are so familiar had yet to be imagined by even the most industrious and profit-minded Americans. Those artifacts of southern difference—collected, preserved, shared with family and friends, and described in journals, letters, and diaries—played a vital role in establishing and reifying the stereotypes and assumptions about the South that made sectional antagonisms seem irreconcilable in the years before the Civil War.

NOTES

This essay is revised from a chapter in my dissertation, "Strangers in a Strange Land: Northern Travelers and the Coming of the American Civil War" (Ph.D. diss., University of South Carolina, 2006).

1. Joseph Holt Ingraham, *The South-West, by a Yankee*, vol. 1 (1835; Readex Microprint, 1966), 197.

2. Ibid., 198–204.

3. Ibid., 204–5.

4. Ibid., 206.

5. In 1837, the *American Railroad Journal* estimated that "travel last year between Charleston and Savannah, and the northern cities alone, amounted to between 50 and 60,000 passengers" (*American Railroad Journal*, 25 February 1837, 117). I thank Aaron Marrs for this reference.

6. For more on this literature, see William R. Taylor, *Cavalier and Yankee: The Old South and American National Character* (New York: Harper Torchbooks, 1961) and Plaag, "Strangers in a Strange Land." My ideas regarding the North-South binary and its construction have been particularly influenced by Susan-Mary Grant, *North over South: Northern Nationalism and American Identity in the Antebellum Era* (Lawrence: University Press of Kansas, 2000); Eric Foner, *Free Soil, Free Labor, Free Men* (1970; New York: Oxford University Press, 1995), 40–72; Edward Pessen, "How Different from Each Other Were the Antebellum North and South?" *American Historical Review* 85 (December 1980): 1119–49; Richard N. Current, "Two Civilizations—or One? 1780s–1850s," in *Northernizing the South* (Athens: University of Georgia Press, 1983), 17–49; Howard R. Floan, *The South in Northern Eyes: 1831 to 1861* (Austin: University of Texas Press, 1958).

7. See, for example, Ruth B. Phillips, *Trading Identities: The Souvenir in Native North American Art from the Northeast, 1700–1900* (Seattle: University of Washington Press, 1998), 5–6, 9. In *On Holiday: A History of Vacationing* (Berkeley: University of California Press, 1999), Orvar Löfgren credits the birth of the souvenir market to the "eighteenth-century world of the Grand Tour" and briefly mentions Niagara tourists taking home war relics and Native American trinkets. He describes miniaturized souvenirs as "narrative coat hangers," able to support a host of varying meanings and memories unique to each traveler while performing the same basic commemorative function (86–88).

8. For a history of early American postcards, see George Miller and Dorothy Miller, *Picture Postcards in the United States, 1893–1918* (New York: Crown, 1976).

9. Eric J. Leed, *The Mind of the Traveler: From Gilgamesh to Global Tourism* (New York: Basic Books, 1991), 21.

10. Leed's theory on contrastive groups offers an alternative to Benedict Anderson's theories on "imagined communities." Anderson criticizes the idea that nationalism requires an Other, arguing that "nationalism thinks in terms of historical destinies, while racism dreams of eternal contaminations, transmitted from the origins of time through an endless sequence of loathsome copulations: outside history." Given that antebellum Americans came to see one another almost uniformly in terms of "the southern race" and "the Yankee race"—a trope evident in some American travel narratives as early as 1815—nationalism can "dream" in terms of both "historical destinies" and "eternal contaminations." See Benedict Anderson, *Imagined Communities: Reflections on the Origin and Spread of*

Nationalism, rev. ed. (New York: Verso, 1991), 141–50. For more on northern nationalism during the antebellum period, see Grant, *North over South*. Grant and I agree that northern nationalism "rested on opposition to the other section" and that "northern ideology went beyond what might be understood as sectionalism" (9); we disagree about how and when that narrative of southern difference was created and employed, the modalities of that narrative in action when northerners and southerners interacted with one another, and the many complications to the perceived sectional binary that undercut that northern national narrative but simultaneously compelled northerners—and eventually southerners—to nevertheless embrace and reify the narrative, in effect making it self-sustaining.

11. Antebellum travelers did not generally use the word *souvenir* to describe these objects, preferring *memento, keepsake,* or similar constructions. For the most part, the word *souvenir* was used during this period to denote printed material created to recall an occasion or sequence of events, as in a concert program or a wedding announcement.

12. Maurice Halbwachs, *On Collective Memory,* trans. and ed. Lewis A. Coser (Chicago: University of Chicago Press, 1992), 204.

13. See Celia Lury, "The Objects of Travel," in *Touring Cultures: Transformations of Travel and Theory,* ed. Chris Rojek and John Urry (London: Routledge, 1997), 76. Lury argues that objects of travel can be divided into three complicated categories that stress original meanings over the meanings imputed to objects by the travelers who experienced and possessed them (77–80). While Lury's categorization is philosophically intriguing, and I agree with her conclusions about the generalized value of traveling objects to the tourist experience, her categories in fact seem to degrade the very quality that makes a souvenir valuable—personal experience of the object by the individual traveler.

14. See Dean MacCannell, *The Tourist: A New Theory of the Leisure Class* (1967; Berkeley: University of California Press, 1999), 158–60. Nelson H. H. Graburn has made the intriguing point that souvenirs also offer hurried travelers "who cover so much ground so fast" the additional benefit of serving "as cues by which to relive the experience at a slower pace" ("Tourism: The Sacred Journey," in *Hosts and Guests: The Anthropology of Tourism,* 2nd ed., ed. Valene L. Smith [Philadelphia: University of Pennsylvania Press, 1989], 33).

15. Beverly Gordon, "The Souvenir: Messenger of the Extraordinary," *Journal of Popular Culture* 20 (Winter 1986): 135.

16. Susan Stewart, *On Longing: Narratives of the Miniature, the Gigantic, the Souvenir, the Collection* (Durham, N.C.: Duke University Press, 1993), 135.

17. On collections, see ibid., 151–70.

18. My use of the term *marker* here loosely derives from that meant by MacCannell (*Tourist,* 41–42). I use the term strictly to apply to the souveniring aspect of fashioning memory about the South.

19. Mrs. Edwin Lamson, 1855 Journal, 37–39, Lamson Family Papers, Box 1, Folder 3, Massachusetts Historical Society, Boston. A heartbreaking postscript to Lamson's journal—perhaps a consequence of early archival practices—is that neither the Spanish moss nor the clover survives in her letters, highlighting one of the most difficult aspects of scholarly antebellum souvenir hunting for historians.

In most cases, antebellum souvenirs evince themselves almost exclusively through their associated journal and diary entries and/or letters. Without this context or the associations of a commercialized souvenir theme, most other souvenirs are deemed meaningless and probably discarded. For example, in the summer of 2003, as I opened an 1857 railway and steamboat guide at an unnamed facility in New England, three pressed leaves fluttered out of the back pages onto the table. The guide contained no notations as to the origin of the leaves. Carefully replacing the leaves to match the stains on the pages within the book, I took the whole mess up to the archivist and explained what had happened. Unimpressed, the archivist took the guide, removed the leaves and tossed them in the garbage, then handed the book back to me.

20. Stewart posits two subclasses of retained souvenirs, "the three-dimensional [reduced] into the miniature, that which can be enveloped by the body, [and] the two-dimensional representation, that which can be appropriated within the privatized view of the individual subject" (*On Longing*, 142). Some souvenir objects could fall into all three categories, depending on symbolic associations. Purchased at the market as a symbol of southern material culture (mattress ticking), Lamson's Spanish moss, for example, would fall into the commercial category; picked from a live oak tree as a feature of southern landscape (Spanish moss was one of the most frequent symbols of southern antiquity, mystery, deterioration, and even death), it was merely a representative souvenir; picked from the live oak tree at Chalmette for its battlefield associations, it was decidedly historical. In Lamson's case, regardless of its operative mode of symbolic function, the moss was inextricably linked with southern difference.

21. Sidney Walter Martin, "A New Englander's Impressions of Georgia in 1817–1818: Extracts from the Diary of Ebenezer Kellogg," *Journal of Southern History* 12 (May 1946): 258 (entry for 7 January 1818).

22. John Frey to Henry Frey, 26 November 1829, 3, Frey Family Papers, 1793–1917, New-York Historical Society, New York.

23. "An Invalid," *A Winter in the West Indies and Florida* (New York: Wiley and Putnam, 1839), 157–58.

24. See Frank O. Spinney, "A New Hampshire Schoolmaster Views Kentucky," *New England Quarterly* 17 (March 1944): 89. For more on the use of the sounds of slavery's horrors in abolitionist presentations at the North, see Mark M. Smith, *Listening to Nineteenth-Century America* (Chapel Hill: University of North Carolina Press, 2001), 156–85.

25. Anne Whitney to "My dear Sarah," 26 January 1851, Anne Whitney Papers, Wellesley College, Wellesley, Mass.

26. "A New-Englander," "Journal of a Trip to the Mountains, Caves and Springs of Virginia," *Southern Literary Messenger* 4 (August 1838): 517. See also T. Addison Richards, "The Landscape of the South," *Harper's New Monthly Magazine*, May 1853, 721–22, wherein the sublimity of the landscape of the South is repeatedly compared with that of the North.

27. See George Cheyne Shattuck Diary, 31 January 1835, 2 February 1835, Massachusetts Historical Society, Boston.

28. Ralph D. Gray, "A Tour of Virginia in 1827: Letters of Henry D. Gilpin

to His Father," *Virginia Magazine of History and Biography* 76 (October 1968): 448–49 (letter of 12 September 1827); see also 461–63 (letter of 16 September 1827), for a similar sublime comparison and description of Natural Bridge and comparison to Niagara.

29. James Kirke Paulding, *Letters from the South, Written during an Excursion in the Summer of 1816*, vol. 1 (New York: Eastburn, 1817), 170.

30. Walter D. Smith Diary, 10 April 1847, Walter D. Smith Diary and Letters, 1842–61, South Carolina Historical Society, Charleston.

31. Charles Clinton, *A Winter from Home* (New York: Trow, 1852), 4.

32. Levi Lincoln Newton to Rejoice Newton, 20 May 1847, Newton Family Papers, Box 2, Folder 3, Letters of Levi Lincoln Newton and Other Family Members, 1834–70, American Antiquarian Society, Worcester, Mass.

33. H. Larry Ingle, "Joseph Wharton Goes South, 1853," *South Carolina Historical Magazine* 96 (October 1995): 319–20 (letter of 5 February 1853), 323 (letter of 8 February 1853).

34. Gray, "Tour of Virginia," 447 (letter of 12 September 1827).

35. Ibid., 455 (letter of 15 September 1827).

36. J. Orin Oliphant, *Through the South and West with Jeremiah Evarts in 1826* (Lewisburg, Pa.: Bucknell University Press, 1956), 89 (entry for 16 February 1826).

37. Mr. and Mrs. Ledyard Lincklaen, Letter-Journal of a Trip to Cuba & the Southern States, 10 February 1857, 12 February 1857, 13 February 1857, New-York Historical Society, New York.

38. Ibid., 13 February 1857, 16 February 1857.

39. Whether historical locations within the South were thought of as "belonging" to the South throughout the antebellum period is unclear. By 1859, however, sectional ownership of history and place had become part of the dialogue on sectional distinction, so much so that those wishing to mute sectional discord invoked these sites as the common property of all Americans. For one example, see Virginia governor Henry A. Wise's speech to the Knights Templars of Massachusetts and Rhode Island: "We meet you and greet you by the mystic tie of brotherhood which exists in every land. We meet you as patriots,—men of the same common country. You are no strangers here in Virginia. . . . I go to your land, and although no man knows me, and though I own no house there, yet there is one house, the Hancock House, that old ball-room of the Boston Tea Party, which is mine as well as yours. Faneuil Hall is there, which is mine too. And here in Virginia is Mount Vernon, and that is yours; and here are Yorktown and Old Raleigh, and they are yours. And Virginia is yours also!" (qtd. in *Memoir of the Pilgrimage to Virginia of the Knights Templars of Massachusetts and Rhode Island, May, 1859* [Boston: Williams, 1859], 45–46). Other speeches offered on this journey, which was apparently undertaken to "improve relations" between New Englanders and Virginians in the midst of sectional strife, amplify and echo the unifying theme of Wise's speech; see, for example, 98–101.

40. Qtd. in Donald B. Cole and John J. McDonough, eds., *Witness to the*

Young Republic: A Yankee's Journal, 1828–1870 (Hanover, N.H.: University Press of New England, 1989), 43 (entry for 23 May 1834).

41. "Journal of Travels, 1849–1851," South Carolina Historical Society, Charleston.

42. Smith Diary, 28 March 1847.

43. Shattuck Diary, 27 January 1835.

44. "A Jersey Man in the Old Dominion," *Southern Literary Messenger,* December 1839, 805.

45. T. P. Coulston (lyricist), Carrol Clifford (composer), and C. Everest (arranger), "Washington's Tomb: Ballad" (Philadelphia: Coulston, 1850). For a fascinating look at the ways in which Mount Vernon functioned as a sectional football—southerners claiming the estate as their own in response to efforts in the 1830s to remove Washington's remains to Washington, D.C., and, later, both northerners and southerners arguing that Mount Vernon should be preserved to preserve the Union—as well as other examples of antebellum souveniring at Mount Vernon, see Jean B. Lee, "Historical Memory, Sectional Strife, and the American Mecca," *Virginia Magazine of History and Biography* 109 (2001): 255–300.

46. *Memoir of the Pilgrimage,* 174–76. For an antebellum work in which early historical tourism of Virginia destinations is overtly promoted, see "An Ex-Member of Congress," *My Ride to the Barbecue; or, Revolutionary Reminiscences of the Old Dominion* (New York: Rollo, 1860).

47. Phillips has already exposed one variety of such transacted objects—the Native American souvenir—in her study of the souvenir trade in native North American art in the Northeast. Alternately called *knickknacks, trinkets, geegaws, bric-a-brac, curiosities,* and even *mementos,* such items had a popularity with travelers in the Northeast that rested "on their success in conveying recognizable—and acceptable—concepts of difference (*Trading Identities,* 5–6, 9).

48. John Pierpont Jr. to father, 1 June 1852, in George H. Gibson, "Georgia Letters of John Pierpont, Jr., to His Father," *Georgia Historical Quarterly* 55 (Winter 1971): 559.

49. Almira Coffin to Mattie H. Osgood, Hollis, Maine, 9 May [1851?], 1–2, Almira Coffin Letters, South Carolina Historical Society, Charleston.

50. Herbert A. Kellar, "A Journey through the South in 1836: Diary of James D. Davidson," *Journal of Southern History* 1 (August 1935): 372. Davidson's views on the South highlight the continuing interregional divisions in the minds of southerners at the same time that northerners began to perceive all of the states south of the Potomac and east of the Mississippi as a unified, cohesive region.

51. "Here I purchased from the land lord's daughter, a rare specimen of the *fine arts* in Emmanuel County. It consisted of a drawing, made with a pen, in red and black ink, of a horse, Negro, Camel, Elephant, a variety of Birds, etc., all very tastefully ornamented with checks, stripes, dots, and diamonds. So far the picture must have been a fancy piece, or else represented those species known only to the artist. It was, I understood the production of a teach of the A.B.C., who but for

this exuberance of talent would never have been heard of beyond his neighbour-hood" (Simri Rose, "Diary of Travel in the North," 15 June 1830, 3, typescript, Hermione Ross Walker Papers, Section II, Book/Vol. 1, microfilm copy, Southern Historical Collection, University of North Carolina at Chapel Hill).

52. For more on the creation of commercialized images of the South, see Plaag, "Strangers in a Strange Land."

53. See, for example, Richards, "Landscape of the South."

54. Dr. Katherine Grier, personal conversation, September 2003. I thank Grier for drawing my attention to this unique brand of travel commemoration through material culture.

55. Edward Beyer, *Album of Virginia; or, Illustration of the Old Dominion* (Richmond: Virginia State Library, 1980). According to the pamphlet accompanying the modern edition of the *Album,* Beyer received significant press coverage in the *Richmond Dispatch,* which reported on 19 May 1856 that he had "considerable success in obtaining subscriptions to his Virginia scenes" (vi).

56. "Lithographic Establishment by L. F. Citti," *First Annual Directory for the City of Richmond* (Richmond, Va.: West, 1859), 158; "Lithographic Establishment by Hoyer & Ludwig," *Second Annual Directory for the City of Richmond* (Richmond, Va.: Ferslew, 1860), 196. The 1860 directory shows Citti still in operation at a separate address.

57. Coulston, Clifford, and Everest, "Washington's Tomb"; Francis Buck, "Blue Ridge Quick Step" (Richmond, Va.: Taylor, 1847); J. E. Magruder, "Berkeley Springs Schottisch" (Baltimore: Miller and Beacham, [1857]); F. Seibert, "Natural Bridge Schottisch" (Baltimore: McCaffrey, 1857); G. George, "Richmond Schottisch" (Baltimore: Miller and Beacham, [1853]).

58. Other examples include such minstrel songs as "A Darkies Life Is Always Gay," "Way Down South in Alabama," "I Wish I Was in Old Virginny," "Darkie's Our Master's Gone to Town," and "Poor Dinah, or Who Stole the Toddy." See Bernard Covert, "The Dismal Swamp" (Boston: Ditson, 1852); Charles White, "De Floating Scow of Old Virginia" (Philadelphia: Lee and Walker, circa 1840s); Charles White, "Oh Carry Me Back to Old Virginny," as sung by Christy's Minstrels (Boston: Ditson, [1844–57?]); Charles White, "Oh! Carry Me Back to Old Virginny," as sung by Christy's Minstrels (New York: Holt, 1848); Charles White, "Carry Me Back to Ole Virginny" (Philadelphia: Ferrett, [1847–50?]); all other titles are from the cover sheet for the Holt version of "Carry Me Back."

59. A. F. Winnemore, "Farewell to Georgia" (Boston: Reed, 1847); A. F. Winnemore, "Away to de Sugar Cane Field" (Boston: Reed, 1847); B. Williams, "Dandy Jim, from Carolina" (New York: Firth and Hall, 1843).

60. For an excellent history of South Carolina photographers, see Harvey S. Teal, *Partners with the Sun: South Carolina Photographers, 1840–1940* (Columbia: University of South Carolina Press, 2001).

61. "Carvalho's Grand Sky-Light Daguerrean Gallery," *Directory of the City of Charleston for the Year 1852* (Charleston, S.C.: Councell, 1851), 188; Smith Diary, 12 May 1847.

62. "The Charleston Bazaar," *Directory of the City of Charleston, to Which Is Added a Business Directory, 1860,* vol. 1 (Charleston, S.C.: Ferslew, 1860), front

matter. For an example of a traveler who purchased a daguerreotype, see
Cathell, Journals, microfilm, 31 March 1852, p. 209, Southern Historical Colle
tion, University of North Carolina at Chapel Hill.

63. Gibson, "Georgia Letters," 573.

64. Samuel Thorne, *Journal of a Boy's Trip on Horseback, 1848,* ed. Samuel
Thorne Jr. (New York: privately printed, 1936), 4. Thorne's and Pierpont's examples emphasize an important distinction between the ephemeral souvenir and
items shipped for use value. A traveler who brought home a crate of oranges
or a pouch of tobacco typically did so to have something to consume that was
otherwise difficult to obtain in the North. Therefore, unless a traveler has specifically noted or implied the symbolic value of such objects, they have not been
considered here as souvenirs. This consumer behavior—shipping southern goods
to northern friends and family members for use value only—frequently appears
in northern travel accounts. Thorne's experience differs in that peas and strawberries were available at the North—just not in early April—and sending them
home was a way of symbolically conveying climatic difference. In his case, the
ephemeral memory had to suffice. Likewise, items gathered specifically for collection or specimen purposes—such as the "petrifactions of shell fish" that Welcome Arnold Greene gathered in Kentucky (only to later observe with chagrin a
slave boy amusing himself by launching them toward the river from the balcony
of Greene's boardinghouse)—do not qualify as ephemeral souvenirs, in that their
function was for scientific rather than symbolic purposes. See Alice E. Smith, *The
Journals of Welcome Arnold Greene: Journeys in the South, 1822–1824* (Madison: State Historical Society of Wisconsin, 1957), 169 (entry for 20 July 1823).

65. Stewart, *On Longing,* 142.

66. I am deeply indebted to Kathleen Hilliard for graciously but relentlessly
grilling me on my theory about ephemeral souvenirs and their various forms.

67. John Hammond Moore, "The Abiel Abbot Journals: A Yankee Preacher in
Charleston Society, 1818–1827," *South Carolina Historical Magazine* 68 (July
1967): 120–21.

68. Sophia E. Dreer to Henry A. Dreer, 8 August 1841, 2, Library of Virginia,
Richmond.

69. Almira Coffin to Mattie H. Osgood [?], 1 February 1851, Coffin Letters.

70. "I must say here by way of tantalizing our folks in imagination: I do wish
I could thrust my head into the sitting room of 134 Orange St. just to breathe
into it a little of this balmy [C]olumbus air;—twould disgust them with the rest of
Feb. Mff! Mff! how the circumambient sweeps in at that open window. Mff! how
sweet it smells—just from those orange isles of the sea I know how mellow the
tint of your blue sky! how the sun light m[e]lts through it! Then how summery
the look of the horizon. But you of the North—I wish I could write a shiver!"
(Cyprian P. Willcox Diary, 1 February 1845, 83, typescript corrected against
manuscript, Hargrett Collection, University of Georgia, Athens).

71. Ibid., 3 March 1845, 85.

Branding Dixie

Selling of the American South, 1890–1930

Karen L. Cox

Story of the Confederate States is going with a whoop! It is the best chance of the whole year to make money. . . . The book just hits the nail right on the head. . . . If for any reason you can't possibly take hold of it quickly, won't you do some friend, as well as us, a favor by calling attention to this great money-making opportunity? —B. F. Johnson Publishing, Richmond, Virginia, circa 1895

The B. F. Johnson Publishing Company's attempts to recruit salesmen for one of its many publications in southern history and literature captures the energy of late nineteenth-century marketing as well as the rise of mass consumerism. It combines the language of profit with that of promise. As Johnson himself wrote in 1895 to a potential salesman shortly after publication of the book, "We are offering you a chance to make money never equaled before." Then he continued, "It is a book for which the people have been waiting for years, *and they want it*. The name alone will secure an order in hundreds of cases."[1]

Johnson's entrepreneurial spirit was, on some level, at odds with what he proposed to sell—a book that touted the Confederate past. Johnson used the tactics of modernity—marketing and advertising—to promote a book written in the antimodern tradition of the Lost Cause. The *Story of the Confederate States,* Johnson explained to a salesman from Tennessee, told the true tale of the efforts to "establish a separate Southern Confederacy" and of the heroism of southern soldiers. Yet even as Johnson wrote of the need to preserve such stories, he was guided more by profit than sentiment. As he explained, this was a "money-making" opportunity for the right salesman, who stood to benefit from the sale of "dozens, scores, hundreds, and even thousands of copies."[2]

50

Johnson's story illustrates the earning potential associated with selling Dixie—in this case, the South's version of the Civil War. Books represented one of several means of profiting from the sale of the Lost Cause. Moreover, southern businesses were not alone in their efforts to tap into the market for all things Dixie. Northern entrepreneurs—book publishers, producers of consumer goods, and music publishers—also recognized the profitability of employing the Dixie brand. On both sides of the Mason-Dixon Line, businessmen sought to capitalize on the marketing and consumption of a Dixie that incorporated the mythology and traditions of the southern past.

Distinctions existed, however. Southern advertisements of consumer items produced in the region tended to use a more martial iconography, applying images of Confederate generals or the battle flag to promote their products. Northern ad firms also found southern images useful for marketing products, yet these images tended to draw attention away from southern militarism and postwar racial violence, focusing instead on the ease of southern life. Thus, tranquil plantation scenes and disarming racial stereotypes were employed to suggest a life of leisure, a docile servant population, and happy-go-lucky race relations. This version of Dixie offered an idyllic counterpoint to modernity—specifically, to rapid urbanization and industrialization—that created what historian T. J. Jackson Lears calls "feelings of unreality." In the South, however, those feelings of unreality were less about urbanization and industrialization than about the rise of enfranchised African Americans during Reconstruction and about the populist challenge to white supremacy in the late nineteenth century. Either way, according to Lears, companies offered products that ameliorated those anxieties through what he identifies as a "therapeutic ethos" in advertising.[3]

Whether the advertising was martial in spirit, as practiced among southern companies, or focused on the sentimental and exotic, as manifested in the North, both regions help to illustrate the profitability of branding Dixie (that is, the South) in the age of modern advertising and the emergence of a mass consumer society. Dixie became a brand in a broad sense, and as a brand it conveyed the values of the product as well as the values of white society.[4] As Grace Elizabeth Hale writes, "By 1930, DixieBrand meant a regional identity made or marketed as southern." Once identified with easily recognizable—and abstracted—symbols, the selling and consumption of Dixie could take place both inside and outside of the region with little heed to the changes affecting the lived South.[5]

The Road to Reconciliation

Understanding the emergence of Dixie as a brand requires understanding the South's evolution after the Civil War as well as its changing relationship with the North. White southerners emerged from defeat by embracing the ideology of the Lost Cause, which allowed them to honor the defeated in the immediate aftermath of the war. After Reconstruction and the return of home rule, southerners celebrated Confederate veterans as heroes and the cause of southern nationalism as just. The Lost Cause phenomenon of the late nineteenth century helped to perpetuate the mythology of the Old South and provided a strong bulwark against modernity and the New South creed favorable to regional industrialization.[6]

The South's relationship with the North underwent significant changes in the decades following the Civil War. White southerners resented Reconstruction and deplored any rights of citizenship granted to blacks; furthermore, southern whites considered military occupation an insult added to injury. Although the "tragic era" remained a significant part of Confederate memory, when it ended in 1877 and former Confederates renewed their claim to governing the South, the road to reconciliation with the North appeared within reach.

At war's end, many northerners too wanted a swift reconciliation with the South, and that sentiment subsequently strengthened. As David Blight argues, the North's interest in reconciliation with the South overshadowed one of the primary outcomes of the war—emancipation. Shoring up a national brotherhood based on Anglo-Saxon supremacy overshadowed the enforcement of the Reconstruction amendments ratified to guarantee the civil liberties newly awarded to the freed slaves. More importantly, the South represented an enormous market for the northern economy. The North's historical amnesia, moreover, meant that southern governments were free to treat their black citizens as they pleased. The result, according to Blight, was that within the politics of Civil War memory, the northern reconciliationist view blended with the South's white supremacist view to eclipse the black memory of the war as about emancipation. By accepting the South's historical revisionism, northerners met a major condition for reconciliation with the white South. This development paved the way for what Nina Silber calls the "romance of reunion," expressed through veterans' reunions of the Blue and Gray as well as in popular culture.[7]

A Changing Economy

In addition to the social reconciliation of northern and southern whites, the process of cultural reconciliation that emerged between the regions can be understood through the examination of the production and consumption of consumer goods in the rapidly changing U.S. economy during the last quarter of the nineteenth century, changes that made branding Dixie possible. Most significantly, the shift from an economy based primarily on agriculture to one increasingly based on industrial production and mass consumption led to changes in the marketplace. Indeed, the end of the nineteenth century marked the rise of the national mass market. Urbanization contributed to this change, as did the significant growth of the national rail network. According to historian Richard Tedlow, "The completion of the new transportation and communication infrastructure made it possible to distribute goods nationally."[8]

New technology created machines that were faster and could produce thousands of units of a product, from cigarettes to breakfast cereals. Production was possible on a scale never before imagined, as were the accompanying profits. This type of production helped meet consumer demands in far-flung markets and created consumers for a variety of luxury goods. Mass production contributed to another important nineteenth-century development—mass marketing and the development of brands.

The South certainly did not experience the same manufacturing growth as the North, despite the best efforts of Henry Grady and other champions of the New South creed. Even though the South served as the North's "colonial economy" for several decades following the Civil War, by the end of the nineteenth century, southern citizens were consumers in the national economy, if not through mail-order catalogs then through magazines with national circulations or regional magazines in which northern companies advertised. Indeed, the emergence of modern advertising in popular magazines linked northerners and southerners as consumers of like products and, in many cases, the values reflected in the marketing of those products.[9]

The Emergence of Modern Advertising

For most of the nineteenth century, the majority of advertising appeared in newspapers. When advertisements appeared in literary magazines, editors usually confined such items to the rear of the journal because of the general disregard for advertising. Religious magazines—some of the most popular publications between the mid-nineteenth and early twentieth centuries—were the exception. Such publications profited handsomely from advertising, stimulated by the controversies between the emergent Fundamentalist and Social Gospel movements as well as the debate over evolution sparked by publication of Charles Darwin's *On the Origin of Species* (1859) and *The Descent of Man* (1871).[10]

Patent-medicine hawkers and insurance companies often purchased the most ad space in nineteenth-century newspapers and magazines and remained important sources of advertising revenue into the early twentieth century. Yet between 1865 and 1900, advertising assumed an even more important role in the marketplace. The rise of marketing across the spectrum of American business enterprises corresponded to the rise of mass production and consumption as well as the expansion of popular magazines. By the end of the century, popular magazines had higher circulations than religious and literary publications, a development spurred by expanding modern advertising expenditures. That advertising, aimed at selling luxury goods to middle-class consumers, resulted directly from the rise of mass production.[11]

By the dawn of the twentieth century, businesses developed marketing strategies to facilitate mass consumption, thereby signifying changes in advertising. A competitive market saturated with similar products required companies and entrepreneurs to mark their product as somehow unique. As one scholar puts it, "Advertising came to be the major communications link between mass production and mass consumption." Advertising, which for most of the nineteenth century did little more than describe a product and its purpose in simple language, now incorporated slogans and hyperbolic messages to appeal to consumers. More importantly, manufacturers sought to sustain their customer base by creating a "supername—a brand."[12]

Before the emergence of brands, soap was soap; with the creation of brands, *Ivory* or *Pear's* immediately conveyed not just soap but soap with supposedly unique qualities assigned by the manufacturer. The rise of brand-name advertising proved effective, as consumers increasingly depended on brands to assure them of "real or perceived quality." Brand-name advertising rapidly expanded in the early twentieth century.[13] Moreover, brands and messaging in advertising not only attracted new consumers because of quality but also, according to Lears, created new customers based on perceived cultural values associated with the product.[14]

Advertising Values

Branding and consuming Dixie can best be understood through an examination of advertising as a medium that can both reflect and reinforce cultural values. Richard Pollay, who has written extensively on the history of advertising, argues that "whether advertising imagery reflects the present or the future, it supports an image of society, and that is enough to warrant our attention." Not all of a society's cultural values are reinforced, however, and those values conveyed through advertising have social and cultural implications. This phenomenon is particularly evident in the way Dixie was branded.[15]

What did it mean to brand Dixie? How was the South branded and what was conveyed in advertising in the pivotal period between 1890 and 1930? For the purposes of this essay, Dixie serves as both symbol and brand. The actual word *Dixie*, when used in the message of an advertisement, symbolized something much broader than a geographic region. It conveyed ideas about landscape and memory, race and class, a rural rather than urban society, an agricultural rather than industrial economy, and an antimodern rather than modern worldview. In numerous instances, the term *Dixie* cast its meaning through the lens of the Confederate past. The Dixie brand conveyed a product that represented a region and a regional identity. When used as part of a product name, as in Dixie Cigarettes or Dixie Nerve and Bone Liniment, it often (though not exclusively) meant the product was manufactured in the South.[16]

The cultural meaning of *Dixie*, moreover, varied between regional and national publications. While regional magazines constituted an obvious place to brand Dixie and to employ the rhetoric of the Lost Cause and the Old South, national advertisers also employed those messages. They capitalized on northern sentiments about reconciliation with the South. Thus, branding Dixie in national magazines might include images of a plantation or a black servant on a product to suggest that the product offered some amelioration from the stress and anxiety associated with rapid urbanization and industrialization. The manufacturers of Gold Dust Twins washing powders, for example, advertised "Let the Gold Dust Twins do your work," suggesting that the product, like docile and obedient servants, provided the consumer with more leisure time. Such advertising also came at a time when southern values on race gained traction nationwide, particularly as northern whites reacted negatively to the influx of ethnic immigrants from southern and eastern Europe.

Branding Dixie in the South was a relatively simple proposition. A healthy market for all things Dixie encouraged the proliferation of regional imagery in advertising at the turn of the twentieth century. Sales of monuments and pro-Confederate books, for example, allowed regional businesses to create new consumers of Confederate products by branding those products as having been made in the South or using iconography instantly recognized by southern consumers raised on the Lost Cause mythology. They could literally purchase Confederate memory. Martial icons such as the Confederate battle flag and Robert E. Lee, for example, regularly appeared in advertisements and instantly conveyed messages to consumers about proper regional identity and values. Popular literature and eventually the film *Birth of a Nation* also marketed the Ku Klux Klan to southern consumers. Yet D. W. Griffith's epic, based on Thomas

Dixon's best-selling novel *The Clansman,* also appealed to northern audiences. Again, the shared cultural values of white supremacy and racism were sold to both northerners and southerners.

Icons of the Old South, especially the mammy, often depicted as a large black woman wearing a kerchief (most recognizably, Aunt Jemima), appeared with less frequency in regional advertising but were favored by northern manufacturers who advertised nationally.[17] Southern businesses more often employed images of southern industry and Confederate heritage during this period, as southern race relations were not conducive to romanticized images of blacks in advertising, even though southern whites thought that the uncle and the mammy served as ideal role models for the younger generation of blacks. Northern publishers and businesses, conversely, marketed to a broader national audience that bought into these stock images of docile and happy black servants because they represented a life of leisure to consumers whose lives in the urban-industrial North were anything but leisurely.

This essay discusses the branding of Dixie within the region based on advertising found in the *Confederate Veteran,* a regional monthly published between 1893 and 1932 with a circulation of around twenty thousand. The magazine provides an obvious choice for examining the advertisement of Confederate culture and is useful for identifying regional businesses as well as national advertisers that recognized a niche market among consumers of the popular publication.

Advertising in the *Veteran* (the shorthand used by contemporaries) reflected trends in modern advertising. Just like national magazines, the *Veteran* hosted ads for patent medicines and insurance companies, railroads and private schools, and domestic goods that appealed to women, whom manufacturers increasingly recognized as their most important consumers. What differentiated ads placed by southern businesses from those placed by northern enterprises was the link to the Confederacy, either through language or through regional icons.[18]

Among the regular advertisements of patent medicines was Dr. G. H. Tichenor's "Antiseptic Refrigerant for Wounds." Tichenor's medicine was manufactured in New Orleans, and its label incorporated a small group of Confederate soldiers hoisting the battle flag. While the product itself claimed to heal wounds "quicker and with less pain on man or beast than any compound known," it was vetted by the fact that George Tichenor was a Confederate veteran. The brand was pure Dixie, made in the South by a physician whose military service had taught him firsthand about the dangers of flesh wounds. The perceived quality of the product, moreover, was directly linked to an image of honor, the heroic southern soldiers holding aloft the Confederate flag.[19]

Dr. G. T. Tichenor of New Orleans used his battlefield
experiences to certify the effectiveness of his antiseptic
product, as seen here in an ad from the April 1906 issue
of *Confederate Veteran*.

Railroads and tobacco companies often lured consumers not only by associating products and services with the Confederacy but also by offering Confederate-related mementos, as in this ad for Stars and Bars Tobacco from the March 1906 issue of *Confederate Veteran*.

The South's various tobacco companies were some of the earliest businesses to adopt advertising budgets and tap postwar nostalgia for the Lost Cause. The American Tobacco Company advertised nationally, yet smaller regional companies also placed a Dixie spin on their advertisements. In 1906, Taylor Brothers of Winston-Salem, North Carolina, advertised its "Stars and Bars" chewing tobacco by appealing directly to veterans and with the purchase of a plug of tobacco offered consumers a "Stars and Bars" calendar "with all Confederate flags in colors, and a history of each flag." Richmond, Virginia, tobacco manufacturers Allen and Ginter, which never advertised in the *Veteran*, manufactured Dixie Cigarettes and pioneered a new advertising gimmick, collectible trading cards. By 1929, Edgeworth Tobacco, also of Richmond, exploited the new technology of radio through its own station, WRVA, which adopted the slogan "Down Where the South Begins." In addition to promoting the link between its station and the "capital of the Southland," the cigarette manufacturer promoted the links between its company and the Confederate history of the Richmond area, telling its listeners, "Our station endeavors to send to you the spirit of hospitality, graciousness and charm that characterizes the Southland."[20]

Souvenirs—essentially luxury items—frequently appeared for sale in the *Veteran*. S. Thomas and Brothers of Charleston, South Carolina, sold "Confederate buttons, souvenir spoons, pictures of Fort Sumter, President Jefferson Davis, Gen. Lee, Gen. Johnston, Gen. Gordon, [and] Gen. Hampton." S. N. Meyer of Washington, D.C., described his "Ladies' Belt Plates" with the raised letters "C.S.A." as "handsome and useful souvenir[s]." The manufacturer of "The Game of Confederate Heroes" classified the item as both a family souvenir and a means of fund-raising for a worthy cause—the preservation of Confederate memory. The game consisted of fifty-two cards "divided into thirteen books," a reference to the thirteen states recognized by the Confederacy as having seceded from the Union. The cards featured color illustrations of Confederate military and political leaders, and the proceeds from the sale of the game went to the Sam Davis Monument Fund in Nashville, Tennessee. As luxury items, these products used the Dixie brand for appeal, and the ads suggested that such items were, like Confederate "relics," sacred.[21]

Increasing rail travel required that railroad companies advertise, and here again, the Dixie brand was evident. The earliest railroad advertisements listed nothing more than times of service, but practices changed with the advent of additional rail lines and tourism travel. Between 1900 and 1920, the *Veteran* regularly included ads for the Dixie Flyer as well as the Cotton Belt Route. The Nashville, Chattanooga, and St. Louis Railroad and the Illinois Central ran the Dixie Flyer along tracks stretching from Chicago to Florida variously promoted as the Dixie Route, the Lookout Mountain Route, the Battlefields Route, and the Dixie Line. Traveling through Dixie on a train that carried the same name helped to brand the route. The St. Louis Southwestern Railway, operator of the Cotton Belt Route from St. Louis into Texas, lured veterans to a reunion in the Lone Star State by offering its travelers a "free picture of Gen. Lee" along with a copy of his farewell address "suitable for framing." In this instance, the South's most honored hero of the Civil War was used to brand the rail service.[22]

Some advertised items met specific market demands. Uniforms for attending reunions of Confederate veterans or of the Blue and the Gray represented a niche market for both northern and southern companies. Both M. C. Lilley and Company of Cincinnati and (after 1910) the Pettibone Company of Louisville, Kentucky, exploited the demand for reproduction uniforms. As the aging veteran population dwindled, Nashville's National Casket Company appealed to consumers with the message that "Confederate Veterans should be buried in Confederate gray broadcloth-covered caskets." Recognizing that its products were not a necessity for burial, the company accentuated the emotional appeal of the Lost Cause to sell its Confederate-themed caskets. The Dixie Artificial Limb Company fulfilled a real need among both Confederate veterans and their descendants who lost limbs during the Spanish-American War. J. C. Griffin, who managed the Nashville-based company, advertised to its potential customers to abandon the "OLD PEG LEG," which caused embarrassment, in favor of his "improved willow wood limbs." For amputees considering new wooden arms or legs, the idea that the manufacturer was based in Dixie may have afforded some additional psychological comfort.[23]

The most frequent categories of goods advertised in the *Veteran* between 1890 and 1930 were monuments and books. Monuments represented the most public symbols of the Lost Cause, and between 1895 and the First World War, hundreds were placed on the southern landscape, efforts spearheaded by the United Daughters of the Confederacy as a way of honoring their Confederate forbears. Thus, monument companies found a ready-made market for their products. Two companies—the Muldoon Monument Company of Louisville, Kentucky, and the McNeel Marble Company of Marietta, Georgia—advertised regularly in the *Veteran* between 1910 and 1920, targeting their ads directly at the Daughters. Muldoon claimed to be the "oldest and most reliable" company, responsible for "nine-tenths of the Confederate Monuments in the United States." The advertisements often employed the image of a Confederate soldier cast in stone, and the companies celebrated their history of working with the Daughters to build monuments throughout the South.

Publishers of southern history and literature filled the pages of the *Veteran* as well as national literary magazines with ads. Pro-southern and pro-Confederate literature was the order of the day in the early twentieth century, and both regional and national publishers sought to meet and heighten consumer demand. Publishers in the major literary centers of New York, Philadelphia, and Chicago advertised in the *Veteran,* as did noted southern companies such as Richmond's B. F. Johnson, Baltimore's Page Publishing, and the University Press of Nashville.

New York publishers published as much racist literature set in Dixie as southern publishers did, which begs the question of why white southerners were convinced that northern histories of the war misrepresented Confederate history. Although part of the answer may lie in the fact that northern publishers indeed put out literature condemning the Confederate rebellion, southerners may also have preferred to buy their books from B. F. Johnson rather than from Scribner as a means of both supporting regional businesses and expressing southern pride. To tap the southern market, Yankee companies had to clearly demonstrate their Confederate sympathies before gaining the hard-earned dollars of southern consumers. For example, Neale Publishing, though headquartered in New York's famous Flatiron Building, emphasized that white southerners with Confederate sympathies had founded the firm.[24]

A plethora of other northern companies also sought to exploit the demand for pro-Confederate goods. The profitability of the Lost Cause attracted the entrepreneurial interest of a wide range of businesses. An Ohio uniform manufacturer specializing in fraternal regalia for a variety of national organizations attempted to meet the needs of men attending

THE COUCH BEAUTIFUL

It is not what you pay for, but what you get, that needs your attention in our line. Confederate Veterans should be buried in Confederate gray broadcloth-covered caskets. See that all your friends are laid away in NATIONAL caskets, the standard of *quality* everywhere. Inquire of your undertaker.

National Casket Company
NASHVILLE, TENNESSEE

In this May 1912 *Confederate Veteran* ad, National Casket sought to attract southern customers by promoting the company's loyalty to the Confederacy.

Confederate veterans' reunions. Flag companies in New York and New Jersey filled consumer demand by manufacturing, selling, and advertising Confederate flags and bunting. Branding Dixie extended into the national marketplace as both northern and southern manufacturers associated the quality and value of their products with the qualities and values that northern advertisers and subsequently consumers associated with the South. The association of quality with southernness thereby alleviated southerners' hesitancy to contribute to the North's economic might.

Print and later radio and television advertising demeaned blacks by creating stereotypical images that regularly appeared in national marketing campaigns. The black mammy and uncle caricatures appealed to white consumers nationwide, because the image often presented blacks as docile servants who willingly cared for their white employers. Furthermore, these faithful servants projected the image of leisure to which white middle-class consumers aspired. Significantly, the ad campaigns that branded Aunt Jemima and Maxwell House (based on a real Nashville hotel) as icons of the Old South were developed by a prominent New York advertising agency, J. Walter Thompson.[25]

The Thompson agency successfully employed black stereotypes and southern style, influencing other advertisers, who used similar images in their ad campaigns. New York publisher E. P. Dutton and Company advertised a book *ABC in Dixie: A Plantation Alphabet* (1904) by using a cartoonlike figure of an elderly black man in a top hat and tails that suggested the male house servants of the Old South. Indeed, according to the ad, the book offers "verses and pictures of the old plantation types." The book formed part of Dutton's catalog of juvenile literature meant to "appeal to the little folks, whether they have been in Dixie land or not." Many consumers fell into the latter category.[26]

National advertisements suggestive of "southernness" were not limited to black stereotypes alone. *Life* magazine included a number of national advertisements beckoning consumers of all things reminiscent of the Old South. Gorham, a manufacturer of silverware, advertised in *Life* in 1928 that its Colfax line was "a delightful reflection of southern hospitality," much like that used by the "charming hostesses of the Colonial South." A Philadelphia distillery ad campaign for Dixie Belle Gin promoted an image of upper-class leisure often associated with the planter South. J. B. Lippincott, a Philadelphia book publisher, carried a large inventory of romance novels in which northern men married southern women, the literary symbol of sectional reconciliation.[27] While Coca-Cola emerged as the best-known manufacturer based in the South during this period, the company was committed to being national in its appeal, even though the company's chair, Asa Candler, was staunchly Confederate in his sympathies. Other southern companies, however, participated in projecting the Old South, Dixie brand. In a 1924 issue of *Life,* Mississippi's Natchez Baking Company advertised its Ole Missus Fruit Cake as "made in Dixie." Nunnally's, an Atlanta-based candy manufacturer, advertised its chocolates as renowned "ever since the old days of the storied South." Using the image of a southern belle being wooed by her beau, the candy was described as having "subtle undertones of flavor that emphasize so delightfully its Southern witchery," well before Margaret Mitchell introduced the world to Scarlett O'Hara.[28]

An important advancement in advertising during the 1920s and 1930s was what historian Roland Marchand calls the "social tableaux." Advertisements of this type usually depict a "slice of life" and serve as reflections on society. While advertisers remained focused on profits, these tableaux depicted scenes reflective of contemporary cultural values, attempting to make products synonymous with that culture. The ad's message is not simply a slogan but an entire story created by the scene. The advertised item becomes a memory trigger, transporting the consumer back through time.[29]

One example of the social tableau that perpetuates the Dixie/Old South theme is an advertisement for Crab Orchard Whiskey, distilled in Louisville, Kentucky. The slice of life is a scene of the old Crab Orchard Springs Hotel, where people came for such "Southern delicacies as barbequed squirrel" or "roast 'possum and candied yams." They washed it down, of course, with bourbon whiskey, "a flavor which even the flower of old-time Kentucky's gentility praised." Crab Orchard Whiskey, in this case, was branded as old-fashioned Dixie, with the accompanying value of being associated with southern gentility. It became, according to its ads, "America's fastest-selling whiskey."[30]

Sounds of Dixie

Perhaps the most entertaining and effective way marketers branded Dixie was through popular culture, especially the sale of sheet music about the region. Before there was radio, there was parlor music, and between 1890 and 1930, sheet music on various Dixie themes reached the height of popularity. In the 1890s, white audiences helped popularize the genre of music about the South known as coon songs. By 1910, those songs had been replaced by the music of Tin Pan Alley, with more of a focus on the South generally rather than specifically on southern blacks, although racial stereotypes remained present in both the lyrics and in the artwork that appeared on sheet music covers. Interestingly, this music was not being produced in the South or by southern musicians but in the North.

New York City's Tin Pan Alley musicians and songwriters wrote hundreds of songs about the South, often using *Dixie* in the titles. Music publishers in New York, Detroit, and Chicago sold thousands of copies of these piano pieces, which were played at home and made popular by vaudeville acts such as the Misses Campbell, who achieved fame through their rendition of the song "You're as Dear to Me as 'Dixie' Was to Lee."[31]

Ironically, Jewish immigrants living in New York City who had never laid eyes on the American South wrote most of these Dixie songs. Irving Berlin composed several pieces on Dixie, including "The Dixie Volunteers" (1917) and "When It's Night Time Down in Dixieland" (1914). His publishing company, Waterson, Berlin, and Snyder, produced numerous other Dixie-themed pieces. Jerome H. Remick, who operated publishing offices in Detroit as well as New York, was responsible for a substantial portion of the market for sheet music on Dixie, including such titles as "Down South Everybody's Happy" (1917).

"Are You from Dixie?" "How's Ev'ry Little Thing in Dixie?" "When the Sun Goes Down in Dixie," and "She's Dixie All the Time" touted the leisurely pace of life in the South as the antithesis of modernity. Songwriters again and again told of days gone by or of a life they wished they had enjoyed or perhaps missed. The lyrics reveal a fascination with the "exotic" South, a place in a warm climate with happy-go-lucky blacks, genteel white women, and a rural landscape awash in moonlight and magnolias. The lyrics from "Dixie Lullaby" (1919), published in St. Louis, offer a typical description of the romanticized South:

There's a tale that they tell about Dixie
It's heaven on earth so they say,
With the birds and the flowers where I spent happy hours
And the tho't of it takes me away

CHORUS
Down in Dear old Dixie where the flowers bloom
Down in Dear old Dixie in the month of June
Floating down the river in a birch canoe
And singing love's song to you
In the fields of cotton where I used to roam
On the old plantation of my Southern home,
Back in Alabamy, back beside my mammy
That's my Dixie Lullaby.[32]

Isaac Goldberg, who lectured and wrote about American popular music, published his treatment of the genre in *Tin Pan Alley* (1930). In it, he relates the story of famous lyricist Gus Kahn, who was asked why the "song boys" of the North wrote about the South. Kahn replied that

Sheet music, such as for the song "Are You from Dixie?" (1915), celebrated the pastoral scenery of a South little changed by the Civil War. (Courtesy of the Library of Congress)

"Southern place-and-State names lent themselves to rhyming." Goldberg added what he believed to be a "deeper reason" for the fascination the South held for so many northern songwriters. "Paradise," he wrote, "is never where we are. The South has become our Never-never Land—the symbol of the Land where the lotus blooms and dreams come true."[33]

For Goldberg, the South was an exotic place. The region was branded so often, in so many different marketing ploys, that perceptions of the South—indeed, southern identity itself—became detached from reality. For songwriters as well as for the ad men who sought to brand the region, the South increasingly represented a respite from the afflictions of modernity. If, for northerners, "paradise" was never where they were, then "Dixie" was paradise, even if the reality did not match the myth. Only the idea of Dixie was needed to make it seem real, and the nation's consumers ate it up with a spoon.

NOTES

1. B. F. Johnson Publishing to J. T. Nolen, B. F. Johnson Papers, Virginia Historical Society, Richmond.

2. Ibid.

3. T. J. Jackson Lears, "From Salvation to Self-Realization: Advertising and the Therapeutic Roots of Consumer Culture, 1880–1930," in *The Culture of Consumption: Critical Essays in American History, 1880–1980,* ed. Richard Wightman Fox and T. J. Jackson Lears (New York: Pantheon, 1983), 7.

4. The numerous secondary sources on the history of advertising in the United States during the late nineteenth and early twentieth centuries include Frank Presbrey, *The History and Development of Advertising* (New York: Doubleday, Doran, 1929); Fox and Lears, *Culture of Consumption*; Stephen Fox, *The Mirror Makers: A History of American Advertising and Its Creators* (New York: Morrow, 1982); Roland Marchand, *Advertising and the American Dream: Making Way for Modernity, 1920–1940* (Berkeley: University of California Press, 1985); Richard S. Tedlow, *New and Improved: The Story of Mass Marketing in America* (New York: Basic Books, 1990); James D. Norris, *Advertising and the Transformation of American Society, 1865–1920* (New York: Greenwood, 1990).

5. Grace Elizabeth Hale, *Making Whiteness: The Culture of Segregation in the South, 1890–1940* (New York: Pantheon, 1998), 146–47.

6. On the Lost Cause, see Charles Reagan Wilson, *Baptized in Blood: The Religion of the Lost Cause, 1865–1920* (Athens: University of Georgia Press, 1980); Gaines M. Foster, *Ghosts of the Confederacy: Defeat, the Lost Cause, and the Emergence of the New South, 1865–1913* (New York: Oxford University Press, 1987). On the New South creed, see Paul Gaston, *The New South Creed: A Study in Southern Mythmaking* (New York: Knopf, 1970).

7. David Blight, *Romance and Reunion: The Civil War in American Memory* (Cambridge: Belknap Press of Harvard University Press, 2001); Nina Silber, *The*

Romance of Reunion: Northerners and the South, 1865–1900 (Chapel Hill: University of North Carolina Press, 1995).

8. Tedlow, *New and Improved*, 14; Fox, *Mirror Makers*, 22. See also Jib Fowles, *Advertising and Popular Culture* (Thousand Oaks, Calif.: Sage, 1996), 32–33.

9. Tedlow, *New and Improved*, 11. On the South as a "colonial economy" of the North, see C. Vann Woodward, *Origins of the New South, 1877–1913* (Baton Rouge: Louisiana State University Press, 1951).

10. Norris, *Advertising and the Transformation of American Society*, 29.

11. Ibid., 31, 33; Fox, *Mirror Makers*, 28–35.

12. Tedlow, *New and Improved*, 14.

13. Norris, *Advertising and the Transformation of American Society*, 99; Tedlow, *New and Improved*, 14–15.

14. Lears, "From Salvation to Self-Realization," 6–14.

15. Russell W. Belk and Richard W. Pollay, "Images of Ourselves: The Good Life in Twentieth Century Advertising," *Journal of Consumer Research* 11 (March 1985): 888. Important works on advertising and cultural values include Fowles, *Advertising and Popular Culture*, 28–29; Marchand, *Advertising and the American Dream*; Monica Brasted, "The Reframing of Traditional Cultural Values: Consumption and World War I," *Advertising and Society Review* 5, no. 4 (2004), 1; T. J. Jackson Lears, *Fables of Abundance: A Cultural History of Advertising in America* (New York: Basic Books, 1994); Susan Strasser, *Satisfaction Guaranteed: The Making of the American Mass Market* (New York: Pantheon, 1989).

16. Hale, *Making Whiteness*, 146. Hale's arguments about buying and selling within the region as well as imagery of the region itself are useful, though her analysis of advertising focuses on black stereotypes in national advertising.

17. On the use of blacks in advertising, see Marilyn Kern-Foxworth, *Aunt Jemima, Uncle Ben, and Rastus: Blacks in Advertising, Yesterday, Today, and Tomorrow* (Westport, Conn.: Greenwood, 1994); M. M. Manring, *Slave in a Box: The Strange Career of Aunt Jemima* (Charlottesville: University Press of Virginia, 1998), 9. See also Hale, *Making Whiteness*, 121–98.

18. *Confederate Veteran* was published in Nashville, Tennessee, from 1893 until 1913 by Sumner A. Cunningham and from 1913 until 1932 by Edith A. Pope, Cunningham's secretary.

19. "Tichenor's Antiseptic Refrigerant for Wounds" (advertisement), *Confederate Veteran*, April 1906.

20. "Stars and Bars Tobacco" (advertisement), *Confederate Veteran*, March 1906; Allen and Ginter Trading Cards, Benjamin Meade Everard Scrapbook, 1889–1890, Virginia Historical Society, Richmond; *Souvenir Radio Log, WRVA, Richmond, Virginia*, "Down Where the South Begins," the Edgeworth Tobacco Station (Richmond, Va.: Larus, 1929), Virginia Historical Society, Richmond.

21. "S. Thomas & Bro." (advertisement), *Confederate Veteran*, circa 1910; "S. N. Meyer" (advertisement), *Confederate Veteran*, April 1906; "The Game of Confederate Heroes" (advertisement), *Confederate Veteran*, June 1899.

22. "Cotton Belt Route" (advertisement), *Confederate Veteran*, February 1902.

23. M. C. Lilley and Pettibone advertised in the *Veteran* between 1900 and 1920; "The Couch Beautiful" (advertisement), *Confederate Veteran*, May 1912; "Dixie Artificial Limb Company," *Confederate Veteran*, February 1906.

24. Robert K. Krick, *Neale Books: An Annotated Bibliography* (n.p.: Morningside, 1977), iv.

25. Kern-Foxworth, *Aunt Jemima, Uncle Ben, and Rastus*, 29–41; Hale, *Making Whiteness*, 151–68; Manring, *Slave in a Box*, 79–100.

26. "ABC in Dixie" (advertisement), *The Critic*, December 1904.

27. "Gorham Silver" (advertisement), *Life*, 5 October 1928; "J. P. Lippincott Holiday Books" (advertisement), *Town and Country*, 23 November 1912.

28. "Ole Missus Fruitcake" and "Nunnally's" (advertisements), *Life*, November 1924, August 1920.

29. Marchand, *Advertising and the American Dream*, 164–68.

30. "Crab Orchard Whiskey" (advertisement), *Life*, 1 June 1935.

31. Isaac Goldberg, *Tin Pan Alley: A Chronicle of the American Popular Music Racket* (New York: Day, 1930); "You're as Dear to Me as 'Dixie' Was to Lee" (New York: Feist, 1917).

32. "Dixie Lullaby" (St. Louis: Dixon-Lane, 1919).

33. Goldberg, *Tin Pan Alley*, 45–46.

The Riddle of the Horny Hillbilly

Patrick Huber

Ever since I purchased a *Dukes of Hazzard* lunch box at a central Missouri flea market in 1991, I have avidly collected tacky southern souvenirs. My collection of southern kitsch currently contains more than four hundred items, including hillbilly postcards; outhouse-shaped salt and pepper shakers; an "American by Birth, Southern by the Grace of God" T-shirt; a Hank Williams Jr. shot glass; miniature rebel flags; a "Coon Hunters Do It All Night" bumper sticker; a "Music City, U.S.A." ashtray; cans of faux possum roadkill; bags of "hillbilly bubble bath"; and dozens of tourist-oriented speech guides, cookbooks, and lifestyle manuals with titles such as *The Official Redneck Handbook, How tuh Live in the Kooky South: A Fun Guide Book fer Yankees, Hillbilly Cookin' Mountaineer Style,* and *Speakin' Suthern Like It Should Be Spoke!*[1] But none of them intrigues me as much as the Horny Hillbilly, the crown jewel of my collection. I first encountered the Horny Hillbilly in 1992 at a combination Texaco station–tourist trap a dozen miles west of Cookeville, Tennessee, called STOP, whose billboards touted its Elvis postcards and two-for-a-dollar hot dogs. STOP boasted one of the widest selections of tacky southern souvenirs on the entire stretch of Interstate 40 between Raleigh and Nashville, and whenever I passed through Middle Tennessee, I often spent a few minutes browsing the store's aluminum shelves and turnstile racks, searching for something new to add to my growing collection. The moment I saw the Horny Hillbilly I recognized what a fantastic article of tastelessness I had stumbled upon for just $1.49. I knew I had to buy it.

For anyone who has not seen one, the Horny Hillbilly is a small plastic figurine, manufactured in China, that depicts a stereotypical southern mountaineer, complete with a floppy felt hat, flowing black beard, and ancient squirrel rifle slung over his shoulder. He is barefoot and squats on his haunches, with his legs spread wide. Out of his britches protrudes a monstrous, erect tallywhacker, and his enlarged genitals make him resemble West African fertility statues or some images of the Greek god Pan. On the lid of the figurine's cardboard box are emblazoned a Confederate battle flag and the painfully bad pun, "THE SOUTH SHALL RISE AGAIN."[2] The figurine is currently sold at tourist shops, roadside attractions, and truck stops in southern Appalachia and the Ozarks, but it is also marketed in locations relatively far removed from the southern mountains, including at that celebrated mecca of tackiness, South of the Border, on Interstate 95 in Dillon, South Carolina.[3] In terms of its calculated tastelessness, the Horny Hillbilly ranks right up there with plastic dog poop, fake rubber vomit, boob-shaped ice cubes, and snaggled Bubba teeth.

On the surface, the Horny Hillbilly might appear to be merely a grotesque novelty or gag gift, destined at best to become a dust collector, and most of the tourists and travelers who encounter this figurine probably never give it a second thought. But I believe that this souvenir merits serious consideration. I have long attempted to unravel what I call the riddle of the Horny Hillbilly, particularly the puzzling association of a fully aroused and generously endowed Snuffy Smith mountaineer with the Confederacy and the Lost Cause. What does this figurine signify? Who buys it (other than me)? And what imaginative, enterprising huckster hatched the crackpot scheme of selling tourists a hillbilly souvenir with an oversized boner? Not surprisingly, the Horny Hillbilly has generated little scholarly research, so there are unfortunately no definitive answers to the last two questions.[4] Several attempts to trace the inventor through the U.S. Patent Office have thus far proven unsuccessful. Nor do any reliable sales figures or market research studies exist, so it is impossible to know how many of these souvenirs have been snatched off the shelves over the years by New Yorkers, New Englanders, midwesterners, and even bona fide southerners themselves, if they do indeed buy such things. ("After all," the late *Atlanta Constitution* newspaper columnist and humorist Lewis Grizzard remarked, "how many southerners have you ever seen paying money to visit a reptile farm?")[5] Although we do not know who purchases these figurines or why, I believe we can come to some historical understanding of this object and its cultural significance, and this essay represents an attempt to do just that—to solve, at least in part, the riddle of the Horny Hillbilly.

First, I am convinced that this mass-marketed souvenir of southern kitsch, although tacky and tasteless, can tell us much about the modern American South, its popular representations in the national imagination, and collective historical memories of the region. As a souvenir, the Horny Hillbilly figurine operates on at least two different levels of memory. On its most basic level, the figurine, like all souvenirs, generally speaking,

Though made in China, the Horny Hillbilly figurine represents the complex history of the American South since the Civil War. (Photo by author)

functions as a private memorial that commemorates a particular place and time of a tourist's travels, both enshrining and stimulating those memories.[6] I clearly remember, for example, the particular Christmas 1992 road trip across Middle Tennessee during which I purchased my Horny Hillbilly. But more importantly and far more interestingly, the Horny Hillbilly also encapsulates collective historical memories about the American South, particularly through its invocation of the Confederacy and the Lost Cause. In broadest strokes, the Horny Hillbilly, with its intriguing blend of sexuality, politics, and memory, reflects several important themes of twentieth-century southern history, including the rise of post–Second World War southern tourism, the evolution of pernicious hillbilly stereotypes, the commodification of southern mountain culture, and the distortion of collective historical memories about the mountain South. I cannot claim to have unlocked all of the secrets of this curious piece of southern kitsch, but I do know that the Horny Hillbilly, itself amazingly complex in its multiple possible meanings, reveals how modern tourism has put both the negative stereotype of the hillbilly and the romantic mythology of the Lost Cause to commercial use and in so doing has fundamentally shaped the cultural representations and collective memories of the mountain South.[7]

One way to begin unraveling the riddle of the Horny Hillbilly is to examine the figurine within the historical context of the rise of post-1945 southern tourism and the related evolution of southern mountain stereotypes. Although travelers and pleasure seekers have visited the southern colonies since at least the eighteenth century, the national increase in consumerism, affluence, and automobile travel after the Second World War rapidly expanded the South's modern tourism industry. The multi-billion-dollar Interstate Highway Act of 1956, signed by President Dwight Eisenhower, led to the construction of a network of highways across the region and in turn fueled the rapid growth of a roadside tourism industry of resorts, motels, theme parks, fast-food restaurants, and gas stations. Soon, as Tim Hollis's wonderfully nostalgic *Dixie before Disney: One Hundred Years of Roadside Fun* (1999) attests, tens of thousands of tourists and vacationers were visiting Rock City, alligator farms, Mammoth Cave, Civil War battlefields, Dogpatch U.S.A., and other southern roadside attractions. By 1958, tourists spent two billion dollars a year in the region. Today, the southern tourism industry generates tens of billions of dollars annually.[8]

Since at least the 1890s, tourists and vacationers have happily carted home cheap, gaudy, mass-produced souvenirs to commemorate their Dixie excursions, and the Horny Hillbilly represents only one of literally thousands of inexpensive (and often tacky) southern souvenirs sold since the end of the Second World War.[9] But its date of origin remains difficult to determine. According to my best estimate, these souvenirs probably appeared on the market at least by the 1970s and may have been available a decade earlier, when open discussion of sexuality became less taboo. Like other hillbilly souvenirs, the Horny Hillbilly figurine primarily intends to satisfy tourists' expectations and reinforce their preconceptions of southern Appalachia and the Ozarks by symbolizing the imagined core characteristics of those who inhabit these particular subregions. No icon is more closely associated with the mountain South than the hillbilly.[10] The hillbilly himself possesses a long and tangled history in American popular culture. He is, in fact, one of the most powerful and enduring southern stereotypes, a stock character who has appeared for the better part of a century in magazine articles, novels, movies, and, more recently, television programs. The Horny Hillbilly figurine, with its exaggerated, grotesque features, reflects common stereotypes of southern mountaineers as shiftless, barefoot, gun-toting, and horny hillbillies. As a form of commodified mountain culture, this souvenir illuminates how heavily the expansive tourism industry of southern Appalachia and the Ozarks depends on the hillbilly stereotype.

The "discovery" of the hillbilly coincided with the invention of southern Appalachia and to a lesser extent of the Ozarks, and his introduction into the American popular imagination began, for all intents and purposes, after the Civil War. Starting in the 1870s, *Atlantic Monthly, Harper's Weekly, Lippincott's Magazine, Scribner's Monthly,* and other middle-class magazines published scores of travel accounts and local-color articles about the strange highlanders of southern Appalachia. Southern mountaineers originally were portrayed chiefly as primitive but noble folk of undiluted Anglo-Saxon ancestry who, living an isolated existence far from modern civilization, maintained the nation's rugged pioneer virtues and folkways. Articles with titles such as "Our Contemporary Ancestors in the Southern Mountains" (1899) and "The Southern Mountaineer: Our Kindred of the Boone and Lincoln Types" (1900) celebrated so-called mountain whites as conservators of these cherished virtues and customs that elsewhere seemed to be rapidly vanishing in an increasingly modern urban-industrial America.[11] Ironically, the invention of southern Appalachia as an idyllic, preindustrial Eden frozen in the eighteenth century coincided with sweeping social and economic transformations as railroads penetrated the mountains, introducing a brisk tourist trade and exposing the region's abundant natural resources to the exploitation of logging and coal-mining companies. But in a nation undergoing large-scale industrial development, urban growth, and immigration, southern Appalachia came to represent, in the words of historian C. Brenden Martin, "a symbolic counterpoint to the progressive thrust of modern urban society," and its mountain whites were seen as noble primitives who, though sorely in need of social and cultural uplift, preserved the nation's pioneer folkways and purest Anglo-Saxon bloodlines.[12]

The prevailing image of the venerable, noble mountaineer did not last long, however. After the turn of the twentieth century, the image of southern mountaineers as depraved hillbillies quickly eclipsed this portrayal of quaint and dignified mountain whites. In 1900, for example, in one of the first published usages of the term, the *New York Journal* described the "Hill-Billie" as "a free and untrammeled white citizen of Alabama, who lives in the hills, has no means to speak of, dresses as he can, talks as he pleases, drinks whiskey when he gets it, and fires off his revolver as the fancy takes him."[13] Southern mountaineers increasingly came to be perceived as ignorant, backward people ridiculously out of step with emerging modern America and prone to little more than feuding, moonshining, idleness, and diddling livestock. Although earlier local-color writers and missionaries attributed the cultural persistence of pioneer virtues and folkways among mountain whites to their prolonged isolation, this same supposed isolation emerged by the 1920s as the chief explanation for what was increasingly seen as their cultural degeneracy.[14] When tens of thousands of southern mountaineers migrated from Kentucky, Tennessee, and West Virginia to midwestern cities during the Great Depression and the Second World War, the image of the hillbilly deteriorated even further. "Skid row dives, opium parlors, and assorted other dens of iniquity collectively are as safe as Sunday School picnics compared with the joints taken over by clans of fightin', feudin' Southern hillbillies and their shootin' cousins," remarked the *Chicago Tribune* in the mid-1950s. "The Southern hillbilly migrants, who have descended like a plague of locusts in the last few years, have the lowest standard of living and moral code (if any), the biggest capacity for liquor, and the most savage tactics when drunk, which is most of the time."[15]

By the 1920s, however, enterprising civic boosters and businessmen in southern Appalachia and the Ozarks had begun to embrace the imposed cultural representation of the hillbilly and, softening it somewhat with humor, harnessed it to their developing tourism industry. Although undoubtedly embarrassing to those residents who wanted to demonstrate how their mountain communities embraced modern progress and civilization, the hillbilly image provided these regions with a distinct and marketable identity of authenticity and local color that proved highly profitable.[16] After the Second World War, tourist attractions and other businesses increasingly traded on the hillbilly image to draw out-of-towners and their dollars. The hillbilly soon emerged as the dominant icon of the tourism industry in the mountain South. Hill-Billy Village in Pigeon Forge, Tennessee; the Hillbilly Inn Restaurant in Branson, Missouri; the Hillbilly Hideaway restaurant and country music opry in Walnut Cove, North Carolina; the Hillbilly Junction gift shop in Tiptonville, Tennessee; the now-defunct Dogpatch U.S.A. theme park near Harrison, Arkansas; and dozens of other commercial businesses relied on the hillbilly image to keep their cash registers ringing.[17] Southern Appalachian towns even organized hillbilly festivals, such as Hillbilly Days in Pikeville, Kentucky, in the heart of the state's depressed eastern coalfields, to help give their struggling economies an infusion of much-needed tourist dollars. Pikeville, the scene of the courtroom trials related to the celebrated Hatfield-McCoy feud, has been hosting its celebration for almost thirty years, and today it regularly attracts upward of one hundred thousand revelers.[18]

As early as the 1930s, as part of their commodification and marketing of southern Appalachian and Ozark culture, local entrepreneurs began selling souvenirs and postcards that traded on the stereotypical hillbilly image.[19] And today, hillbilly souvenirs and novelties are big business in these regions. For example, the Mallard Cove Trading Company, located in Shell Knob in the Missouri Ozarks, specializes in what it calls "hillbilly humor" souvenirs and bills itself as the "premier source for all your hillbilly souvenir and novelty needs." On its Web site, the firm markets a host of gag novelties, including hillbilly toothbrushes (a piece of dried corncob attached to a twig), hillbilly flashlights (a kitchen match mounted on the end of a cedar block), hillbilly bubble bath (a bag of dried red beans), and hillbilly desktop calculators (a wooden cutout of a hand with the five fingers numbered).[20] Unlike racist souvenirs depicting African Americans, which slowly evolved between the 1880s and the 1950s, the exaggerated stereotypes represented in hillbilly souvenirs have remained largely unchanged since the 1930s. Common motifs include outhouses, feuds, moonshine jugs, hound dogs, corncob pipes, rifles and shotguns, and bare feet. Virtually all of these motifs are unabashedly derogatory, representing hillbillies as lazy, drunken, ignorant, violent, unsophisticated, poor, and filthy, to shorten a very long list.[21] But few souvenirs currently on the market depict the supposed sexual voraciousness and deviancy of hillbillies as explicitly as the Horny Hillbilly.

Hillbillies, I suspect, are not really any hornier than anyone else. But since at least the first decade of the twentieth century, white, middle-class Americans have relentlessly portrayed southern mountaineers as sexually insatiable, projecting sexual anxieties and fears onto hillbillies almost as often and as intensely as onto African Americans.[22] Early twentieth-century missionaries, settlement house workers, and writers, for example, regularly commented on the perceived sexual impropriety and loose morals of southern mountaineers. Writing in *The Highlanders of the South* (1910), the Reverend Samuel Hunter Thompson observed, "Far up in the mountains . . . the moral relations of the sexes are hardly more sacred than among animals." "In the backwoods [of the Ozarks]," echoed Charles Morrow Wilson in *Outlook and Independent* magazine in 1929, "sexual intercourse has been traditionally regarded as one of the more casual turns in vital experience. To [Ozarkers] virtue seems not necessarily heroic."[23] Three decades later, similar attitudes surfaced in James A. Maxwell's 1956 *Reporter* article, "Down from the Hills and into the Slums," which quoted a Cincinnati resident who complained that the city's recently arrived Kentucky migrants "drink too much" and that their sexual standards "would shame an alley cat."[24] Mountain fecundity and inbreeding continue to figure prominently in depictions of hillbillies in novels, films, comic strips, and other products of mass culture. One hillbilly-themed postcard, titled "Ozark Hillbilly Weddin'," for example, shows a reluctant groom, his pregnant bride, and her shotgun-toting father. The crude humor of this "shotgun wedding" tableau plays on the widely accepted stereotype of southern mountaineers' lax sexual morals and overwhelming reproductive urges.[25]

This perceived sexual promiscuity and unbridled lustfulness also finds expression in the phrase *horny hillbilly,* which apparently dates to around the 1960s.[26] The soft-core porn film industry has a "horny hillbilly" subgenre, and during the 1960s and 1970s, Russ Meyer and lesser-known directors churned out dozens of these low-budget, drive-in flicks with suggestive titles such as *Mudhoney* (1965), *Moonshine Love* (1970), *Midnight Plowboy* (1971), and *The Pigkeeper's Daughter* (1972).[27] Since then, *horny hillbilly* has become a relatively common expression in American speech, as any Internet search will confirm. The turn of phrase is often used in reference to former president Bill Clinton of Arkansas. For example, in 1998, after the Monica Lewinsky scandal broke, a columnist for *The Age* Webzine referred to the embattled president as "the Ozarks Casanova" and "the horny hillbilly."[28]

But in the national imagination, hillbillies represent far more than mere yokel fornicators and adulterers. They are also often cast as savage barbarians with frightening sexual appetites, a sort of current-day white counterpart of the post-Reconstruction "black brute."[29] Moreover, hillbillies are often associated with a full range of aberrant sexual behaviors considered illegal, immoral, or taboo, including incest, rape, pedophilia, and bestiality. The sexual habits of Chicago hillbilly migrants "with respect to such matters as incest and statutory rape," remarked Albert N. Votaw in a 1958 *Harper's Magazine* article, "The Hillbillies Invade Chicago," "are clearly at variance with urban legal requirements." Similarly, Maxwell quoted a Cincinnati police officer as saying, "Incest is another matter which a lot of mountaineers see differently than we do. They usually come from small, isolated communities where there's a considerable amount of inbreeding anyway, and they can't see what it's any business of the police what they do with their sex life. Just a few days ago, for instance, one of them looked at me as though I'd lost my mind when I told him that he was under arrest for having intimate relations with his stepdaughter. 'Hell, she ain't even a cousin,' he told me."[30] A current joke trades on the same perverse sexual behaviors. Question: "What's a hillbilly virgin?" Punch line: "An ugly third-grader or a girl who can outrun her brothers."[31]

The pernicious stereotype of the incestuous hillbilly is widespread in American popular culture, but equally damaging is the image of hillbillies as vicious, predatory sodomizers, as portrayed in such popular Hollywood films as John Boorman's *Deliverance* (1972) and Quentin Tarantino's *Pulp Fiction* (1994). In the aftermath of the September 11 terrorist attacks, to cite another example, a Web blogger proposed that an appropriate punishment for Osama bin Laden, should he be captured, would be to incarcerate him in the Huntsville, Texas, penitentiary, where he could serve as "some horny hillbilly's bitch."[32] The expression *horny hillbilly* obviously is not a flattering one, but it can be used somewhat humorously. When journalists and fans ask if she is Roman Catholic because she comes from a large East Tennessee family, country-pop diva Dolly Parton is fond of remarking, "Naw, we ain't Catholic. We're just horny hillbillies!"[33]

As Parton's quip suggests, this pernicious stereotype of the oversexed hillbilly remains pervasive even among southern mountaineers. Many of the bawdy stories contained in Vance Randolph's classic *Pissing in the Snow and Other Ozark Folktales* (1976), which he collected in southwestern Missouri and northwestern Arkansas between the 1920s and 1950s, revolve around the popular stereotypes of the promiscuous and incestuous hillbilly. Such stories also demonstrate how insider- and outsider-generated stereotypes often overlap. "Jack and His Family," which Randolph collected from an informant in Joplin, Missouri, in 1934, is a case in point. With their parents away, the story goes, two Ozark siblings named Jack and Jenny take off all their clothes and lie down on the cabin floor to escape the summer heat. The siblings begin to caress one another. In the midst of their petting party, Jack's "pecker" swells up so big that his sister exclaims, "My goodness, I never seen anything so big only on a jackass, and maybe that's how they come to name you Jack!" Jack mounts his sister, and in the throes of intercourse, he exclaims, "My God, Jenny, I never had it so good in my whole life! Why you're lots better than Maw!" "Yeah," responds Jenny, "that's what Paw always says."[34] Randolph's collection reveals how, like Dolly Parton, some Ozarkers embraced the jokes about incest and other derisive stereotypes projected onto them as a way of defusing such ugly images and diminishing their psychological impact.

Again, like the image of the mythical black brute in the New South white imagination, the image of the sex-mad hillbilly is reinforced by the stereotype of his oversized, unruly, and unsocialized penis. Several of the bawdy stories in *Pissing in the Snow* refer to the abnormally large size of hillbillies' anatomy, with scattered allusions to "that long-peckered boy," "big long tallywhacker," and "God-awfullest tool you ever seen."[35] The oversized genitals of the Horny Hillbilly figurine portray graphically the cultural representations of southern hillbillies as the literal embodiment of a primitive white hypermasculinity. As J. W. Williamson explains in *Hillbillyland: What the Movies Did to the Mountains and What the Mountains Did to the Movies* (1995), the hillbilly is perceived as fiercely independent, ruggedly masculine, and prone to haphazard violence as the mood strikes him. He is "theatrically lazy but remains virile." He revels in the lowdown masculine pleasures of drinking, loafing, and fighting, while his womenfolk perform all the chores on his ramshackle farm. But the stereotype of the well-hung hillbilly casts him as essentially a subhuman beast—little more than an animal with uncontrollable sexual desires—rather than a civilized human being. The Horny Hillbilly figurine combines two of the most common but seemingly contradictory depictions of mountaineers in the American imagination. He is on the one hand a harmless country bumpkin and on the other a threatening sexual predator. As Williamson writes, "The distance between the hillbilly as comedy and the hillbilly as threat is amazingly short." Thus, the Horny Hillbilly combines the dueling images of the goofy, comic-strip mountaineer and the lustful, depraved sexual monster—a sort of Li'l Abner and Jack the Ripper rolled into one.[36]

Perhaps the most perplexing aspect of the riddle of the Horny Hillbilly, however, concerns its evocation of the Confederacy and the Lost Cause. At first glance it might strike readers as decidedly odd that this souvenir connects the hillbilly, the defining symbol of southern Appalachia and the Ozarks, with the rebel battle flag, the defining symbol of the Confederate States of America. Outside of perhaps the black mammy, no more readily recognizable icons of the American South exist than the hillbilly and the Stars and Bars. But it is no coincidence that kitsch moguls selected the hillbilly to represent a bellicose, rising South. The clever combination of these two southern icons was a commercially calculated decision, and the Horny Hillbilly figurine reveals how the post-1945 southern tourism boom and the civil rights movement transformed the souvenirs sold in the mountain South.

Sometime after the Second World War, as historian C. Brenden Martin notes, hillbilly souvenirs began to replace Sambo, mammy, and pickaninny souvenirs in the theme parks, roadside attractions, and gift shops of southern Appalachia. At Gatlinburg and Pigeon Forge, Tennessee, for example, souvenirs often combined the "hillbilly image" with "powerful symbols of the Deep South—namely, rednecks and the Confederate flag." These hybrid souvenirs, Martin argues, became increasingly popular after 1960 "as more and more whites traveled from the Deep South to spend their vacations in Sevier County." Martin attributes the growing popularity of hillbilly souvenirs paradoxically to both the heightened racial sensitivities and the heightened racial animosities sparked by the civil rights movement. During the 1960s, as the production of overtly racist souvenirs caricaturing African Americans declined, owners of tourist shops switched to selling "the racially charged symbols of Dixie to attract and satisfy their overwhelmingly white clientele" from former Confederate states, particularly Georgia, Alabama, and Mississippi. Such souvenirs depicting stereotypical poor white southerners apparently were deemed inoffensive to tourists, and the popularity of these souvenirs increased in part as a result of television programs such as *The Beverly Hillbillies* (1962–70) and *Hee Haw* (1969–92), which reinforced the image of a kinder, gentler, less-threatening hillbilly. The heyday of hillbilly kitsch had dawned.[37]

The Horny Hillbilly symbolizes the white masculine mountain South but also serves as a remarkably clever, if overly optimistic, symbol for an unconquered and unvanquished, rebellious Confederate South. Nothing I have ever seen so clearly connects the concepts of southern white manhood and sexual virility, on the one hand, to Confederate nationalism and the Lost Cause anthem that "The South will rise again," on the other.[38] Writing two decades before the humbling U.S. withdrawal from Vietnam, esteemed historian C. Vann Woodward argued that the American South was distinguished from the rest of the nation by its tragic history of devastating defeat in the Civil War and military occupation during Reconstruction.[39] Indeed, according to historian Nina Silber, the

Confederacy's humiliating defeat in "The Late Unpleasantness" sparked a crisis in southern manhood, a symbolic emasculation of the southern slaveholding aristocracy, at least in the eyes of middle-class northerners. For northern men, the Union victory served as "a confirmation of their moral righteousness and superior civilization," writes Silber, and reinforced their image of "a feminized, and, therefore, illegitimate Confederate government."[40]

Perhaps the best examples of this symbolic emasculation of southern manhood are the apocryphal stories, widely reported in the northern press in May 1865, that as the Confederacy was collapsing, Jefferson Davis attempted to evade pursuing Union troops by donning a bonnet and hoop skirt to disguise himself as a southern belle. Dozens of song sheets, cartoons, and lithographs lampooned the petticoated Confederate president, among them "Jeff's Last Shift," "The Chas-ed Old Lady of the C.S.A.," and "Jeffie-Davis—The Belle of Richmond." "Ultimately, then," concludes Silber, "through their general discussions and through their depictions of Davis, Northerners painted a picture of emasculated Southern men . . . and a Southern system that had been thoroughly and utterly feminized."[41]

However, the Horny Hillbilly, with its unusually large, erect penis—an obvious symbol of male potency and power—aggressively counters this inherited image of a weak and feminized Confederate South and in its Lost Cause anthem defiantly promises a rebirth of a new Confederate nation. As early as 1864, even before the Confederacy was officially vanquished, southern rebels began promising that "the South will rise again."[42] And to this day, southern partisans and neo-Confederates continue to promise a national resurrection. So far, however, "The South will rise again" appears to be little more than an empty slogan (though the Republican Party's recent stranglehold on national political power could be interpreted as the partial fulfillment of such a prophecy given southerners' prominence within the party's ranks). Ultimately, though, the Horny Hillbilly suggests the absurdity of the notion that the Confederate South will ever rise again. The only uprising this mountaineer is capable of stimulating is an erection. Within this plastic novelty figurine, the complicated issues of secession, the Civil War, and the Lost Cause are effectively reduced to a ridiculous, lustful ridge runner and his frustrated sexual urges. The Confederate South remains impotent, despite the many grandiose Lost Cause promises to the contrary. But associating a sexually excited, well-hung hillbilly with an insurgent, rebellious Confederacy reveals much about the gendered images and political discourse surrounding the way we think about the post–Civil War South.[43]

One last significant aspect of the riddle of the Horny Hillbilly involves the erasure of southern history and the distortion of collective memory.

The Horny Hillbilly powerfully illustrates the historical amnesia about the mountain South found in modern regional tourism, particularly the popular but skewed historical memory of southern Appalachia as a bastion of secessionism and southern nationalism during the Civil War. As several historical studies of the region have argued, many of the hill folk in western North Carolina, eastern Tennessee, and northern Alabama were diehard Unionists who fought against the Confederacy during the conflict Lost Cause partisans deceptively labeled the "War between the States."[44] But the Horny Hillbilly essentially revises the historical record regarding the mountain South's opposition to secession and the Confederacy. It unabashedly promotes a historically inaccurate image of a white Confederate South solidly united in its defense of states' rights, secession, and the southern homeland against northern aggression, a widely accepted but erroneous view embraced by many white southerners today. As such, the Horny Hillbilly reveals how southern tourism and mass-marketed souvenirs have both influenced and reflected the collective memories and cultural representations of southern Appalachia and the Ozarks.[45] It also demonstrates that much of whatever southern distinctiveness and identity still persists in twenty-first-century postmodern America is sustained in significant part by the southern tourism industry itself.

Although I appreciate the many levels of meaning encapsulated within this figurine, I am still struggling to solve the riddle of the Horny Hillbilly. I plan some day to donate my prized figurine, along with my entire southern kitsch collection, to an archive or museum, where these artifacts can be preserved, exhibited, and studied by other historians and American studies scholars. Until then, my Horny Hillbilly sits inconspicuously on a bookshelf in my history department office, hidden away inside its box. Only on rare occasions do I show it to colleagues or visitors. Not everyone, after all, can appreciate this Dogpatch Dirk Diggler for the compelling cultural artifact that it is. Some folks have an awfully hard time seeing beyond that tallywhacker.

NOTES

For critical readings, encouragement, and suggestions, the author thanks Brooks Blevins, Tad Brown, Fitzhugh Brundage, Liz Cummins, Steve Fisher, Ellen Furlough, Anthony Harkins, Anne Goodwyn Jones, Lynn Morrow, Ted Ownby, David Roediger, Kris Swenson, David Whisnant, J. W. Williamson, and Lisa Yarger. Special thanks go to Kathleen M. Drowne, Bucky Huber, Midge Huber, the late Paul A. Huber, Nan Morein, and Anthony Stanonis.

1. These objects are housed in the author's private collection of southern kitsch, which he half-jokingly calls the Popular Culture Representations of the American South Museum, established in July 1992. Outside of black collectibles

(see n.4), the historical and popular literature on kitschy southern souvenirs is quite limited. See, for example, Sue Bridwell Beckham, "We Have Met the South and It Is Us: Southern Souvenirs and the American Image," *Prospects* 11 (1986): 247–59; Charles Reagan Wilson, "Southern Tacky Anonymous: A Member in Good Standing," *Southern Living* 28 (February 1993): 178; Tim Hollis, *Dixie before Disney: One Hundred Years of Roadside Fun* (Jackson: University Press of Mississippi, 1999), esp. 12, 13, 23–24, 38–39, 47, 100, 157; Victor Margolin and Patty Carroll, *Culture Is Everywhere: The Museum of Corn-Temporary Art* (Munich: Prestel, 2002), 22–23. Few archives, museums, and institutions currently work actively to collect southern kitsch. To my knowledge, only the Center for the Study of Southern Culture at the University of Mississippi in Oxford, the Southern Historical Collection at the University of North Carolina at Chapel Hill, and the Museum of Corn-temporary Art in Chicago boast collections of these regional souvenirs. The Center for the Study of Southern Culture's souvenir collection actually belongs to historian Charles Reagan Wilson, an avid collector of what he calls "southern tacky." The Southern Historical Collection's "Southern Tacky Collection," amassed by staff members over the past twenty-five years, contains about three hundred items, according to the archive's online catalog, while the Museum of Corn-temporary Art houses Florida souvenirs and perhaps other southern-related kitsch.

2. Nowhere on its box is this plastic souvenir identified as the Horny Hillbilly, but the same figurine is marketed under that name in a psychedelic-patterned, purple-and-black box without the Confederate battle flag and the slogan on the lid. Thus, I have adopted the name to refer to the souvenir packaged in the Confederate battle flag box.

3. See, for example, Russell Underwood, "Under the Big Sombrero," *Southern Exposure* 21 (Winter 1993): 4–5.

4. Even fewer studies of hillbilly and redneck souvenirs exist. See, for example, J. W. Williamson, *Hillbillyland: What the Movies Did to the Mountains and What the Mountains Did to the Movies* (Chapel Hill: University of North Carolina Press, 1995), 3–5, 8–9; Roger Lyle Brown, *Ghost Dancing on the Cracker Circuit: The Culture of Festivals in the American South* (Jackson: University Press of Mississippi, 1997), 78–79; C. Brenden Martin, "To Keep the Spirit of Mountain Culture Alive: Tourism and Historical Memory in the Southern Highlands," in *Where These Memories Grow: History, Memory, and Southern Identity,* ed. W. Fitzhugh Brundage (Chapel Hill: University of North Carolina Press, 2000), 259–60; Leland Payton and Crystal Payton, *See the Ozarks: The Touristic Image* (Springfield, Mo.: Lens and Pen, 2003), 52–59.

In contrast, the racist African American–themed souvenirs (such as pickaninny rag dolls and Aunt Jemima and Uncle Mose salt and pepper shakers) that sold in the American South chiefly between the 1890s and 1950s have generated an extensive historical and collectors' literature. For a sampling of this literature, see Douglas Congdon-Martin, *Images in Black: 150 Years of Black Collectibles* (West Chester, Pa.: Schiffer, 1990); Kenneth W. Goings, *Mammy and Uncle Mose: Black Collectibles and American Stereotyping* (Bloomington: Indiana University Press, 1994); Dawn E. Reno, *The Encyclopedia of Black Collectibles: A*

Value and Identification Guide (Radnor, Pa.: Wallace-Homestead, 1996); Grace Elizabeth Hale, *Making Whiteness: The Culture of Segregation in the South* (New York: Vintage, 1998), 146–47, 151–68; Larry Vincent Buster, *The Art and History of Black Memorabilia* (New York: Potter, 2000); Lynn Casmier-Paz, "Heritage, Not Hate? Collecting Black Memorabilia," *Southern Cultures* 9 (Spring 2001): 43–58. Today, the Black Memorabilia Collectors Club and its official magazine, *Black Ethnic Collectibles,* are devoted exclusively to collecting, selling, and appraising these objects, and Bill Cosby, Oprah Winfrey, Whoopi Goldberg, Julian Bond, and Henry Louis Gates Jr. are among the prominent collectors of black memorabilia.

5. Qtd. in Hollis, *Dixie before Disney,* 3.

6. On the memorial function of souvenirs, see Nelson H. H. Graburn, foreword to *Souvenirs: The Material Culture of Tourism,* ed. Michael Hitchcock and Ken Teague (Aldershot, Eng.: Ashgate, 2000), xii; Michael Hitchcock, introduction to *Souvenirs,* ed. Hitchcock and Teague, 1.

7. Souvenirs, after all, are objects whose cultural meanings are neither fixed nor singular. Rather, souvenirs offer ambiguous and multiple meanings and are interpreted differently across time and region by different people, depending on each person's relationship to the objects. As Hitchcock notes, "Souvenirs do not comprise a unified set of objects and cultural meanings, though they often hint at the experience sought by tourists" (introduction, 11). My understanding of the Horny Hillbilly as a complex cultural artifact has been heavily influenced by the insightful arguments of Hitchcock and of literature scholar Tony Hilfer, who contends that one faulty assumption about the artifacts of popular culture is that they are "universally simple and banal" and lack "the complexity and resonance of high art." Such artifacts are "deemed simple," he argues, because scholars either dismiss them out of hand as lowbrow kitsch—and hence unworthy of intellectual scrutiny—or "read [them] simplemindedly" ("'Wreck on the Highway': Rhetoric and Religion in a Country Song," *John Edwards Memorial Foundation Quarterly* 21 [Fall–Winter 1985]: 116). Although Martin never discusses the Horny Hillbilly in "To Keep the Spirit of Mountain Culture Alive," his superb essay has shaped much of my argument about this souvenir's significance for the mountain South's tourism industry.

8. On the post-1945 southern tourism boom, see, for example, Thomas D. Clark, *The Emerging South* (New York: Oxford University Press, 1961), 131–37, 142; Hollis, *Dixie before Disney*; Richard D. Starnes, introduction to *Southern Journeys: Tourism, History, and Culture in the Modern South,* ed. Richard D. Starnes (Tuscaloosa: University of Alabama Press, 2003), 6–7, as well as other essays in this fine collection.

9. On the origins of the southern souvenir market, see Charles Reagan Wilson, "Southern Tacky Anonymous," 178. Moreover, as an imported product manufactured overseas, the Horny Hillbilly reflects the American South's increasing integration into a global market economy. Earlier models of the figurine may have been made domestically, but since at least the 1990s, the Horny Hillbilly has been manufactured in the Republic of China. What do Chinese factory workers think

of these figurines? Do they even know what a hillbilly is? And do they wonder what brand of ginseng supplements he takes?

10. On the stereotypical features of souvenirs, see Graburn, foreword, xiii.

11. William Goodell Frost, "Our Contemporary Ancestors in the Southern Mountains," *Atlantic Monthly,* March 1899, 311–19; William Goodell Frost, "The Southern Mountaineer: Our Kindred of the Boone and Lincoln Types," *American Review of Reviews* 21 (March 1900): 303–11; Brown, *Ghost Dancing,* 76; Martin, "To Keep the Spirit of Mountain Culture Alive," 251. My discussion of the invention of southern Appalachia and the Ozarks draws heavily on Henry D. Shapiro, *Appalachia on Our Mind: The Southern Mountains and Mountaineers in the American Consciousness, 1870–1920* (Chapel Hill: University of North Carolina Press, 1978); David E. Whisnant, *All That Is Native And Fine: The Politics of Culture in an American Region* (Chapel Hill: University of North Carolina Press, 1983); Allen W. Batteau, *The Invention of Appalachia* (Tucson: University of Arizona Press, 1990); Lynn Morrow and Linda Myers-Phinney, *Shepherd of the Hills Country: Tourism Transforms the Ozarks, 1880s–1930s* (Fayetteville: University of Arkansas Press, 1999); Brooks Blevins, *Hill Folks: A History of Arkansas Ozarkers and Their Image* (Chapel Hill: University of North Carolina Press, 2002).

12. Martin, "To Keep the Spirit of Mountain Culture Alive," 252.

13. Qtd. in Archie Green, "Hillbilly Music: Source and Symbol," *Journal of American Folklore* 78 (July–September 1965): 204. On the origins and early usage of the term, see also Patrick J. Huber, "Rednecks and Woolhats, Hoosiers and Hillbillies: Working-Class Southern Whites, Language, and the Definition of Identity" (master's thesis, University of Missouri at Columbia, 1992), 106–7; Anthony Harkins, *Hillbilly: A Cultural History of an American Icon* (New York: Oxford University Press, 2004), 48–57.

14. On the emergence and development of the hillbilly stereotype, see J. W. Williamson, *Hillbillyland,* esp. 1–4; Batteau, *Invention of Appalachia,* 127–32; Harkins, *Hillbilly,* esp. 47–69, 103–40.

15. Qtd. in Albert N. Votaw, "The Hillbillies Invade Chicago," *Harper's Magazine,* February 1958, 65–66.

16. As early as the 1930s, for example, John T. Woodruff, a Springfield hotelier and member of the local chamber of commerce, expressed concern that the commercial exploitation of the hillbilly image to promote the Missouri Ozarks would only reinforce tourists' stereotypical views of local residents. "The typical Ozarkian is no hillbilly at all," Woodruff remarked, "but a high-minded, patriotic and God-fearing citizen. Never get the idea that is rampant today that they are uncouth, illiterate and mean, and possessed of none of the finer sensibilities" (qtd. in Payton and Payton, *See the Ozarks,* 55).

17. Martin, "To Keep the Spirit of Mountain Culture Alive," 259. On the development of tourism in the southern mountains, see Martin, "To Keep the Spirit of Mountain Culture Alive," 249–69; Morrow and Myers-Phinney, *Shepherd of the Hills Country;* Payton and Payton, *See the Ozarks;* Blevins, *Hill Folks,* esp. 262–65, for a discussion of Dogpatch U.S.A.; Brooks Blevins, "Hillbillies and the

Holy Land: The Development of Tourism in the Arkansas Ozarks," in *Southern Journeys*, ed. Starnes, 42–65, which also contains an extensive discussion of Dogpatch U.S.A.

18. On Pikeville's Hillbilly Days, see Brown, *Ghost Dancing*, 65–89; Harkins, *Hillbilly*, 11, 218–19; *New York Times*, 20 October 1996. Highlands, North Carolina, near Asheville, hosted a similar festival, Highlands Hillbilly Days, during the 1950s. See Harkins, *Hillbilly*, 263 n.26.

19. Payton and Payton, *See the Ozarks*, 52–61.

20. Mallard Cove Trading Web site, http://www2.mo-net.com/~mmalard/new .htm (accessed 21 October 2001); Brown, *Ghost Dancing*, 78. For a critical response to such souvenirs, see ABC News.com, "Is 'Hillbilly Humor' Offensive?" http://dailynews.att.net/cgi-bin/news?e=pri&dt=031031&cat=us&st=usrednecko31029 &src=abc (accessed 31 October 2003).

21. Brown, *Ghost Dancing*, 80; J. W. Williamson, *Hillbillyland*, esp. 2–4; Harkins, *Hillbilly*.

22. See, for example, Winthrop D. Jordan, *White over Black: American Attitudes towards the Negro, 1550–1812* (Chapel Hill: University of North Carolina Press, 1968); George M. Fredrickson, *The Black Image in the White Mind: The Debate on Afro-American Character and Destiny, 1817–1914* (New York: Harper and Row, 1971); Joel Williamson, *The Crucible of Race: Black-White Relations in the American South since Emancipation* (New York: Oxford University Press, 1984), 115–18, 121–22, 127–31, 133–34, 178–79, 306–9.

23. Qtd. in John H. Ashworth, "The Virginia Mountaineers," *South Atlantic Quarterly*, July 1913, 195; Charles Morrow Wilson, "Backwoods Morality," *Outlook and Independent*, 9 January 1929, 67; J. W. Williamson, *Hillbillyland*, esp. 1–4; Harkins, *Hillbilly*, esp. 103–40, 205–21.

24. James A. Maxwell, "Down from the Hills and into the Slums," *Reporter*, 13 December 1956, 27.

25. Ozark Hillbilly Weddin' postcard, Vacationland Distributing, Butler, Missouri, printed in Ireland, in author's collection.

26. Although I have not been able to locate the first usage of this expression, the earliest published linkage of the terms *horny* and *hillbilly* likely dates to around the 1960s, shortly before Horny Hillbilly figurines first appeared on the market. The first known published usage of *hillbilly* dates from the *Dallas Morning News*, 22 May 1893, while *horny*, used to mean "sexually excited" or "lecherous," especially in regard to a man, is slightly older, dating at least to 1889. But based on the entries in the second edition of the *Oxford English Dictionary* (1989), this slang word did not gain widespread currency until after the Second World War. One of the characters in J. L. Herlihy's 1965 novel *Midnight Cowboy*, for example, exclaims, "You *are* a gorgeous-lookin' piece, Cass. Gets a guy all horny just *lookin* at you" (*OED Online*, http://dictionary.oed.com [accessed 8 December 2005]).

27. See, for example, David K. Frasier, *Russ Meyer—the Life and Films* (Jefferson, N.C.: McFarland, 1990); Doyle Greene, *Lips, Hips, Tits, Power: The Films of Russ Meyer* (London: Creation, 2004). Several of these films, including *Mid-*

night Plowboy and *The Pigkeeper's Daughter,* have been reissued on DVD by Image Entertainment.

28. A December 2007 Google search on the phrase *horny hillbilly* turned up 898 hits, while the expression *horny hillbillies* yielded another 1,030. Most of these Internet usages appear either on pornography Web sites or on conservative blogs in reference to former president Clinton. For an example of the latter, see Roger Franklin, "Bubba Struggles to Create a Legacy from the Quagmire of Controversy," *The Age,* http://www.theage.com.au/daily/981213/news/news15 .html (accessed 21 October 2001).

29. On the development of the post-Reconstruction "black brute" image, see, for example, Williamson, *Crucible of Race,* 115–18, 121–22, 127–31, 133–34, 178–79, 306–9.

30. Harkins, *Hillbilly,* pp. 110–11, 175–77; Votaw, "Hillbillies Invade Chicago," 65; Maxwell, "Down from the Hills and into the Slums," 28.

31. The author first heard this joke in his hometown of Ste. Genevieve, Missouri, around 1988 from former high school classmate and longtime friend, Michael "Stupe" Papin, one of the community's best joke tellers; a variant of this joke appears in Vance Randolph, *Pissing in the Snow and Other Ozark Folktales* (1976; Urbana: University of Illinois Press, 1986), 80.

32. Unidentified Web site, accessed ca. October 2001, printout in the author's possession.

33. Qtd. in Charlotte Robinson, review of Dolly Parton performance at the House of Blues, Chicago, 17 August 2002, on PopMatters, http://www.popmatters .com/music/concerts/p/parton-dolly-020817.shtml (accessed 20 May 2006).

34. Randolph, *Pissing in the Snow,* 18–19; for more incest-themed stories, see 22, 54, 80–81, 147–48.

35. Ibid., 42, 91, 102; see also 19, 35, 77, 118. The expression *hillbilly pecker*—which is how scandalmonger Albert Goldman refers to Elvis's in a venomous 1981 best-selling biography—usually refers to an uncircumcised penis rather than an oversized one. See Albert Goldman, *Elvis* (New York: McGraw-Hill, 1981).

36. J. W. Williamson, *Hillbillyland,* 2–3, 35.

37. Martin, "To Keep the Spirit of Mountain Culture Alive," 259–61.

38. On the Lost Cause, see Gaines M. Foster, *Ghosts of the Confederacy: Defeat, the Lost Cause, and the Emergence of the New South, 1865–1913* (New York: Oxford University Press, 1987); David W. Blight, *Race and Reunion: The Civil War in American Memory* (Cambridge: Belknap Press of Harvard University Press, 2001).

39. C. Vann Woodward, *The Burden of Southern History,* rev. ed. (1960; Baton Rouge: Louisiana State University Press, 1989), 188–91. Woodward first made this argument in his 1952 presidential address before the Southern Historical Association, subsequently published as "The Irony of Southern History," *Journal of Southern History* 19 (February 1953): 3–19.

40. Nina Silber, "Intemperate Men, Spiteful Women, and Jefferson Davis: Northern Views of the Defeated South," *American Quarterly* 41 (December

1989): 616, 625. This illuminating article forms a chapter in her longer study, *The Romance of Reunion: Northerners and the South, 1865–1900* (Chapel Hill: University of North Carolina Press, 1993), 13–38.

41. Silber, "Intemperate Men, Spiteful Women, and Jefferson Davis," 615, 625–26.

42. A variant of the expression, for example, appeared in print fourteen months before Appomattox. The February 1864 issue of the *Southern Literary Messenger* published a eulogy, written by a New Orleans woman, titled "Last Words of Major Wheat" that included the line, "And soon the South shall rise, boys, all glorious and fair." Even today, cars and trucks can occasionally be seen on southern interstates with bumper stickers reading "Save your Confederate money, boys. The South will rise again!" See "Hermine," "Last Words of Major Wheat," *Southern Literary Messenger* 38 (February 1864): 111.

43. At the same time, the Horny Hillbilly can also be interpreted as a symbol of embattled American manhood and male anxiety. In the wake of the modern feminist movement, affirmative action laws, and the deindustrialization of the nation's economy, the figurine expresses a rising tide of white American masculine alienation and frustration—an invitation to take pleasure in an unfettered masculinity and male dominance that is now believed lost—more than a specific celebration of neo-Confederate nationalism or a negative indictment of mountain backwardness. I thank Jerry Williamson for pointing out this alternate reading.

44. See, for example, John C. Inscoe and Gordon B. McKinney, *The Heart of Confederate Appalachia: Western North Carolina in the Civil War* (Chapel Hill: University of North Carolina Press, 2000); several of the essays in Kenneth W. Noe and Shannon H. Wilson, eds., *The Civil War in Appalachia: Collected Essays* (Knoxville: University of Tennessee Press, 1997). As Martin points out in his study of Gatlinburg and Pigeon Forge, "Ironically, the appeal of Confederate images contradicts the strong pro-Union sentiment in Sevier County during the Civil War. Indeed, the Confederacy is much more popular in Sevier County today than it was in 1861, when the county rejected secession by a vote of 1,302 to 1. Nevertheless, in virtually every place involving tourism, including restaurants, museums, gift shops, and entertainment parks, entrepreneurs blended Appalachian stereotypes with symbols of Dixie" ("To Keep the Spirit of Mountain Culture Alive," 260).

45. Martin, "To Keep the Spirit of Mountain Culture Alive," 249.

PART II

Coloring the Market

Race and Consumerism

Identity Market

W. Fitzhugh Brundage

The confluence of entrepreneurship and identity unites these four essays. Although these essays cover a historical range from the late nineteenth century to the present, all nevertheless expose the marketplace's power to define and alter identity. These essays also reveal the contradictory possibilities that the marketing of identity creates; those possibilities are at times emancipatory, at times restrictive, and at times both.

These essays are especially valuable because they highlight these contradictory consequences while emphasizing the agency of the actors involved, whether they be postemancipation black ministers, Ozark hillbilly reenactors, a South Carolina huckster, or Montgomery preservationists. Simply put, these are not accounts of vast, faceless, inexorable market forces entrapping naive and numbed consumers. The market has shaped American historical identities and representations far more than the state has. Only in the half century following the Second World War did government at both the federal and state levels assume a crucial role in such things as tourism, historic preservation, and historic site management. And even then, the state usually sought to advance the interests of the private sector. Consequently, tourism entrepreneurs, not government officials, usually served as the most significant architects of regional and historical identity.

John M. Giggie grapples with the implications of black consumerism, a topic about which far too little is known. African Americans were obviously consumers even before they enjoyed freedom; the slaves who held personal property and possessed savings accounts were the progenitors of postbellum black consumers. But the scale of black consumption and the meanings attached to it during the postbellum era were clearly unprecedented. Giggie clarifies how, to borrow historian E. P. Thompson's phrase, "the education of desire" took place among blacks.[1]

That black ministers played a role in this "education of desire" is both surprising and predictable—surprising because scholars have had so little to say about this facet of black ministers' activities; predictable because black ministers, as Giggie explains, were ideally situated to serve as intermediaries between merchants and black consumers. In addition, the politics of respectability and the logic of racial uplift transformed consumption into a symbol of racial progress. Giggie's findings should inspire other scholars to ponder all of the myriad ways black churches served as venues for and agents of black consumption. For example, just as white churches routinely hosted church bazaars, typically organized and stocked by white women, so too black churches had comparable traditions.

Giggie's essay also suggests some of the tensions that black ministerial entrepreneurship must have inspired. It is ironic that Booker T. Washington, Carter Woodson, and many other black secular leaders lambasted black ministers for their purported laziness, pointless posturing, and unsuitability to lead African Americans in the transition to modernity. Washington instead should have embraced these black ministers as foot soldiers in his program of racial uplift and economic advancement. Giggie's essay suggests that Washington and his ilk failed to understand that the black church served as an agent of rather than an obstacle to modernization.

It is perhaps a leap from the sacred to the profane to turn from postbellum black ministers to the tourist boomtowns of the Missouri Ozarks and of South of the Border, a fading South Carolina tourist mecca. The Ozark boosters who populate Aaron K. Ketchell's essay apparently have suffered no cognitive dissonance as a consequence of reconciling their relentless pursuit of the tourist dollar with a nostalgia for homespun culture and traditional mores. By tracing the permutations of the "hillbilly" moniker in both the region and the national imagination, Ketchell demonstrates that Ozark residents have been both complicit in and adept at manipulating the hillbilly stereotype. Especially striking is the apparent appeal of the imagined hillbilly and his milieu; the architects of the Ozarks stereotype range from Protestant evangelists to country music impresarios and champions of white racial purity. The Ozarks seem to fulfill a function for modern America that the plantation South served for the antebellum United States. A half century ago, William R. Taylor, in his masterful *Cavalier and Yankee: The Old South and American National Character*, argued that the myth of the planter cavalier in the Old South provided an antidote to the restless mobility and strident materialism of the antebellum United States.[2] Fear and envy sustained the allure of a culture that was immune to acquisitiveness and indiscriminate progress yet was rooted in place and tradition. Ketchell suggests that the Ozarks and their "authentic" culture continued to perform a similar function during the twentieth century. Across the century, both Ozark residents and non-residents reinterpreted the region's culture to bolster shifting ideas about regional and national identity. Yet as often as Ozark culture was used to criticize U.S. institutions and values, it was also used to accommodate residents to those values. While boosters dwell on the region's purported timeless traditions and mores, they nevertheless have presided over a profound and irreversible transformation of the region. And whereas observers previously affirmed the cultural separateness of the region's people, now, in a more pluralist age, they point to a Japanese-born fiddler who draws huge crowds to his curious blend of musical traditions performed in a garish theater. We perhaps should find satisfaction in the fact that contemporary Americans find fellowship through such curious adaptations of Ozark culture. But we would be naive to assume that the meanings we assign to that culture today will not be subject to revision and reinvention in the future.

It seems to defy common sense that something as preposterous and gaudy as South of the Border warrants sustained reflection. Where others see only one of the worst eyesores along the nearly two-thousand-mile length of Interstate 95, Nicole King astutely discerns a telltale manifestation of a complex and contradictory reimagination of southern identity as a commodity. Situated on a literal border of two states and in a metaphorical borderland between the southern hinterland and the demographic (and traffic) free-for-all of Interstate 95, South of the Border vividly demonstrates the ways in which tourism, as a business and as a form of cultural production, can challenge local and regional norms. King sketches an intriguing portrait of Alan Schafer, the entrepreneur responsible for South of the Border. He seems to have possessed an acute if intuitive sense of the license that the tourism industry and his location gave him, a sense that allowed Schafer to transgress so many apparent white southern verities in a peculiarly complex social geography. To the north of Dillon County, where the attraction is located, is Robeson County, North Carolina, the home of one of the largest Native American communities east of the Mississippi. To the southeast is Horry County, which harbored one of the most violent and popular Ku Klux Klan revivals of the late 1940s and early 1950s. And local politics were uncommonly rough-and-tumble, with an entrenched conservative Democratic political machine the norm.

Schafer's astute appreciation of the opportunity represented by the continuous migration of nonsoutherners up and down Interstate 95 made possible his unique enterprise. Because Schafer marketed a fantasy world of kitsch to snowbirds and other nonsoutherners, he maintained a freer hand than promoters of sites such as Colonial Williamsburg, which marketed heritage (complicated by the racial implications of celebrating a colonial community populated with slaves) rather than location and convenience. Put another way, presumably no one travels to South Carolina specifically to visit South of the Border. Whether Schafer consciously recognized the possibilities that his migratory, nonsouthern customer base offered is not clear. But King's essay leaves little doubt that Schafer was a visionary tourist entrepreneur with a keen understanding of evolving consumer tastes. Consequently, the chapter on South of the Border is as much a story of postwar automobile age America as of the American South.

Ironies also abound in Glenn T. Eskew's cautionary account of the commercial and commemorative impulses evident in the remembrance of the civil rights movement in various southern communities. The cast of characters in these various campaigns to preserve and represent the civil rights struggle are often colorful, and this statement certainly holds true in Montgomery, Alabama, where the sacred and the profane seem to be found next door to one another. Eskew also clarifies the evolution of the commemorative campaign, revealing how tourism, economic development, historic preservation, and commemoration have become inextricably linked. Like Dillon County in South Carolina, Montgomery, Alabama, is, in many ways, sui generis. But in broad terms, the story that Eskew tells is suggestive of events in every southern battleground of the civil rights struggle that has subsequently sought to market that heritage.

Virtually every southern city that has recently invested itself in civil rights commemoration suffers from marked economic decay. Downtown Memphis, Montgomery, Selma, Greensboro, and Albany, to take just a few examples, stand among the bleakest urban landscapes in the South. Birmingham, to a degree, remains an exception, but it claims the tremendous advantage of a booming medical industry. Against this backdrop, as Eskew explains, civil rights tourism represents more than a manifestation of predictable collective memory and nostalgia; it also provides a testament to the economic failure of metropolitan Montgomery and other southern cities.

Similarly, civil rights commemoration is a measure of African American political empowerment. Southern blacks in many communities now enjoy the power that white southerners once monopolized—the privilege of etching their past onto the landscape. But just as white southerners sought to harness hallowed memories to all manner of contemporary ambitions, so too black commemoration has been yoked to political ambitions, fund-raising, and neighborhood renewal. That the commemoration of the civil rights movement would eventually exhibit the influence of the marketplace was perhaps inevitable, but Eskew draws attention to some of the individuals who have had an especially large hand in this process as well as the skillful manner in which they wrapped their endeavors in the mantle of racial tolerance. In the process, the boundaries between the cause of social and racial justice and the pursuit of power and profit have sometimes become murky. Here, then, is a cautionary reminder that the memory of the civil rights movement is, like the memory of other chapters in southern history, vulnerable to exploitation.

From the flatlands to the mountainsides and from the bustling interstate highway corridors to the struggling downtowns of the American South, entrepreneurs, consumers, and travelers have tackled questions of identity and memory as well as profits and costs. The stories that follow—of groups, whether black Christians or white Ozark hillbillies, or of individuals, whether Alan Schafer or Morris Dees—speak to a larger narrative of southern engagement with the modern market. Like the good salespeople they were and are, the entrepreneurs recounted in this section have sold more than trinkets and services; they have sold dreams and identity. But like prudent consumers, we should always check under the hood.

NOTES

1. E. P. Thompson, *William Morris: Romantic to Revolutionary* (New York: Pantheon, 1976), 798.

2. William R. Taylor, *Cavalier and Yankee: The Old South and American National Character* (New York: Braziller, 1961).

Refining Religion

Consumerism and African American Religion in the Delta, 1875–1917

John M. Giggie

In 1909, members of the Zion Baptist Chapel in Lonoke, Arkansas, tore down their small, dilapidated, one-story wooden church. Twenty-three years after building it on a cotton plantation in this small rural town east of the state capital, Little Rock, congregants wanted to celebrate their growth as a religious community by constructing a special house of worship. They erected an impressive new church far larger and more lavishly decorated than most of its neighbors. Painted white and boasting a frame construction and a bell tower in the northeast corner, the structure seated about two hundred people in twenty-eight pews carved from golden oak. During services, members sang along with a new Kimball organ and watched the minister consecrate the Lord's Supper on a raised altar platform ringed by three upholstered chairs. Store-bought drapes adorned the windows.[1]

The style and decoration of the new Zion Baptist Church are starting points for analyzing the changing material and consumerist dimensions of black religion under Jim Crow in the Arkansas and Mississippi Delta, a historic center of rural African American life.[2] Here, black Baptists and Methodists, most of whom toiled as plantation workers and tenant farmers in the local cotton economy, experimented with ways of integrating their faith with the market. Throughout Reconstruction and until the First World War, large numbers of blacks steadily migrated to the Delta, chasing the dream of landownership and the seductive promises dangled by unscrupulous labor agents. These agents, employed by white Delta landowners and speculators desperate for a new and bigger workforce after slavery's demise, rode by horse and rail to every state that had flown the Confederate flag and spun wondrous tales of cheap plentiful land and high wages to any black person who would come and work. Thousands arrived to sow their ambitions in the Delta soil. From 1870 to 1910,

when 90 percent of all black Americans lived in the South, blacks ac-
counted for approximately 75 percent of the Delta's overall population.[3]
The area ranked first nationally in the total number of black-majority
counties, some of which possessed a ratio of blacks to whites that ran as
high as fifteen to one.[4]

By the early twentieth century, most Delta blacks understood the sheer
size of churches like Zion Baptist and its interior furnishings as emblems
of a large, vibrant, and prosperous congregation. Any black or white
visitor to the area might also have done so, but likely without a keen
appreciation for how the design and ornamental features formed part of
the rich local culture of home and church adornment that slowly evolved
within African American religious life after Reconstruction.[5] White congregations certainly made similar associations as the mass market penetrated the hinterlands. And much of what followed in the black community, such as calls for respectability, for moral home environments, and
for women to serve as moral guardians of domestic spaces, had parallels
within white congregations. But the burdens of Jim Crow, racism, and
poverty gave special meaning to the material goods enjoyed by blacks. In
this culture, blacks imbued material things with spiritual meaning and
used them to structure, organize, and represent their physical world.
They enmeshed architectural forms, church furnishings, and domestic
consumer commodities in a dense cultural web of denominational loyal-
ties and racial associations that provided a critical means of communi-
cating and constituting sacred belief.[6] For African Americans, material
objects symbolized and sustained religious conviction and racial uplift.

In the late nineteenth-century Delta, several transformations in transportation and the economy made possible the growth of this new material culture of African American religion—the rapid expansion of the
railroad and the postal delivery service, the emergence of inexpensive
domestic commodities as a key feature of American capitalism, and the
rise of black preachers and newspaper editors as salesmen pitching many
of these commodities to rural African Americans.[7] This steady infusion of
the latest consumer and literary goods into the region introduced many
residents to new products and ideas about personal dress, home life, and
church beauty. However, Delta blacks could afford only a few of these
new commodities because they often lacked enough money, credit, and
autonomy to acquire what they wanted. Their purchases were limited
primarily to simple clothing, home furnishings, Bibles, religious tracts,
books, lithographs of scenes from the Old Testament, and visual images
of black leaders. Still, they made these items the basis of an ideology of
religious material culture that represented their developing ideas about
the consumer market, gender, and religious identity. They established

the critical use of commodities in homes and churches as an important cultural mechanism in building Baptist and Methodist communities and fashioning images of refined black consumption. The shared experience of consumption, in turn, promoted a sense of denominational and black identity that strengthened fellowship among Delta churches.

This essay focuses on the historical relationship between spiritual life and consumerism among African Americans in the Delta from the end of Reconstruction to the First World War, when, in an abrupt reversal of earlier migration patterns, tens of thousands of blacks, unable to realize the dreams planted by labor agents, fled the region in search of better jobs and race relations in the Midwest and North. Confronting a society in flux, Delta blacks turned to the emerging consumer economy as one way of building and supporting religious communities that promised not only a measure of relief from the evolving culture of segregation but also progress in the effort to improve the race. How precisely did African American Baptists and Methodists—in this case, the vast majority of them rural agricultural workers—appropriate and modify aspects of modern consumer culture to fashion a range of visual statements about the proper nature of citizenship and spiritual identity?[8] Such an analysis promises to shed new light on the ways in which poor black southerners articulated shifting ideas about racial politics and gender through their religious material culture.

The home was the crucial locale in the making of this new material culture of religion. Although Delta blacks had always seen home life as fundamental in producing good Baptists and Methodists, the dawn of the twentieth century brought a burgeoning interest in domestic spaces and the ideological construction of the "black Christian home," an idealized setting in which proper design and decoration theoretically nurtured the manners and morality of all who lived there. Here parents taught children how to read and follow the Bible's precepts in their daily lives. The black Christian home was also an extension of the church, a place on whose walls hung images of black heroes and symbols of African American Protestantism and whose inhabitants dressed plainly and behaved in an orderly fashion. By looking more like houses of worship, homes supposedly became more spiritual spaces and made the teachings of Jesus easier to recall and follow.

At the heart of the concept of the black Christian home and religious material culture in the Delta lay changing notions about black women. During the late nineteenth century, many black women echoed religious leaders and proclaimed themselves the chief curators of the black Christian home. They claimed primary responsibility for developing their households as symbols of sensible consumption, models of cleanliness, and centers for raising literate, law-abiding, and devout children. Their work promised tangible political benefits: it overturned caricatures of African Americans as unruly profligates; enabled a new generation of blacks to understand bills of sale, court orders, and labor contracts; and instilled boys and girls with the education and moral vision to become leaders of the next generation. But this work also carried a more immediate payoff. By enhancing the cultural significance of black women's role in establishing the black Christian home and portraying its success as vital to the community's progress, these women created a fresh means of earning a measure of social and religious authority at a time when traditional opportunities for political advancement were fast closing for them and for all blacks.[9]

The expansion of African American material Christianity in the Delta coincided with the elaboration of domestic religion among northern white urban Protestants and Catholics, many of whom were first- or second-generation immigrants from the British Isles and southern Europe. Noteworthy similarities existed between the two groups. In both cases, individuals bought objects of religious significance and either wore them or placed them throughout their homes. These objects did not simply mirror a style or mode of religious decoration but served as physical components of rituals and theologies that celebrated the sacredness of the family, promoted middle-class aspirations, and strengthened the moral fiber of the local community and nation. Women bore the chief responsibility for overseeing this aspect of religion.[10]

Yet in important ways, black Baptists and Methodists in the Delta fostered a distinctive material culture, although it was smaller in scope than that nurtured by whites in the urban North. Absent was the thick display of embroidered crosses, statues of Jesus, silver-plated crucifixes, holy water receptacles, and ceramic figurines of saints that crowded the mantels and home altars of Protestants and Catholics living in Boston, New York, and Philadelphia. Delta blacks carefully selected and utilized their religious objects in ways that reflected their specific geographic locale and fit their cultural needs. They relied on such items to help standardize devotional practices and unify denominational culture across the rural Delta. Furthermore, they embedded religious objects in overlapping narratives of spiritual and racial uplift that identified the black Christian home as a crucible of moral reform and enlightenment, thereby equipping them with ideas and practices that lessened, though never eliminated, the ill effects of white supremacy. And black women considered religious items and the black Christian home to be elements in the renewal of their political authority in the church and community during the Jim Crow era.

"Improving" Black Religion

Popular interest in religious material culture among Delta blacks soared during the late nineteenth century as changes in the consumer market intersected with new ideas about individual and societal refinement. The growing availability of inexpensive domestic and literary commodities—whether through plantation commissaries, general stores, traveling salesmen, or itinerant preachers who also worked as peddlers—introduced a range of material ingredients from which to fashion and express notions of public and private decorum. A central element in this effort to refine black religion in the Delta, directly affecting how Delta blacks invested consumer goods with spiritual meaning, was the ethic of respectability. Beginning in about the 1890s, black church officials went to great lengths to popularize "respectability" as a chief element in a broad code of ethics and behavior. They widely defined *respectability* as a series of conservative moral values, attitudes, and behaviors that offered subscribers deeper faith, improved prosperity, and greater public respect from blacks and whites. Although no panacea for injustice, respectability's key elements of temperance, order, neatness, sexual purity, propriety, and manners also promised to lift many racial burdens. In particular, these behaviors challenged popular images of blacks as unclean, unruly people incapable of responsibly exercising the privileges of freedom or acting within the boundaries of white bourgeois morality.[11]

Black leaders' exhortations for their followers to live more respectably brimmed with implicit assumptions about class identity. These leaders generally equated the highest form of southern black life with idealized notions of middle-class existence. Like white urban reformers evaluating improvements in lifestyle and livelihood among ethnic immigrants crowding northern cities, black community elders measured African American progress in the Delta by calculating how closely blacks emulated Victorian notions of manhood, womanhood, and gentility.[12] In reality, however, Delta blacks, in large part because of their poverty, stood little chance of living middle-class lives, thus frustrating the ambitions of respectability's staunchest spokespeople. Still, African American leaders embraced the broad spirit of respectability by linking patterns of consumption to the hope of racial uplift, even if most did not meet every middle-class standard.

Respectability explicitly linked an ideal of disciplined character to frugal routines of individual consumption. Proponents insisted that blacks avoid overspending and buying frivolous items, such as gilded tableware or lacy clothing, because indiscriminate use of income diverted coins from church coffers and inflamed negative stereotypes of blacks as spendthrifts. Advocates of the respectability ethic permitted the purchase of a specific market item only when it augmented their objectives. To show-case a public representation of thrift and self-esteem, for example, blacks were encouraged to buy only plain clothing and to keep themselves clean and well-groomed. To project an image of a disciplined people, blacks should buy brushes, buckets, and cleaning agents—and should use them frequently.[13]

In this sense, respectability became part of the larger racial program of social improvement and disciplined consumption championed nationally by black spokespersons such as Booker T. Washington and locally by leaders including Arkansas Delta minister Elias Camp Morris, president of the Arkansas Baptist Convention and the National Baptist Convention.[14] In his 1901 address to graduates of Little Rock's Arkansas Baptist College, one of the nation's largest black Baptist colleges, Morris situated respectability in the context of the wider effort to advance Delta blacks' morality and fortune. He argued that the recent progress of the black race was spectacular: blacks had become "surrounded with schools and churches, and hav[e] so many educated preachers and competent teachers." Such success, however, meant that "much more will be expected of us in the future." And as the twentieth century commenced, Morris continued, "we will be expected to be better citizens, such as will not dodge the tax collector, no matter if we are discriminated against. We are to be better neighbors by . . . respecting and paying due regard for our neighbors' rights and possessions. Crime among our people must be lessened." A future of continued improvement and acceptance by white southerners required the graduates of Arkansas Baptist College to embrace the ethic of respectability—"to be the advocates of purity and right in every quarter," "to teach the people . . . the lessons which will inculcate the habits of cleanliness, economy, decision," and to "keep their surroundings clean."[15]

Like Morris, national and local black leaders of the Methodist Episcopal Church encouraged their followers to embrace the ethic of respectability as a means of improving their material and moral condition. In a series of essays, they extolled the importance of respectability by recalling the biblical story of Exodus. Their choice of context was obviously significant. Exodus enjoyed wide popularity among African American Christians as the scriptural narrative of bondage and liberation that most closely paralleled their own historical circumstances.[16] "It was forty years after Israel left Egypt before Canaan could be reached because of unreadiness. It has been about forty-five years since our race left physical slavery and gathered at this Jordan swollen with questions, doubts, and arguments, pro and con, respecting the fitness and ability of the race." The ethic of respectability promised to prepare the race to wield the duties and responsibilities of freedom with aplomb and maturity: "Let us decide that this preparation to enter every sphere and department of American civilization shall be [with] a better appearance." The "preparation" specifically called for "good thoughts in the brain and good principles in the soul, together with a clean body, clean teeth, well-combed hair, and clothes on in good shape."[17]

Respectability also gained a measure of popular approval because of its application in minimizing illness. The emphasis on habits of cleanliness in private and public life implicitly attacked the health hazards and consequent mortality that plagued African Americans in the Delta. Malaria, typhoid, and pregnancy and childbirth took a severe toll, especially in the most rural areas, where medical care was poorest. Blacks often traveled a full day to reach the nearest hospital, only to discover that no one there would treat them. In Mississippi's Sunflower County, the high mortality rate hit black children hardest. By the time most black women reached forty-five years old, they had birthed seven or eight children but had lost three or four to illness or infection. By contrast, white women of the same age had generally birthed five children and lost only one or two.[18]

In addition to promising relief from illness, many preachers extolled the value of respectability as part of a broader effort to standardize ritual practices and educational qualifications for the ministry. By so doing, they hoped to strengthen denominational solidarity and create a more enlightened and orderly black public. The lingering elements of "slave religion"—a term they applied derisively to indicate practices of ecstatic worship, the use of uneducated men and sometimes women as preachers, and the popular faith in the supernatural that had been common among blacks under bondage—that thrived in some Delta communities emerged as the favorite targets of reform-minded clerics. In particular, church officials desperately wanted members to resist spontaneously breaking into bouts of shrieking, crying, dancing, hand clapping, and foot stomping during services. To accomplish this goal, religious leaders urged their congregations to strictly regulate when congregants should sing by adopting hymnbooks and training choirs.[19] Reformers also hoped to ensure that a person could no longer earn a certificate to preach simply by standing up in church or at a revival, extemporizing from a biblical passage in front of the congregation, and thereby gaining popular approval. The Baptist and Methodist churches passed new rules requiring that every candidate for the pulpit be a man, demonstrate a basic level of literacy, and pass a written and oral exam on biblical knowledge administered by a group of pastors drawn from the local church district. Between 1889 and 1891, church officials with the Southeastern Baptist District Association of the Arkansas Delta passed "a law forbidding churches to examine and ordain young ministers. . . . The object of this law was to transfer the examination of applicant for ordination to the association, so as to meet the fast growing demand for a more qualified ministry."[20] Ministers strictly enforced the regulations. In 1905, those serving on the qualification board "examine[d] Brother B. J. Cobb for the ministry. After a very [im]partial examination in the branches proscribed by the association and the Bible, he was pronounced incompetent and referred back for study."[21]

Decorating the Black Christian Home

The growth of the consumer market, the ethic of respectability, and the ongoing clerical interest in refining the religious lives of Delta blacks ultimately fueled the development of the idea of the black Christian home. During the late nineteenth century, Delta preachers began to believe that the physical traits of the home profoundly influenced the overall character of its inhabitants. The cleanliness of the floors, the selection of the prints and photos hanging on the walls, and the decoration of the rooms served as important vehicles for forming the residents' values and disposition and, more generally, the collective future of the race. An 1899 editorial in the *Christian Index,* the organ of the Colored Methodist Episcopal Church, opened by stating that black Christian homes "have a far greater influence in shaping the destinies of nations and of a people than we commonly imagine."[22] The official newspaper of blacks within the Methodist Episcopal Church, the *Southwestern Christian Advocate,* advanced a similar proposition. In one article, "Begin a Movement for Better Homes," a group of black ministers asserted, "We do not believe one will be either as good a man or as worthy a citizen without the inspiration which a comfortable and happy home lends."[23]

The rhetoric of the black Christian home, like that of respectability, warned against extravagance and wastefulness. Profligacy was a grave sin with serious consequences: spendthrifts incurred debt, forfeited rent or mortgage payments, and ultimately jeopardized their chances of living in homes. The need for financial and moral restraint in the black Christian home was a central theme of the Arkansas Baptist Mothers' Conference held in Pine Bluff in September 1894. In "Ten Evils That Result from Fashionable Dress," Laura F. Brown of Mount Holly identified the frittering away of time and money as the worst. "Time is Wasted. Think of the tucks, ruffles, and laces that are sometimes used that are not at all necessary." The price of ignoring the cultural proscriptions of the black Christian home and respectability was too high. "Many are homeless. Many are living in rented homes and on mortgaged farms because of fashionable dress. . . . It leads both men and women into debt."[24]

The call for black Christian homes in the Delta slowly swelled into a multidenominational chorus of black leaders exhorting congregants to wisely purchase and display physical goods. Such calls articulated a specific relationship between black morality and the design and decoration of domestic spaces, arguing that an individual's morality, ethics, and even education depended greatly on the visual setting of the home. Black Christians must "use money [previously] spent for tobacco, whiskey, and snuff in buying homes and subscribing to books, papers, magazines, etc., for their children," urged Memphis resident Ida B. Wells. In an 1888 article in the *Christian Index,* she argued that blacks "are to be taught personal, individual, family and race pride, the necessity of culture, by beautifying their homes and cultivating their minds."[25] Wells suggested that the most important items for beautifying a black home were religious books and especially pictures. Editors at the *Christian Index* were blunter. In a weekly feature called "Advice," they explained that "in the decoration of a home each article tells a story of its own; the small ornaments . . . and especially the kinds of pictures and books. [W]e should always be careful to get good ones, instead of showy ones which are offensive to people."[26]

The stress on "good pictures" as a constitutive feature of the black Christian home also stemmed from pragmatic and philosophical considerations. Visual images, especially those cut out from the pages of black religious newspapers, were inexpensive, accessible, and fairly simple to distribute. Many clergymen valued this ability to control, at least in part, what black Baptists and Methodists tacked to the walls of their homes because of the popular belief that religious images possessed the power directly to affect the character and morality of their viewers. For example, in a February 1899 front-page editorial, "The Sacredness of the Home," an unnamed minister instructed readers of the *Christian Index* about what type of religious pictures to display—"pictures that we will not tire of looking at," images that "the more we see [them], the more their beauty grows upon us."[27] This clergyman never clearly defined what he meant by the phrase "beauty grows upon us," yet he obviously believed that regularly gazing at a religious picture produced spiritual benefits.

Because "good pictures" became essential elements in the black Christian home, clerics did not mince words when describing the moral suitability of pictures for hanging. "Do not decorate your homes with pictures representing shows, theaters, minstrels and saloons," read the *Christian Index*'s "Advice" column during the first week of March 1892.[28] In an article with the straightforward title "What Kind of Pictures to Hang on Your Walls," published in the *Southwestern Christian Advocate,* the Reverend G. I. Izard declared anathema "any depiction of W. Duke, Sons & Co.'s tobacco manufacturing establishment" or "different theaters, circus shows, base ball playing . . . representing sin in the blackest form." In contrast, he continued, "it is better and will prove more beneficial to the young to have on your walls a picture showing the arrest, crucifixion, burial, resurrection and ascension of our Lord and Savior Jesus Christ."[29]

The strong didactic tone present in these examples, however, betrayed an anxiety and ambivalence about relying on the market as a key resource for creating the black Christian home. While furnishing visual images deemed appropriate for the home, the market also produced images that potentially subverted morality. To counter this paradox, black religious leaders asserted their role as judges of consumer goods. As early as 1877, officials of the North Mississippi Conference of the African Methodist Episcopal Church, a region that included most of the Mississippi Delta, provided pictures of bishops to congregants who paid their "dollar money"—that is, their yearly assessments.[30] Other denominations eventually followed suit. Beginning in the spring of 1891, the *Southwestern Christian Advocate* sold pictures of bishops to members of its Methodist Episcopal churches. "Many of our readers would gladly possess the pictures of our bishops if they only knew where to get them. In order to accommodate them, we have arranged to supply them with a beautiful cabinet group photograph of all our bishops, for the small sum of 25 cents."[31]

For black Christians unable to spare even a few cents to buy portraits, editors started to print them as a regular newspaper feature. In the summer of 1894, the *Southwestern Christian Advocate* inaugurated a "Picture Gallery," which offered a picture and brief biography of a different cleric every two to three weeks. The features were intended to be cut out and tacked up somewhere inside the home. The portraits quickly became a hit with readers, according to the newspaper. "In thousands of the homes of our constituency those pictures with the brief history of their originals will be found." The editors' excitement, however, reflected not only their belief that the popularity of the pictures signaled public approval of the black Christian home but also more practical financial considerations. The "Picture Gallery," they happily pointed out, helped to "greatly augment and accelerate . . . the increased circulation of the SOUTHWESTERN."[32] Perhaps spurred by the apparent popular and commercial success of the "Picture Gallery," editors at the *Christian Index* created "Our Picture Gallery" in 1900, introducing the series by announcing that "we shall insert, every week, the portrait of some preacher of our Church, accompanied by a short biography of the same name." They invited local preachers to mail in personal histories along with "$2.00 and your picture."[33]

During the 1890s, editors of black religious newspapers also published sketches of famous figures in African American history who were not church leaders. Readers of the *Southwestern Christian Advocate* enjoyed pictures of Frederick Douglass and Abraham Lincoln, the latter usually printed during the weeks before the anniversary of the Emancipation

Proclamation and advertised as "rugged cuts" of the president who freed the slaves.[34] At other times, black religious leaders sold mass-produced decorations specifically designed as religious wall hangings. In honor of Thanksgiving 1895, editors at the *Southwestern Christian Advocate* offered a framed print of a landscape oil painting called *American Beauty.* They provided few clues about the print itself other than it "form[ed] a beautiful ornament for the high, narrow wall spaces for which it is so difficult to obtain pictures of the proper style."[35] Similarly, in 1896, the editors at the *Baptist Vanguard* offered a wall hanging of the Emancipation Proclamation by stressing its value as "a beautiful ornament for any parlor in the country."[36] For decades, Delta blacks apparently decorated their homes with these types of pictures cut out or purchased through black religious newspapers and church publications. Investigating the living conditions of black sharecroppers in the Delta during the 1920s, federal agents noted that homes contained few expensive, store-bought decorations. Instead, blacks commonly covered their walls with pictures from newspapers and magazines.[37]

One sign of the growing importance of visual images to black religious culture in the Delta during the 1890s was the sudden interest shown by Catholic missionaries in securing fresh supplies of prints and pictures for use in their evangelical labors. In August 1898, the Reverend Thomas Plunkett, a Josephite brother and director of the Colored Industrial Institute, a small Catholic school in Pine Bluff, Arkansas, penned an urgent note to his superior, Reverend Joseph Slattery. Plunkett asked not only for items customarily used in Catholic worship and devotion—"one dozen rosary beads, two dozen hymn books, and two or three dozen small religious medals"—but also "all the pictures of Colored men and Saints you can afford," which were essential to the goal of winning converts because "only by such means [can] we . . . expect to do much with those attending the Institute."[38] Plunkett's demand for pictures that resonated with black culture, however, also represented a persistent tension gnawing at many black Protestants over the expanded use of mass-produced goods both in the making of black Christian homes and more generally in nurturing greater levels of public refinement. Not every religious image—and certainly not one featuring a black Catholic—was appropriate. Even more worrisome was the fact that not all black Baptists and Methodists possessed the critical faculty to select the proper images for their homes. For black Baptists and Methodists to develop a sensible religious material culture, some additional figure needed to act as the guardian of standards and decorum.

The duty of ensuring that only proper visual images decorated the black Christian home eventually fell to black women. Indeed, by the 1890s, the most important person in this mission was widely assumed to be the female authority figure in the household—mother, wife, daughter, sister, aunt, or grandmother.[39] Women oversaw the household's upkeep and adornment, organized its daily rituals, and, most importantly, supervised the teaching of faith, decorum, and literacy to its residents. In 1893, Priscilla Scott defined black women's preeminence in the black Christian home in a paper presented at the joint meeting of two Arkansas groups, the Women's State Baptist Association and the State Baptist Sunday School Convention. According to Scott, a woman's "home ought to be the greatest pleasure and her most precious privilege. Home is the kingdom of women and she should be the reigning Potentate. A father, a mother, children, a house, and its belongings constitute a home [as] the most delightful place in the world."[40]

The rapid evolution of women's religious associations like the one in which Scott participated helped to promote the idea of black women as chief curators of the black Christian home. During the late nineteenth century, these associations functioned in part as local and state-level forums in which women could share and articulate a set of popular goals that included broadening and politicizing women's leadership in the home. For example, the Arkansas Women's Southeast District Association, which included representatives of four Delta counties, organized in 1897. Its original objectives included "to get parents interested in daily family devotion [and] to discuss subjects that will help to raise a higher moral standard in the homes of many of our people."[41] Delegates explicitly defined women's chief obligations to society as creating black Christian homes and educating children. At the annual meeting in 1907, the Committee on Mothers and Children reported that "we find that the hand that rocks the cradle rules the world [and] that the responsibilities of mothers are many in training their children to reach perfect manhood and womanhood."[42] Several years later, at another annual meeting, Mrs. M. B. Hacker spoke about "the making of good men." She argued that it is "our duty as mothers to make our boys good. It requires all of their youthful days to do this. The Bible is an excellent agent to use in this great task. It is a standard because all during the ages it has stood the test. Let us teach our boys the precepts of this book." Hacker concluded by reminding her audience of Baptist women that "government begins with the family, and law must begin where government begins. Maintain a certain law for your family and see that your boy obeys these laws."[43]

Like women's groups operating at the district level, statewide associations also emerged as venues where black women clarified their duties in the black Christian home. On this larger public stage, black women often seized the opportunity to address audiences—sometimes numbering in the thousands—to deliver bolder assessments of the social and racial implications of women's domestic work. When Sister S. C. Shanks, the president of the Arkansas Baptist Women's Association, summarized black women's crucial contributions to the progress of the race, she singled out their enduring leadership of the black Christian home as the most important. In a sweeping survey covering the late nineteenth and early twentieth centuries, she stated, "The home and the mother teach the future as well as the present, and their influences must penetrate the very core of our great State." Her main point was that the "call of the mother . . . is not merely to keep watch over her hearthstone, but to prepare the atmosphere in which she lives. . . . If our race is to be reclaimed mentally, morally, spiritually, physically, it must be done through the child [and in] our homes and local churches."[44]

Interracial partnerships between black and white women also at times helped to publicize and enhance the relationship between black women and the black Christian home. For example, Susie Bailey, as colporteur for the white American Women's Home Missionary Society, worked closely with white missionary Joanna Moore to distribute religious literature that had as one of its central goals the moral reform of black Christians. The character of that reform included a set of behaviors and attitudes that directly reinforced the ideal of the black Christian home and women's key role in it. Throughout the Arkansas Delta, Bailey and Moore organized black women into "Bible bands" and "mothers' meetings," teaching participants about the Fireside School, a program of domestic Christian education in which women pledged to read the Bible regularly with their families, pray daily with their children, and become models of conservative temper, disposition, style of dress, and spending. The Fireside School, according to its promotional literature, led to the "purification and elevation of the home life" and women's recognition of their "responsibility to God for the training of His children in the home."[45]

In their mothers' meetings, Bailey and Moore distributed a variety of instructional pamphlets and tracts designed to help women build and sustain black Christian homes. Along with such publications as *For Mother while She Rocks the Cradle, Conversion of Children,* and *Bible Stories That Entertain and Instruct the Little Ones,* Bailey and Moore offered a range of Bibles, including versions with large print and large print with durable bindings, pocket editions, and illustrated editions.[46] They taught about the school's notion of righteous living, which, in its insistence on training children to be moral and purchasing spiritual books and magazines, closely resembled the core principles of the black Christian home. In an unpublished essay explaining why she labored to establish the schools, Bailey stated that she firmly believed that "every home should be a place of happiness but it can not be unless there are good rules and the children required to obey them." Mothers "should not neglect the religious training of their children. Every parent should resolve to do his whole duty by . . . carr[y]ing his children to God night and morning. And also buying them good books and subscribing to little religious newspapers. . . . And above all let each child have his own bible."[47] Bailey also distributed to her audiences copies of *Hope*, the monthly magazine published for blacks by the American Women's Home Missionary Society. Its editors reinforced the need for black women to dress and act modestly: "Any woman is too tightly dressed when she cannot raise her arms straight above her head and clasp her hands; who cannot stoop to tie her shoe or pick up a pin without any unpleasant pressure around the waist. Tight lacing is a crime that casts a heavy burden upon the coming generation and makes the present unfit for its duties. It ruins the digestions."[48]

The public effort to place women at the center of the black Christian home in the Delta hardly seems to constitute, at first glance, a notable social change. Indeed, it appears merely to add a veneer of moral import to traditional labors. After all, the Delta's black women had for years cooked, cleaned, carried water, washed clothes in pots of hot water, nursed infants, and supervised children. As members of agricultural families, they also turned the earth, planted, hoed, weeded, harvested crops, fed animals, and tended vegetable gardens.[49] Under the banner of the black Christian home and during decades of political marginalization for black women, however, these activities assumed a fresh degree of cultural meaning.

The black Christian home's heightened political significance for black women in the Delta represented in large part a response to the recent transformations of political authority and power in the region. Racial violence and disfranchisement profoundly inhibited African American women's ability to exercise political influence as they had during Reconstruction. No longer did they enjoy the same degree of opportunity to participate in political rallies, party hustings, and orchestrated efforts to sway the votes of male friends and relatives. Matters only worsened as black male fraternal orders largely exclusive of women developed as a new part of the civic culture of the Delta. In this context of political disempowerment, black women found modest opportunities to exercise social leadership by helping to organize denominational schools, Sunday schools, women's associations, and young people's groups.[50] As a complement to these public labors, they also constructed their role as leaders of the black Christian home. They stressed that in their homes they shaped the future of their families, communities, and race. Within their households, they influenced the contours of black society in ways that did not fully replace the lost forms of political participation but nevertheless promised a renewed degree of authority and satisfaction.

The gendered political resonance of the black Christian home sprang more generally from the work of female black Baptist theologians from across the South who revised popular views of women's character and domestic authority. Virginia Broughton, Mary Cook, and Lucy Wilmot Smith contradicted stereotypes of women as delicate, plastic, and prone to manipulation. Based largely on an exegesis of the Old Testament that emphasized a history of women raising the men who would lead the ancient Hebrews out of bondage and a trend in liberal Protestant theology that ascribed religiosity to women as a distinctive and inviolable trait, Broughton, Cook, and Smith argued that women inherently possessed a powerful capacity to shape the thoughts and actions of men, especially within the confines of the home.[51] Katherine Davis Tillman described this special power of women to affect the development of the black family in an 1885 article she penned for the *African Methodist Episcopal Church Review* after touring the South. "The home is an institution for which we are indebted to Christianity. It is of equal importance with the school and church. . . . It is in the home that our women, and indeed all women, are seen either at their best or their worst."[52]

One type of black Christian home carried special significance in every black community. Of all the black homes in an area, none was more important than the local parsonage in publicizing the standards of the black Christian home and the material culture of black religion. The home of the pastor and his family theoretically functioned as a type of community showcase, offering visitors a glimpse of a model of what to purchase and how to organize themselves and their domiciles. The parsonage also publicly demonstrated the domestic work and achievements of the pastor's wife. In "The Much Needed Parsonage," Carrie Mitchell Price, who lived on a cotton plantation in the Mississippi Delta with her husband, a minister with the Methodist Episcopal Church, urged her peers to improve their parsonages. "Let the wives adorn [the house's] walls with pictures and surround it with shade trees[,] grass[,] plots and flowers."[53] An editorial published in the *Southwestern Christian Advocate* at the turn of the century more directly emphasized the parsonage's disciplinary value to the black community, describing it as "the model home of the community. It is more frequently visited than most homes are generally, and from the parsonage the housekeepers of the community not only get the impression of the ability of the preacher's wife to make a home, but get their ideal of home-making." The piece concluded by pointing out that "the parsonage represents the community life as no other single home does. It represents the combined industry, home ideals, and aesthetic tastes of the community."[54]

At the same time that Delta blacks fashioned new standards for the decoration of their homes, they also reinvented norms of decoration for their churches. In both cases, African Americans invested certain commercial goods and styles of adornment with spiritual and social significance and created a religious material culture that registered their notions of beauty, progress, respectability, and godliness. By the turn of the century, pastors and their flocks struggled to create houses of worship whose size, design, and amenities represented the community's refinement.

When fashioning standards of church beauty, Delta blacks took cues from nationwide changes in style and adornment. During the late nineteenth and early twentieth centuries, leading white and black evangelical congregations across the country built new churches and refurbished older ones with stained wood, wainscoting, moldings, cornices, frescos, wallpaper, carpet, upholstery, rich color schemes, and modern heating and lighting systems.[55] The parent church for African Methodist Episcopalians, Mother Bethel in Philadelphia, Pennsylvania, underwent a highly publicized renovation in the late 1880s. A national fund-raising effort transformed a church deemed "as plain as a Quaker's coat, and perfectly free from ornament" by Bishop Daniel Alexander Payne. The new Mother Bethel contained a magnificent series of stained glass windows done "in the colors of the rainbow, with all the tints and hues of the precious stones mentioned in the Revelation of St. John xxi.11–21." They formed "a glorious scene of divine beauty, and so profuse as to resemble the magnificence of the starry heavens."[56] Church leaders hoped that the new Mother Bethel might inspire congregations throughout the nation and exhorted members to pay far closer attention to the physical appearance of their churches. In 1908, African Methodist Episcopal clerics attending the General Conference passed a resolution stating that "architecture is the art of building according to principles which are determined, not merely by the ends of the edifice it is intended to serve, but by consideration of beauty and harmony."[57]

In the Delta, of course, most black communities lacked the capital to purchase stained glass windows of any type and simply could not afford to imitate the level of beauty achieved by Mother Bethel. Yet they still participated in a regional variation of this national trend of church adornment. Developing a local visual aesthetic for black Baptist and Methodist churches, they built new houses of worship or renovated old ones, embellished them with richly colored walls and ceilings, and outfitted them with a modest range of handsome furnishings and amenities.

The emerging visual aesthetic of black churches included a new definition of clerical pastoral success. Beginning in the late 1870s, the ownership of a church with a pulpit, a bell, and finished pews was symbolically almost as important an indicator of progress for a minister and his congregation as the number of souls saved. In their quarterly and annual reports, southern missionaries with the African Methodist Episcopal Church portrayed their victories by describing the physical state of their houses of worship. Presiding elder R. F. Harley judged the effort of Elder Murry, whose territory included the northern tip of the Delta, by assessing the material condition of his church. Murry had "a splendid unfinished frame church, 40 × 60, with [a] fourteen foot ceiling. Elder Murry has succeeded in paying off many of the debts. . . . He has plastered it overhead and has purchased a bell."[58] Combining details about the church's construction, dimensions, purchases, and freedom from debt, Harley revealed the categories that he consulted to evaluate the success of his charge.

A black church's appearance often depended directly on the congregation's financial status. Members of Little Rock's First Baptist Church, the oldest and wealthiest black church in the capital city and therefore something of a model for other churches within the state, lavished attention on the construction of a new building in the mid-1880s as part of a campaign to promote the church's venerable status. Through the addition of eye-catching architecture and new consumer goods, congregants publicly demonstrated the importance of their church and hoped to attract new members. Probably the most ornate black Protestant church in the vicinity of the Delta, the new building was constructed from red brick and outfitted "with two front entrances, spires on both sides, a pipe organ, beautifully engraved windows, steam heat, . . . electric lights and fans, a balcony and a large bell that was [originally] purchased in 1869."[59]

When congregants installed a pipe organ in their church, as did members of First Baptist in Little Rock, they selected one of the most popular material symbols of prosperity for any black religious community in the Delta. It was also one of the most expensive, typically costing between one and two hundred dollars. During the Third Annual Session of the Arkansas Baptist Sunday School Convention in June 1886, participants discussed how organs were "really indispensable to denominational progress."[60] Two years later, members of this group emphasized the importance of organs as a badge of progress by including a new statistic in their annual report. In between columns labeled "Converts in S.S. School" and "Value of Property," a new column appeared under the heading "Schools with Organs." Eighteen of the sixty-seven schools, most of them located in the Delta and housed in or adjacent to churches, had organs.[61] The rising popularity of organs became obvious from the published minutes for the 1904 Baptist Missionary and Educational Convention of Tennessee, which featured a full-page advertisement for National Baptist Organs. The promotion appeared opposite the title page and bore the open endorsement of the Reverend R. H. Boyd, secretary of the National Baptist Publishing Board.[62] The popular interest in creating fancier and more elaborate churches at times fired a friendly competition among the leading Baptist ministers in the southern part of the Arkansas Delta, who scrambled to build houses of worship more beautiful than those of their colleagues. During the early 1890s, according to a local black Baptist historian, a "great rivalry in church building was begun, and many nice, and some real fine churches were constructed." These local competitions strengthened a shared sense of corporate identity as respectable, organized, and progressive black Christians. The church historian explained, "Revs. I. G. Bailey, W. H. Allen, W. W. Booker, A. Gross, S. D. Douglass, and others built nice churches and this raised the Baptists very much in the estimation of the public. . . . The Baptists now ceased to be called back numbers, but instead were called a progressive set of church workers."[63]

Few black religious institutions in the Delta were elaborately designed or decorated, of course. Most churches were supported by poor agricultural workers who struggled to raise money to purchase fancy goods. Congregants usually built simple houses of worship decorated with a few wall hangings and perhaps a set of electric lights. During his 1883 visit to the Mississippi Delta, New Yorker Clarence Deming reported that "along with every large plantation for hundreds of miles . . . goes the inevitable Negro church." Most such structures had a "rough, barn-like exterior, whitewashed, and with seating capacity for perhaps a hundred auditors. Within are coarse benches, cobwebbed board walls, a long desk and platform made of unfinished lumber, a dingy kerosene chandelier with one or two lights, and behind the so-called pulpit a line of tawdry colored prints pasted on the boards depicting scriptural themes like Moses and the burning bush, the ark on Ararat, and Daniel with the lions." Although most churches lacked bells, they were greatly desired. One poor congregation wanted a bell so badly, according to Deming, that church members improvised by "substitut[ing] a rusty buzz-saw hung by a rope [that], when struck by a stone, g[ave] a . . . cracked note to summon worshippers together."[64]

Deming's description of the common black church in the Mississippi Delta loosely matched that of the Arkansas Delta. Here, churches also tended to be simple white frame one-story buildings measuring about fifty by seventy-five feet. Such structures had shingle roofs, single doors that served as the front entrances, and sets of double doors in the back. Four broad windows opened on both sides of the longer walls and provided natural light in the daytime for the one hundred or so people who could sit comfortably in the ten pews. Few of these buildings possessed bell towers or even bells. Lithographs of biblical figures or black heroes sometimes were tacked onto the walls. Oil lamps illuminated most interiors at night; only the better-off churches enjoyed electric lights. During the winter months, wood heaters kept away the cold.[65]

The architectural and ornamental features recorded by observers of black churches in the Delta after Reconstruction serve as reminders of the importance of domestic commodities and consumerism in the religious lives of African American Baptists and Methodists. Although few blacks from the region published accounts during the late nineteenth and early twentieth centuries revealing how their faith was changing, the style and design of their homes and churches, their statements about dress and respectability, and their enshrinement of black women as curators of an emerging material culture of black spiritual life help illuminate the matter. In the midst of Jim Crow, Delta blacks integrated a range of cheap domestic commodities and notions of proper living into their religion and gave rise to modern African American expressions of public taste, domestic and sacred space, and gender. The range of these goods was narrow because blacks struggled to secure sufficient money and access to sample, see, and buy what they wanted. Yet these blacks still adapted, borrowed, and modified selected aspects of the evolving consumer market to add new dimensions to their spiritual lives that simultaneously defined them as consumers, citizens, and Christians at a time when many white southerners did not.

NOTES

1. "Zion Chapel," Works Project Administration—Historical Records Survey, Box 417, Folder 29, "Missionary Baptist," Special Collections, University of Arkansas at Fayetteville.

2. On the history of the Mississippi Delta, see esp. J. William Harris, *Deep Souths: Delta, Piedmont, and Sea Island Society in the Age of Segregation* (Baltimore: Johns Hopkins University Press, 2001); John Willis, *Forgotten Time: The Yazoo-Mississippi Delta after the Civil War* (Charlottesville: University Press of Virginia, 2000); Robert L. Brandfon, *Cotton Kingdom of the New South: A History of the Yazoo Mississippi Delta from Reconstruction to the Twentieth Century* (Cambridge: Harvard University Press, 1967); James C. Cobb, *The Most Southern Place on Earth: The Mississippi Delta and the Roots of Regional Identity* (New York: Oxford University Press, 1992); Valerie Grim, "Black Farm Families in the Yazoo-Mississippi Delta, 1920–1970" (Ph.D. diss., Iowa State University, 1990); Sidney Nathans, "'Gotta Mind to Move, a Mind to Settle Down': Afro-Americans and the Plantation Frontier," in *A Master's Due: Essays in Honor of David Herbert Donald,* ed. William J. Cooper Jr., Michael F. Holt, and John McCardell (Baton Rouge: Louisiana State University Press, 1985) (focusing on Tunica County). The literature on the Arkansas Delta is not

as large. See Fon Gordon, *Caste and Class: The Black Experience in Arkansas, 1880–1920* (Athens: University of Georgia Press, 1995) (concentrating on blacks in the Delta); Jeannie M. Whayne, *A New Plantation South: Land, Labor, and Federal Favor in Twentieth-Century Arkansas* (Charlottesville: University Press of Virginia, 1996); Willard B. Gatewood Jr. and Jeannie M. Whayne, eds., *The Arkansas Delta: Land of Paradox* (Fayetteville: University of Arkansas Press, 1993); Willard B. Gatewood Jr., "Sunnyside: The Evolution of an Arkansas Plantation, 1848–1945," *Arkansas Historical Quarterly* 50 (Spring 1991): 5–29; Donald C. Alexander, *The Arkansas Plantation, 1920–1942* (New Haven: Yale University Press, 1943). For studies that treat both the Mississippi and Arkansas Deltas, see Nan E. Woodruff, "African-American Struggles for Citizenship in the Arkansas and Mississippi Deltas in the Age of Jim Crow," *Radical History Review* 55 (Winter 1993): 523–54; Nan E. Woodruff, *American Congo: The African-American Struggle for Freedom in the Delta* (Cambridge: Harvard University Press, 2004).

3. U.S. Bureau of the Census, *The Social and Economic Status of the Black Population in the United States: An Historical Overview, 1790–1978* (Washington, D.C.: U.S. Government Printing Office, 1979), 13–20. In 1870, 91 percent of all black Americans lived in the South; in 1910, the number was 89 percent. For the purposes of this report, the Census Bureau defined the South as a region encompassing all of the former Confederacy plus Delaware, Maryland, West Virginia, Kentucky, Oklahoma, and the District of Columbia.

4. U.S. Bureau of the Census, *Negro Population, 1790–1915* (Washington, D.C.: U.S. Government Printing Office, 1918), 35–36, 46–49, 51, 115, 125, 127, 129, 131, 569–73, 777, 782, 784, 787–88.

5. On the relationship between material things and identity, see Leigh Eric Schmidt, *Consumer Rites: The Buying and Selling of American Holidays* (Princeton: Princeton University Press, 1995), esp. 3–32, 105–75; Grant McCracken, *Culture and Consumption: New Approaches to the Symbolic Character of Consumer Goods and Activities* (Bloomington: Indiana University Press, 1988); Arjun Appadurai, ed., *The Social Life of Things: Commodities in Cultural Perspective* (Cambridge: Cambridge University Press, 1986). On the multiple links between mass-produced items and popular identity and on how consumers use market objects in ways unforeseen and unintended by their producers and advertisers, see Lawrence Levine, "The Folklore of Industrial Society: Popular Culture and Its Audiences," *American Historical Review* 97 (December 1992): 1369–99; Lawrence Levine, *Highbrow/Lowbrow: The Emergence of Cultural Hierarchy in America* (Cambridge: Harvard University Press, 1988); Clarence Taylor, *The Black Churches of Brooklyn* (New York: Columbia University Press, 1994), xvi–xvii, 24, 69–70; Kathy Peiss, *Cheap Amusements: Working Women and Leisure in Turn-of-the-Century New York* (Philadelphia: Temple University Press, 1986), 11–15; Roy Rosenzweig, *Eight Hours for What We Will: Workers and Leisure in an Industrial City, 1870–1920* (Cambridge: Cambridge University Press, 1983), 208–21; John F. Kasson, *Amusing the Million: Coney Island at the Turn of the Century* (New York: Hill and Wang, 1978).

6. For theoretical insights on religious material culture, see David Morgan and Sally M. Promey, *Visual Culture of American Religions* (Chicago: University of

Chicago Press, 2001); David Morgan, *Visual Piety: A History and Theory of Popular Religious Imagery* (Berkeley: University of California Press, 1998); Schmidt, *Consumer Rites*; Colleen McDannell, *The Christian Home in Victorian America, 1840–1900* (Bloomington: Indiana University Press, 1986); Colleen McDannell, *Material Christianity: Religion and Popular Culture in America* (New Haven: Yale University Press, 1995); Robert Orsi, *Madonna of 115th Street: Faith and Community in Italian Harlem, 1880–1950* (New Haven: Yale University Press, 1990); Robert Orsi, *Thank You, St. Jude: Women's Devotion to the Patron Saint of Hopeless Causes* (New Haven: Yale University Press, 1998); Diane Winston, *Red Hot and Righteous: The Urban Religion of the Salvation Army* (Cambridge: Harvard University Press, 1999).

7. On southern black preachers and newspaper editors as salesmen, see John M. Giggie, "Preachers and Peddlers of God: Ex-Slaves and the Selling of African-American Religion in the American South," in *Commodifying Everything: Relationships of the Market*, ed. Susan Strasser (New York: Routledge, 2003), 169–90.

8. Few works probe rural black religion in the post-Reconstruction South, especially its relationship to consumerism. Important exceptions of works that focus wholly or in large part on black religion in the rural South for this period include David W. Wills, "Exodus Piety: African American Religion in an Age of Immigration," in *Minority Faiths and the American Protestant Mainstream*, ed. Jonathan Sarna (Urbana: University of Illinois Press, 1998), 136–88; William Montgomery, *Under Their Own Vine and Fig Tree: The African-American Church in the South, 1865–1900* (Baton Rouge: Louisiana State University Press, 1993); Stephen Ward Angell, *Bishop Henry Turner and African-American Religion in the South* (Knoxville: University of Tennessee Press, 1992); Nell Irvin Painter, *Exodusters: Black Migration to Kansas after Reconstruction* (New York: Norton, 1976); Steven Hahn, *A Nation under Our Feet: Black Political Struggles in the Rural South from Slavery to the Great Migration* (Cambridge: Harvard University Press, 2003). Works that focus wholly or in large part on rural blacks for this period but pay little attention to the role of religion include Woodruff, *American Congo*; Greta deJong, *A Different Day: African American Struggles for Justice in Rural Louisiana, 1900–1970* (Chapel Hill: University of North Carolina Press, 2002); J. William Harris, *Deep Souths*; Willis, *Forgotten Time*; Whayne, *New Plantation South*; Cobb, *Most Southern Place*; Leon F. Litwack, *Trouble in Mind: Black Southerners in the Age of Jim Crow* (New York: Knopf, 1998); Neil R. McMillen, *Dark Journey: Black Mississippians in the Age of Jim Crow* (Urbana: University of Illinois Press, 1988).

9. On the changes to black women's politics in the postemancipation South and especially women's turn to the household as a renewed source of moral and political authority after disfranchisement, see Elsa Barkley Brown, "Negotiating and Transforming the Public Sphere: African American Political Life in the Transition from Slavery to Freedom," *Public Culture* 7 (Fall 1994): 107–46; Glenda Elizabeth Gilmore, *Gender and Jim Crow: Women and the Politics of White Supremacy in North Carolina, 1896–1920* (Chapel Hill: University of North Carolina Press, 1996), 31–61, 119–31; Tera Hunter, *"To 'Joy My Freedom": Southern*

Black Women's Lives and Labors after the Civil War (Cambridge: Harvard University Press, 1997), 21–44; Jane Dailey, *Before Jim Crow: The Politics of Race in Postemancipation Virginia* (Chapel Hill: University of North Carolina Press, 2000), 1–14, 22–47; John M. Giggie, "'Disband Him from the Church': African Americans and the Spiritual Politics of Disfranchisement in Post-Reconstruction Arkansas," *Arkansas Historical Quarterly* 60 (Autumn 2001): 245–64.

10. McDannell, *Christian Home*, xiv–xvi, 6–12, 12–16, 21, 26, 35–36, 39, 42, 45–48, 73, 109–14; McDannell, *Material Christianity*, 2–3, 4–5, 69–72, 223, 271–74; Anne C. Loveland and Otis B. Wheeler, *From Meeting House to Megachurch: A Material and Cultural History* (Columbia: University of Missouri Press, 2003), 1–3, 61–62, 240.

11. Evelyn Brooks Higginbotham, *Righteous Discontent: The Women's Movement in the Black Baptist Church, 1880–1920* (Cambridge: Harvard University Press, 1993), 14–15, 145, 185–229. See also Evelyn Brooks Higginbotham, "African-American Women's History and the Metalanguage of Race," *Signs* 17 (Winter 1992): 257–67. On the views of whites and especially white landowners toward the spending habits of blacks, see Ted Ownby, *American Dreams in Mississippi: Consumers, Poverty, and Culture, 1830–1899* (Chapel Hill: University of North Carolina Press, 1999), 62.

12. See, most recently, Michele Mitchell, *Righteous Propagation: The Politics of Racial Destiny after Reconstruction* (Chapel Hill: University of North Carolina Press, 2005), 10–12, 154–58.

13. See, for example, Mrs. L. C. Thompson, "Women's Work in the Church," *Christian Index*, 14 November 1896. See also the calls for cleanliness issued forth by member of the Baptist Women's Convention in 1905 in Higginbotham, *Righteous Discontent*, 193.

14. See Booker T. Washington, *Up from Slavery: An Autobiography* (New York: Doubleday, Page, 1907), 163–75.

15. E. C. Morris, "Annual Address at the Closing of the Arkansas Baptist College," in *Sermons, Addresses, and Reminiscences and Important Correspondence, with a Picture Gallery of Eminent Ministers and Scholars* (Nashville: National Baptist Publishing Board, 1901), 130–31.

16. On the Exodus motif among enslaved black Americans, see Albert J. Raboteau, *Slave Religion: The Invisible Institution in the Antebellum South* (New York: Oxford University Press, 1978), 311–21; Eugene Genovese, *Roll, Jordan, Roll: The World the Slaves Made* (New York: Oxford University Press, 1972), 253–81; Timothy L. Smith, "Slavery and Theology: The Emergence of Black Christian Conscience in Nineteenth-Century America," *Church History* 31 (December 1972): 502–3. On its usage during and after slavery, see Albert J. Raboteau, "African-Americans, Exodus, and the American Israel," in *African-American Christianity: Essays in History,* ed. Paul E. Johnson (Berkeley: University of California Press, 1994), 1–17; Albert J. Raboteau, *Fire in the Bones: Reflections on African American Religious History* (Boston: Beacon, 1995), 17–37; Wills, "Exodus Piety," 136–88; Floyd T. Cunningham, "Wandering in the Wilderness: Black Baptist Thought after Emancipation," *American Baptist Quarterly* 4, no. 3 (1985): 268–81.

17. Reverend C. A. Tindley, "Practical Suggestions toward Material Progress," in *Methodism and the Negro*, ed. I. L. Thomas (New York: Eaton and Mains, 1910), 300, Schomburg Library, New York Public Library, New York.

18. J. William Harris, *Deep Souths*, 154–56, 160–61, 363 (table 20), 397 n.19. On death and disease, see Grim, "Black Farm Families," which uses a series of extensive interviews with elderly black Delta residents. For the Arkansas Delta, see Elizabeth Anne Payne, "'What Ain't I Been Doing?': Historical Reflections on Women and the Arkansas Delta," in *Arkansas Delta*, ed. Whayne and Gatewood, 129, 131–33. See also, more generally, Marian M. Davis, "Death and Nineteenth Century Arkansas: Frequencies in Causes of Death in Three Arkansas Counties during 1850 and 1880" (honors thesis, University of Arkansas, Fayetteville, 1988); Stewart E. Tolnay, "Fertility of Southern Black Farmers in 1900: Evidence and Speculation," *Journal of Family History* 18 (December 1983): 314–32.

19. David D. Daniels III, "The Cultural Renewal of Slave Religion: C. P. Jones and the Emergence of the Holiness Movement in Mississippi" (Ph.D. diss., Union Theological Seminary, 1992), 64–79, 178–88; Jerma Jackson, *Singing in My Soul: Black Gospel Music in a Secular Age* (Chapel Hill: University of North Carolina, 2004), 12–14.

20. L. W. Blue, *History of the Southeastern District Baptist Association of Arkansas* (n.p., 1903), Bailey-Thurman Papers, Box 4, Folder 17, Special Collections, Emory University, Atlanta, Ga.

21. *Proceedings of the Twenty-third Annual Session of the South-East Bapt. Asso[ciatio]n. Held with the First Bapt. Church, Rev. W. W. Booker, Pastor. Wilmot, Arkansas, Nov. 1906* (Little Rock: Baptist College Power Press, 1907), 17, Bailey-Thurman Papers, Box 5, Folder 27.

22. "The Sacredness of Home," *Christian Index*, 16 February 1899.

23. "Begin a Movement for Better Homes," *Southwestern Christian Advocate*, 5 July 1900 (hereafter cited as *SWCA*). See also Iola, "The Minister Out of the Pulpit," *Christian Index*, 12 May 1888.

24. *Minutes of the Second Mothers' Conference Held in Pine Bluff, Arkansas, September 8th, 9th, & 10th, 1894* (Atlanta: Byrd, 1894), 16–17, in African-American Baptist Associations—Arkansas: 1867–1952, microfilm, roll 14, Arkansas Historical Commission, Little Rock.

25. "The Minister Out of the Pulpit," *Christian Index*, 12 May 1888.

26. "Aesthetics," *Christian Index*, 28 January 1900.

27. "The Sacredness of the Home," *Christian Index*, 16 February 1899.

28. "Advice," *Christian Index*, 5 March 1892; "The Minister Out of the Pulpit," *Christian Index*, 12 May 1888.

29. Rev. G. I. Izard, "What Kind of Pictures to Hang on Your Walls," *SWCA*, 19 June 1900.

30. *Minutes of the First Session of the North Mississippi Annual Conference of the African Methodist Episcopal Church Held in Edward Chapel, Coldwater, Miss., from November 15th to 19th, 1877* (Vicksburg, Miss.: Rogers and Groome, 1878), 15, Mississippi Department of History and Archives, Jackson.

31. "Reading Culture," *SWCA*, 21 May 1891.

32. "Picture Gallery," *SWCA*, 23 August 1894.

33. "Our Picture Gallery," *Christian Index*, 16 February 1900.

34. The Douglass print appears in J. Z. Hartzell, "Our Southern District Campaign," *SWCA*, 6 June 1895; the Lincoln print appears in *SWCA*, 30 December 1897, 29 December 1898, 28 December 1899, on the back pages of each edition.

35. "Our Thanksgiving Gift to Everyone of Our Readers," *SWCA*, 23 November 1893.

36. *Arkansas Baptist Vanguard*, 6 April 1896.

37. Dorothy Dickens, *A Nutrition Investigation of Negro Tenants in the Yazoo-Mississippi Delta* (n.p.: Mississippi Agricultural Experiment Station, 1928), 10–11.

38. Rev. Thomas Plunkett to Rev. Joseph Slattery, 31 August 1898, 19-K-8h, Slattery Papers (before 1904), Mill Hill Fathers Archives, Josephite Fathers Archive, Baltimore, Md.

39. Higginbotham, *Righteous Discontent*, 97. On the use of domestic spaces as arenas for the enactments of cultural proscriptions, see Liz Cohen, "Embellishing a Life of Labor: An Interpretation of the Material Culture of American Working-Class Homes, 1885–1915," in *Common Places: Readings in American Vernacular Architecture*, ed. Dell Upton and John Michael Vlach (Athens: University of Georgia Press, 1986), 261–78.

40. *Minutes of the Women's State Baptist Association and the State Baptist Sunday School Convention, Held with the St. John Church, New Port, Arkansas, June 19–24, 1893* (n.p., n.d.), 5, in African-American Baptist Associations—Arkansas: 1867–1952, microfilm, roll 14. In 1897, an author known as "Sadie C. M." published an article, "Women's Education," in which she argued that "man endears himself to his family by his constant endeavors to support it and do that which will promote happiness, but woman is around the hearth implanting in the youthful minds the beauty and obligation of the future life and its responsibilities" (*Christian Index*, 26 January 1897).

41. Blue, *History*, 46.

42. *Minutes of the Eleventh Annual Session of the Women's Southeast District Association Held with the Mt. Carmel Church, Warren[,] Ark. Rev. R. A. Adams, Pastor. Aug. 23–25, 1907* (Little Rock: Baptist Vanguard Power Press, 1908), 4, Bailey-Thurman Papers, Box 5, Folder 52.

43. *Minutes of the Seventeenth Annual Session of the Baptist Women's Southeast Arkansas Association Held at the First Baptist Church, Crosset, Ark., August 23–26, 1913* (Los Angeles: Bailey, 1913), 6–7, Bailey-Thurman Papers, Box 4, Folder 44.

44. *Minutes of the Forty-fourth Annual Session of the Arkansas Baptist Women's Association Which Convened with the First Baptist Church, Dermott, Arkansas, June 1918* (Los Angeles: Bailey, 1913), 11, Bailey-Thurman Papers, Box 4, Folder 36.

45. *Tidings*, February 1911, Bailey-Thurman Papers, Box 5, Folder 50.

46. *Price List of Hope: Bibles, Fireside School Books, Etc. Sold at Fireside School Headquarters* (Nashville: n.p., 1908), 1, 2, 3, Bailey-Thurman Papers, Box 1, Folder 7.

47. Susie Bailey, "The Training of Children," n.d., Bailey-Thurman Papers, Box 4, Folder 9.

48. *Hope,* October 1893, 8, Bailey-Thurman Papers, Box 5, Folder 55.

49. J. William Harris, *Deep Souths,* 154–55; Elizabeth Anne Payne, "'What Ain't I Been Doing?'" 130, 135–38, 139–43. On the broader topic of rural black women's labor, see Jacqueline Jones, *Labor of Love, Labor of Sorrow: Black Women, Work, and the Family from Slavery to the Present* (New York: Basic Books, 1985); Jacqueline Jones, *The Dispossessed: America's Underclass from the Civil War to the Present* (New York: Basic Books, 1992); Jacqueline Jones, "Encounters, Likely and Unlikely, between Blacks and Poor White Women in the Rural South, 1865–1940," *Georgia Historical Quarterly* 76 (Summer 1992): 333–53.

50. Gilmore, *Gender and Jim Crow,* 31–61, 119–31; Hunter, "To 'Joy My Freedom," 21–44; Mitchell, *Righteous Propagation,* 135, 137.

51. Higginbotham, *Righteous Discontent,* 128–36.

52. Katherine Davis Tillman, "Afro-American Women and Their Work," *African Methodist Episcopal Church Review* 11 (April 1885): 497–98. See also Mrs. Alice Jean Parham, "The Women We Need," *SWCA,* 6 June 1895.

53. Mrs. Carrie Mitchell Price, "The Much Needed Parsonage," *SWCA,* 8 June 1899. See also Rev. J. W. Jackson, "A Confidential Talk with Ministers' Wives," *SWCA,* 14 June 1900.

54. "Why Improve the Parsonage?" *SWCA,* reprinted in *Methodism and the Negro,* ed. Thomas, 293–94. The date of the editorial is not provided. It was likely published around 1908 or 1909 because the other articles and reprinted editorials in the book were composed or published during those years.

55. Loveland and Wheeler, *From Meetinghouse to Megachurch,* 34, 46, 48, 53, 57; Jeanne Kilde, *When Church Became Theater: The Transformation of Evangelical Architecture and Worship in Nineteenth-Century America* (New York: Oxford University Press, 2002).

56. Daniel Alexander Payne, *History of the African Methodist Episcopal Church* (1891; New York: Arno, 1969), 463, qtd. in Loveland and Wheeler, *From Meeting House to Megachurch,* 58.

57. *Minutes of the Twenty-third Quadrennial Meeting of the General Conference of the African Methodist Episcopal Churches* (Philadelphia: AME Publishing House, 1908), 64, qtd. in Taylor, *Black Churches,* 22.

58. Rev. R. F. Harley, Letter to the Editor, *Christian Recorder,* 10 May 1878. See also Sister Havvy Hill, Letter to the Editor, *Arkansas Baptist Vanguard,* 10 December 1896. Outside of the Delta, see B. W. Roberts, "A Word from the Isle of the Sea [Key West, Florida]," *Christian Recorder,* 4 January 1877; Rev. W. R. Harris, "Letter from Forsyth, Georgia," *Christian Recorder,* 2 September 1880.

59. "First Baptist Church," Works Project Administration—Historical Records Survey, Box 417, Folder 31, "Baptist."

60. *Minutes and Statistics of the Third Annual Session of the Arkansas Baptist Sunday School Convention Held at the Centennial Baptist Church, Helena, Ark., on the 10, 11, and 12 Days of June, 1886* (Helena, Ark.: Golden Epoch, 1886),

6, in African-American Baptist Associations—Arkansas: 1867–1952, microfilm, roll 14.

61. *Proceedings of the Eighth [sic] Annual Session of the Arkansas Baptist Sunday School Convention Held with the First Baptist Church, Little Rock, August 20th and 21st, 1888* (n.p., n.d.), 16, in African-American Baptist Associations—Arkansas: 1867–1952, microfilm, roll 14; Loveland and Wheeler, *From Meetinghouse to Megachurch,* 57.

62. *A Journal of the Proceedings of the Seventeenth Anniversary of the Baptist Missionary and Educational Convention of Tennessee Held with First Baptist Church, Murfreesboro, Tenn., July 13th–19th, 1904* (Nashville: National Baptist Publishing Board, 1904), in the State Conventions and General Associations of the Nashville, Tennessee Area Affiliated with Various National [Negro] Baptist Conventions, 1865–1929, West Tennessee Association, 1887–1889, microfilm, Tennessee State Library and Archives, Nashville.

63. Blue, *History,* 18–19.

64. Clarence Deming, *By-ways of Nature and Life* (New York: Putnam's, 1884), 359–60.

65. See the following documents, some of which include sketches and rough diagrams of churches: "Salem," Works Project Administration—Historical Records Survey, Box 416, Folder 19, "Missionary Baptist"; "Providence," Works Project Administration—Historical Records Survey, Box 434, Folder 2, "Methodist [AME]"; "Little Bethel," Works Project Administration—Historical Records Survey, Box 435, Folder 4, "Methodist [AME]."

Hillbilly Heaven

Branson Tourism and the Hillbilly of the Missouri Ozarks

Aaron K. Ketchell

Pearl Spurlock, the first tour guide in Branson, Missouri, often told her guests, "God has to keep people chained up in heaven for fear they'll come to the Ozarks and become hillbillies." Within a place renowned for its religiously oriented tourist offerings and often labeled the buckle of the Bible Belt, it might seem surprising that Spurlock sanctified this icon. Most well known in the popular imagination as shabbily clad, apparently drunken, sexually promiscuous, impoverished, and indolent, the hillbilly persona seems a perplexing choice for alliance with Ozark, particularly Branson, tourism. However, local people's and boosters' uses of this moniker reveal a situation far more complex than the stereotypes would indicate. In fact, the hillbilly figure represents a time-tested merger of this persona and a wide variety of regional values, a union that has often positioned the hillbilly as a favorable symbol of Ozark morality.[1]

Branson began attracting vacationers as early as the 1910s, with most visiting sites made famous in Harold Bell Wright's place-defining novel, *The Shepherd of the Hills* (1907). Said to have been outsold only by the Bible in the early decades of the twentieth century, this work tells the story of a messianic city dweller who moves to an isolated Ozark mountain village populated by simple country folk. Wright's book valorized both the physically and spiritually curative qualities of the Ozark hills and praised the simple yet virtuous character of their residents. Glorifying the inherent sanctity of Branson and its environs, the protagonist states, "There is not only food and medicine for one's body; there is also healing for the heart and strength for the soul in nature. One gets very close to God . . . in these temples of God's own building." In this passage and many others, the author expresses attitudes echoed by visitors, who came to embrace a vision of blessed nostalgia within rapidly modernizing America.[2]

Shortly after the publication of *The Shepherd of the Hills,* a local industry emerged to provide tourists access to the sites and people described in the novel. Such literary tourism remained the chief Branson draw until 1960, when Silver Dollar City and the Shepherd of the Hills Farm debuted. Silver Dollar City currently attracts more than two million guests per year to its presentation of late nineteenth-century Ozark culture and its unique rendering of Christian-guided "family values." Since its inception, the theme park has offered patrons a sometimes anachronistic fusion of the Missouri frontier, preindustrial craftsmanship, and simple faith. Only a few miles down the road, the Shepherd of the Hills Farm has enacted Wright's novel on a nightly basis for more than forty years, has welcomed as many as 250,000 guests annually, and has often ranked as the No. 1 outdoor drama in the United States.[3]

In the 1960s and 1970s, Branson was primarily a regional destination for families looking to partake of Silver Dollar City's offerings, outdoor theater, water sports on area lakes, and a few local musical acts. By 1980, the city attracted close to two million visitors per year, principally from the Midwest and mid-South. The tourism industry began to gain national recognition in 1983, when country legend Roy Clark opened a variety show on Highway 76 (the Branson Strip). Other stars of the genre, such as Boxcar Willie and Mickey Gilley, soon followed suit. By 1989, more than twenty theaters lined the Strip, attracting nearly four million patrons.[4]

All observers of Branson's tourism history mark 1991 to 1994 as the city's boom years. During that period, the number of both lodging rooms and restaurant seats increased by nearly 10,000, the number of indoor theater seats swelled from 22,788 to 50,065, and construction values skyrocketed from roughly $20 million to nearly $140 million. In 1994, 5.8 million guests came to the area for its entertainment offerings, welcomed by a host of new stars, including Andy Williams, Tony Orlando, the Osmonds, Kenny Rogers, and Wayne Newton. Through a variety of attractions that blended wistful retellings of a premodern American culture and an unwavering, popularly arbitrated devotion to Christian theology and precepts, the city became a national phenomenon that today counts more than 7 million visitors per year.[5]

Although Branson's growth has resulted from many factors, the idea that local residents possess inherent virtue has been integral to the success of a values-driven market since Wright first celebrated the righteous Ozarker. Hazel Dagley Heavin highlighted this theme in a 1949 poem, "Hillbilly." The poet bestowed numerous merits on this label, including honesty, simplicity, neighborliness, industriousness, and other qualities that did not leave "much room for sin." Although a diligent worker, the hillbilly also was said to possess a love of recreation that was often conjoined with religious sentiment. He could "Dance all night and sees no wrong, / Conscience clear as he plods along, / Singin' an old camp meetin' song." The poem concluded with an allusion to paradise that mimicked Spurlock's vision of the otherworldly realm full of those sympathetic to the Ozark worldview: "Near the throne of God where the angels stay / They'll point with pride at him and say: / 'That's a hillbilly!'"[6]

Heavin's ode is complicit in historical processes that have hallowed the Ozark hillbilly, but it also suggests the dual nature and indefinite constitution of that character. The consensus holds that the hillbilly is materially impoverished yet morally rich, destined for a life of agricultural toil yet content with whatever bounty nature may offer, and grounded in ethical standards despite outsider perceptions of hillbilly depravity. These ambiguities position the emblematic Ozarker as a classic trickster figure. Any investigation of the Ozark hillbilly must, therefore, wrestle with elements of contradiction to reveal the ways hillbilly imagery has underscored a cohesive system of religious and philosophical principles while illuminating issues that jeopardize the integration of piety and pleasure in Branson.

The Ozark Trickster

As religion scholar S. G. F. Brandon has noted, the trickster's many "guises" include "deceiver, thief, parricide, cannibal, inventor, benefactor, magician, perpetrator of obscene acts," and a host of other roles that reflect "common occurrence in human experience." This multiplicity of characteristics makes any attempt at an all-encompassing definition a tenuous undertaking. Over the past fifty years, scholars have identified tricksters in Greek mythology, in African American folklore, and even within American popular culture icons such as Bugs Bunny and Bart Simpson. In light of this variation, ubiquity may safely be added to a set of defining attributes mired in what William J. Hynes has labeled as "polysemous diversity and endless semiotic activity."[7]

Recent scholars have drawn on Victor Turner's work to suggest that a liminal nature is possibly the only universally defining feature of the trickster. According to Turner, "The attributes of liminality . . . are necessarily ambiguous" because they "elude or slip through the network of classifications that normally locate states and positions in cultural space." By reworking a sacred/profane dualism to demonstrate the overlapping nature of those categories within lived existence, Turner and fellow scholar Mary Douglas have offered an analytical template that resists defining the signifier as good/evil or creative/destructive. Turner viewed society as a constant interplay of structure and antistructure (or hierarchical organization and egalitarian aspirations), and Douglas's landmark study of cultural boundary making describes the ways that purity and impurity create "unity in human experience." Their scholarship, therefore, refuses to limit tricksters to a singular construction and instead focuses on representations immersed in changeable, conflictive meanings.[8]

The juxtaposed functions embedded in these characterizations and the inability to situate them as wholly benevolent or malevolent prompted folklorist Barbara Babcock-Abrahams to write, "The distinctive feature of trickster tales (like Trickster himself) may well be their ability to confound classification." Like other tricksters, the hillbilly represents cherished regional standards but also embodies social taboos. The imagined southern mountaineer offers residents and tourists the opportunity safely to mock established ethical dictates (think of the Horny Hillbilly figurine) but at the same time solidifies them via a process of only symbolic inversion (who, after all, would want to be or even meet a real-life Horny Hillbilly?). The hillbilly thus provides the foundation for Branson-area consumer culture even while representing a host of ideologies and behaviors that are contrary to the values marketed by the local tourism industry. He is, in other words, "of the margins yet somehow of the center."[9]

Examining the uses of the hillbilly motif in Branson demonstrates that the term and its embodiments have indeed permitted locals to represent their collective values (religious or otherwise) and to demarcate the merits of the Ozarks from those of America at large. By ambivalently modeling the worldview of a culture, the southwest Missouri hillbilly (in all its forms) has affirmed and negated ethical understandings, thereby mimicking ethnologist Klaus-Peter Koepping's description of tricksters as "the chaos on which order depends." The contradictory hillbilly image, however, has provided Missourians a profitable opportunity. The Ozark region was smaller in size and population than Appalachia, was obviously more distant from eastern urban centers, and possessed fewer natural resources such as coal. Consequently, the Ozarks have historically received less attention—much to area boosters' delight, since such attention often depicted hillbillies in a negative light. Missouri Ozarkers also escaped the stigma borne by Arkansas, a state ridiculed as backward since the antebellum period.[10]

During the late nineteenth century, Americans began associating the qualities of laziness, squalor, and an overall propensity for cultural backwardness with the southern mountaineer. As Henry Shapiro has written, between 1870 and 1900, many Americans felt that the "strange land and peculiar people" of Appalachia did not fit with contemporary conceptions of a homogenous nation. In 1900, a reporter from the *New York Journal* coined the term *hillbilly* and applied it to the residents of Appalachia: "a free and untrammeled white citizen of Alabama, who lives in the hills, has no means to speak of, dresses as he can, talks as he pleases, drinks whisky when he gets it, and fires off his revolver as the fancy takes him." Many of the initial written impressions concerning the southern mountaineer were the product of the Hatfield-McCoy feud of the 1880s. Fought along the Kentucky–West Virginia border, the feud, as routinely described by eastern authors, epitomized a culture of violence within the mountain South, particularly Appalachia. The feud thus created the first iconic images of mountaineers as ominous, savage, and irrational. Coal companies supported such perceptions into the early twentieth century as they repeatedly—and violently—clashed with striking miners within the region. Adding fiscal abnormality to this sense of deviance, New Deal policies portrayed the South as the nation's primary "economic problem." Of particular concern was seemingly backward Appalachia, which received the most radical of New Deal projects, the Tennessee Valley Authority. President Lyndon Johnson likewise concentrated on Appalachia as a central battleground in his War on Poverty. Furthermore, countless manifestations of violent, depraved hillbillies have appeared in popular literature, music, film, and television, with the horrific aspect reaching its pinnacle via the portrayal of inbred and brutal Georgia sodomites in 1972's *Deliverance*. Historian Allen Batteau has described the roots of this characterization as descending from literary and political interpretations that highlighted "the animality and rural cacophony of Appalachia."[11]

Farther from American media centers and less rich in natural resources, the Ozarks have received less scrutiny within American culture. A quick Google search in June 2007, for example, found 150,000 hits for the phrase *Appalachian hillbilly* and just 68,300 hits for *Ozark hillbilly*. Of course, outsider imaginations have produced negative portrayals of Ozark mountaineers as well. Southern hillbillies have long been painted with a broad cultural brush. For example, Henry Rowe Schoolcraft, whose 1818–19 explorations took him throughout southern Missouri, described early white inhabitants as "not essentially different from that which exists among the savages." With an equally harsh tone, H. L. Mencken commented after a trip to the Ozarks in the early 1930s that he saw "dreadful people" who picked lice off their children like "mother monkeys in a zoo." And *New York Times* book reviewer Joe Queenan depicted Branson as a "Mulefuckers Mecca" and "cultural penal colony" in a 1999 book on America's "white trash."[12]

Nevertheless, twentieth-century Ozark commentaries tended to present a more complimentary picture than their Appalachian counterparts. An early 1960s article in *American Mercury* was typically benign when the author wrote that these "hillbillies . . . have no set standard of living, no respect for money, nor fame, nor caste. They know no greed, no envy, no subserviency. These unimpressive men in unimpressive garb, though poor, they seem, are immensely rich." Appalachia certainly has garnered similar praise. And boosters in Appalachia have definitely worked hard to erase negative associations with the region. Moreover, recent scholarship on representations of Appalachian hill folk has revealed a greater degree of self-definition as well as processes whereby natives engaged in complex debates about the nature of regional identity. For example, David Hsiung has argued within his study of upper East Tennessee that Appalachian stereotypes are ultimately rooted in class separation, with many pre–Civil War supporters of railroad projects labeling their neighbors who opposed such ventures ignorant, lazy, and backward. Broadcast nationally, these sentiments became powerful and enduring images of the region as a whole. More specifically addressing Appalachian tourism, Richard Starnes has investigated the link between western North Carolina's tourist industry and the larger national economy. When examining the "invention" of Appalachia at the turn of the twentieth century, the author locates complicity between outsiders defining the region and its people as "strange" or "peculiar" and local boosters who adopted this image for the sake of tourist dollars. Thus, the works of these scholars include a revisionist historiography that seeks to negate rote renderings of regional exceptionalism and to demarcate more nuanced aspects of Appalachian stereotypes that have a closer affinity to the Ozark hillbilly described throughout this essay.[13]

Yet when asked to define hillbilly (and to vote on the accuracy of those definitions) on the Web site Urban Dictionary, users voiced differing perceptions of Appalachian and Ozark hillbillies. One of the five most approved definitions described hillbillies as "isolated denizens of [the] Appalachian Mountains, (Eastern USA) descendants of some of the earliest Scotch-English settlers, who seem to have had some proclivity for naming their children 'William' (familiarly 'Bill') and some not inconsiderable inclination to incestuous sexual congress." Two other definitions identified the hillbilly as "a person who lives in a remote, rural area in the South, often in the Appalachian (or sometimes Ozark) Mountains and therefore is isolated and somewhat out of touch with modern culture" and as "people, primarily in the Appalachian region of the South, who are isolated from civilization and cannot therefore assimilate into modern culture." One definition made no regional reference, merely linking the term to any individual who "shoots 'varmints' with his/her rifle and squaredances in the wee hours of the morning, often at 'hoedowns.'" Only one of the top five definitions made a sole connection to the Ozarks. The author offered a much different image of this hillbilly: "Contrary to popular belief Hillbillies are no smarter or dumber than a person from the city, though Hillbillies tend to enjoy the simpler pleasures in life, are laid back, have a penchant for homemade liquor, and have their own slang words." Not surprisingly, Anthony Harkins, in his recent study of the hillbilly, has noted that hillbilly imagery was more prevalent in Ozark tourist traps than in those of Appalachia.[14]

In light of such perceptions, the controversial decision by CBS programmers to create a reality show version of the popular 1960s television series *The Beverly Hillbillies* makes sense. CBS officials in 2003 ignored the Ozarks, home of the beloved fictional Clampett family of the original program, while searching for a mountaineer clan to whisk off to a Los Angeles mansion. Rather, executives scouted the poorest Appalachian counties of Kentucky to find, in the outraged words of Georgia politician Zell Miller, "toothless illiterates with hookworms and an old man who has impregnated his barefoot, teenage daughter." Protests from across the Appalachian South halted production of the show. Such evidence scattered across the popular culture suggests a meaningful though subtle geographic fissure in perceptions of where hillbillies reside and in what Appalachian or Ozark hillbillies represent. Less couched in terms of senseless violence, sheer slothfulness, contemptuous family relationships, or deplorable ignorance, the Ozark hillbilly presents commentators with a more problematic set of meanings than his Appalachian cousin, especially given the prominence of religion within the Missouri Ozark tourism industry.[15]

According to regional journalist Sarah Overstreet, "Ozarkers know that some of the stereotypical 'hillbilly' characteristics are founded in truth." This candor is demonstrated in a jocular but insightful manner by a 1975 article in a Springfield, Missouri, newspaper that posed the question, "What IS a hillbilly?" To answer, the author offered the experience of a family who had come to the area for a vacation. Arriving in Branson, the father asked a well-dressed man standing on a street corner, "Where can I find a real, live hillbilly?" The local responded, "Why, you're looking at one rah cheer." Because the man's appearance did not match the vacationer's preconceived notions, he responded, "Pshaw and double-pshaw. It's gettin' to whir you can't believe a thing you see or hear. It's also getting to whir you can't tell a hillbilly from people." As the social and cultural history of Branson attests, countless instances exist in which the boundary between hillbillies and hill folk has been expunged.[16]

The line between hillbilly fact and fiction is often revealed within the realm of tourism. In the mid-twentieth century, newspaper commentator Elsie Upton described the hillbilly in a manner that bears striking similarities to other confounding tricksters: the hillbilly has "two distinct meanings" that "vary almost as much as high or low, true or false, good or bad." A native will always "assert himself a hillbilly," and when exercised in this manner, "all that is good, all that is honorable, flows in the term," and it becomes "an eminence worthy of owning." Problems arose, however, when this definition was mediated by nonlocal boosters and vacationers to match extant negative stereotypes. Thus, an evaluation of this regional identity necessitates discussion of the ways that it has been co-opted by residents, given a sometimes hackneyed and exaggerated usage by interlopers, and reinscribed in local identities to encapsulate numerous virtues that resonate with and have been perpetuated by the area's tourism industry. Such an analysis reveals that Ozark inhabitants have negotiated the ramifications of the idiom within daily life and the world of vacationing to craft a predominantly upright and even sanctified variant of the hillbilly employed for both pride and profit.[17]

Although one author wrote in 1911 that "the Hill Billy has a traditional history, reaching into the dim and distant past," this essay does not intend fully to unearth such precedents. Nor will it suggest that an entirely unified hillbilly paradigm has been proffered by Ozarkers since the beginning of the twentieth century. However, evidence from the Ozarks intimates that the characterization of the word has more often been affirmative than negative. Moreover, scrutinizing its many ambiguous uses enables the identification of the signifier's ability to mediate a rather consistent body of ethics. Ozarker Malinda Donaldson demonstrated this play of contradictory meaning in a 1943 essay, writing that the hillbilly "is equally great and humble; he is equally the master and the servant. He is a world, a law, a king in his own right. He draws no line between the King of England and a ditch digger." She continued, "NO matter who you are, or how famous you may be, if you felt your importance or fame in the presence of a Hillbilly he'd make you feel like a fool. And he'd do it with poise and dignity for he never loses face. He's a good neighbor, the best there is, but you can't take liberties or he'll put you in your place." Donaldson concluded by noting the ruse perpetrated by the budding tourism industry: "One thing more that few people know, there are not many Hillbillies in the Ozarks. There never was at any time. Most of us who live in the Ozarks are just hillfolks, pretending to be Hillbillies." Donaldson thus highlighted the ways Ozarkers made a virtue of hillbillyism, a category that represents what is extraordinary about Ozark hill folk and via this function enhances relationships to fundamental values and an exalted regional spirit.[18]

Further exhibiting the ubiquitous and sometimes contentious nature of the characterization, hillbilly terminology has even been taken to court. In 1960, the Springfield, Missouri, court of appeals heard the case of *Moore v. Moore,* in which Lowell Moore sought to divorce his wife, Minnie, on the grounds that she had committed "indignities." Minnie Moore's bevy of alleged indiscretions included disparagingly referring to her in-laws as "hillbillies," the coup de grâce after many years of insults and abuses. In his decision denying the divorce, Judge Ruark wrote, "We suggest that to refer to a person as a 'hillbilly' . . . might or might not be an insult depending upon the meaning to be conveyed, the matter of utterance, and the place where the words are spoken. . . . But without the added implication or inflection which indicates an intention to belittle, we would say that, here in Southern Missouri, the term is often given and accepted as a complimentary expression." Ruark expressed glowing admiration for area mountaineers: "An Ozark hillbilly is an individual who has learned the real luxury of doing things without the entangling complications of *things* which the dependent and over-pressured city dweller is required to consider as necessities. . . . The hillbilly is often not familiar with new models, soirees, and office politics. But he does have the time and surroundings conducive to sober reflection and honest thought, the opportunity to get closer to his God." Ruark then gutted Lowell Moore's claim that his wife had slandered his family: "No, in Southern Missouri, the appellation 'hillbilly' is not generally an insult or an indignity; it is an expression of envy."[19]

Ruark's decision is certainly the most famous judicial pronouncement on the nature of hillbillyism. In the legislative realm, Congressman Dewey Short, the Orator of the Ozarks, most thoroughly expounded on the term. Short was born in Galena, Missouri, just a few miles northwest of Branson, in 1898 and lived in Stone County until he went to college in 1915 and subsequently entered the ministry. While pursing religious credentials, he also continued his studies and attended universities in Berlin and Heidelberg, Germany, and Oxford, England. He eventually taught philosophy and psychology at Southwestern College in Winfield, Kansas, from 1923 to 1924 and 1926 to 1928.[20]

Short served in the U.S. Congress from 1929 to 1931 and from 1935 to 1957, representing the district that included Stone County. Like his independent-minded constituency, he was known for supporting individual initiative and for criticizing Franklin Roosevelt's interventionist New Deal programs. Short's oratorical flair became the talk of Washington, D.C., during the mid-1930s, with national commentators describing his plainspoken yet stinging style as "revivalistic." Despite his vast academic training, worldwide travels, and political fame, Short always emphasized his Ozark upbringing and the values it inculcated in him, stating, "I take pride in the fact that I am a hillbilly from the Ozarks. I like hillbillies. They are frank, candid and honest. Their generosity is unbounded, their hospitality is sincere. They are genuine folks. If they like you, they will die for you; if they dislike you they may let you die. Not all of them are over-industrious for Nature is bountiful, and it is rather easy to live in the Ozarks." This most famous of all self-proclaimed hillbillies again illustrates the many facets of that title. Despite a well-known career as an academic, pastor, and congressman, he insisted on being buried in Galena, where he had always felt most comfortable because locals "do not write their name across the stars" but rather "write it in the hearts" of their fellow human beings. According to Short, such simple "hillbilly" merits "are the things of his greatness."[21]

Amid heated mid-twentieth-century debates over hillbilly terminology, the *Ozarks Mountaineer* came into existence as a periodical meant to rebut negative portrayals of hill folk. Founded in 1952 as a small tabloid featuring stories of political interest for residents of southwestern Missouri, the publication came under new ownership in 1967 and began to attend more thoroughly to Ozark history, folklore, and pioneer life. In that year, the editor addressed the name of the journal in a brief column that spoke to the relationship between "mountaineer" and "hillbilly." Expressing a desire to dispel stereotypes, "project an image of a proud heritage," and look toward a "progressive future," the writer ultimately concluded that these goals could be accomplished by a local renegotiation of the "hillbilly" idiom. Likening that title to nonbelievers' initial derogatory uses of the word *Christian,* the piece claimed that numerous "valuable traditions" were still encapsulated within the moniker and that contrary to recurrent outsider characterizations, "what we are speaks loudest of all."[22]

Staging the Ozark Hillbilly

The definition of the Ozark hillbilly related directly to the cultural conception of the landscape. *The Shepherd of the Hills* may have lamented modernity's encroachment on simple American life, but it also suggested to readers that a place existed where the perceived troubles of industrialization or urbanization could be allayed—a locale populated by folks who, according to the text, "pause in the hurried rush to listen to the call of life" and who serve as examples of "what God meant men and women to be" away from "the shame and ugliness of the world." Thus, the untouched terrain sought by tourists shortly after the novel's publication was also said to be replete with the honest values of country life. While the hills and rivers around Branson could offer vacationing urbanites fleeting solace and time for contemplation, engagement with the region's inhabitants might well be a means of finding sanctuary from the stings of technological progress, social differentiations, and moral relativism.[23]

By 1908, Wright enthusiasts began arriving in Branson eager to meet his fictional characters and partake of their uncomplicated and upright lifestyle. As a writer for the *St. Louis Post-Dispatch* remembered in 1965, "Nobody expected to see Scarlett O'Hara in Georgia, of course, but tourists in the Ozarks did hope to see Old Matt and Young Matt, Uncle Ike, Sammy Lane, and other characters in *The Shepherd of the Hills.*" The primary locus for this literary pilgrimage was the Ross cabin, home of Wright's main characters. The homestead's residents, John and Anna Ross, quickly melded into characters Old Matt and Aunt Molly in the minds of tourists seeking the bona fide individuals on whom the characters were based. A whirlwind of myths concerning the identity of "actual" characters began to arise in the 1910s, thereby creating an image of Branson and the surrounding area as a site of "true" and ongoing premodern culture. In the decades following the work's publication, local residents unabashedly claimed to be prototypes of the story's characters or put forth their kinfolk as such. Via this profit-driven ruse, locals initiated a mode of righteous hillbilly enactment that coursed its way through multiple genres over the twentieth century.[24]

Ozark hillbillies have been portrayed in film since 1915, when the term made its first on-screen appearance in *Billie—the Hill Billy.* This stereotypical story told of a city dweller who travels to the Ozarks, encounters a backwoods family headed by a tyrannical father, falls in love with the daughter, and eventually whisks her away for an urban life. Other early offerings set in the region featured more stock characters (both positive and negative), including a feud between mountain families in *The Big Killing* (1928); depictions of unbridled pedophilic lust in *Child Bride of the Ozarks* (1937); a Nazi-fighting regional heroine in *Joan of Ozark* (1942); and portrayals of poor, antimodern, yet ethical mountaineers in *The Kettles in the Ozarks* (1956). As this limited sample demonstrates, the cinema (like the rest of America) situated Ozark hillbillies within a dichotomy of meaning. Yet Harkins has asserted that because the region was not subject to the degree of outsider scrutiny that plagued Appalachia in the early twentieth century, film producers and viewers more easily defined the Ozarks as "mythic space."[25]

A few residents of Arkansas and Missouri became actors during the 1930s and 1940s. Bob Burns, from Van Buren, Arkansas, starred in numerous B movies that played on hillbilly stereotypes, including *Comin' round the Mountain* (1940), which featured "the only surviving species of the genus homos hillbillicus Americanious." Frank, Leon, and June Weaver, better known as the Weaver Brothers and Elviry, came from Springfield, Missouri, and had been successful vaudeville comedians in the 1910s and 1920s. Between 1930 and 1943, they starred in twelve films that portrayed hillbillies who, aware of the foibles of human nature, used simple astuteness and plain virtue to triumph over city slickers. The director of *Friendly Neighbors* (1940) described both the actors and their characters as "grand, simple, honest, sincere, fun to be around." Finally, Chester Lauck and Norris Goff of Mena, Arkansas, created their Lum and Abner personalities in 1931 and captivated radio audiences with life in the fabled Ozark town of Pine Ridge until 1951. During this run, they also made six movies that played on archetypal mountaineer themes. Although some critics said the fictitious Pine Ridge gave the Ozarks a national "black eye," Lauck responded with the upright hillbilly model: "We have endeavored to depict a good, clean, wholesome, down-to-earth way of life. . . . Those who don't know that type of life want to dream of it. Those who do know it want to return to it. We have tried to picture Pine Ridge as a Shangri-La."[26]

Ozark hillbillies made their first television appearance in 1958 when Jack Benny returned to his supposed roots by portraying fiddler Zeke Benny, who appeared with his Ozark Hillbillies on a single show. Paul Henning truly invented this regional television persona, however, by defining it for a national audience and allying it with modern Branson tourism. Henning was born in Independence, Missouri, in 1911. Prior to creating and producing *The Beverly Hillbillies,* he was instrumental in creating other television programs, including *Fibber McGee and Molly, The Burns and Allen Show,* and *The Bob Cummings Show.* Recounting boyhood Scout trips to southwest Missouri, he asserted, "I fell in love with hillbilly characters. I thought they were independent and had always been a fan of hillbilly humor." When *The Beverly Hillbillies* debuted in 1962, an estimated 50 percent of television viewers watched, making the series America's No. 1 rated show by the end of its first month. The most-watched program of 1962 and 1963, *The Beverly Hillbillies* still boasts the highest rated half-hour individual episode in television history and counts eight episodes among the fifty most viewed. During the show's run, which lasted until 1970, Henning also served as creator and producer of *Petticoat Junction* (1963–70) and executive producer of *Green Acres* (1965–71). These credentials thus make him the undisputed king of rural situation comedy.[27]

Many aspects of *The Beverly Hillbillies* might account for its incredible success. Within a 1960s context of social and cultural upheaval, the show offered simple escapism and a sense of down-home security. Moreover, mountaineers had come to national attention during the 1960 West Virginia Democratic primary when John F. Kennedy made the poverty of Appalachia central to his presidential campaign. On an intellectual level, however, the show possessed an ability to cleverly combine banal comedy with social criticism. By illustrating the idiosyncrasies of consumer culture, censuring the pretense of social elites, epitomizing traditional value systems that necessitated support from family and kin, and modeling a democratic egalitarianism that some observers believed to be rapidly waning in the United States, *The Beverly Hillbillies* possessed many interesting nuances that often escaped commentators of the time. Via these reappraisals, Horace Newcomb has claimed that the program promoted "the moral superiority of rural wisdom" and that the Clampetts functioned as a metaphor for a set of "truly American values."[28]

Most vital for this study, *The Beverly Hillbillies* also instituted a national redefinition of the hillbilly. The program perpetuated a number of patented images, of course, including shotgun-wielding, government-fearing, and moonshining mountaineers; signature attire of plaid shirts, overalls, and slouched hats; superstitious matriarchs (as epitomized by Granny); innate sexuality that is sultry yet immature (as represented by Elly May); and ingrained naïveté cum stupidity (as characterized by Jethro). However, the show represented Ozark rather than Appalachian hillbillies—that is, from pro-Confederate Missouri. And further distancing the Clampetts from the history of brutal coal strikes and the rough world of mining associated with mountaineers, again most notably in Appalachia, the show's family became rich from a different black mineral—oil—accidentally discovered when an errant rifle shot struck crude. A *Saturday Evening Post* writer described Buddy Ebsen (Jed Clampett) as a "hand-me-down philosopher" and repository of folk knowledge. Furthermore, Henning depicted Granny (Irene Ryan), modeled after his mother, as having "the accumulated wisdom of self-sufficient generations." Reflecting on this infusion of integrity into the hillbilly icon, an executive for Filmways (the project's production company) claimed that through "simple, but not stupid" depictions, "the word 'hillbilly' will ultimately have a new meaning in the United States as a result of our show." Again demonstrating hillbilly dualism, viewers beheld a more virtuous construct of that signifier and embraced its moral fortitude and regard for principled (and at times misguided) labor accented by an appreciation for leisure.[29]

In 1967, four episodes of *The Beverly Hillbillies* were filmed at Silver Dollar City in Branson. Aired as the first shows of the 1969 season, they focused on the family members' return to their Ozark home to find a suitable husband for Elly May. Entering the city limits, the cast immediately imbibed the rarified air of the Ozarks, leading Jed to remark, "This clean stuff is going to take some getting used to." Many local celebrities and attractions made cameo appearances, and famous sites from *The Shepherd of the Hills* were mentioned. As a result of the episodes, Silver Dollar City witnessed its greatest one-year increase in visitation to date, and newfound national interest pushed guest totals above one million by the early 1970s. Reflecting on this upsurge and the ways that these fictional Ozark hillbillies facilitated a process of cultural formation, the theme park's executive vice president, Pete Herschend, stated, "*The Beverly Hillbillies* moved Silver Dollar City, and therefore Branson, out of the regional business and into a national attraction. That was *the* change.

That made *the* difference. And this community has never looked back since that time."[30]

As Branson began to establish an identity with variety-show entertainment in the late 1960s, the hard work of playing hillbilly became the bastion of stage rather than screen performers. When the Presley family opened the Ozark Mountain Jubilee (the first theater on the now-famous Highway 76 Strip) in 1967, it featured not only country and gospel music but also the antics of Gary Presley (Herkimer), a comedian labeled by his theater as a "savant hillbilly." Travel writer Bruce Cook utilized typically paradoxical language when describing Presley as "swaggering and sort of dim" on stage but "intelligent" and "direct" outside of this role. Cook further extolled Herkimer as "a remarkable combination of businessman and performer," a characterization that again demonstrates the ambiguities of the hillbilly persona and the ever-present merger of Ozark labor and leisure.[31]

During a performance I attended in the mid-1990s, Herkimer warmed up the crowd in a manner that exhibited the hillbilly's role as mediator of values. The act began with a joke about a chance meeting between Moses and former president George H. W. Bush and then proffered a steady diet of religiously motivated yarns that laid bare the production's ideological vantage. Herkimer made clear that the Presleys' Country Jubilee endorsed Christianity and conservative politics, a civil-religious merger that finds expression in almost every contemporary production. Serving as a prelude to a medley of gospel numbers, his comedy focused on the evangelistic work of preachers and ministers awaiting entrance into heaven. It also included a bevy of jabs at President Bill Clinton's administration and "liberal" politics writ large. For example, Herkimer proposed that he would run for president. After the emcee responded that people would not vote for a hillbilly, Herkimer replied that since enduring the Clinton White House, Americans might very well want a "real clown" in office.

Although Branson's hillbilly comics pepper their acts with humorous comments on religious and political subjects, they also include much material that reflects the bawdy side of hillbilly imagery. In so doing, they further demonstrate the dichotomous nature of their character. The Baldknobbers Jamboree (originally the Baldknobbers Hillbilly Jamboree) was the first musical show in Branson and in 1968 became the second act on the Strip. Over the next three decades, their hillbilly component (the Mabe brothers) mixed humorous discussions of Ozark values with what commentator Lori A. Robbins has called "toilet humor." Creating a template still utilized by all regional comics, they conjoined scatological outhouse wit with jokes about flatulence, senior citizen sexuality, immoderate alcohol consumption, and other "taboo" Branson subjects.

The Mabe brothers and other area jesters thus offer a brand of humor that mimics, though in a tamed manner, the often salacious nature of the imagined hillbilly and, like the antics of their folkloric trickster counterparts, permits guests to laugh at the hopes, fears, and crudities of their common humanity.[32]

Since the late 1960s, the Presleys and Baldknobbers have inspired countless imitators on the Branson entertainment scene. Every venue offers some variant of the hillbilly guise. However, this characterization is not static. Instead, the nebulous imagined hillbilly has adapted to changing social and cultural climates. For example, in 1987, Herkimer began wearing sequined overalls that inspired a move toward this more brassy attire among all area performers. Similarly, Terri Sanders, a participant in the local industry for more than twenty years who plays jester Homer Lee at the Braschler Music Show, attested to the need to "mutate" and "evolve." During a 2002 performance, Sanders lampooned the Latina maids now prominent at local hotels and motels, performed a version of the River Dance, and leveled numerous jokes about Wal-Mart (supposedly the Branson tourist's favorite retail store). Gary Presley astutely addressed the moral vision that undergirds such an ever-transforming yet "simple and ancient" genre when he posited this type of humor as perfect for the Bible Belt.[33]

In an atmosphere sated with performances of the Ozark trickster, Bruce Seaton was the consummate example of the integration of hillbilly enactment, lifestyle, and religious promotion. An Ozark native, he spent fifteen years away from the region before returning in the early 1960s to take a job as a Linotype operator for the *Stone County Republican*. Possessing little knowledge of contemporary machinery, Seaton instead began work on an antique hand press at his editor's print shop at Silver Dollar City. There he realized his true career objective, reenacting a prototypical variant of nineteenth-century pioneer life. Soon thereafter, he entered his family in Branson's Plumb Nellie Days parade. With Seaton attired in overalls and a fake shabby beard, his wife in a tattered calico skirt and bonnet, and their eight barefoot and sullied children, the Seatons won the event's Best Hillbilly Family award on several occasions.[34]

The Seatons' success as hillbilly performers led to a career. Attired in their parade garb and situated around dilapidated cabins or rickety outhouses, the Seatons began selling pictures of themselves to a Springfield photographer. For nearly a decade, they forged a life as professional hillbillies. Their likenesses appeared on postcards, cookbooks, and calendars. Then in 1963, the family further blurred the line between fact and fiction by purchasing a plot of land and a little shack in rural Stone County. In a setting replete with a tar-paper roof and sagging front porch, they butchered and cured their own meats, chopped wood for

The members of the Seaton family, as seen on this postcard circa 1970, transformed themselves into marketable and pious Ozark hillbillies. (From author's collection)

heat, and did their own barbering. Further demonstrating hillbilly ambiguity, Seaton asserted that everything in the house was modern "but it don't look it."[35]

Leon Fredrick, Seaton's former print-shop employer, labeled him "a genuine manufactured hillbilly." Although most of this appearance was forged through pictorial representations, he also constructed his hillbillyism by playing Preachin' Bill in the Shepherd of the Hills pageant. Seaton came to the production shortly after it debuted. Preachin' Bill, while not a major character in Wright's work, nevertheless possesses special significance because he is the first to speak. He declares, "When God looked upon th' work of his hands an' called hit good, he war sure a lookin' at this here Ozark country." Until his death in 1976, Seaton's dual persona as archetypal hillbilly and Ozark-sanctifying vicar melded outwardly disparate roles into a career that typified the virtues of mitigated labor and the encouragement of regional sanctity.[36]

Historian of Appalachian popular culture representations J. W. Williamson has described the hillbilly as "an outlaw on the fringes of the economy" and "the idiot of capitalism." Dissecting the character's market-based function, he states, "If capitalism operates by inducing its workers to believe in the virtues of work and by condemning the evils that interfere with work, such as strong drink, roaming the woods and hunting, and various social indiscretions including murder, mayhem, and bastardy . . . then clearly the hillbilly fool is a warning, a keep-away sign enjoining us to avoid the rocky rural edges outside the grasp of the urban economy." The Ozark hillbilly perpetrates acts prohibited by the ethos of the larger Branson entertainment industry and is thus involved in some of the chicanery mentioned by Williamson. Moreover, constructions of this vague figure have historically been couched in an aversion to capitalist enterprise. However, for nearly a century, area natives have made a merit of simple, independent, and honest work, stressed the equally necessary nature of deserved recreation, and folded these qualities into the hillbilly moniker. Translated into the tourism industry, this ethic as enacted by a seemingly indolent character has been vital to the region's fertile consumer culture.[37]

Willful participation in the stereotype has produced what one Springfield journalist labeled "hillbilly tycoons." In contrast to other business magnates, this mogul does not have to work on Wall Street, engage in a lengthy commute, or "risk his life on the subway." Possessing the ability to change and reshape, the Ozark hillbilly can "go to college and travel in Europe undistinguishable from other tycoons," but after returning to the hills, he "resumes his native character and costume, smokes his corncob pipe, whittles his walnut walking sticks, hitches up his galluses, and watches the dollars roll in." Thus, for this writer and many throughout Branson's history, the hard work of facilitating the recreation of others through enacting hillbillyism has been valorized as an ethic worth cultivating.[38]

Racializing the Ozark Hillbilly

Hillbilly stereotypes and tensions were heightened by a massive outmigration of Appalachian residents in the three decades following the Second World War. Spawned by loss of jobs in the area's coal mines and employment opportunities in northern cities, the diaspora reached its height in the 1950s. In total, more than three million southern Appalachian people abandoned the hills during this period. In 1958, an author for *Harper's Magazine* described such a group in Chicago as resistant to change, clannish, disorderly, drunken, content in their dire poverty, and devoid of a moral code. Representing "the American dream gone berserk," these "hillbillies" "confound[ed] all notions of racial, religious, and cultural purity." Thus, for this writer and many others, when hill folk invaded urban areas, any vestige of quaintness or down-home virtue was lost. The anomalous makeup of mountaineer culture became anathema to majority understandings of propriety, especially in regard to normative whiteness. As the hillbilly often served as an ominous signifier of antimodernism, the term also became indicative of a perilous racial standing. And through Othering these primarily Appalachian migrants

whose authentic whiteness was being called into question, urbanites affirmed historian Matthew Frye Jacobson's contention that "Caucasians
are made and not born."[39]

Again demonstrating the subtle divide between the Ozark hillbilly and
his eastern counterpart and highlighting the play of contradictory meaning inherent in the signifier, boosters in southwestern Missouri more easily preserved the imagined white purity of their mountaineers. Scholars,
especially during the early twentieth century, argued that both Appalachia and the Ozarks served as white refuges, preserving racial purity in
the face of waves of immigration and demographic diversification. But in
the popular imagination, this formulation became more applicable to the
Ozarks as coal companies introduced blacks, Italians, Slavs, and others
to Appalachia—often as strikebreakers—and as miners worked to create
one big (color-blind) union. This is not to say that Appalachian tourism
promoters surrendered their defense of the region's whiteness. Boosters in both regions manipulated their histories. Although most original
immigrants to the Ozarks were Scots-Irish, their settlement was by no
means totalistic. Within the larger Ozark setting, French Creoles were
the first to establish communities along the Mississippi River. By 1840,
remnants of the Cherokee nation had settled near the Trail of Tears in the
western Ozarks, and sizable populations of free blacks existed throughout the area. Yet despite this racial and ethnic variation, Ozark boosters
throughout the twentieth century frequently connected southwest Missouri culture to a monolithic Anglo-Saxon heritage—what they deemed
as the last of its kind in the United States—and by association valorized
the genuine and often sanctified whiteness of the hillbilly icon.[40]

May Kennedy McCord and Otto Ernest Rayburn, the Branson-area's
primary boosters from roughly 1920 to 1970, frequently recruited the
hillbilly to combat the ills of modernity, including a perceived loss of
meritorious whiteness. Dubbed Queen of Hillbillies at her death in 1979,
McCord had a forty-year career as author, radio host, musician, and
folk festival organizer. She is best known for a column, "Hillbilly Heartbeats," published weekly by Springfield, Missouri, newspapers from 1932
to 1943 and reprinted in a number of regional and national publications.
In these pieces, she wrote of the hillbilly with great reverence. In 1933
she penned, "I'm of his tribe and his clan, and I love every bone in his
body. And if I or any contributor of mine ever mis-represents the Hillbilly
may the blackness of the desert hide us, the sand fleas devour us and our
bones bleach till judgment day." McCord also invited readers to offer
comments on her work and thus facilitated a communal sense of hillbilly
pride. In fact, her column became so popular that it generated more letters than all of the newspaper's other features combined. Reflecting on
this community-building project, she declared, "Come on, hillbillies, let's

get together. Let's rave about it all. Write some poetry and some essays and some love letters to the hills!"[41]

Despite her interest in popularizing Ozark life, McCord claimed that her concern did not spring from the lure of tourist dollars. Instead, she continually sought to preserve the culture of "honorable and industrious" Ozarkers who "directly descended from the colonizers of America" and were "the only true Anglo-Saxons left." Affirming this sentiment, a 1930 column featured a poem, "The Hillbilly":

Hillbilly, Hillbilly
Who are you,
Dreaming and dreaming the
Whole day through?
Blood of the Cavalier
Bold and true
Blood of the Puritan
That is you!

Aside from this allusion to religious heritage, such environmentally determined racial superiority was also claimed through Ozark folk songs said to descend from ancient English ballads and "picturesque and lyrical" mountaineer vocabulary said to contain "about 2000 words that can be traced directly to the Elizabethan or Chaucerian periods."[42]

Although McCord was not the first Ozarker to make such declarations, she greatly influenced outsider perceptions of the region because of her role as tour guide for national journalists and scholarly researchers. In the early 1950s, she accompanied a *Life Magazine* writer and photographer into the region and told him specifically that residents shared "the blood of the Seventeenth Century Colonists." Their innate constitutions led to characteristics such as pride, individualism, and community/familial loyalty. During her long career, McCord did much to promote and defend what she believed was a virtuous hillbilly legacy. As with most conceptions of the hillbilly discussed thus far, her vision sought to salvage the Ozark native from occasional claims of backwardness. Yet crucial for this notion was an erasure of regional diversity and a glorification of locally cultivated whiteness.[43]

Until his death in 1960, folklorist, educator, and author Otto Ernest Rayburn served as another ardent voice for the unique and consecrated nature of the Ozark landscape and its residents. Publishing his first magazine aimed at regional boosterism in 1925, he continued to produce monthly journals under a variety of titles for the next thirty-five years. Like others of his time, Rayburn's initial writings often derided the onset of modernity in the hills. He embraced the solace (or idea of solace) that accompanied life in the region. Such "glorious rest" was unavailable amid the "maddening hum of modern machinery" and the "mess of materialistic pottage" found in urban areas. Throughout his career, Rayburn trafficked in such idealism. Seeking to "write not so much of the Ozarks in reality as what the region stands for in the imagination," he frequently waxed poetic about inspirational landscapes, "straight thinking" inhabitants, and the merits of simple living.[44]

Within publications that extolled the region's natural beauty, Rayburn frequently intoned a racial makeup that mimicked its pristine hills and rivers. As the "'seedbed' of Anglo-Saxonism in the United States and the last surviving Elizabethan culture in the western world," his Ozarks represented a "veritable Garden of Eden" exempt from the unseemly aspects of modern life. In 1924, he moved to northwest Arkansas to become school superintendent for the Kingston Community Project. Sponsored by the board of missions of the Presbyterian Church, this initiative extended the town's educational system from only elementary grades to a high school and a summer-session college, thereby creating the "Little Harvard of the Hills." Kingston was the brainchild of the Reverend Elmer J. Bouher, a missionary and preacher, who had come to the Ozarks in 1915. Like Rayburn, Bouher considered the region an Anglo-Saxon preserve. As he wrote to a local, "You and your family have maintained the British character exemplified when their ancestors first settled on the Atlantic seaboard. There is no melting pot in these mountains. Your people have maintained your integrity, habits and racial purity."[45]

Drawing inspiration from an American eugenics movement rising in popularity during the early decades of the twentieth century, Bouher crafted a juxtaposition between the "pure[,] clean-bred," and "sturdy" stock of Ozark Anglo-Saxons cut from the same cloth "as Jackson and Lincoln" and the mounting numbers of southern and eastern European immigrants to the United States. As he suggested in the 1920s, "America's greatest problem today is the flood of immigration from the lower levels of European society that is threatening to submerge and destroy our American ideals." Through this statement, he not only allied the Ozark hillbilly with now-familiar traits of idealism, purity, industriousness, and democratic standards but also implicitly situated the prototypical mountaineer as a racial redeemer in a country overrun with unsavory shades of whiteness. Although Rayburn resisted positing this dynamic in such crisis-ridden terms, he too hoped that this seedbed of Anglo-Saxonism would remain unsullied.[46]

Although the discourse focused on slight permutations of whiteness subsided at midcentury, the modern-day Branson vacation business continues a nearly homogenous racial landscape of white residents, performers, and tourists. Reflecting on this dynamic, travel writer Arthur Frommer has noted the "undeniable racism" of some contemporary local promoters, and a journalist for *Gentlemen's Quarterly* described the town as possessing a "foul smell of bigotry." Despite a plethora of theaters and acts, Branson's current offerings include only a handful of black entertainers. In fact, the only ongoing black headliner is Charley Pride, who arrived in 1994. Pride, a member of the Grand Ole Opry, presents a traditional Nashville sound, and his act seldom if ever includes themes or styles related to African American music. Such an approach therefore suggests that nonwhite performers must engage in an erasure of their racial composition and concomitantly perform a certain variant of whiteness to profit in the local industry.[47]

In light of the area's history of vaunted Anglo-Saxonism, it is at first confounding that Shoji Tabuchi, a Japanese-born entertainer, is currently one of Branson's most popular acts. However, he has worked for many years to gain acceptance by implicating himself in Ozark hillbilly-ism. Trained as a classical violinist, Tabuchi's musical affinities drastically changed when he attended a concert by country music star Roy Acuff. In 1967, Tabuchi moved from Osaka to San Francisco to pursue a career as a country music fiddler. A year later, he received his big break when Acuff invited him to appear at the Grand Ole Opry. In 1981, Tabuchi came to Branson and played at the Starlite Theater. Remaining in town through the 1980s, he was named Instrumentalist of the Year at the Ozark Music Awards from 1984 to 1987. In 1990, he opened his own two-thousand-seat venue and since that time has often been dubbed the King of Branson.[48]

Promotional materials from Tabuchi's theater claim that he "contradicts all ideas about American Country music." Although he does not don hillbilly attire, numerous aspects of his act mirror the incongruous nature of that signifier. A multiplicity of musical genres permeates the show, including jazz, conga, polka, classical, country, and gospel. In the late 1990s, Tabuchi even added a two-thousand-pound Japanese taiko drum to the production. Like the more conventional fiddles and banjos of the hillbilly craft, the instrument was embraced in rapidly modernizing post-1945 Japan as a way supposedly to preserve endangered cultural traditions. Further demonstrating this venue's paradoxical disposition in a Branson context that persistently makes a virtue of simplicity, the theater features a much-discussed ostentatious style. In particular, the auditorium's bathrooms, attired with granite and onyx pedestal sinks, gold-leaf mirrors, marble fireplaces, pool tables, and velvet drapes, are cited as a "must-see." Finally, in a town that regularly derides Las Vegas–oriented glitz and glamour, Tabuchi is the most sequined of all stars, and his site utilizes a host of high-tech theatrics, such as animated laser art, mirror balls, and neon lights.[49]

Despite Tabuchi's eccentricities, his biography and act nevertheless resonate with the hillbilly moral standard, thereby functioning to mostly expunge his ethnicity. Like the acclaimed mountaineer of actuality and lore, his livelihood had humble beginnings, and he rose to prominence only through a virulent work ethic. As with the semimythical hillman and his onstage counterpart, he supports a set of core regional values within his performance. Family is marked as vital to this construct, and Tabuchi's white wife and daughter frequently appear in the show. Christianity is endorsed via numbers such as "The Old Rugged Cross," and every performance is punctuated by a patriotic finale. Finally, Tabuchi has adopted the self-effacing and hackneyed humor of Branson hillbilly comics as a way to both remind and make light of his heritage. One frequently reiterated joke states that he and friend Mel Tillis often fish together, but Tillis is afraid to turn his back for fear that the Japanese star might "eat the bait." Thus, Tabuchi, like Pride, has infiltrated Branson's predominantly white industry by espousing many elements of hillbilly-ism. Considering the demographic makeup of the area's residents and guests, this embrace may be the only way that a nonwhite celebrity could be christened an entertainment king within a region that has often proclaimed its pure racial legacy.

Tricking the Tourists

In the introduction to an anthology of Ozark tall tales, *We Always Lie to Strangers,* folklorist Vance Randolph has written, "There's no harm in 'stretchin' the blanket' or 'lettin' out a whack' or 'sawin' off a whopper' or 'spinnin' a windy' when they involve no attempt to injure anybody. 'A windy ain't a lie, nohow,' said one of my neighbors, 'unless you tell it for the truth.' And even if you do not tell it for the truth nobody is deceived, except maybe a few tourists." Randolph was not a native Ozarker, but no folklorist is more thoroughly associated with the region or has more comprehensively assembled accounts of tourist gullibility at the hands of area natives. His *The Ozarks: An American Survival of Primitive Society* (1931) represented the initial book-length study of the region. Although unabashedly neglectful of the more modern elements of the area's society and culture, he forcefully argued that "the Ozark hill-billy is a genuine American—that is why he seems so alien to most tourists." Enamored with notions of isolation and stubborn traditionalism, Randolph filled pages with comments on virtues long lost in contemporary America. While some saw the nostalgia voiced within *The Ozarks* as folkloric invention, he insisted that it contained "not a line of fiction or intentional exaggeration."[50]

Throughout his life, Randolph tenuously grappled with the ever-increasing stream of vacationers pouring into the hills and their effects on traditional culture. He always said that such things did not interest him, but he nevertheless realized that tourism was good business and wanted hill folk to profit from outsider dollars. Offering opinion on this subject during a speech at a 1934 Eureka Springs, Arkansas, folk festival, he stated, "The professional Ozark boosters would do well to put more of this primitive stuff into their tourist advertising, and not talk so much about our splendid highways and excellent new hotels. [City people] come here to see rugged mountain scenery and quaint log cabins and picturesque rail fences and romantic-looking mountaineers." Via this premise, his much cherished primitivism could actually be protected rather than threatened by outsider interventions. If natives continued to cultivate the illusion of the past, they would both profit financially and preserve aspects of their heritage made available in consumable form.[51]

Randolph documented many natives who took great pride in their ability to deceive city-dwelling tourists. In *Funny Stories about Hillbillies* (1944), he cited an individual who avowed it was "taken as a compliment to be called a liar," and another who professed, "You can hear anything in Stone County except the truth." Such yarns continue to be spun for modern-day Branson visitors. Commenting on the hillbilly's image within the contemporary vacation industry, the co-owner of Presley's Country Jubilee, Raeanne Presley, who was elected mayor of Branson in 2007, has stated, "In the mind of the people that live here that would call themselves a hillbilly, that didn't mean stupid. It might have meant that they were uneducated but it never meant that they weren't smart." She continues, "So, that's what carries over and what Gary [Herkimer] tries to do with his comedy [in the Presleys' Country Jubilee]. Although you might laugh because he didn't pronounce the word right or he used it incorrectly in a sentence or he looked kind of silly in his clothes, the end of the joke is always that he outsmarted the other guy." The comedic style celebrated rather than derided hillbillies. Presley explained, "That's why I think people are not insulted by that. The play is the smart city guy and the dumb hillbilly but the dumb hillbilly wins. . . . The people that might consider themselves hillbillies are never insulted by that. Usually the ones that don't want the Ozarks known for hillbillies aren't hillbillies." Deliberate backwardness or an intentional lack of knowledge may then be securely adjoined to the myriad ambivalences that characterize the Ozark trickster. By deceiving sojourners in such a manner, the hillbilly fortifies virtues of simplicity, individualism, and relaxed industriousness. Such chicanery furthers a sense of Otherness in the minds of outsiders and assists in the cultivation of mountaineer pride. Behind the veil of ignorance is astuteness, just as underneath a shroud of debauched stereotypes lies a multifarious set of regional values.[52]

Tricksters play tricks. Utilizing a strategy of deception, they achieve ends that are self-serving, culturally necessary, or a mixture of the two. The hillbilly trickster has effectively enacted this process within the Ozark tourism industry for nearly one hundred years. Words from countless natives throughout this period suggest a complicit involvement in the practice, an involvement that was necessary for the construction of the region's vast consumer culture. Likewise, many people have embraced the moniker as a badge of honor and used it to denote a cohesive group of ethical and religious dictates that lie beneath the tourist's misperceptions, foibles, and follies. Reducing the function of the hillbilly trickster to a singularity does a disservice to the richness of the semiotic tradition and pigeonholes a signifier with a demonstrable ability to resist coherent description. Positioned on the margins of an Ozark construct of propriety, the figure also resides at the center of the tourism enterprise. Stationed within a mythical lifestyle of indecency and squalor, it also bears connotations of admired simplicity and deep-seated morality. Within a vacation industry intent on offering a strictly delineated portrait of principled thought and action, the ambiguous hillbilly has simultaneously granted reminders of that which imperils its authority and presented an ideological map that charts the path for its continuance.

NOTES

1. For Spurlock's quotation, see Fred Pfister, *Insiders' Guide to Branson and the Ozark Mountains* (Guilford, Conn.: Insiders' Guide, 2002), 25. While conducting fieldwork in Branson, I heard numerous versions of the quotation.

2. Asa Don Dickinson, *The Best Books of Our Time, 1901–1925* (New York: Wilson, 1928), 201; Harold Bell Wright, *The Shepherd of the Hills* (1907; Gretna, La.: Pelican, 1994), 284. According to Dickinson, Wright was the third-most-popular American writer between 1895 and 1926 and the first in popularity between 1909 and 1921.

3. Crystal Cody, "Silver Dollar City Hits Slump," *Arkansas Democrat-Gazette,* 8 August 2003; Michael Lewis Frizell, "A History of *The Shepherd of the Hills* Dramatizations: The Branson Productions" (master's thesis, Southwest Missouri State University, 1996), 61–66.

4. Don Zimmerman, "Country's Mecca in Missouri," *USA Today,* 24 June 1994; Kathy Buckstaff, "Despite Pains, Growth Moves Ahead," *Springfield News-Leader,* 26 February 1995; "First There Was Nashville . . . Then Came Branson," *Atlanta Journal-Constitution,* 4 July 1993.

5. Zimmerman, "Country's Mecca"; Buckstaff, "Despite Pains, Growth Moves Ahead"; "First There Was Nashville."

6. Hazel Dagley Heavin, "Hillbilly," *Rayburn's Ozark Guide* 21 (1949): 76.

7. S. G. F. Brandon, "Trickster," in *A Dictionary of Comparative Religion*, ed. S. G. F. Brandon (New York: Scribner's, 1970), 623; William J. Hynes, "Inconclusive Conclusions: Tricksters—Metaplayers and Revealers," in *Mythical Trickster Figures: Contours, Contexts, and Criticisms*, ed. William J. Hynes and William G. Doty (Tuscaloosa: University of Alabama Press, 1993), 215.

8. Victor Turner, *The Ritual Process: Structure and Anti-structure* (Chicago: Aldine, 1969), 95; Mary Douglas, *Purity and Danger* (London: Penguin, 1970), 13.

9. Barbara Babcock-Abrahams, "'A Tolerated Margin of Mess': The Trickster and His Tales Reconsidered," *Journal of the Folklore Institute* 11 (1975): 165; Robert D. Pelton, *The Trickster in West Africa: A Study of Mythic Irony and Sacred Delight* (Berkeley: University of California Press, 1980), 3.

10. Klaus-Peter Koepping, "Absurdity and the Hidden Truth: Cunning Intelligence and Grotesque Bodily Images as Manifestations of the Trickster," *History of Religions* 24, no. 3 (1985): 193; Gordon Morgan and Peter Kunkel, "Arkansas' Ozark Mountain Blacks: An Introduction," *Phylon* 34 (Third Quarter 1973): 285.

11. Henry Shapiro, *Appalachia on Our Mind: The Southern Mountaineers in the American Consciousness, 1870–1920* (Chapel Hill: University of North Carolina Press, 1978), x; Archie Green, "Hillbilly Music: Source and Symbol," *Journal of American Folklore* 78 (July–September 1965): 204; Allen W. Batteau, *The Invention of Appalachia* (Tucson: University of Arizona Press, 1990), 132.

12. www.google.com (accessed 7 June 2007); Milton D. Rafferty, ed., *Rude Pursuits and Rugged Peaks: Schoolcraft's Ozark Journal, 1818–1819* (Fayetteville: University of Arkansas Press, 1996), 63; H. L. Mencken, "Famine," *Baltimore Evening Sun*, 19 January 1931; Joe Queenan, *Red Lobster, White Trash, and the Blue Lagoon* (New York: Hyperion, 1999), 166.

13. Julia McAdoo, "Where the *Poor* Are *Rich*," *Ozark Guide Yearbook* (Reeds Spring, Mo.: Pipes, 1962), 13, 83; David Hsiung, *Two Worlds in the Tennessee Mountains: Exploring the Origins of Appalachian Stereotypes* (Lexington: University Press of Kentucky, 1997); Richard Starnes, *Creating the Land of the Sky: Tourism and Society in Western North Carolina* (Tuscaloosa: University of Alabama Press, 2005).

14. *Urban Dictionary*, http://www.urbandictionary.com/define.php?term =hillbilly (accessed 7 June 2007); Anthony Harkins, *Hillbilly: A Cultural History of an American Icon* (New York: Oxford University Press, 2004), 215–16.

15. "Beverly Hillbillies?" *Los Angeles Times*, 11 February 2003.

16. Sarah Overstreet, "Some of the Stereotypes May Be Founded in Truth, but Mostly It's Pure Hollywood Fiction," *Springfield News-Leader*, 10 March 1985; Dale Freeman, "What is a Hillbilly?" *Springfield News and Leader*, 2 February 1975. Another piece of Ozark wit further illustrates the difficulties that arise when tourists attempt to identify "authentic" hillbillies. According to this account, "An old native of the White River Valley, after being queried from time to time by tourists looking for a hillbilly, was once more asked by a New Englander where he might find one. After he was informed that he was talking to a hillbilly and finding that the native looked no different than any one else, he commented;

'These natives aren't like they used to be, are they?' To which the old native replied, 'No, nor they never were.'" See "Ozark Wit and Humor," *White River Valley Historical Quarterly* 1 (Spring 1962): 6.

17. Elsie Upton, "Hillbilly," *Rayburn's Ozark Guide* 19 (1948): 23.

18. Charles H. Hibler, *Down in Arkansas* (Kansas City, Mo.: Smith, 1911), 33; Malinda Donaldson, "The Hillbilly," *Arcadian Life Magazine*, Spring–Summer 1943, 16–17.

19. *Moore v. Moore*, 337 SW 2d 781 (1960).

20. *History of Stone County, Missouri* (Marionville, Mo.: Stone County Historical Society, 1989), 236; "Political Shepherd of the Hills," *Rayburn's Ozark Guide* 18 (1948): 26; Joel D. Treese, ed., *Biographical Directory of the American Congress, 1774–1996; the Continental Congress, September 5, 1774, to October 21, 1778; and the Congress of the United States, from the First through the 104th Congress, March 4, 1789, to January 3, 1997* (Alexandria, Va.: CQ Staff Directories, 1997), 1819.

21. *History of Stone County*, 236–37; "Genuine Folks," *Rayburn's Ozark Guide* 18 (1948): 20; "The Hillbilly," *Rayburn's Ozark Guide* 48 (1956): 4.

22. "Hillbillies—To Be or Not to Be," *Ozarks Mountaineer* 15, no. 5 (1967): 12. In one of the first issues of the *Ozarks Mountaineer*, a native Ozarker added further nuance to the magazine's negation of the hillbilly idiom. Cora Pinkley Call asserted that despite outsider characterizations, a great diversity of people and lifestyles existed in the region. Thus, the mountaineer was "not a curiosity." Although the author sought to debunk a variety of stereotypes, she concluded that two overarching regional attributes could be identified—a "strength of character" and a "oneness of purpose to serve the Almighty" ("We Are Mountaineers, Not 'Hill-Billies," *Ozarks Mountaineer* 2, no. 4 [1953]: 10).

23. Wright, *Shepherd of the Hills*, 292, 259, 288.

24. "There's Gold in Those Ozark Hills," *St. Louis Post-Dispatch*, 29 August 1965, qtd. in Lynn Morrow and Linda Myers-Phinney, *Shepherd of the Hills Country: Tourism Transforms the Ozarks, 1880s–1930s* (Fayetteville: University of Arkansas Press, 1999), 32.

25. J. W. Williamson, *Hillbillyland* (Chapel Hill: University of North Carolina Press, 1995), 37–38, 39–40, 62, 55; Harkins, *Hillbilly*, 160.

26. Harkins, *Hillbilly*, 161; Wade Austin, "The Real Beverly Hillbillies," *Southern Quarterly* 19 (Spring–Summer 1981): 83–94, 86–90; Ken Parker, "Shangri-La," *Rayburn's Ozark Guide* 28 (1951): 23.

27. Anthony Harkins, "The Hillbilly in the Living Room: Television Representations of Southern Mountaineers in Situation Comedies, 1952–1971," *Appalachian Journal* 29 (Fall 2001–Winter 2002): 99–109; "Come 'n Listen to My Story 'bout a Man Named . . . Paul," *Independence Examiner*, 3 February 2001, http://www.examiner.net/stories/020301/fea_02030100.shtml (accessed 22 May 2004).

28. Harkins, "Hillbilly in the Living Room," 114; Horace Newcomb, "Appalachia on Television: Region as Symbol in American Popular Culture," in *Appalachian Images in Folk and Popular Culture*, ed. W. K. McNeil (Knoxville: University of Tennessee Press, 1995), 322–23.

29. Richard Warren Lewis, "The Golden Hillbillies," *Saturday Evening Post,* 2 February 1963; "The Corn Is Green," *Newsweek,* 3 December 1962. Reflecting on the dialectic of meaning found within *The Beverly Hillbillies*'s characterizations, eastern Tennessee correspondent and radio commentator Mack Morris has written, "We alternately seem to swing, as a regional group, from one image to another in the eyes of much of the rest of the nation. . . . This swing from one extreme to the other occurs with remarkable regularity . . . and is enough to set up a sort of schizophrenia—as a matter of fact, I think it has, in us and in the rest of the country regarding us—which may explain the popularity of 'The Beverly Hillbillies'" (qtd. in Ronnie Day, "Pride and Poverty: An Impressionistic View of the Family in the Cumberlands of Appalachia," in *Appalachia Inside Out—Culture and Customs,* ed. Robert J. Higgs, Ambrose N. Manning, and Jim Wayne Miller [Knoxville: University of Tennessee Press, 1995], 376).

30. "Back to the Hills," *The Beverly Hillbillies,* 24 September 1969, CBS; Pete Herschend, interview by author, Branson, Mo., 24 September 2002.

31. Bruce Cook, *Welcome to Branson, Missouri: The Town That Country Built* (New York: Avon, 1993), 156–57.

32. Lori A. Robbins, "A Lyin' to Them Tourists: Tourism in Branson, Missouri" (master's thesis, University of Mississippi, 1999), 82.

33. Ron Sylvester, "Branson's Style Definition Changes with Musical Scene," *Springfield News-Leader,* 23 May 1993; Terri Sanders, interview by author, Branson, Mo., 16 September 2002; Cook, *Welcome to Branson,* 157.

34. Jane Bennett, "How to Be a Professional Hillbilly," *Springfield Leader and Press,* 6 September 1970; Leon Fredrick, *Ozarks Hillbilly Editor* (Branson, Mo.: Fredrick, 1995), 176–79.

35. Bennett, "How to Be a Professional Hillbilly."

36. Fredrick, *Ozarks Hillbilly Editor,* 179; Bennett, "How to Be a Professional Hillbilly"; Wright, *Shepherd of the Hills,* 13–14.

37. Williamson, *Hillbillyland,* 27.

38. Dorothy Roe, "Ozark Hillbilly: Tycoon with 'Fringe Benefits,'" *Springfield Daily News,* 9 August 1965.

39. Harkins, "Hillbilly in the Living Room," 100; Jacqueline Jones, *The Dispossessed—America's Underclasses from the Civil War to the Present* (New York: Basic Books, 1992), 209, 212; Albert N. Votaw, "The Hillbillies Invade Chicago," *Harper's Magazine,* February 1958, 64–66; Matthew Frye Jacobson, *Whiteness of a Different Color: European Immigrants and the Alchemy of Race* (Cambridge: Harvard University Press, 1998), 4.

40. Milton D. Rafferty, *The Ozarks: Life and Land* (1980; Fayetteville: University of Arkansas Press, 2001), 41–66.

41. "'Queen of the Hillbillies' Reigns No More," *Springfield Leader and Press,* 22 February 1979; May Kennedy McCord, "Hillbilly Heartbeats," *Springfield Leader and Press,* 6 August 1933; May Kennedy McCord, "Hillbilly Heartbeats," *Rayburn's Ozark Guide* 37 (1953): 33.

42. *History of Stone County,* 238; May Kennedy McCord, "Hillbilly Heartbeats," *Ozark Life,* January 1930, 16.

43. May Kennedy McCord, "The Vanishing Ozarker," *Rayburn's Ozark Guide* 36 (1953): 55.

44. Otto Ernest Rayburn, "Rayburn's Roadside Chat," *Ozark Life*, September 1929, 3; Otto Ernest Rayburn, "Rural Musings," *Rayburn's Ozark Guide* 20 (1949): 3.

45. Otto Ernest Rayburn, *Ozark Country* (New York: Duell, Sloan, and Pearce, 1941), 36; Otto Ernest Rayburn, "Progress in the Ozarks," *Rayburn's Ozark Guide* 35 (1953): 3; Ethel C. Simpson, "Otto Ernest Rayburn, an Early Promoter of the Ozarks," *Arkansas Historical Quarterly* 58 (Summer 1999): 164; Abby Burnett, *When the Presbyterians Came to Kingston: Kingston Community Church, 1917–1951* (Kingston, Ark.: Bradshaw Mountain, 2000), 38–39.

46. Simpson, "Otto Ernest Rayburn," 162–63; Burnett, *When the Presbyterians Came,* 186–87.

47. Arthur Frommer, *Arthur Frommer's Branson!* (New York: Macmillan Travel, 1995), 34; Jeanne Marie Laskas, "Branson in My Rearview Mirror," *Gentlemen's Quarterly,* May 1994, 174; Bill Smith, "Branson Attracts Few Blacks," *St. Louis Post-Dispatch,* 23 July 1995.

48. Tom Uhlenbrock, "From Japan with Love . . . for Country Music," *St. Louis Post-Dispatch,* 21 April 2002; Suzanne Morrissey, "King of Branson," *Country America,* November 1997, 72; Martin Booe, "A Fiddlin'," *USA Weekend,* 2–4 April 1993.

49. Shoji Tabuchi Theatre press packet, 1998; Tammy Felton, "Shoji Tabuchi Features Awesome Japanese Drumming!" *Travelhost,* June–July 1997, L10; Toni Stroud, "Branson, Mo.: Many Attractions but Music Is King," *Minneapolis Star Tribune,* 14 July 1996.

50. Vance Randolph, *We Always Lie to Strangers: Tall Tales from the Ozarks* (New York: Columbia University Press, 1952), 3; Vance Randolph, *The Ozarks: An American Survival of Primitive Society* (New York: Vanguard, 1931), 22, v.

51. Otto Ernest Rayburn, *Forty Years in the Ozarks* (Eureka Springs, Ark.: Ozark Guide, 1957), 89–90.

52. Vance Randolph, *Funny Stories about Hillbillies* (Girard, Kans.: Haldeman-Julius, 1944), 5–6; Raeanne Presley, interview by author, Branson, Mo., 27 September 2002.

Behind the Sombrero

Identity and Power at South of the Border,
1949–2001

Nicole King

Travelers on Interstate 95 see an imposing neon sombrero rising in the distance. The two-hundred-foot Sombrero Tower is the first sign of South Carolina's famous tourist complex, South of the Border. From the observation deck inside the sombrero, visitors can view the vast 350-acre compound littered with a miniature golf course, a truck stop, a campground, garishly decorated motels, souvenir shops, restaurants, amusement rides, and strange animal statues. Beneath the layers of kitsch, however, rest layers of controversy. South of the Border created controversy when it opened in 1949 because its primary purpose was to sell beer to residents of the conservative, rural counties on the North Carolina–South Carolina border. Owner Alan Schafer, the Jewish southerner and the mastermind of South of the Border's constant evolution, also engendered controversy with his outspoken nature and behind-the-scenes political dealings. The icon of Pedro, South of the Border's cartoonish mascot, became controversial because of the ethnic stereotype the figure embodies.

By looking behind the sombrero and the kitsch appearance of South of the Border, this chapter explores the interactions among identity, politics, and power, especially as they offer commentary on the racial and ethnic conflicts in the American South. Focusing on the production side of the story—that is, the discourse shaped by Schafer—elucidates the connections between economic gain and social change. The size and power of South of the Border's kitsch aesthetic affords the site a special position both inside and outside South Carolina's dominant white value system. Expanding the often simplistic dichotomy of black-white race relations in the South, South of the Border functions as a complex borderland where real and imagined identities mingle and clash.

The name *South of the Border* denotes the physical border between the states of South and North Carolina; however, the various connotations of the space create a much more complicated picture. As cultural

The Sombrero Tower, seen here in 2001, provides a vantage point for visitors interested in seeing the sprawling South of the Border grounds. (Photo by author)

This sign (shown in 2001) welcomes visitors to the South of the Border complex near Dillon, South Carolina. (Photo by author)

historian Gloria Anzaldúa writes in the preface to *Borderlands/La Frontera*, "Borderlands are physically present wherever two or more cultures edge each other, where people of different races occupy the same territory, where under, lower, middle and upper classes touch, where the space between two individuals shrinks with intimacy."[1] This essay traces the evolution of the burgeoning tourist conglomerate in the context of a rapidly changing post-1945 South, where change was closely related to shifting race relations.[2]

The power to construct South of the Border was tied to the history and vision of one individual, Alan Schafer. He manipulated social and historical forces while developing a multi-million-dollar business that has thrived for more than five decades. While he navigated the social environment, Schafer also created a multifaceted built environment with a Mexican border-town theme. Critically analyzing South of the Border's social and built environment over time foregrounds the hybrid identities that emerged from increased prosperity, mobility, and diverse cultural contact in the South following the Second World War.[3]

Alan Schafer's South of the Border

From the time he opened his roadside business in 1949 until his death in 2001, Schafer made all the major decisions in constructing South of the Border, from designing its aesthetic to defining its political role within Dillon County. The story of South of the Border is Schafer's because he obtained the power to construct the physical and rhetorical space of his tourist empire. In an article on South of the Border's fiftieth anniversary, reporter Anna Griffith wrote, "Schafer is as big a character as the 97-foot-tall sombrero-wearing Pedro that guards over his kingdom. He's as much a study in contrast as the clashing shades of pink, aqua and fuchsia his designs favor."[4]

Schafer was a political powerhouse as well as a successful businessman. He described himself to a journalist as a "knee-jerk liberal, bleeding-heart Democrat."[5] He served as chair of the Dillon County Democratic Party from 1963 to 1981.[6] Schafer even blended his colorful political critiques into South of the Border's advertising. One upside-down billboard read, "South of the Border—sign planned in Washington. Pedro feex later OK?"[7] Schafer's South of the Border exemplified trends in American roadside culture and tourism; however, his travel spot also challenged the demure and conservative facade of small-town southern culture and thereby undermined the dominance of elite whites and the institutional segregation prevalent in the region.[8]

In the tumultuous period following the Civil War, Alan Schafer's grandfather, Abraham, a recent German Jewish immigrant, bought a small farm in Little Rock, South Carolina, and established a mercantile business.[9] By the time Alan Schafer's father, Samuel, was born in 1888, prominent local citizen James Dillon had assisted in the procurement of nearby land for a railroad station and a small town. The new town of Dillon thrived from the railroad traffic, and development of the area led the state legislature to carve Dillon County out of the northern part of Marion County in 1910.[10]

Samuel Schafer and his first wife, Wilhelmina (Heller) Schafer, had two children, including Alan, born in 1915. His mother died in the 1918 influenza epidemic, and Mag Hines, a black woman who worked for and lived with the Schafer family, raised him and his siblings. Thus, Alan Schafer's close relationship with the area's African American community began early in his life.[11]

Dillon County experienced its share of economic hardships in the early twentieth century, and Alan Schafer learned from them. "The bank took the farm in the '20s and that's why I hate banks. And that's why I've never borrowed any money," Schafer told a journalist.[12] During the 1930s, one-third of South Carolina's farms were mortgaged, and almost three-fourths of the state's farmers survived on borrowed money. By 1931, the state's deficit had swelled to $5 million ($49.9 million by today's standards).[13] However, depression-era Dillon County also experienced some economic hope with the construction of a major road. Highway 301 became known as Dillon's Gold Coast because, as Durward Stokes wrote in his study of the county, a "new era in transportation had begun which proved to be profitable in many ways for the county and its citizens."[14]

To tap the market opened by the highway, the Schafers created the Schafer Distribution Company in the 1930s and forged the business into one of the South's most successful beer distribution operations. Alan Schafer returned home from the University of South Carolina in 1933. After Abraham Schafer's death, Samuel asked his son to go into business with him. The young Schafer had an idea—sell the family's country store and concentrate on the beer business. At the Schafers' store, patrons could buy groceries on credit but had to pay cash for beer. As a young and observant entrepreneur in training, Alan noticed that even during tight times, beer produced cash. Beer, not tourism, was his first business venture.[15]

As Jews, the Schafers skirted the cultural stigma associated with selling alcohol that would have affected the white southern Baptists and other religious conservatives who dominated the area.[16] Schafer later attributed the success of his business to "loyalty in the black accounts," pointing to a possible coalition between the area's small Jewish community and its large African American population.[17] According to Stokes, with the "hard work and the managerial genius of the younger Schafer," the distribution business flourished, and by 1950 its territory had expanded from the Carolinas as far as Miami, Florida.[18] As the business grew, so too did the Schafer family's cultural and political influence in the area.

Samuel Schafer was a well-respected member of the local Jewish community. Abraham Schafer had been one of the first Jews to settle in what eventually became Dillon County, and the family remained the only Jews in Little Rock during Alan's childhood.[19] Samuel Schafer helped build the first synagogue in the area in 1942, although Dillon County's Jewish community remained small, growing only to fifty members by 1978.[20]

In addition to establishing himself as a leader in the Jewish community, Samuel Schafer proudly served as a member of the Democratic Party's executive committee, the only viable political party in the area during the early and mid-twentieth century. After his father became ill, however, Alan Schafer felt that the Democrats failed to honor his father's contributions, explaining, "When the election came up in 1944, Dad had gone to the Sloan-Kettering [medical center]. I asked a guy I thought was a friend of his to elect Dad an honorary committeeman [of the Democratic Party]. The guy promised he would, but they didn't. And it damn near broke my father's heart." Alan Schafer saw this slight as unforgivable. "Early on I made up my mind if I ever got a chance to cut those bastards' throats, I would," he said.[21] Samuel Schafer died in 1945; however, his son's vendetta against Dillon's political establishment did not.

The Second World War marked both the rise of Alan Schafer and a major shift in southern life. Schafer worked locally with the military police from 1943 to 1945, thereby remaining involved in his community and in the family business despite the war.[22] Schafer thus witnessed firsthand the region's dramatic changes during this time. In 1940, for example, more than three-quarters of South Carolina's population lived in rural areas or towns smaller than twenty-five hundred, and the state contained the lowest population of foreign-born residents in the country.[23] But, as historian Pete Daniel writes, "The war challenged [southern] provincialism, offered employment, and reshaped society. After the war, [soldiers] could not fit their experiences or expectations back into the South of the 1930s."[24] South Carolina historian Walter Edgar calls particular attention to veterans' desire to facilitate positive change in race relations in their state. Edgar points out, however, that the "enthusiastic young veterans wanted to change South Carolina, but they faced the opposition of the county elites who preferred the status quo."[25]

Wartime opportunities for employment and service by African Americans along with the rumblings of civil rights activism began to erode white supremacy even in provincial Dillon County. In 1948, taking advantage of the postwar South's changing nature, Schafer embarked on two progressive campaigns in politics and business. As a consequence of a recent Supreme Court decision, Democratic primaries, the "real elections" in Dillon County at the time, opened to blacks in 1948.[26] But few white South Carolinians warmed to the idea of black voters. The same year, in response to President Harry Truman's decision to integrate the U.S. military, a group of southern Democrats including South Carolina governor Strom Thurmond formed the States' Rights Democratic Party (the Dixiecrats), with Thurmond serving as the party's presidential candidate. Thurmond's opposition to African American civil rights won him every county in South Carolina except for Anderson and Spartanburg, located upstate.[27]

Schafer continued to swim against South Carolina's political tides. He often discussed his involvement in the 1948 primary: "I went out and registered every black citizen in the Little Rock precinct. Then I took control of that nucleus of 140 to 150 voters and I've had it ever since." As a result, Schafer placed himself at the center of the local tensions over political and racial power. He explained, "With that black base, I took over the county machine. The Ku Klux Klan used to follow the trucks of my beer distributing company around. I was a pariah in the white community." Although Schafer was white, he was not quite "lily-white," as he called his political enemies.[28] Schafer presented himself as seizing control of the emerging black vote rather than viewing blacks as controlling their own voices or political power. Schafer's language—"I took control" and "I took over the county machine"—leads to the question of whether he was co-opting the emerging African American vote for his personal political power or forming a coalition based on shared power.

To local conservative whites, the distinction mattered little. Black voting meant black (and Jewish) empowerment. Schafer's alliance with African Americans thus spurred a backlash. He explained, "Boycotts against my beer company were organized. Crosses were burned in front of my home. Groups of Klansmen began following my beer trucks around, urging white retailers to not buy beer from that 'nigger lover' Schafer." The passage of time failed to abate the furor. According to Schafer, "The Klan continued this harassment through the years, holding rallies aimed at me just 3 miles south of South of the Border and then driving in a Kavalcade through the S.O.B. premises as a warning."[29] Such efforts at intimidation were not surprising, considering many white southerners' fervent opposition to desegregation at this time. Schafer's work with the African American community placed him solidly outside the norm for white southerners.

In October 1948, just a month after the primary, Schafer paid every employee of his beer distribution business, which had a four-thousand-dollar-per-week payroll at the time, in two-dollar bills to show "that legally controlled alcoholic beverages contribute a vital share to the prosperity and well-being of the Town, Country, and State."[30] These bills flooded the area and made an impression. In addition to illustrating the vital role of legal alcohol, Schafer wanted to show that he was an economic and political force, not easily silenced through boycotts or threats. Schafer promoted the sale and consumption of alcohol and crossed the color line to work with the black community at the moment of its emergence on the political scene. Schafer's status as a Jewish southerner gave him the fluidity to inhabit these social borderlands. In addition, the wealth and upward mobility he acquired through his business acumen certainly offered him additional possibilities for social interaction.

Schafer skillfully used his hybrid identity to his advantage, especially as a means of combating criticism. When the Jewish Anti-Defamation League sent him a letter of complaint concerning the "almost-Kosher" Virginia ham he advertised at South of the Border, he replied, "I'm almost Kosher myself." Schafer explained, "There is a power to being Jewish—you hear about persecution, but most people think you're a lot smarter than you are. It's a nationwide syndrome." Journalist Rudy Maxa clarified, "Schafer is a southerner when it suits him. He is also Jewish when it suits him."[31]

In *Blacks in the Jewish Mind,* Seth Forman points out that although the 1915 lynching of Jewish businessman Leo Frank in Atlanta is well known, "these kinds of actions were tempered by countervailing Southern ideas concerning the equality of all white men, the overriding concern with the subordination of Blacks, and the usefulness of the Jewish presence as merchants and artisans." Jews in the South negotiated their "delicate situation"—their livelihood often depended on not rocking the boat—by attempting to be accepted by whites in the dominant culture of white supremacy.[32] The other choice was to challenge white supremacy and risk retribution. As a businessman and political figure, Schafer would have to negotiate this social borderland as he opened and ran South of the Border.

Schafer understood the importance of manipulating physical as well as social borderlands when he selected the location for South of the Border. He chose when and where to open the small business in reaction to the fact that Robeson County in bordering North Carolina went dry—no alcohol could be bought or sold there. No longer able to distribute beer in the area, Schafer decided to draw the beer drinkers to him. In 1949, Schafer procured a small piece of land in Hamer, South Carolina, a small town seven miles north of Dillon, and set up an eighteen-by-thirty-six-foot store, which he called the South of the Border Beer Depot. The simple spatial placement of the store on the southern side of the state line gave South of the Border its name and contributed to its lasting identity.[33]

Schafer claimed that Governor Thurmond told him to serve food in addition to beer to avoid controversy.[34] Schafer eventually changed the name from "beer depot" to "drive-in" and added a ten-seat grill. A December 1949 South of the Border ad in the *Dillon Herald* announced "a new kind of drive-in restaurant" where patrons could "eat, drink," and "be merry." The establishment now served "deliciously toasted sandwiches, made to order while you wait. Every sandwich a meal in itself. Sliced chicken, corned beef, pastrami—plus all regular style sandwiches." Lest patrons forget the establishment's primary purpose, however, large, bold letters proclaimed, "Beer by the case," and the store ran a promotion where the first one thousand cars would receive a free bottle of wine. Less flatteringly, Schafer later remembered the offerings as "grilled cheese. Grilled ham. Peanut butter and jelly. That was the whole menu, except for soda and coffee—and beer, of course."[35] Selling food did not automatically make South of the Border a socially acceptable space, but it helped disguise the socially distasteful beer market. Schafer manipulated the built environment of South of the Border and its border businesses as he manipulated his identity and the social and political boundaries of Dillon County. Schafer became skilled at maximizing or minimizing controversy in accordance with his and his tourism empire's needs.

In addition to facilitating an alcohol trade unpopular with many locals during the 1950s, South of the Border soon began to offer accommodations to tourists passing through. The Interstate Highway Act of 1956 changed the nature of American car culture and strengthened Schafer's hand within Dillon County. During the 1950s, South of the Border grew from a small diner that served beer to include a cocktail lounge, a motel, a gas station, and a souvenir shop.[36] By the mid-1960s, South of the Border had expanded to include even more attractions—a barbershop, a drugstore, a package store, novelty and variety shops, a post office, outdoor recreation facilities, a racetrack for go-carts, and an immense 104-foot statue of Pedro weighing seventy-seven tons. The massive Pedro held a South of the Border sign and contained four miles of wiring.[37] In 1961, Schafer capitalized on the Civil War centennial by adding the ironically named Confederateland, U.S.A., which included a museum of Confederate memorabilia, to South of the Border's attractions.[38] In 1962, South of the Border began to sell fireworks, which were (and remain) illegal in North Carolina.[39] In December 1964, the *Dillon Herald* announced that Interstate 95 would pass right by South of the Border.[40] Many observers, including Edgar, have suspected that Schafer somehow "finagled" the construction plans to ensure that South of the Border not only came within view of drivers but that the federal highway included two exits that poured customers directly into the tourist complex.[41] Schafer denied that his money and power influenced the location of the exits, explaining that in 1957, when the Eisenhower administration "first issued the interstate map, I went with Rep. [John] McMillan to see the Bureau of Public Roads. We had 60 rooms at that time, and I said. 'Should we expand or not?' Every map they had showed the interstate would cross the border right at our point, so we went ahead and expanded."[42]

The roadside motel, an emerging phenomenon, had a questionable moral status through the 1950s. John Jakle and Warren Belasco, historians of roadside American culture, point out that early motels "developed an unsavory reputation in the popular media." Both use as evidence J. Edgar Hoover's famous 1940 attack on motels, in which he claimed that "behind many alluring roadside signs are dens of vice and corruption."[43]

As more and more motels sprouted across the American landscape, motel referral organizations appeared. Such "chains," explains Jakle, comprised "independently owned motels whose owners adhere to set standards and aid one another by supporting national advertising and a reservation and referral system."[44] According to Schafer, this system did not fit the progressive nature of his emerging tourist empire because of the racial politics of the time. And his attitude certainly did little to endear him to area whites already suspicious of South of the Border. Schafer opened his first motel in 1954, the same year the U.S. Supreme Court handed down its *Brown v. Board of Education* decision banning segregated public schools and thereby polarizing the South.[45] In 1979, Schafer told Maxa, "In 1954, we were admitted to what was then a mutual referral organization [of motel owners] but within 18 months were asked to resign, which we did. The reason (never stated openly, but told to us personally by the top brass) was that we accepted Negroes on equal basis with anyone else who had the $$$." Schafer defended his progressivism regarding race: "Of course, we were the first major motel/restaurant south of Washington who *from the start* always had an open door policy—first come, first served. And also we checked only the color of their money, not their skins."[46] In the early 1980s, a Schafer associate reiterated the claim that even before the federal government demanded it, Schafer served blacks at South of the Border: "There was never a sit in at South of the Border. There was a demonstration conducted by the Ku Klux Klan in retaliation for his opening these facilities to black people."[47] At that same time, Gloria Blackwell, a black professor teaching in Atlanta who had grown up with Schafer in Little Rock, also described his efforts on behalf of African Americans. Blackwell regarded Schafer "almost like a brother," and the two had worked together to educate and register black voters. According to Blackwell, "I can speak for the citizens—for the black citizens in Little Rock and Dillon County, and we have always seen him as, first a friend, for things that had to do with civil rights, education, health, welfare, any of those efforts; in those efforts we worked together. . . . Everything he has ever done has been consistent with a philosophy of dedication to the improvement of human rights."[48]

Despite such public encomiums, little hard evidence substantiates Schafer's claim that South of the Border was an integrated space from the beginning. The ads and articles in the *Dillon Herald* from the 1950s and 1960s do not mention African American patrons, and the Carolina Studios Photographic Collection at the University of South Carolina's South Caroliniana Library shows images only of black workers, not patrons.[49] And ads run by South of the Border from this era offer no evidence that South of the Border openly welcomed African Americans. Even if he catered to blacks in some way, Schafer was not foolish enough to publicly proclaim his stance at that time. Economic tactics, often referred to as "the squeeze," were used to punish black or white South Carolinians who supported integration. Segregationists, as Edgar notes, applied "social ostracism, economic boycott, and political pressure . . . to force politically correct views."[50] The region surrounding South of the Border was notorious for its Ku Klux Klan activities, many of them organized by James "Catfish" Cole, an evangelical minister and general huckster from Marion County, South Carolina, bordering on Dillon. One of Cole's targets was the large American Indian population in neighboring Robeson County, North Carolina, and a 1958 Klan rally there provoked a massive protest by the county's Lumbee Indians, with both factions armed.[51] But Alan Schafer's tourist trap welcomed the Lumbee. According to Karen Blu, the Lumbee "proclaimed, whether correct[ly] or not, 'You can get *anything* [at South of the Border].' When it was illegal to sell beer, wine, and liquor in Robeson (as it was in 1967), Indians seeking to purchase any of these items legally often drove to this South Carolina tourist center, where they could also be entertained by the passing parade of, to them, strange people with strange ways."[52]

For groups marginalized by segregation laws, South of the Border clearly supplied a space where the rules of the racial caste system could be bent if not broken. Some form of spatial segregation similar to that described by cultural historian Andrew Hurley likely divided South of the Border. Hurley describes diners as compartmentalized "into different sections and rooms" that allowed customers to use the facilities "in a variety of different ways [and] kept people who had no desire to associate with one another at a distance." If a public facility "achieved a diverse following, it was as much the result of proprietors' efforts to keep people apart as to mix them together."[53] Schafer said that South of the

Border "accepted" black patrons, but he did not explain the conditions of that acceptance. Integrating leisure space could be a dangerous and even deadly undertaking in South Carolina during the 1950s and 1960s. In 1968, for example, three black South Carolina State college students were killed and twenty-seven others were injured by police when racial tensions escalated as a result of efforts to desegregate a bowling alley in Orangeburg.[54]

The broadness of Schafer's claim to be the first decent restaurant open to African Americans between Washington, D.C., and Miami negates the existence of black-owned businesses in the region. Furthermore, with strident opposition to desegregation in the South during this time, it seems unlikely that an integrated bar, restaurant, and motel would have flourished as South of the Border did during the 1950s and 1960s. However, South of the Border's customers were not just locals. Although travelers may have been less concerned with upholding southern segregation, they likely would have thought twice about rubbing elbows with patrons of color.

Throughout the 1960s, Schafer ran weekly informational ads under the headline "Pedro's Borderlines" in the *Dillon Herald*. The ads listed new employees and included employee announcements such as marriages, births, awards, and college acceptances. "Pedro's Borderlines" also showed that many regional community groups, such as the Boy Scouts, local schools and businesses, supper clubs, dance clubs, and historical societies, frequently used South of the Border as a community gathering space. While serving the local community, South of the Border successfully appealed to the growing working and middle-class tourist market. For example, the four March 1965 "Borderlines" ads included letters from happy tourists from Vermont; Washington, D.C.; New York; Connecticut; Virginia; and Maryland.[55]

Appealing to various consumers created an odd Yankee-Confederate amalgamation at South of the Border. From a 1952 ad announcing "Confederate Cooking!! (Yankee Style)" to various Yankee/Confederate jokes scattered throughout the "Pedro's Borderlines" series in the 1960s, it is clear that South of the Border was literally making Yankee/Confederate distinctions laughable.[56] However, that did not prevent the site from profiting from the glorification of the Lost Cause at Confederateland, U.S.A. During a time when many white southerners rallied around images of a romanticized Old South and the Lost Cause as a means of fending off calls to guarantee blacks' civil rights and to enforce desegregation, South of the Border mocked rather than sentimentalized these icons of the past in its advertisements.

Schafer's negotiation between the locals and the Yankee tourists is apparent in a 1965 "Pedro's Borderlines" that announced a new shoe, bag, and hosiery department at South of the Border. The announcement ends by advising the locals, "Hurry Senoritas, before ze Yankees clean out ze best numbers in ze Easter Rush!"[57] Furthermore, one August 1962 "Pedro's Borderlines" begins "Pedroland Invaded!" and quips, "There were so many people beating their way to pedro's doors Monday that five YANQUI SOLDIERS landed in a helicopter to beat the heavy traffic for lunch. If thees keep op, pedro may hav' to build LANDING STRIP ... then, YANQUI soldiers breeng all the buddies!" This extension of hospitality to "Yanqui" soldiers contrasted in the same ad with a segment labeled "Confederateland Flash" announcing the lowest score at Confederateland Golf with a picture of a stout and stereotypical Mexican figure wearing the uniform of a Confederate soldier.[58]

South of the Border's growth increased Schafer's success, wealth, and power. By 1981, Schafer had become the largest single employer in Dillon County; his employees, he claimed, included more than 100 American Indians and 250 African Americans.[59] One newspaper went so far as to describe Schafer, who had never won election to any public office, "as one of the most powerful politicians in South Carolina."[60] In February 1980, he received a position on the South Carolina Highway and Public Transportation Commission, an appointment that marked the peak of his official political power. He fell from that perch just a few months later when he was charged with buying votes in the 1980 Democratic Party primary in Dillon County. Schafer ultimately pled guilty to the charges, which stemmed from the presence of a box containing absentee ballots at South of the Border, and accepted a sentence of three and a half years in federal prison plus a twelve-thousand-dollar fine. Schafer nevertheless remained defiant, claiming that absentee ballots allowed African Americans to vote without harassment.[61]

He continued to defend himself from prison in a letter to the *Dillon Herald,* claiming that vote buying had been "business as usual" in Dillon County for years and that the racist underpinnings of the election and the history of disenfranchising the county's black voters made Schafer feel that "the rightness of my motives justified the means."[62] In 1982, Schafer took a more contrite tone, publicly apologizing for his crime on the front pages of the *Dillon Herald*: "I do not condone what I did. I am deeply ashamed for myself; for my family; for the Democratic Party and for the many friends I feel I have let down. My transgressions were not for personal profit nor for political power nor political gain. They were motivated by what I believed to be the best of reasons—love of the underdog, a fear of the concentration of power."[63] Repentance did not equate with submission, however. Although he pledged that such offenses "will never happen again," he also vowed "always, as long as God gives me strength, [to] fight for the poor, the underprivileged, and against the concentration of power in any man. This is what my life has stood for. I seek no recognition for it. I have never sought wealth for its own sake, but for what good I could do with it for my fellow man. Whatever may happen to me, these feelings will go with me to the grave."[64] By 1994, Schafer had become less apologetic and sentimental, and he again began to maintain his innocence: "I did absolutely nothing wrong, I just had a chicken shit bunch of lawyers." Although he personally was out of politics, his conviction "doesn't mean I can't give the sons of bitches who are still in it hell."[65]

Schafer also refused to let his time in prison stop the expansion of his constantly changing kitsch emporium, working to ensure that South of the Border appealed to the broadest possible consumer base. In the mid-1980s, the South Carolina Legislature quietly and with no debate passed a measure, sponsored by state senator—and Schafer friend—Jack Lindsay, that made video gambling legal in the state.[66] Between 1996 and 1999, Schafer added first the Silver Slipper and then four more video gambling establishments to South of the Border's amusements.[67] The issue of video gambling came to play a pivotal role in South Carolina's 1998 gubernatorial race, which pitted Republican incumbent David Beasley, an opponent of video gambling, against Democrat Jim Hodges, who largely dodged the issue. Operators of video gambling establishments, including Schafer, put a great deal of money into the Hodges campaign and ran negative advertisements against Beasley. A few weeks before the election, Beasley's campaign filed suit against Schafer and another video gambling mogul, Fred Collins, to stop the ads and force the men to divulge how much they had spent on the anti-Beasley advertisements. A judge refused the request, and after the election, won by Hodges, the Beasley campaign dropped the suit. The 1998 race was the most costly and nasty gubernatorial race in modern South Carolina history, but Schafer and video gambling appeared triumphant.

However, the legislature passed a Hodges-backed measure that required that the video gambling issue be decided by a popular referendum to be held in November 1999. But a month before the vote was to be held, the South Carolina Supreme Court ruled that by holding such a referendum, the legislature would unconstitutionally delegate its lawmaking responsibilities to voters. The court upheld the part of the law that stipulated that if no referendum were held, video gambling would become illegal as of 1 July 2000, and the video gambling parlors closed.[68] As South Carolina's most visible icon of tourism on the busy Interstate 95 corridor, South of the Border also suffered as a result of the boycott of South Carolina launched in the summer of 2000 by the National Association for the Advancement of Colored People as a result of the state's refusal to remove the Confederate flag from the statehouse grounds.[69]

Despite these setbacks, Schafer's unflagging dedication to his business resulted in continued growth and national publicity for South of the Border. A 1963 article in the *Union Daily Times* described South of the Border as "the object of much publicity throughout the southeast" and perhaps "the most publicized single tourist attraction on the famous north-south Route 301."[70]

In 1986, *Roadside America*—"the modern traveler's guide to the wild and wonderful world of America's tourist attractions"—featured the site.[71] The *Washington Post* named South of the Border the tackiest place in the Mid-Atlantic in 1996, prompting the *Columbia State* to quip, "Aside from quibbling over the Post's geographical acumen (just where does the South begin these days?) we'd have to say this award seems long overdue."[72] In 2001, *USA Today* listed South of the Border among the "10 Great Places to Stop the Car and Take a Look," while *American Heritage* dubbed it one of America's best roadside attractions.[73] Schafer ran his tourist empire until right before his death in 2001, often putting in twelve-hour days, seven days a week, even while battling prostate cancer and leukemia.[74]

Politicizing Pedro: The Strange Career of an Icon

Not everyone was pleased by the Mexican border-town theme and abounding image of Pedro sheltered beneath the imposing Sombrero Tower. Some observers saw the image as tasteless ethnic stereotyping, a controversy stimulated by contemporary concerns with political correctness and the emerging role of Latinos within American life. The strange career of Pedro further complicates South of the Border's story and Alan Schafer's philosophy of equality.

Pedro most obviously illustrates the relationship of the United States to Mexico; however, rather than presenting any realist depiction, the image more succinctly embodies how the South imagines and exoticizes Mexico and Mexicans. Cultural historian Helen Delpar traces the "flowering of cultural relations between Mexico and the United States" to the 1920s while pointing out that this "development of cultural relations could be replete with distortion and misunderstanding."[75] Fellow scholar Dirk Raat writes that beginning in the 1940s, "all things Mexican were the rage" in the United States, as exemplified by various Mexican art exhibits in New York City. In the realm of popular culture, "western" themes had influence in a variety of areas, including the architecture of American motels. According to Jakle, "Motor courts with facades integrated

Pedro (shown in 2001) is a recurring image in South of the Border advertising. (Photo by author)

around interior courtyards were reminiscent of Spanish haciendas, especially when they were constructed of stucco to simulate adobe. Motels with names such as El Rancho and Casa Grande appeared from coast to coast."[76] South of the Border's motels and its larger cultural landscape borrow from such cultural interpretations of Mexico.

Raat sees ethnocentrism as a form of collective egocentrism, "the habit of ordering the world so that components away from the 'self' diminish in value." Pulling from the words of cultural geographer Yi-Fu Tuan, Raat elaborates, "'We' are at the center, and as people are perceived as moving away from the center they are proportionally dehumanized."[77] In the instance of Pedro, the use of humor eases the discomfort created by this process of dehumanization. Are these representations completely free floating, or do they relate to real human or social conditions? An analysis of imagery at South of the Border and the official discourse explaining it shows how representations are innately connected to the political realities of the South's location in a global context.[78]

"South of the Border (A Short History)," a public relations document, poses and answers the question of how Pedro came about. In an informal style meant to appeal to tourists, the story explains, "Well, Mr. Schafer went to Mexico to establish import connections and met two young men. He helped them get admitted to the United States, and they went to work at the motel office as bellboys for several years. People started calling them Pedro and Pancho, and eventually just Pedro."[79] During Schafer's 1981 sentencing hearing, his lawyers brought up the story of the two Mexican boys to demonstrate his magnanimous nature, one of the major themes of the testimony on Schafer's behalf.[80]

The narrative of Pedro and Pancho moves further toward the dehumanizing and cartoonesque in *Pedro Presents South of the Border's Award Weening Billboards,* a short Schafer publication containing images of the early billboards.

In 1950, pedro, hitch-hiking down U.S. 301, on his way back to Mexico, got lost. Arriving at a place called Hamer, S.C., almost starving, he stopped at a farm, scrounged some bread and cheese and went back to the road to catch a ride.

A Hungry Yankee saw him, hit the brakes, and offered him $5 for the sandwich. pedro immediately decided that at $5 for a nickel's worth of cheese and a slice of bread, this was the place for him!

So pedro bought a wheel of cheese, 3 loaves of bread, borrowed a tobacco crate, and set up business by the side of the road. Sadly, no one stopped.

Desperate, pedro grabbed a board and wrote on it: SANWEECH $5. The Yankees still kept whizzing by. A day later, the bread getting stale, pedro changed the sign: SANWEECH $1. Six or eight people stopped. pedro was in business. Soon, he changed the sign again: SANWEECH 50 cents. Business Boomed! pedro sent for hees brother, pancho. They added another crate, and wrote two more signs, reading SANWEECH 10 cents. They were mobbed!

In the Mad Rush, pancho was run over by a New York Cab Driver who had no insurance. pedro decided queek, he better get off the road. Off the road, not so many Yankees pulled in to buy the Sanweech. So, pedro put up more Signs, and More, and More. An' pedro leev happily Ever Seence! Hope you are the same.[81]

This publication offers a revisionist history of South of the Border, changing its origins from a beer store operated by the shrewd, controversial Schafer to a sandwich stand operated by the disarmingly cartoonish Pedro. The "Mexi-speak"—incorrect grammar that mimics broken English spoken with a Mexican accent—appears throughout the "heestory," a parallel to the way in which southerners are often objects of derision as a consequence of their accents.[82] Pedro is depicted as the owner and creator of South of the Border throughout the complex and its official publications, including literature welcoming visitors and asking for their opinions of the services. It is almost as if Pedro is the public performance of Schafer's alter ego, an outsider who has exploited southern culture for economic gain. Yet strangely, *pedro,* a proper noun, is never capitalized within the booklet's narrative, while *Yankee* and *New York Cab Driver* are.

Pedro has been featured on almost three hundred billboards from Pennsylvania to Florida, all of them created by Schafer.[83] These billboards function as roadside material culture that illustrates the changing nature of the Pedro stereotype. In a 1997 article in North Carolina's *Raleigh News and Observer,* G. D. Gearino explains the shift in public sentiment. In the beginning, South of the Border "drew unhappiness because it was a peddler of beer; no one cared about it being a peddler of stereotypes."[84] "Pedro's Borderlines" from the 1960s show the lack of concern with the ethnic stereotyping Pedro represents. Instead, to the consumers visiting

South of the Border, Pedro seemed to represent authenticity and humor. A "Pedro's Borderlines" from 1965 announces, "Zee International Club of Dillon High School" came to South of the Border and "enjoyed a real Mexican Diner in the Acapulco Room these pas' week as part of their study program."[85] A couple from Fort Dodge, Iowa, wrote a letter asking Pedro to send a few copies of the menus "so that we might show our children your wonderful sense of humor."[86]

In 1979, Schafer dismissed claims that Pedro was "an unfair stereotype of the lazy, crafty Mexican." When accused of ethnic stereotyping, he admitted that he "plays on being Jewish in a small, Southern community." Schafer continued, "Once, a Mexican embassy guy wrote to a senator from New Mexico saying the embassy was hot, that we gave employers a bad image of Mexicans. I told the senator we had 100 good-paying jobs, above the minimum wage, with chances for advancement, and he should send some Mexicans down. I never heard from him again. They lost a chance to give jobs to 100 Mexicans."[87] Schafer seemingly made no distinction between representations and actual people. He also failed to recognize that Pedro might represent and perpetuate a problem that closely resembled the injustice against blacks he so strongly opposed.[88]

Over the years, as *Roadside America* observed in 1986, Schafer toned down the Mexi-speak on the billboards.[89] Gearino's article described a similar shift in the Pedro image: "Pedro, once shown in his swarthy, mustachioed glory, returned to the almost abstract image he enjoyed on a 1950s-era menu—a design that almost completely hides his face (although, curiously, he still seems to rest a lot)."[90] Schafer held fast to his mascot, however, unapologetically sneering, "We've had complaints for years that our advertising is insulting to the people of Mexico. You get all that politically correct stuff. [People] don't get the joke."[91] In 1994, he boasted, "I stay politically incorrect all the time. Even people who come in bitching and complaining spend money."[92] Yet just three years later, Schafer admitted, "We have to communicate with the present generation. These baby boomers do not have a sense of humor."[93] What is politically correct, of course, changes with the times, a phenomenon that may explain Schafer's reluctance fully to accept the political correctness of the 1980s and 1990s. Being politically incorrect remained acceptable to Schafer as long as his business made money.

During the final years of Schafer's life, Pedro almost completely disappeared from the billboards, replaced by a simple serape and sombrero on the corner of the billboards, which can be read as a commitment to more sensitive advertising.[94] With the changes in political correctness and the number of Latinos moving to South Carolina more than tripling between 1990 and 2000, perhaps Schafer thought the ethnic stereotype might cut into his profits.[95]

The images and stories of Pedro may not be "authentic" or "real," yet the mind-set and emotions they represent are. Examining the strange career of Pedro demonstrates how a politics of exclusion has moved from the realm of actual physical occupancy to that of representation. Is this a sign that the postmodern shift from truth and reality to representation and simulation not only is the province of privileged intellectuals but also has been growing up in the provinces—the small-town South—all along?

All Those Souvenirs

The numerous and strange souvenirs displayed at South of the Border further expose the complex cultural and economic relationship between the South and the global tourist trade. Regarding the Mexican embassy's complaint, Schafer countered, according to one reporter, with a "red hot" letter "in which he suggested the embassy perhaps instead should focus on the $1.5 million in merchandise he imports from Mexico."[96] For Schafer, money often lay at the heart of the racial and ethnic discourses at South of the Border—from his profession that South of the Border "checked only the color of their money, not their skins" to his argument that the money he spent in Mexico trumped his use of an ethnic stereotype.

South of the Border is a space that offers much to the discussion of positive and negative aspects of increased cultural exchange. The site turns hybrid identities into dollars. In 1995, Schafer opened Pedro's Africa Shop. In the summer of 2000, a sign at the entrance proclaimed to visitors, "This shop is dedicated to the millions of Americans whose ancestors came from Africa. We have hundreds of authentic artifacts (mostly made by hand) in present day Africa. And hundreds more to remind you of the joy and sorrows of African-American history in our great country. We hope you enjoy this shop and perhaps take home a souvenir of your visit to Pedro's South of the Border." On that visit, however, I found a handwritten note taped to an "authentic" African artifact—labeled "Coloninisation [sic] Figure"—in the shop: "This carving represents a French colonial figure. When colonialists first came to Africa from Europe many young girls would keep dolls such as this so that their own children might be as prosperous as the new visitors." Selling supposedly authentic African handcrafts without any understanding of the complex history of colonization can create problems. Such a stance is even more problematic in the South, with its legacy of slavery, especially when suggesting African admiration of European might.

Encounters such as this one with the African handcrafts at South of the Border symbolize the difficulties of cross-cultural understanding and the problems of commodifying cultures. The tourist trade clearly complicates southern culture while commodifying and thereby simplifying cultures. South of the Border, for example, memorializes the African American experience by selling "authentic" souvenirs from Africa in a Mexican-themed tourist spot created by a progressive Jewish man in the predominantly Anglo, conservative, and Protestant American South.

In the aptly titled "Into the Future: Tourism, Language and Art," Peter Wollen discusses how "art, in particular, has developed a special relationship with tourism as its artisanal base has been reshaped as a department of the souvenir industry." Discussing the "circulation of images and discourses," Wollen writes, "The flow from low to high and from periphery to core has been discussed in terms of appropriation and innovation, while the opposite flow has been seen as vulgarization and its end product has been dismissed as kitsch."[97] Wollen sees kitsch not as a degraded form of trash or the antithesis of art. Rather, in his view, "modernism is being succeeded not by a totalizing Western postmodernism but by a hybrid new aesthetic in which the new corporate forms of communication and display will be constantly confronted by new vernacular forms of invention and expression."[98] South of the Border should be critiqued for its complexities—represented as much by the juxtaposition of plastic Horny Hillbillies molded in China and wooden statues of Frenchmen carved in Africa as by the outlandish decor—and not disregarded simply because of its status as a kitsch roadside attraction.

South of the Border can also symbolize the fading distinction between high and low culture. Artist and photographer Ruben Ortiz Torres exhibited a photo depicting South of the Border's Sombrero Tower in a 1998 art show. He did not simply celebrate the kitsch of the tower but rather utilized the structure as a critique of cultural appropriation. The artist compared the photograph to one taken in Guatemala: "In Guatemala they do this dance which is called the Dance of the Mexicans, and a Guatemalan guy dresses as a Mexican guy. He wears the same iconography, the big hat, the gun—they've seen Mexican films from the 1930s—so there's the gun, the tequila, whatever." The artist believed that the photos and their subjects "convey more information about Guatemala and South Carolina than they do about Mexico." He explained, "For me, what all this means is that whenever we see any representation—no matter how objective or scientific—it's always telling us more about who's doing it than what's being represented."[99] With this understanding, the Sombrero Tower, South of the Border, and the merchandise sold there speak most clearly of Alan Schafer's culture and the perspectives he gained during his life in the South.

Concluding Schafer's Story

The rise of South of the Border is primarily a story about power and identity in the context of commercialized leisure. Schafer worked below the surface and sometimes above the law to "give those bastards"—that is, the ruling white elite—"hell." Schafer inhabited both dominant and subordinate positions. His power came from his qualified whiteness, his wealth, and his connections. The fact that he was not "lily-white" and did not completely defer to the local elite and to white supremacy made him a threat to the dominant white southern society. His understanding that his beer distribution business succeeded because of "loyalty in the black accounts" led to his professed focus on "the color of their money, not their skin" within South of the Border. Perhaps late in life he shifted the nature of his billboards to avoid offending the growing population and purchasing power of Latinos. Schafer took risks, but he ultimately understood the complexities of his consumers' identities, tastes, and preferences.

Schafer often framed South of the Border as a place that had almost constructed itself. As he told one journalist, the creation of South of the Border was "all an accident. We didn't anticipate the tourists." Schafer was pushed into the food-service business to obtain social acceptability. In addition, he claimed that his souvenir trade began when a northern salesman stopped at South of the Border without enough money to get home. "He had a station wagon filled with plush toys—bears, elephants. So I bought them. I took about a five-times markup, and I put these animals on all the shelves, and in three weeks they were gone. And I said, 'Jesus.'" Schafer also reported that travelers' demand pushed him into the motel business: "They'd aim for South of the Border after seeing our signs, thinking that we had a motel here." Schafer explained, "For a while, we had them sleeping on the floor in the dining room. Then I thought, 'Well, this is silly, to have them staying here for free.'"[100] The supposed accidents imply that the consumers (the tourists and local patrons) played an important role in how South of the Border evolved. The story of Alan Schafer is important, but it must be complicated further by examining how people perceived, interacted with, and consumed South of the Border as a product. Why people stop at South of the Border is not an accident but rather an important part of the roadside attraction's history and allure.

Schafer intently listened to the voice and the power of patrons' dollars. In making a profit, Schafer influenced and was influenced by social change. In the news story about Schafer's death, Anna Griffin wrote, "Schafer's life story has two central themes: Occasional shows of compassion and frequent examples of shameless commerce."[101] Does it matter if the motivations for social change stem from a belief in equality or a desire to make a profit? In America's commercial culture, change usually results from a combination of both impulses. South of the Border's story shows that social change and economic success are not mutually exclusive but are often closely linked. The story also demonstrates that spaces of enjoyment and leisure can also be serious sources for social history.

In a 1993 article, "Under the Big Sombrero," a journalist explained that some people find South of the Border distasteful because "for them South of the Border is emblematic of the New South, a monument to greed and bad taste, a place Elvis might have loved in his later years."[102] South of the Border is indeed bright, garish, and extreme, but that is part of its challenge to the normative ideals of what it means to be southern and who gets to be southern. South of the Border began by being tacky because it pushed booze and catered to different races. Today it is seen as tacky because of its proclivity toward neon and its offensive depiction of Mexicans. Examining South of the Border as a southern space expands the stereotype of moonlight and magnolias to encompass bright neon sombreros and "almost-kosher" country ham.

NOTES

1. Gloria Anzaldúa, *Borderlands/La Frontera: The New Mestiza,* 2nd ed. (San Francisco: Aunt Lute, 1999), preface.

2. Race and ethnicity are the central lenses of analysis for this essay. Yet other aspects of identity and power—for example, class—also play a part in South of the Border's history.

3. The few academic texts on South of the Border include an entry in Charles Reagan Wilson and William Ferris, eds., *Encyclopedia of Southern Culture* (Chapel Hill: University of North Carolina Press, 1989); Maria Rogal, "South of the Border: Down Mexico Way" (2000), http://mariarogal.com/pdf/sobweb.pdf (accessed October 2001); Nicole King, "The Story of South of the Border: A Southern Construction of Space" (master's thesis, University of New Mexico, 2001); Laura Koser, "Planned by Pedro: South of the Border, 1950–2001" (master's thesis, University of South Carolina, 2005).

4. Anna Griffin, "South of the Border Turning 50," *Myrtle Beach Sun News,* 19 March 2000.

5. Brett Bursey, "Meet Alan Schafer, Grandmaster of Tack," *The Point,* October 1993.

6. Rudy Maxa, "South of the Border Down Carolina Way," *Washington Post,* 7 January 1979.

7. Lawrence Toppman, "You're a Beeg Wiener at Pedro's, You Never Sausage a Place," *Toronto Star,* 27 January 1990.

8. Koser, "Planned by Pedro," does an excellent job locating South of Border within the context of American roadside culture.

9. Durward T. Stokes, *The History of Dillon County, South Carolina* (Columbia: University of South Carolina Press, 1978), 123.

10. Ibid., 127–28.

11. Herbert Ravenel Sass, ed., *The Story of the South Carolina Low Country* (West Columbia, S.C.: Hyer, 1956), 410; Maxa, "South of the Border," 16.

12. Bursey, "Meet Alan Schafer."

13. Walter Edgar, *South Carolina: A History* (Columbia: University of South Carolina Press, 1998), 485, 489.

14. Stokes, *History of Dillon County,* 360.

15. Griffin, "South of the Border Turning 50"; Sass, *Story of the South Carolina Low Country,* 410.

16. Stokes, *History of Dillon County,* states that most county residents who practiced formal religion were Baptist, Presbyterian, or Methodist.

17. "The Alan Schafer Story," *Dillon Herald,* 29 April 1982.

18. Stokes, *History of Dillon County,* 123, 376.

19. Ibid., 297; "Sentence Proceedings before the Court," *Dillon Herald,* 24 November 1981, in "Alan Schafer Story."

20. Stokes, *History of Dillon County,* 297; Maxa, "South of the Border."

21. Maxa, "South of the Border."

22. Sass, *Story of the South Carolina Low Country,* 411.

23. Edgar, *South Carolina,* 513.

24. Pete Daniel, *Lost Revolutions: The South in the 1950s* (Chapel Hill: University of North Carolina Press, 2000), 9. For the Second World War's importance to southern culture, see George Brown Tindall, *The Emergence of the New South, 1913–1945* (Baton Rouge: Louisiana State University Press, 1967); Pete Daniel, "Going among Strangers: Southern Reactions to World War II," *Journal of American History* 77 (December 1990): 888–91; Neil McMillen, ed., *Remaking Dixie: The Impact of World War II on the American South* (Jackson: University Press of Mississippi, 1990); Charles Chamberlain, *Victory at Home: Manpower and Race in the American South during World War II* (Athens: University of Georgia Press, 2003).

25. Edgar, *South Carolina,* 571. For a discussion of the changes in South Carolina after the Second World War, see Edgar, *South Carolina,* 512–52.

26. The Supreme Court ruled in 1944 that blacks could not be denied the right to vote in Texas Democratic primaries. South Carolina acted swiftly to make primaries "private affairs," beyond the reach of federal laws. In 1948, Judge J. Waties Waring finally opened the primaries to black voters, opining, "It is time for South Carolina to rejoin the Union" (Edgar, *South Carolina,* 515–16, 519).

27. Ibid., 520–21.

28. Maxa, "South of the Border." Schafer later retold the same story in "Alan Schafer Story."

29. "Alan Schafer Story."

30. Koser, "Planned By Pedro," 10; "Will Flood County with $2.00 Bills," *Dillon Herald,*, 26 August 1948; "Schafer $2 Bills in Circulation," *Dillon Herald*, 2 September 1948.

31. Maxa, "South of the Border."

32. Seth Forman, *Blacks in the Jewish Mind: A Crisis of Liberalism* (New York: New York University Press, 1998), 34–35.

33. Joseph Melvin Schafer, interview by Dale Rosengarten and Klyde Robinson, 11 July 1995, 30–32, Jewish Heritage Project, Robert Scott Small Library, College of Charleston, Charleston, S.C.; Griffin, "South of the Border Turning 50"; "South of the Border (A Short History)" (2000). This document was given to me when I met with Suzanne Pelt, head of public relations at South of the Border, in 2000. It appears to be the document given to journalists or other interested parties throughout the years because the information within the piece reappears in articles on South of the Border over the past twenty years.

34. Bursey, "Meet Alan Schafer"; Schafer, interview, 31–32. Alan Schafer's brother, Joseph Schafer, explained that Alan originally opposed the sale of food because it was too much trouble. However, the Dillon County sheriff, according to Joseph, complained (Schafer, interview). Social codes, if not the law, clearly pushed South of the Border to diversify its focus beyond beer.

35. "South of the Border (A Short History)"; Earl Swift, "South of the Border Is the Big Enchilada of East Coast Tourism," *Baltimore Sun*, 14 April 1996.

36. "The History of South of the Border," in *Discover Dillon County: Quietly Progressive South Living* (Dillon: Dillon County Chamber of Commerce, 1994), 10.

37. Ibid.; "History of South of the Border," 10.

38. Bev Ballard, "Palmetto Pathways," *Union Daily Times*, 10 June 1963.

39. *Dillon Herald*, 16 November 1962; Charles Hillinger, "The Big Bang; Business Booms All Year Round at the Nation's Biggest Fireworks Stand," *Los Angeles Times*, 4 July 1989. During the late 1990s, Schafer led the way in Dillon County with video gambling establishments. The games were not legal in North Carolina; however, North Carolinians made a large part of the consumer base in neighboring South Carolina (Catherine Pritchard, "North Carolinians Place Their Bets," *Fayetteville Observer-Times*, 2 March 1997). It was illegal to advertise video gambling in South Carolina. Schafer placed the signs advertising the Silver Slipper (South of the Border's first video gambling establishment) a few yards away in North Carolina, while the Silver Slipper was located in South Carolina.

40. "NC Highway Commission Proposes I-95 Route to SC Line," *Dillon Herald*, 16 December 1964.

41. "Roadside Legacy," *St. Petersburg Times*, 21 July 2001.

42. Maxa, "South of the Border."

43. John Jakle, "Motel by the Roadside: America's Room for the Night," in *Fast Food, Stock Cars, and Rock 'n' Roll: Place and Space in American Pop Culture*, ed. George O. Carney (Lanham, Md.: Rowman and Littlefield, 1995), 180; John Jakle, Keith Sculle, and Jefferson Rogers, eds., *The Motel in America* (Baltimore: Johns Hopkins University Press, 1996), 16–17; Warren Belasco, *Ameri-*

cans on the Road: From Autocamp to Motel, 1910–1945 (Baltimore: Johns Hopkins University Press, 1979), 168.

44. Jakle, "Motel by the Roadside," 184; Jakle, Sculle, and Rogers, Motel in America, 138–39.

45. For the effects of the 1954 Supreme Court decision on South Carolina, see Daniel, Lost Revolutions, 195–96, 228–50; Edgar, South Carolina, 522–29.

46. Maxa, "South of the Border."

47. "Sentence Proceedings before the Court," in "Alan Schafer Story."

48. Ibid.

49. Koser, "Planned by Pedro," 35–37, discusses the pictures of South of the Border's workers in the Carolina Studios Photographic Collection. Studies of how consumers understood, used, and remember the roadside attraction are needed.

50. Edgar, South Carolina, 526–27.

51. Timothy B. Tyson, Radio Free Dixie: Robert F. Williams and the Roots of Black Power (Chapel Hill: University of North Carolina Press, 2001), 79; Daniel, Lost Revolutions, 208.

52. Karen I. Blu, The Lumbee Problem: The Making of an American Indian People (1980; Lincoln: University of Nebraska Press, 2001), 12.

53. Andrew Hurley, Diners, Bowling Alleys, and Trailer Parks: Chasing the American Dream in Postwar Consumer Culture (New York: Basic Books, 2001), 83.

54. Jack Bass and Jack Nelson, The Orangeburg Massacre (Macon, Ga.: Mercer University Press, 1986); Hurley, Diners, Bowling Alleys, and Trailer Parks, 190.

55. "Pedro's Borderlines," Dillon Herald, 5, 11, 18, 25 March 1965.

56. Dillon Herald, 9 October 1952. There was also a billboard for South of the Border that read "Confederate Cookin' Yankee Style!" The images on the billboard included a Confederate flag and the American flag on the right side and a sombrero and serape on the left. The image can be found in Pedro Presents South of the Border's Award Weening Billboards, n.d. (sold in the souvenir shops at South of the Border).

57. "Pedro's Borderlines," Dillon Herald, 18 March 1965.

58. Ibid., 8 August 1962.

59. "Sentence Proceedings before the Court," in "Alan Schafer Story."

60. "Schafer, Two Others Named in Indictment," Columbia Record, 29 June 1981.

61. "Schafer to Learn How Much Prison Time He Must Serve," Columbia Record, 10 February 1982; Anne Marshall, "Suspended Councilman Pleads Guilty to Three Counts of Vote Fraud," Columbia Record, 13 July 1981; Jack L. Truluck, "Probe Narrowing in Dillon County Vote Buying Saga," Columbia State, 2 February 1981. During the 1980 Democratic primary, the contested election was for the sheriff's office. Roy Lee, the incumbent and a Schafer ally, had recently appointed the first black deputies in Dillon County's history. Greg Rogers, Lee's challenger, was supported by his father, Pete Rogers, another major Dillon County political player. Schafer accused the Rogers camp of attempting to challenge the integration of public offices in the county. Individuals from both sides

were convicted of buying votes. The absentee ballots were sent through the mail, making the crime a federal offense. The authorities located the absentee ballot box at South of the Border. Therefore, it is logical to conclude that South of the Border was a space for local political action as well as a tourist attraction.

62. "Alan Schafer Story."

63. In "Alan Schafer Story," South of the Border's owner explained that "Pete Rogers had already secured the election of his son-in-law, Jack McInnis, to the Dillon County seat in the S.C. House of Representatives." Therefore, Schafer reasoned that the elder Rogers was attempting to become a "one-man dictator" in Dillon County. "If Rogers could win the Sheriff's office, he would control the top three Dillon County political offices in his immediate family." In the hotly contested election, Rogers received 4,686 votes to Lee's 3,905. However, Lee received 1,265 absentee ballot votes to Rogers's 81 (Truluck, "Probe Narrowing").

64. "Alan Schafer Story."

65. Bursey, "Meet Alan Schafer."

66. Will Moredock, *Banana Republic: A Year in the Heart of Myrtle Beach* (Charleston, S.C.: Frontline, 2003), 45. Moredock explains that the change in the budget bill was not noticed until lawyers pointed it out in a 1988 case where the owner of a convenience store with video gambling machines was sued. In 1991 the state Supreme Court upheld the ruling. During the 1990s in South Carolina, the industry grew rapidly. By 1999, the industry brought in $2.8 billon with more than thirty thousand machines throughout South Carolina ("S.C. Court Rejects Video Gambling Referendum," *Washington Post*, 14 October 1999).

67. "South of the Border (A Short History)." After the Silver Slipper, Schafer opened the Golden Eagle in 1997 and the Orient Express and Pedro's Hideaway in 1998. The Golden Eagle was the smallest poker mall (as they were called by the industry) and the only one not open twenty-four hours a day.

68. Michael Sponhour, "Gov.-Elect Hodges Wants Final Step in S.C. Video Poker War to Be a Statewide Referendum," *Columbia State*, 19 November 1998; Cliff LeBlanc and Douglas Pardue, "Video Poker Operators Says [*sic*] Court Will Put Them Out of Business," *Columbia State*, 29 April 1999; Cliff LeBlanc, "No Poker Vote, S.C. Supreme Court Decision Halts Games by July 1, 2000," *Columbia State*, 15 October 1999; "S.C. Court Rejects Video Gambling Referendum"; David Firestone, "South Carolina High Court Derails Video Poker Games," *New York Times*, 15 October 1999.

69. The Confederate flag debate also hurt Beasley's 1998 reelection campaign for governor. In 1996 he professed that "he had been shown—through prayer and Bible reading—that the Confederate flag should come down." This was a reversal from his previous stance, and it greatly angered his conservative base. Beasley tried to avoid the issue, but, like video gambling, it fueled his 1998 defeat (Moredock, *Banana Republic*, 39).

70. Ballard, "Palmetto Pathways."

71. Jack Barth and Doug Kirby, *Roadside America* (New York: Simon and Schuster, 1986), 15–16. South of the Border is also featured in the new and updated *Roadside America* (New York: Simon and Schuster, 1992), 107–10.

72. Eva Zibart, "Tack Mentality," *Washington Post,* 12 July 1996; "Talk about Town," *Columbia State,* 24 July 1996.

73. "10 Great Places to Stop the Car and Take a Look," *USA Today,* 3 August 2001; John Margolies, "The Best Roadside Attractions," *American Heritage,* April 2001, 18.

74. Griffin, "South of the Border Turning 50."

75. Helen Delpar, *The Enormous Vogue of Things Mexican: Cultural Relations between the United States and Mexico, 1920–1935* (Tuscaloosa: University of Alabama Press, 1992), vii–viii.

76. W. Dirk Raat, *Mexico and the United States: Ambivalent Vistas* (Athens: University of Georgia Press, 1992), 196–97; Jakle, Sculle, and Rogers, *Motel in America,* 45.

77. Raat, *Mexico and the United States,* 1; Yi-Fu Tuan, *Topophilia: A Study of Environmental Perception, Attitudes, and Values* (Englewood Cliffs, N.J.: Prentice Hall, 1974).

78. For two recent collections that address the U.S. South in a global context, see Deborah Cohn, ed., *Look Away: The U.S. South in New World Studies* (Durham, N.C.: Duke University Press, 2004); James L. Peacock, Harry L. Watson, and Carrie R. Matthews, eds., *The American South in a Global World* (Chapel Hill: University of North Carolina Press, 2005).

79. "South of the Border (A Short History)."

80. "Sentence Proceedings before the Court," in "Alan Schafer Story." Schafer's generosity is well documented. Stokes, *History of Dillon County,* points out that Schafer gave extensively to "worthy religious, charitable, scientific, literary, and educational causes" on the local, state, and national levels (377). In an interview with the author in July 2000, Suzanne Pelt, public relations manager at South of the Border, pointed out that Schafer gave on average a quarter of a million dollars per year to worthy charities and highly valued education. Pelt also gave me a copy of the 6 July 2000 *Dillon Herald* with a front-page story and picture of Schafer presenting a twenty-five-thousand-dollar check to the Dillon County chapter of the Red Cross.

81. *Pedro Presents South of the Border's Award Weening Billboards.*

82. Barth and Kirby, *Roadside America,* coined the term *Mexi-speak* to refer to South of the Border's advertisements.

83. Rather than outsource the billboards to another business, Schafer created Ace-Hi Advertisements, which designed and created all of the numerous advertisements for Schafer's businesses.

84. G. D. Gearino, "Hasta la Vista, Pedro: South of the Border's Politically Incorrect Mascot Gets a Makeover, but Don't Think He's Running Scared," *Raleigh News and Observer,* 17 October 1997.

85. "Pedro's Borderlines," *Dillon Herald,* 26 February 1965.

86. Ibid., 8 April 1965. Schafer chose the letters that appeared in "Pedro's Borderlines," and his purpose was to promote his business. The owner filtered the letters from tourists that have become part of the public record.

87. Maxa, "South of the Border."

88. The ethnic stereotype of Pedro is a part of a similar discourse of ethnocentrism and prejudice. However, it is different than segregation and disenfranchisement. For example, the fight for civil rights in the 1950s and 1960s was primarily about the access to political power through voting and the access of actual embodied persons to public places, such as schools, restaurants, movie theaters, etc. The more recent discourses of political correctness often focus on representations of people or ideologies, such as Pedro or the Confederate flag. This is not to say that the two are not innately intertwined; however, Schafer seems to be more comfortable with the 1950s and 1960s civil rights model that deals more with people's conditions and access to places.

89. Barth and Kirby, *Roadside America*, 16.

90. Gearino, "Hasta la Vista, Pedro."

91. Ibid.

92. Cathy Lynn Grossman, "Bordering on the Absurd: 1,000 Acres of Kitsch on the Road," *USA Today,* 29 June 1994.

93. Gearino, "Hasta la Vista, Pedro."

94. After Schafer's death, however, Pedro reemerged in full force on South of the Border's billboards. South of the Border's built environment often paralleled the trajectory of Schafer's life. During the last years of his life, Schafer changed the Cancun Saloon into the Antique Shop. While this seems to metaphorically symbolize the late stage of Schafer's life, I am sure that the decision, like most of Schafer's concerning his business, primarily involved profits. However, it is still striking that a business that began simply to sell beer no longer has a bar, though beer is still sold at the various restaurants.

95. Helena Oliviero, "Population Triples in 1900s," *Myrtle Beach Sun News,* 16 March 2001.

96. Gearino, "Hasta la Vista, Pedro."

97. Peter Wollen, *Raiding the Icebox: Reflections on Twentieth-Century Culture* (Bloomington: Indiana University Press, 1993), 190, 209.

98. Ibid., 209–10.

99. Valerie Takahama, "Seeing Where Cultures Come Together," *Orange County (California) Register,* 24 September 1998.

100. Swift, "South of the Border Is the Big Enchilada"; Griffin, "South of the Border Turning 50."

101. Anna Griffin, "South of the Border Creator Schafer Dies," *Myrtle Beach Sun News,* 21 July 2001.

102. Russell Underwood, "Under the Big Sombrero: Fear and Loathing at South of the Border," *The Point,* October 1993.

Selling the Civil Rights Movement

Montgomery, Alabama, since the 1960s

Glenn T. Eskew

A partnership of public and private groups in the South has created a civil rights industry that sells the bitter legacy of race hatred while celebrating the ostensible triumph of racial equality enshrined in the congressional reforms of the 1960s. Subsidized by local, state, and federal resources but largely managed by private entities, these memorials to the movement buttress a new American ideology that promotes tolerance. Black and white participants in the post-1945 struggle against segregation at first organized to observe important anniversaries and remember their comrades in a personal manner. Yet the promise of tourist dollars attracted governmental entities that beginning in the 1980s worked with the largely nonprofessional volunteers to finance the building of institutes and museums. Spontaneously occurring in a variety of southern locales previously noted as sites of racial conflict, all the independent efforts recounted the fight against white supremacy, the acquisition of minority access to the American system, and the success of black political empowerment. They set their heroic stories against a Montgomery-to-Memphis refrain that placed local events within the context of Dr. Martin Luther King Jr.'s leadership. As a result, visitors to the Rosa Parks Museum in Montgomery, the King Memorial National Historic Site in Atlanta, the Birmingham Civil Rights Institute, or the National Civil Rights Museum in Memphis receive similar messages symbolized by the ubiquitous display of monochromatic life-cast mannequins riding on a bus, sitting in at a lunch counter, protesting with signs, or marching to freedom.

In revisiting the past, however, some activists saw the potential of memorializing the movement as a way to reiterate the ideological goals of the struggle. They incorporated as educational eleemosynary groups rather than not-for-profit political action committees and hired staff to supplement interpretive exhibits with primary- and secondary-school lesson plans that promoted diversity. Assisted by nonprofit corporations that raised money for liberal causes, the civil rights commemorations received institutional support that added teaching tolerance to the nation's K–12 curriculum. The museums and institutes consequently became tangible expressions of diversity as inculcated throughout American schools. The memorialization of the movement in Montgomery, Alabama, reveals the evolution of civil rights commemoration from a marking of actual sites related to the struggle to the creation of abstract symbols of tolerance used for ideological purposes in America.[1]

Old Montgomery

Municipal leaders proudly boasted of Montgomery's heritage as the Cradle of the Confederacy, but for the two decades after King's murder in 1968, local people largely ignored its dual role as the birthplace of the modern civil rights movement, leaving that commemoration work to others. These efforts fell in with the larger struggle over historic preservation in Montgomery that concerned members of the public had waged for decades against the prophets of progress. With much of its downtown nineteenth-century built environment up to the State Capitol intact into the 1970s, the city existed in a sleepy haze that romanticized the antebellum past. Consequently, the historic streetscape from the period of the Montgomery Bus Boycott also remained largely untouched. As in other southern cities, local preservationists advocated the creation of historic districts and worked with state preservation officers in the Alabama Historical Commission to get their nominations through the National Park Service and listed on the National Register maintained by the U.S. Department of the Interior. Montgomery's role as regional center during the late antebellum, war, and postbellum years, which coincided with the height in popularity of Italianate architecture, led that style to dominate in the city, especially in residential architecture. Particularly well suited for the sunny South, the look featured bracketed eaves overhanging long verandas anchored by asymmetrical towers. It also found expression as Renaissance revivalism in commercial buildings, all of which gave Montgomery's built environment a distinctive flair.[2]

With the post-1945 sprawl of Montgomery's suburbs, the downtown stagnated as properties declined in value and became vacant. The federal interstate transit system, which promoted new subdivisions on the outskirts of town, also cut through older residential areas like a knife, cleaving neighborhoods in half and destroying whole blocks of antebellum Montgomery, especially between Court and Union Streets. Responding to the decline in real estate values, investors razed historic buildings and constructed new offices or parking lots or both, as happened on Court Square with urban renewal money during the 1960s. Yet this concrete bunkerlike three-story building remained in scale with its neighbors and did not alter the look of Montgomery's skyline.

Local preservationists worked to halt the destruction by emphasizing the city's architecture through the Landmarks Foundation of Montgomery, headed by its president, James Loeb. Wanting to tap into the one hundred thousand tourists who visited the State Capitol annually, Landmarks started preparing in 1972 and finished two years later a driving tour guide and map that featured many of the downtown antebellum houses as well as Dexter Avenue Baptist Church. By 1978, Loeb served on the Montgomery Historical Development Commission, which stressed adaptive use of the city's architectural infrastructure. Incentives such as the provisions of the federal Tax Reform Act of 1976 and the general cost of rehabilitation, which often came in at under half that of new construction, spurred a series of redevelopment projects in the downtown area, such as Union Station and the warehouses on Commerce Street. The city government promoted informational meetings such as a 1979 seminar, "The Past Can Be Profitable," which evaluated "recent economic benefits available from adaptive use of historic structures." As property owners embraced the strategies, it appeared that what remained of Montgomery's historic built environment might be preserved.[3]

Up on Goat Hill, state legislators slowly implemented elements of the Olmstead Brothers 1930 master plan for a governmental complex surrounding the antebellum Capitol by knocking down old residences on the nearby streets and building attractive governmental structures suitably scaled to the site in a planned fashion. Yet the conservative solons favored strict fiscal restraint in government and declined to use public monies to build enough office space to accommodate Alabama's growing civil service. In Washington, Congress started chipping away at the tax advantages for preservation, an effort that culminated with the passage of the eviscerating Tax Reform Act of 1986. Tommy Gallion, a local attorney and the chair of Montgomery's Downtown Unlimited, believed that the act "scuttled" the area's redevelopment by removing the economic incentives that had made many of the projects feasible. Gallion thought the change in the federal tax code "a real tragedy for historical renovation, the final guillotine." No longer encouraged to rehabilitate structures, developers began creating a new cityscape by clearing away the old look of Montgomery that had persisted since the bus boycott.[4]

Though dramatic changes would soon come to the Montgomery skyline, the movement to safeguard civil rights had already made headway. The first major memorialization of the movement in Montgomery occurred on 3 June 1974, with the designation of the Dexter Avenue Baptist Church as a National Historic Landmark. The recognition came just before the twentieth anniversary of Rosa Parks's arrest, which movement veterans observed with a December 1975 service and workshops at the church, which constituted an active "site of memory." Speakers who had participated in the Montgomery Bus Boycott twenty years earlier used the occasion to stress current concerns for racial justice. The president of the Montgomery Improvement Association, Johnnie Mae Carr, called for the federal government to launch an investigation into King's assassination and to designate his January birthday a national holiday. A host of civil rights celebrities joined her on the roster, including Rosa Parks, the Reverends Ralph Abernathy and Martin Luther King Sr., and Coretta Scott King. Although the event functioned as a family reunion of sorts and perhaps even a ritual in an evolving civic religion, it was not an exercise in heritage education and tourism.[5]

Yet civil rights pilgrims already had started to come to Montgomery to see the sites related to the bus boycott. At first the congregation at Dexter Avenue Baptist Church accommodated the visitors with brief tours of the sanctuary where King had preached, but the tours proved disruptive to staff and sporadic at best for visitors. More often than not, the pilgrims found the church locked. In 1979, under pastor G. Murray Branch, the congregation worked with state officials and local preservationists to restore the building's original Italianate look, an effort that required "correcting all deficiencies on the exterior" and stripping away the concrete entrance steps and glass doors used during the bus boycott, replacing them with something deemed more historically appropriate for a nineteenth-century building. The inside also experienced total "refurbishing," with extensive space downstairs allocated for the painting of a memorial mural depicting moments in the civil rights struggle. Parishioner and Carver High School art teacher John W. Feagin headed a team of artists that designed and painted the mural over a number of years. The congregation dedicated the restoration on Easter, 6 April 1980, and marked the occasion by changing the church's name to the Dexter Avenue King Memorial Baptist Church. Signifying its imprimatur, Landmarks Foundation of Montgomery unveiled a historical marker on 22 June, explaining the Italianate architecture and recounting the role of King and the congregation in the bus boycott. Feeling that they now had something to show, members sold one-dollar tickets to tour the church and view the mural in an exercise that basically comprised Montgomery's civil rights heritage tourism for most of the 1980s—that is, until a modest sculpture was erected just up the hill and around the corner.[6]

Morris Dees Comes to Montgomery

The dedication of Montgomery's Civil Rights Memorial in 1989 marked a transitional moment in a life filled with transitions for Morris Dees.

The son of a cotton farmer who managed the black field hands on rented plantation lands in nearby Mount Miegs, Morris Seligman Dees Jr. grew up experiencing the contradictions in the South's racial customs, whereby the law upheld segregation but common practice revealed a shared culture. Rather than defend white supremacy, Dees developed a sense of racial egalitarianism and a resentment of class privilege. His father sent him to the University of Alabama, where Morris launched a variety of enterprises with fellow law student Millard Fuller. Pooling resources and talents, the two invested in rental property but found success with Bama Cake Service, an enterprise conducted through the mail whereby parents could special order personalized birthday cakes for their kids. Other products followed. Earning their law degrees in 1960, the entrepreneurs relocated to Montgomery, hung out their shingle, and incorporated as Fuller and Dees. Using the postal service to reach a customer base had proven irresistible, and the two men conceptualized strategies to continue marketing their products to targeted audiences. They thought of a way to profit from civic group fund-raising campaigns by providing Lions Clubs or Pilot Clubs with personalized cookbooks for chapters to sell at a markup. The Future Farmers of America raised money locally by selling Fuller and Dees tractor cushions embossed with the group's logo. The men marketed plastic holly wreaths to other charities. Within three years, sales exceeded one million dollars through direct mail operations. Once they became multimillionaires, both men changed their outlook on life and put their marketing skills to other uses, Fuller with Habitat for Humanity and Dees with the Southern Poverty Law Center.[7]

At first disinterested observers of the civil rights movement, Dees and Fuller witnessed indigenous protests and were irrevocably changed. In his autobiography, Dees recalled the events of 1955–56: "Although the birth of the modern civil rights movement took place right in my backyard, I didn't pay much attention to it. The 381-day Montgomery Bus Boycott, triggered when Rosa Parks refused to give up her seat to a white person, passed me by completely." Feeling both "frightened and disgusted," Dees watched the Ku Klux Klan–led riot on the University of Alabama campus during Autherine Lucy's attempt to integrate the school in 1956 and later spoke out against this violent contradiction in Christian teachings during Sunday school. Yet when vigilantes stopped the Freedom Ride after its arrival in Montgomery in 1961, Dees successfully defended one of the Klansmen arrested for assault in the melee. Not until a bomb exploded at Birmingham's Sixteenth Street Baptist Church, killing four black girls on a Sunday morning in 1963, did Dees and Fuller begin serious soul-searching. In the spring of 1965 they escorted several ministers to Selma, and although the two lawyers returned to Montgomery rather than join the march, later that week they watched the thousands of black and white demonstrators walk up Dexter Avenue and, from the shadow of the State Capitol, over which flew the Confederate battle flag, listened to King's peroration, "How Long, Not Long." That fall, Fuller sold his share of the mail-order company to Dees for one million dollars, gave the money to charity, and moved his family to the interracial Koinonia Christian commune outside Americus, Georgia, where he later developed the ideas for Habitat for Humanity. In 1969, Dees sold the company to Times Mirror for six million dollars. The same year, he and noted black attorney Fred Gray filed suit to integrate Montgomery's all white YMCA.[8]

A series of civil rights cases had earned Dees the ugly sobriquet "nigger lover" and convinced him of the need for legal advocacy for race reform. In 1968, he joined Gray and teachers associated with historically black Alabama State College in an unsuccessful suit to stop the building of a branch campus of Auburn University in Montgomery's white suburbs. The next year, Dees defended the right of peace activist and Yale University chaplain William Sloane Coffin to speak when denied a podium at Auburn. With Gray, Dees forced the integration of the Alabama State Patrol. In a bribery case involving a right-wing Alabama legislator, Dees joined fellow University of Alabama graduate and Montgomery attorney Joe Levin Jr. on the defense. Their success convinced the two to open a new firm that specialized in "exciting and socially significant cases": in early 1971, they incorporated as the nonprofit Southern Poverty Law Center (SPLC) with the goal of fighting "the effects of poverty with innovative law suits and educational programs." Yet people in Montgomery still viewed them as "Levin & Dees, the firm with the businessman and the collection lawyer that had achieved a few fluke victories against the big boys in some gadfly cases." A combination of events quickly changed that perspective.[9]

While the center filed occasional suits ending some forms of racial discrimination, it struck gold with a death penalty case, not because of its expertise in the courtroom but because it tapped the racist tragedy for direct-mail purposes to fund future civil rights litigation. The SPLC's involvement in the defense of Joan Little, a black prisoner in North Carolina who murdered a white jailer as he allegedly attempted to rape her, brought the case to national attention and, when recounted in two million letters mailed to potential donors, raised $350,000 for the center in 1975.[10]

Dees realized the lucrative potential of promoting liberal causes and white guilt. He had sensed this opportunity when working as a fund-raiser for George McGovern's 1972 presidential campaign. Death penalty cases proved more attractive to donors than suits over brown lung disease. But when outbreaks of Ku Klux Klan activity occurred in Greensboro, North Carolina, and Decatur, Alabama, in 1979, Dees hit on a volatile mix perfect for target marketing. That year Dees set up Klan-watch to monitor white supremacist groups and document hate crimes that the SPLC might later engage through court trials. When a judge in Colbert County, Alabama, refused to marry an interracial couple, the center successfully intervened. Likewise, the SPLC came to the aid of Vietnamese fishermen harassed by the Klan in Texas. To publicize the threat of white supremacy groups, the center published *The Ku Klux Klan: A History of Racism and Violence* and produced a documentary that received an Academy Award nomination, distributing both to schools, religious groups, and community centers across America in 1982. In 1984 the center filed suit against the United Klans of America over the wrongful death of Michael Donald, a nineteen-year-old black man whom Klansmen had lynched in Mobile in 1981. The decision handed down in 1987 bankrupted the Klan, and, although Donald's mother collected only $51,875 of the $7 million judgment, the SPLC marketed the case in direct-mail solicitations that acquired millions of dollars for its endowment. Dees had mastered the technique of defending pro bono poor people in hate crimes involving other poor people and then using the trial as the subject for fund-raising. Awash in money, the center socked the donations away in its endowment, which had already grown to more than $12 million by 1985.[11]

To symbolize the multi-million-dollar enterprise with its twenty-six full-time employees, Dees constructed a bombproof building on a prominent point in downtown Montgomery as the SPLC's new headquarters. His success against the Klan had won him the hatred of white supremacists. Assassins had attempted to kill him, and in July 1983 an arsonist set fire to the center's offices on Hull Street. In 1983, he hired architect Robert Cole to design an eleven-thousand-square-foot tamper-resistant structure with state-of-the-art security measures such as electronic gates and sprinkler systems, all encased in gray enamel panels and one-way bulletproof glass windows in a postmodern style Dees compared to the recently completed High Museum of Art in Atlanta. Local critics called it the Poverty Palace. The site fronted the intersection of Washington Avenue and Hull Street and offered a commanding panorama of downtown Montgomery, from the bend in the Alabama River to the State Capitol, captured in part by obscuring the view from the antebellum Swan-Seibels-Ball-Lanier House, which the center owned as an investment. At one time, Dees considered rehabilitating the exquisite Italianate structure for use by the SPLC, but the pressing security needs that he now confronted seemed more easily resolved by building a new facility that, once completed, left the old house empty and a potential shelter for assassins intent on killing him. In addition, Dees realized that by altering the city's built environment, he could thumb his nose at his social critics and emphasize the constant danger in which he found himself. He thus paved the way for a dramatic shift within the preservation movement and the commemoration of Montgomery's history.[12]

Reconstructing Montgomery

Montgomery's flirtation with adaptive use of historic structures ended when the 1986 federal tax law removed the practice's attraction for developers. The city government under Republican mayor Emory Folmar kicked off the demolition by bulldozing the brick Italianate Saffold House, one of seventeen Montgomery buildings found worthy of documentation by the Historic American Buildings Survey in 1935. Under the newspaper headline "Page of History 'Wiped Aside' in Demolition," Loeb dismissed criticism of the Landmarks Foundation for failing to save the property with the pitifully honest statement, "We can't tend to everything." Indeed, Landmarks had its hands full just trying to restore the several houses it had moved out of the way of the bulldozers building Interstate 85 to Atlanta and Interstate 65 to Birmingham. In 1988, preservationists circled around the Seibels House, which Genevieve White of the Landmarks Foundation of Montgomery called the city's "prime preservation challenge." It too fell to the wrecking ball in 1988 when Dees had the site cleared and then sold the lot to the Retirement System of Alabama (RSA). As the bricks and plaster crumbled and the deep eaves of the bracketed roof gave way, Montgomery remembered its antebellum grandeur. Civil rights activist Virginia Durr, who had visited the house as a child, recalled its beautiful parlor furniture, velvet drapes, and role as a fashionable "social center." Marilyn Sullivan, an architect and planner who had struggled to save the building, compared its destruction "to ripping a masterpiece painting out of its frame just to substitute a new painting." Architectural historian Robert Gamble of the Alabama Historical Commission described the house as "state-of-the-art design," and noted, "We are virtually erasing an entire architectural era." Dees called the empty building a "hazard" and retorted, "We just wanted to get the house off the property." As understandable as Dees's actions might have been regarding this particular demolition, his comments also revealed a callous disregard for historic preservation and an emerging ahistorical and adaptable view of the past that would reappear in his efforts to teach tolerance through the SPLC.[13]

In the face of progress, Montgomery's historic frame buildings fared better than the city's brick structures, especially during the building boom of the late 1980s and 1990s. In several cases, purchasers such as the RSA, headed by investment banker David Bronner, donated to Landmarks a structure and the money necessary to move it to clear a lot for new construction. The RSA, which received its investment capital from the pension plans of Alabama public school teachers, found a partner willing to acquiesce to such projects in the worn-down historic preservationists who accepted compromised sites as a way to save the historic buildings. Founded in 1968, Landmarks Foundation of Montgomery had undertaken as its first project the restoration and interpretation of the Italianate Ordeman-Shaw House on North Hull Street. Volunteers opened the antebellum brick townhouse to the public in 1971. Landmarks soon had redeveloped several blighted properties along Hull Street, filling in empty spaces with saved historic buildings moved to the area to create "Old Alabama Town," an architectural petting zoo of nineteenth-century structures. By the 1990s, the living history museum compound had grown to include six city blocks. On other downtown sites swept clean of their history, the RSA erected multistoried buildings and rented office space to state employees and the lobbyists who dominate Alabama government. With Bronner's signature green roofs, marble entrances, and brassy finishes, the RSA high-rises gave Montgomery's downtown skyline a shiny corporate gloss.[14]

Federally funded progress claimed a variety of Montgomery's historic sites, many of them related to the civil rights era. Tax dollars constructed an interstate system through the city: Interstate 85 in the 1960s obliterated the white neighborhood of antebellum and Victorian houses between Court and Union Streets, and Interstate 65 in the 1970s divided Montgomery's black neighborhoods along Holt Street. Whether feuds between President Lyndon Johnson's administration and Alabama governor George Wallace's cronies caused the poor design or whether racists in the Alabama Department of Transportation sought revenge for the civil rights struggle, the outcome was the building of two federal highways that irreparably damaged the urban landscape. While Landmarks managed to move historic houses, the interstates hastened the decline of Montgomery's black neighborhoods, in particular around Holt Street Baptist and other churches involved in the bus boycott. The highways hemmed in historically black Alabama State College so that expansion required the school to condemn a local restaurant frequented by movement leaders. The subsequent growth of Montgomery's downtown hospital came at the expense of a number of black middle-class houses on Jackson Street, where Dexter Avenue Baptist Church maintained its parsonage. While in 1986 a state agency placed historical markers in front of civil rights sites such as E. D. Nixon's house and Trinity Lutheran Church, the highways destroyed the look and feel of downtown Montgomery's skyline and the surrounding neighborhoods that had persisted since the days of the boycott. Oddly enough, the destruction of historic settings by the interstates and high-rise corporate offices had little impact on Montgomery's memorialization of the movement because that process occurred in the abstract, disconnected from some particular locale associated with the struggle.[15]

The dedication of the Civil Rights Memorial in front of the SPLC on 5 November 1989 brought living leaders of the movement and the families of the victims to Montgomery for a somber ritual featuring Maya Lin's moving sculpture. More than four hundred people reflected on the sacrifices of the forty individuals killed during the struggle whose names appear on the monument. The mother of Andrew Goodman recalled the murder of her son and two others in Philadelphia, Mississippi, in 1964 with the observation that "this tragedy is not private," adding, "It is part of the public consciousness of the nation." The program featured comments by Rosa Parks and an address by Julian Bond, whose association with the SPLC dated back to its 1971 origins, when Dees asked Bond to serve as its first president. Dees hoped the dedication of the memorial would heal what he saw as a persistent racial divide in the city, so he planned the day's events to bring Montgomery's black and white leaders together to revisit the past through the message of the memorial while promising a brighter future through the center's work. To his disappointment, few locals attended. Nonetheless, the day marked a transition in Dees's life, the mission of his nonprofit agency, and the memorialization of the civil rights struggle in Montgomery.[16]

As a monument, the Civil Rights Memorial works beautifully. Dees suggested in his autobiography that after attending the 1987 state convention of the National Association for the Advancement of Colored People (NAACP), where he spoke on the martyrs of the movement and was asked to identify some of the people he had cited, he realized the need for a memorial to the fallen. In February 1988, the SPLC contacted Maya Lin and asked her to consider designing something suitable. Seven years had passed since the unveiling of her striking Vietnam Veterans Memorial in Washington, D.C. While criticized in some circles for its minimalist look—two long black walls of polished granite banked in the earth with the names of fifty-eight thousand veterans who died in the war chiseled into its surface—the public had embraced the sobering monument with an emotional outpouring of grief. Lin agreed to consider Dees's project. Since she knew little about the movement, having been born about the time of the Freedom Rides, the SPLC mailed her the video series *Eyes on the Prize* and the center's booklet on the Klan. After absorbing the materials, Lin accepted the commission and flew to Montgomery. Over lunch with Dees, she sketched out on a paper napkin a curved wall of black granite carved with the quotation from the biblical book of Amos that King had cited at the March on Washington: "We will not be satisfied until 'justice rolls down like waters and righteousness

Funded by Morris Dees's Southern Poverty Law Center, Maya Lin's Civil Rights Memorial recalls forty martyrs of the modern civil rights struggle. The striking monument was dedicated at a November 1989 ceremony that kicked off the regional effort to memorialize the movement. (Courtesy of the Southern Poverty Law Center)

like a mighty stream.'" This, Lin explained, represented the universal piece of the sculpture, and she envisioned something specific stationed in front, with the two elements connected. Within a few weeks, Lin had completed the assignment and returned to Montgomery with a model showing the missing specific as an inverted cone of black granite, the center of which percolated water that covered the smooth flat surface of the circular top, filling the carved white letters identifying the forty martyrs with dates and explanations of their murders that radiated out like spokes in a wheel. Behind this short black table, water poured over the black wall etched with King's quotation while white granite paved the plaza around the monument, offering visitors a place to pause and reflect. An advocate of touching sculpture, Lin designed the Civil Rights Memorial for fingers to feel the names of the dead through the cool water and for people to see their reflections, linking them to the past. "It's the kind of thing that requires patience, awareness and added sensitivity," she said just before its dedication. In explaining the aesthetic quality of the monument as "dissimilar elements maintaining equilibrium," she noted, "things can look different . . . but still be the same."[17]

The SPLC's installation of the Civil Rights Memorial proved a stroke of genius on the part of Dees. In addition to the $5 million a year he raised through direct-mail solicitations, which helped fund the center's $25 million endowment in 1989, he collected $650,000 in contributions earmarked for Lin's sculpture. The polished stone brilliantly underscored the center's work to bring to justice the perpetrators of hate crimes while also signifying a subtle shift into "teaching tolerance." Increasingly, memorialization of the civil rights movement in Montgomery meant promoting personal commitments to tolerance and the creation of abstract interactive displays such as Lin's sculpture rather than preservation of sites linked to the historic past. And others in Montgomery could not help but notice how Dees's skillful celebration of the movement padded the SPLC's endowment.

Through its Civil Rights Education Project, the SPLC supplemented its previous Klan publications and videotape with *Free at Last*, an extensive booklet on the movement that told the stories of the forty victims featured on the memorial. Noted authors of civil rights histories David Garrow, Taylor Branch, and Juan Williams assisted the staff in producing the booklet, which the center pitched as "designed for classroom use" and sold at bulk rates. Recognizing the power of this contribution, the National Education Association awarded Dees its Martin Luther King Jr. Memorial Award in 1990. The success of *Free at Last* revealed room in the market for pedagogical materials on the civil rights movement, so to exploit that need Dees launched *Teaching Tolerance* in 1991. The SPLC sent forty-six thousand schools abbreviated copies of the Blackside video

Eyes on the Prize subsidized by Pepsi and "education kits" that featured lesson plans on diversity training. Led by Sara Bullard, the SPLC's staff filled the "free to educators" magazine *Teaching Tolerance* with "high quality educational materials to help teachers promote interracial and intercultural harmony in the classroom." In time, noted historian John Hope Franklin and child psychologist Robert Coles joined as advisers to the biannual publication later edited by Jim Carnes. The materials proved financially rewarding, as the SPLC's endowment skyrocketed from just under thirty-four million dollars in 1990 after the memorial's dedication to fifty-two million dollars by 1994. Rather than spending the increased revenues on its civil rights activities, the center banked its endowment, becoming the wealthiest civil rights organization (and one of the wealthiest charities) in America. Selling an abstract ideology of tolerance cut the center loose from hustling white guilt derived from concrete examples of racial injustice. *Teaching Tolerance* soon reached millions of schoolchildren, while only thousands visited the Civil Rights Memorial.[18]

On the eve of the SPLC's dedication of Lin's sculpture, Dees addressed Montgomery's Rotary Club on the need to develop heritage tourism in the city. He suggested that the Civil Rights Memorial could "spur the city's development of other related attractions." Comparing Montgomery to Williamsburg, Virginia, Dees thought more should be done to revitalize the downtown through adaptive use of vacant buildings, a comment some historic preservationists in the audience must have found particularly galling, given the fate of the Seibels House. Dees proposed relating Montgomery sites to the Civil War and the civil rights movement. "I think in some way we're coming to grips with our past and can see it in a positive light," he told the gathering of elite white businessmen and civic leaders, adding, "I don't see it as a racial thing. I see it as an opportunity for us to put a good face forward for this city and this nation." Dees then enticed the crowd with the description of a multi-million-dollar civil rights museum that the SPLC contemplated building on an adjacent lot and that would, in Disney fashion, use the entertainment world's latest technology to tell the story of the movement. Although Dees has yet to open such a museum, Rotarians assisted other civic leaders in developing big plans for capitalizing on Montgomery's legacy of racial hatred for heritage tourism purposes.[19]

The federal government joined in the memorialization of the movement by designating the fifty-four miles from Selma to Montgomery a National Historic Trail in 1996. Georgia congressman John Lewis, who had suffered brutality at the Edmund Pettus Bridge in 1965 but had come to epitomize the success of the subsequent Voting Rights Act, spearheaded the effort, convincing his colleagues in 1990 to approve the funding necessary to recommend the route to the National Park Service.

Speaking in support of the initiative at a public hearing in August 1991, the Montgomery Improvement Association's Carr identified the SPLC memorial and the King site in Atlanta as evidence of a new interest in civil rights tourism. By 1995, the state of Alabama had endorsed the effort, calling the route a National Scenic Byway and leveraging money from the federal Intermodal Surface Transportation Efficiency Act for the building of trailheads, one of which would be located in Montgomery. In July 1999, Alabama's Department of Transportation completed its master plan for the roadway, but rather than place the five-million-dollar trailhead downtown near the State Capitol, where the historic march ended, it recommended the site of suburban St. Jude's Hospital, where the marchers had stayed the night before. Under the administration of President Bill Clinton, Washington money poured into Montgomery to finance federal ventures in heritage tourism.[20]

In conjunction with the trail effort, the federal government authorized the construction of a massive annex to and the renovation of its historic courthouse downtown on Church Street. The original structure, built in 1933 by the Works Progress Administration, not only housed the courtroom in which Judge Frank M. Johnson Jr. handed down many significant civil rights rulings but also was the site of the 1961 Freedom Ride riot, which spilled over from the adjacent Greyhound bus station on Court Street. During the courthouse work, the federal government's General Services Administration used the nearby abandoned bus station as an office, agreeing to turn that building over to state and local officials when the construction project finished in early 2001. Reflecting a legal system on steroids, the architect tacked monstrous new Greek Revival wings onto the original neoclassical building, giving the courthouse a sweeping plaza and overall appearance that local critics compared to the Reichstag. As a way to offset the damage done to the historic setting by the $50 million addition, federal officials promised $325,000 to be used in interpreting the civil rights legacy of the bus station site. The Montgomery Improvement Association, headed by its president, Carr, and the Alabama Historical Commission established the Greyhound Bus Station Restoration Committee and hired the Boston firm Main Street Designs to conceptualize exhibitions for the proposed museum, which they hoped to open in time for the fortieth anniversary of the event in May 2001. Yet state and local funding became an issue, and the forlorn bus station sat empty.[21]

Federal dollars subsidized the building of the Rosa Parks Museum that Troy State University Montgomery erected on the site of Parks's 1955 arrest in front of the historic Empire Theater. Ironies abounded as the bus stop became a battleground of a different sort when historic preservationists fought college officials over the demolition of the first air-conditioned theater in the South, where legendary country singer Hank Williams had gotten his start. The upstart urban branch campus of the rural college from Troy, Alabama, had bought several blocks of downtown Montgomery, rehabilitating some historic buildings as classrooms and offices but bulldozing dozens of others to make space for parking lots. Administrators in the overwhelmingly white institution watched from their suites in the Davis Theatre across the street from the Empire as hundreds of tourists stopped to read a historical marker erected by the Alabama Historical Commission in 1990 identifying the site. The plaque explained that in 1955, as white moviegoers exited the theater to board the bus, the segregated middle ground gave way and the driver demanded that Parks surrender her seat. She refused, provoking a boycott that lasted a year and started the modern civil rights movement. The reverse of the plaque mentioned that Williams had won a singing contest on the Empire's stage, launching his country music career.

By 1996, college administrators realized that they could deflect criticism for demolishing the Empire by replacing the historic theater with a memorial to Rosa Parks. The idea originated with college president Glenda Curry, who envisioned "honoring Parks with bricks, mortar and memorabilia that would draw people from near and far." Curry's top aide, Cameron Martindale, recalled, "We could see all the people reading the marker and taking pictures. We knew it had a lot of potential." To finance the museum and library, Troy State sold the nearby historic Bartlett Building to the federal government so that it could be razed for the courthouse expansion. Alabama's congressional delegation intervened to up the price tag from Washington's initial offer of $2.5 million to Troy State's demand for $7.5 million, which it claimed represented the true replacement value of the Bartlett site. With the additional $5 million, Troy State razed the Empire Theater and erected the Rosa Parks Library and Museum.[22]

To win the support of movement members, the white college administrators first courted Parks and her advisers and then appointed a blue-ribbon panel of black advisers, all the while retaining complete control over the venture. In 1997, President Curry, accompanied by the black member of the school's board of trustees, visited Parks in Detroit, convinced her of their sincerity, and won her blessing. Civil rights veterans Carr and Gray sat on the advisory board. The groundbreaking occurred on 22 April 1998, with a gala ceremony attended by five hundred people at which Parks received a standing ovation. Announced Mayor Folmar, "This is more than a testimony to sticks and stones, no matter how beautiful the building will be. It is a tribute to courage." As Troy State University Montgomery's first new building, the museum and library joined the old Paramount Theater, renovated as the Davis Theatre for the

To deflect criticism of its decision to demolish a historic theater to build a library at the site where the Montgomery police arrested Rosa Parks, Troy University added to the building a museum that celebrates the subsequent yearlong bus boycott. (Courtesy of Troy University/Kevin Glackmeyer)

The Rosa Parks Museum in Montgomery includes several monochromatic life-cast mannequins in different settings, depicting the bus boycott in a fashion that has come to characterize the exhibits that memorialize the civil rights movement in other museums across the nation. (Courtesy of Troy University/Kevin Glackmeyer)

Performing Arts, and an old hotel renamed Whitley Hall, both of which fronted the opposite side of Montgomery Street. In her comments, Curry emphasized that a "library is the heart of a university, and Troy State's heart will be engraved with Rosa Parks' name." Officials announced that Disney World had donated to the college an oversized mural of Parks and other civil rights leaders that it had used for a black heritage celebration. Curators searched for relics to exhibit in the museum space.[23]

Forty-five years after the historic arrest, Troy State University Montgomery opened the Rosa Parks Library and Museum with great fanfare on 1 December 2000. State Farm Insurance Company subsidized the day's proceedings. Civil rights celebrities joined more than one thousand people in the dedication of the ten-million-dollar facility. Women of the movement, including Coretta Scott King, Mamie Till-Mobley, and Carr, offered tributes to Parks. Alabama's governor, Don Siegelman, and U.S. Senator Jeff Sessions provided remarks for the occasion, as did Martindale, the new college president, who kissed Parks and said, "Just as you have brought us all together to this historic occasion, may the influence of your life continue to hold us together in unity." Chancellor Jack Hawkins declared the event the "day that the Lord has made," and announced, "Social change would not have been possible without the sacrifices of pioneers like Mrs. Rosa Parks." The ceremony revealed all the hallmarks of the new civic religion memorializing the movement.[24]

The architectural firm of Sherlock, Smith, and Adams designed the fifty-five-thousand-square-foot building that housed the museum, with a gift shop on the first floor, a library with twenty-five thousand volumes on the second floor, and a computer lab on the third floor. Eisterhold Associates of Kansas City conceptualized the exhibit space, which combines traditional displays with state-of-the-art technology. Visitors enter a room decorated with a panoramic photograph of the city showing the untouched skyline from the 1950s. An eight-minute video that uses interviews with participants establishes the feel of race relations in Montgomery in 1955. Transitlike folding doors click open, ushering the audience into a space in which computer-generated images on a vintage bus reenact the scene of Parks's arrest. The confrontation ends with other doors opening into a more conventional space filled with typical museum artifacts. One of the choice items, a restored 1955 Chevy Bel Air station wagon, is displayed as a taxi used during the boycott by Holt Street Baptist Church. Monochromatic life-cast mannequins fabricated by Superior Exhibits and Design sit inside the vehicle. While touring the site, the ailing eighty-seven-year-old Parks smiled when she saw a huge bronze bust of her head without her ubiquitous glasses, which she hated seeing on herself in photographs. Perhaps she also agreed with what Iota

Responding to the overwhelmingly positive public reaction to its Rosa Parks Museum, Troy University added a children's wing that features "time-travel rides" on the Cleveland Avenue bus. Visitors confront holographic figures from the past discussing slavery, the Civil War and Reconstruction, and the Jim Crow South prior to the Montgomery Bus Boycott. (Courtesy of Troy University/Kevin Glackmeyer)

To capture the tourist dollars of the thousands of people who stop by the Civil Rights Memorial in Montgomery, Morris Dees opened a museum that places the names carved into the stone memorial into an abstract ideology of tolerance. (Courtesy of the Southern Poverty Law Center)

Phi Lambda sorority president Lillian Parker told a journalist after viewing the exhibits: "It's fitting. . . . [I]t keeps the [civil rights] cause in your face." In the gift shop, Troy State University Montgomery sold books and posters about the civil rights movement, T-shirts printed with multicultural messages, and a variety of objects featuring Parks's image, including key chains and a three-hundred-dollar cookie jar bust with a removable pillbox hat for a lid. Seven thousand people toured the museum during its opening weekend.[25]

Trying to capitalize on the growing civil rights tourism trade, the Dexter Avenue King Memorial Baptist Church renovated its historic parsonage and turned the house next door into an interpretative center with a gift shop that sells such items as the one-dollar memorial parsonage fly swatter in yellow, red, or green plastic. Encouraged in the enterprise by the State of Alabama, which paid to print thousands of brochures for the Dexter Parsonage Museum, the mostly volunteer staff guides tourists through the seven rooms furnished to look as they did when King lived there from 1954 until 1960. The cement front porch still retains the small crater made when a dynamite bomb exploded in 1956, blowing out the front windows of the house but sparing the lives of King's wife and daughter and a visiting friend. A PowerPoint presentation places King's pastorate in the context of church history, paying special attention to the activist tenure of his predecessor, Vernon Johns. The low-key site with its modest appearance offers a sharp contrast to Montgomery's other civil rights venues. Also missing is the ideological agenda of teaching tolerance.[26]

With the Dexter Parsonage Museum and King Memorial Baptist Church, the Rosa Parks Museum, the proposed Greyhound Freedom Ride site, the St. Jude trailhead, and the Civil Rights Memorial, the number of Montgomery civil rights tourist sites competing for the time and money of travelers appeared to have reached a saturation point. Yet like the Troy State University Montgomery administrators, Morris Dees watched the thousands of tourists stop at the monument in front of the SPLC, take a picture, and leave, with nowhere else on the site to tour and nothing to buy. So he had an idea. He decided to turn his 1980s-era postmodern building into a museum and educational resource called the Civil Rights Memorial Center and the Wall of Tolerance, hiring Eisterhold Associates to design the facility. Dees already had moved the SPLC into a new and bigger office across Washington Avenue that local critics referred to as the Hotel Beirut because of its postmodern international appearance with stainless steel bombproof siding. Turning the Poverty Palace into a museum enabled Dees to explain to tourists who paid a small admission fee (free to contributors) the background story behind the monument and the sacrifices made by the forty martyrs featured in its design. It also offered an opportunity to recruit new members and collect donations for the SPLC.[27]

Although the dedication of the Wall of Tolerance was "not a Montgomery happening," more than 15,000 people showed up on 23 October 2005 for the event, with 250,000 more exploring the museum via the Internet. Dees estimated that between fifty and seventy-five local black people—none of them politicians or ministers—and an equal number of local white people attended. The rest of those who joined the gathering were SPLC supporters from around the country eager to tour the new facility. Entering the museum, visitors wander into the Overlook section—constructed on the former front grounds of the Seibels House but now situated above the memorial—where observation-deck-style telescopes pinpoint key locales in downtown Montgomery associated with the struggle for racial justice. This local story intersects with displays of newspaper headlines identifying not only the forty "Martyrs to a Movement" but also "The Forgotten" who died as victims of intolerance. A collage of photographs announces that "The March Continues," with pictures of people in the United States carrying a banner that reads "Fight Lesbian and Gay Oppression" and of international activists struggling against patriarchy and racial and ethnic discrimination. Every thirty minutes, the museum shows Jim Carrier's film, *Faces in the Water*, which tells the stories behind the names on Lin's monument. With a soundtrack similar to Aaron Copeland's "Adagio for Strings," the film sends its viewers on an emotional roller-coaster ride that empties its audience into a vast open space before which towers the Wall of Tolerance. Against this edifice roll down names, including those of Morris Dees and anyone else who pledges "to work in their daily lives for justice, equality and human rights."[28]

Despite occasional negative publicity about Dees and the SPLC's fundraising activities, people continued to donate money. The first serious criticism appeared in February 1994 as an investigative series in the *Montgomery Advertiser* by reporters Dan Morse and Greg Jaffe. The articles documented the defection of several key SPLC employees over Dees's vision for the Klanwatch program as well as over the absence of African Americans in daily decision-making positions. A November 2000 exposé in *Harper's Magazine* by Ken Silverstein described the center's budget, explaining that it had assets of $120 million in 1999 but spent less than 10 percent of that amount, with the majority going into the printing and distribution of *Teaching Tolerance*. According to that critique, nearly $6 million subsidized fund-raising, while less than $3 million paid for legal services. Nonetheless, the SPLC had added to its arsenal against racism materials to combat Holocaust deniers, militia groups, and gay bashers. Although it took on few court cases, the center had won its trial against Texas vigilantes who illegally policed the border with Mexico and had helped to lock away neo-Nazis in California. By 2006, the SPLC actively supported migrant tree planters and Hurricane Katrina construction workers through the Immigrant Justice Project. Its Intelligence Project led workshops with law enforcement agencies on white supremacist groups in the United States. Twice a year, the SPLC continued to distribute for free to educators more than six hundred thousand copies of its award-winning magazine, *Teaching Tolerance*, with its pedagogical tips on using multimedia in multicultural studies and dealing with bullies on the bus.[29]

Dees recognized film as a key tool for tolerance training. Since its video on the Ku Klux Klan, the SPLC has dabbled in documentary, winning awards for its efforts. During the 1990s, it mastered a form of docudrama that proved seductive to secondary school teachers and reflected a sensibility physically exhibited by the profusion of civil rights memorials that merged the past and present (like the faux bus doors that usher patrons through the Rosa Parks Library and Museum or the interactive impulse spurred by Lin's sculpture). A film about Rosa Parks, *Mighty Times*, won an Academy Award, as did *The Children's March*. But unlike the strict attention to academic rigor that marked Henry Hampton's *Eyes on the Prize* a decade earlier, the SPLC's films, produced by Tell the Truth Pictures, are of questionable historical accuracy. Directed and produced by Robert Hudson and Bobby Houston in association with Home Box Office, the docudramas mix actual film footage and still photographs with re-created images in a fashion that blurs the line between reality and fiction. For dramatic effect, people not involved in the historic events are interviewed as if they were participants. While the scripts follow the typical master narrative, the story line uses sleight of hand to promote its message of tolerance.[30]

The blurring of truth (and of time) fit the SPLC's abstract memorialization of the movement that saw as its true mission—in addition to raising money—the promulgation of a new civic religion promoting diversity. In a show of genius, Dees had combined an intangible ideology with the ephemeral donation. As a "crusade," the "Tolerance Movement" of the "National Campaign for Tolerance," as Dees's promotional literature explained, would "help rebuild a sense of fairness and community for our divided nation" by paying for pedagogical materials that would "inspire fair play and help stop the pain of intolerance." For "a tax-deductible gift of $15, $25, $50 or whatever you can spare," people could add their names—or those of anyone they chose—to the Wall of Tolerance. A continual stream of letters from the computer database flowed down the twenty-by-forty-foot curved black granite backdrop covered with running water that appeared to join the memorial out front. The technology broadcast on the wet shiny surface the personalized digital images of everyone who had taken "a stand against hate, injustice and intolerance." Visitors could access a computer control panel to search for someone who had taken the pledge. Or, perhaps even more importantly, they could at that moment swear their support for tolerance, type their own names, and then see them join in the continual flow of witnesses who had paid the price and stood up for justice. It was a brilliant idea.[31]

With *Teaching Tolerance*, the SPLC provided schools with the materials necessary to inculcate an abstract ideology suitable for and reflective of the emerging civil rights industry. With the Wall of Tolerance, Dees had developed another fund-raising approach that offset a decline in direct-mail solicitations. Whereas, at its height, the center claimed a mailing list of twenty million addresses, by 2006 that number had dropped to fewer than five million people. Dees explained the decline by suggesting that "all the Eleanor Roosevelts were dying off" and that the American Civil Liberties Union and NAACP similarly suffered. He noted that few people respond to e-mail solicitations for money, but he did not dwell on the Internet's capacity for reaching new audiences, as demonstrated by the number of hits the SPLC's Web site receives. The endowment certainly had not suffered, approaching $175 million by the end of 2006, with the center drawing around 5 percent to add to its annual budget, which that year totaled $28 million.[32]

Thus, in addition to public investment at the local, state, and federal levels, private contributions have subsidized the construction of monuments to the movement that provide a tangible shape to an otherwise ambiguous message. What began as veterans of the struggle gathering to remember past events at sites of memory has become a civil rights industry that manufactures an ahistorical interpretation of the social movement as a means of promoting a new American civic religion of tolerance. In Montgomery, whites who had no involvement in the historic civil rights struggle control the most successful of the city's commemorations, and the black veterans of the movement who participate in heritage tourism work along the margins. While historic preservationists fought a losing battle to preserve Montgomery's Italianate look, movement memorialists assisted in the redevelopment of the city's skyline. Now sensing the profits to be made, Rotarians and other municipal leaders in Montgomery hustle a tourism package that embraces the Cradle of the Confederacy's dual legacy as the birthplace of the modern civil rights movement.

NOTES

1. The work of Pierre Nora and his colleagues on memory as an interpretative tool in French history has influenced my thinking on the relationship of civil

rights memorials to the construction of a national ideology. See Pierre Nora, ed., *Rethinking France: Les Lieux de Memoire*, vol. 1, *The State*, trans. David P. Jordan (Chicago: University of Chicago Press, 2001); Pierre Nora, ed., *Realms of Memory: The Construction of the French Past*, vol. 3 (New York: Columbia University Press, 1998). The controversial scholarship of Norman G. Finkelstein has also prompted my analysis of the selling of the civil rights movement. See Norman G. Finkelstein, *The Holocaust Industry: Reflections on the Exploitation of Jewish Suffering* (London: Verso, 2000). The use of civic religion to explain the consumption of Confederate defeat and white supremacy in the Bourbon South provides a useful point of departure when considering the sanctification of civil rights celebrities. See Charles Reagan Wilson, *Baptized in Blood: The Religion of the Lost Cause, 1865-1920* (Athens: University of Georgia Press, 1980). For similar analyses on a national scale used to defend white supremacy, see David W. Blight, *Race and Reunion: The Civil War in American Memory* (Cambridge: Belknap Press of Harvard University Press, 2001); Kirk Savage, *Standing Soldiers, Kneeling Slaves: Race, War, and Monument in Nineteenth-Century America* (Princeton: Princeton University Press, 1997). On the use of a historic site of memory for ideological and commercial purposes, see Jim Weeks, *Gettysburg: Memory, Market, and an American Shrine* (Princeton: Princeton University Press, 2003). For an informed exploration of the relationships among monuments, heritage, and ideology, see John R. Gillis, ed., *Commemoration: The Politics of National Identity* (Princeton: Princeton University Press, 1994). See also the first collection that seriously explored southern memory, W. Fitzhugh Brundage, ed., *Where These Memories Grow: History, Memory, and Southern Identity* (Chapel Hill: University of North Carolina Press, 2000). For a discussion of methodology and memorialization, see Alon Confino, "Collective Memory and Cultural History: Problems of Method," *American Historical Review* 102 (December 1997): 1386–1403. The difficulties of commemorating negative sites are addressed in Kenneth E. Foote, *Shadowed Ground: America's Landscapes of Violence and Tragedy* (Austin: University of Texas Press, 1997). On civil rights memorialization, see Glenn T. Eskew, "Memorializing the Movement: The Struggle to Build Civil Rights Museums in the South," in *Warm Ashes: Issues in Southern History at the Dawn of the Twenty-first Century*, ed. Winfred B. Moore Jr., Kyle S. Sinisi, and David H. White Jr. (Columbia: University of South Carolina Press, 2003), 357–79; Renee C. Romano and Leigh Raiford, eds., *The Civil Rights Movement in American Memory* (Athens: University of Georgia Press, 2006).

2. The Italianate is documented in Mary Ann Neeley, *Montgomery: Capital City Corners* (Dover, N.H.: Arcadia, 1997); Robert Gamble, *The Alabama Catalogue: A Guide to the Early Architecture of the State* (Tuscaloosa: University of Alabama Press, 1987), 92–106, 323–29. Gamble picked up on the significance of the Italianate in Montgomery's architectural heritage (Robert Gamble, interview by author, 13 October 2006).

3. Responding to postwar demolitions such as the city's destruction of the Dickerson-Arnold-Greil Home, Ralph Hammond noted, "Montgomery has had more of its ante-bellum mansions razed than any other city in Alabama. Literally by the dozens they have been torn down to make way for new homes, new apart-

ments, and modern business establishments" (*Ante-Bellum Mansions of Alabama* [New York: Bonanza, 1951], 154). See also *Montgomery Advertiser*, 12 February 1974; *Alabama Journal*, 13 April 1978, 23 May 1978; Montgomery Historic Development Commission, "The Past Can Be Profitable," 5 February 1979, program, vertical file on historic preservation, Montgomery Public Library, Montgomery, Ala.

4. Olmstead Brothers, Master Site Plan, the Capitol Grounds, Montgomery, Alabama, 28 April 1930, map showing "General Plan for Improvements," Alabama State Planning Board, July 1945, and "State of Alabama, Site Plan of Capitol Group," State Building Commission, 7 February 1973, vertical file on state Capitol, Montgomery Public Library, Montgomery, Ala.; Montgomery *Advertiser*, 24 March 1992.

5. *Dexter Avenue King Memorial Baptist Church: A Brief History* (Montgomery: Alabama Bureau of Tourism and Travel, 1998); *Montgomery Advertiser*, 6 December 1975.

6. *Dexter Avenue King Memorial Baptist Church: A Brief History*; *Dexter Avenue King Memorial Baptist Church: Reverend Dr. Martin Luther King Jr. from Montgomery to Memphis, 1955–1968* (Montgomery: State of Alabama Bureau of Tourism and Travel, 1996).

7. Millard Fuller and Diane Scott, *Love in the Mortar Joints: The Story of Habitat for Humanity* (Piscataway, N.J.: New Century, 1980), 33–53; Morris Dees with Steve Fiffer, *A Season for Justice: The Life and Times of Civil Rights Lawyer Morris Dees* (New York: Scribner's, 1991), 51–103. Dees revised the epilogue in a reprinting of the book, *A Lawyer's Journey: The Morris Dees Story* (Chicago: American Bar Association, 2001).

8. Dees with Fiffer, *Season for Justice*, 77–78, 83–85, 89–92; Fuller and Scott, *Love in the Mortar Joints*, 51–75.

9. Dees with Fiffer, *Season for Justice*, 97–98. Dees and Gray had a public falling-out over Dees's testimony before the U.S. Senate Judiciary Committee when it debated Gray's nomination for the post of U.S. district judge for middle Alabama. See Fred Gray, *Bus Ride to Justice* (Montgomery, Ala.: New South Books, 1995), 294–97; Morris Dees, interview by author, 9 October 2006. Joining cofounders Dees and Levin as the third key administrator at the law center was J. Richard Cohen, who now serves as president and chief executive officer.

10. James Reston Jr., *The Innocence of Joan Little: A Southern Mystery* (New York: Times Books, 1977), 143–46. See also Fred Harwell, *A True Deliverance* (New York: Knopf, 1980), 123–38, 274–75, which notes that after the 1975 Little mailing at the favorable postage rate for nonprofits, membership in the SPLC doubled from 70,000 to 150,000, while its annual revenues reached $2.5 million in "public support" tax-exempt donations.

11. Reston, *Innocence of Joan Little*; Harwell, *True Deliverance*. A decade before, the Southern Christian Leadership Conference had found similar success using its direct-action campaigns as material for direct-mail solicitations, raising hundreds of thousands of dollars; see Glenn T. Eskew, *But for Birmingham: The Local and National Movements in the Civil Rights Struggle* (Chapel Hill: University of North Carolina Press, 1997), 314–16. In addition to its special report, *The*

Ku Klux Klan, the SPLC's Klanwatch, later renamed the Intelligence Project, publishes the quarterly *Intelligence Report*, providing the latest information available on white supremacist and other hate groups. Through educational workshops, the SPLC provides this and similar information to law enforcement agencies.

12. *Alabama Journal*, 26 October 1984; *Montgomery Advertiser*, 26 June 1984, 1 January 1985, 30 September 1986. Ironically, on the night of Alabama's secession, as bonfires and parties lit up the Montgomery skyline, looming above the celebration sat the Unionist Seibels's house in stunning darkness (Gamble, interview).

13. *Montgomery Advertiser*, 14 January 1986. Although a feud existed between Seibels and Confederate President Jefferson Davis, Seibels's granddaughter headed the effort in 1900 to save Montgomery's best-known Italianate mansion, the White House of the Confederacy ("City Losing Old Mansion to Neglect," *Montgomery Advertiser*, 1988, Historic Homes vertical file, Montgomery Public Library, Montgomery, Ala.; *Alabama Journal*, 19 May 1988). While Dees permitted the destruction of the Seibels house, he donated some of the outbuildings to Landmarks.

14. *Montgomery Advertiser*, 18 October 1989; Mary Ann Neeley, *Old Alabama Town: An Illustrated Guide* (Tuscaloosa: University of Alabama Press, 2002), xvi–xvii, 6–7, 14–21.

15. *Montgomery Advertiser*, 4 July 1999, 26 February 2000.

16. *Atlanta Journal-Constitution*, 26 October 1989, 6 November 1989; "Civil Rights Memorial Dedication Ceremony" (program), 5 November 1989, Civil Rights Memorial vertical file, Montgomery Public Library, Montgomery, Ala.; Dees, interview.

17. Dees with Fiffer, *Season for Justice*, 332–33; *Time*, 6 November 1989.

18. *Free at Last: A History of the Civil Rights Movement and Those Who Died in the Struggle* (Montgomery, Ala.: Civil Rights Education Project of the Southern Poverty Law Center, n.d.); *Teaching Tolerance*, Spring 2000. Since the dedication of the Civil Rights Memorial, the SPLC has distributed a number of brochures, including *Forty Lives for Freedom*. Within a decade of its dedication, the memorial had attracted nearly 250,000 visitors; see *Montgomery Advertiser*, 4 March 2000. See also *Montgomery Advertiser*, 13 February 1994, which lists the SPLC with $52 million in reserve, the American Civil Liberties Union with $14.3 million in assets, and the NAACP Legal Defense and Education Fund with $16.9 million in assets. Dees explained that the SPLC entered the field of pedagogical materials because of the exorbitant expense of similar resources produced by the Anti-Defamation League and Simon Wiesenthal Center. Dees credited Bullard with developing much of the concept of "teaching tolerance" (Dees, interview).

19. *Alabama Journal*, 24 October 1989. A week later, *Time* quoted Dees as saying, "Montgomery fought the movement at every turn but I think it can be a very positive cathartic thing for the city to face up to its past" (*Time*, 6 November 1989). Dees later restated his belief that people interested in heritage tourism "are interested in both Civil War and civil rights history" and explained that he had talked with Disney's Michael Eisner about creating an American Experience Theater–type venue in Montgomery that could interpret both events in a process

he defined as "essentially entertainment" but one that no doubt would carry a message of teaching tolerance (Dees, interview).

20. *Montgomery Advertiser*, 30 August 1991, 5 July 1999, 12 February 2000, 3 August 2000; *Long-Range Interpretive Plan, Selma to Montgomery National Historic Trail* (Harpers Ferry, W.Va.: Department of the Interior, National Park Service, Harpers Ferry Center Interpretive Planning, 2003). While celebrating King Day in 2007, Montgomery mayor Bobby Bright said that he would lead an effort to erect a monument to King, possibly at the foot of the Capitol steps, where the historic march ended in 1965 (*Atlanta Journal-Constitution*, 16 January 2007).

21. *Montgomery Advertiser*, 14 June 1999, 18 February 2000, 30 September 2000.

22. Ibid., 10 December 2000; Wayne Greenhaw and Kathy Holland, *Montgomery: Center Stage in the South* (Chatsworth, Calif.: Windsor, 1990), 41, 47, 55, 66. "Troy State University gears its classes to working adults, with class meetings scheduled in the evenings and in several locations" (Greenhaw and Holland, *Montgomery*, 47). While the college deserves commendation for rehabilitating two of Montgomery's historic buildings, had it followed the lead of other more sensitive schools such as the Savannah College of Art and Design, it would have realized the benefits of using an entire area downtown as a campus and renovated the Empire into a library and museum.

23. *Birmingham News*, 23 April 1998; *Montgomery Advertiser*, 4 December 1995, 20 October 2000, 10 December 2000. Troy State renovated the Paramount in 1989, and the Montgomery Symphony and Troy State Orchestra now use the facility for concerts (Greenhaw and Holland, *Montgomery*, 55).

24. *Rosa Parks Library and Museum Dedication Program*, 1 December 2000, vertical files, Montgomery Public Library, Montgomery, Ala.; *Montgomery Advertiser*, 2 December 2000. Other civil rights celebrities scheduled to appear included Ambassador Andrew Young, the Reverend Jesse Jackson, Martin Luther King III, Maya Angelou, and Juanita Abernathy (*Montgomery Advertiser*, 17 November 2000).

25. *Rosa Parks Library and Museum Dedication Program*; *Montgomery Advertiser*, 1 December 2000, 2 December 2000, 9 December 2000, 10 December 2000. A group ticket for the museum tour costs $5.50.

26. Dexter Parsonage Museum brochure, printed by the State of Alabama. A survey distributed by the center asks visitors to "tell us what you think about our museum!" A combined group ticket for the parsonage and church costs four dollars.

27. Dees, interview. The SPLC paid Eisterhold Associates $556,010 for its museum design services (SPLC IRS 990 for 2004).

28. Dees, interview; SPLC Web site, www.splcenter.org (9 October 2006). See also *Civil Rights Memorial Center and Wall of Tolerance* (brochure) (Montgomery: SPLC, 2005).

29. See "Rising Fortunes: Morris Dees and the Southern Poverty Law Center," *Montgomery Advertiser*, 13–18 February 1994; Ken Silverstein, "The Church of Morris Dees," *Harper's Magazine*, November 2000, 56–57. A critical portrait

of Dees appears in John Egerton, *Shades of Gray: Dispatches from the Modern South* (Baton Rouge: Louisiana State University Press, 1991), 211–36. See also *Teaching Tolerance*, Spring 2000, Fall 2005. IRS Form 990 for the SPLC, covering fiscal year 1 November 2004–31 October 2005, listed assets worth more than $160 million, legal fees of more than $4.5 million, and educational expenses totaling $14.6 million. For his work as president, Cohen received $235,620, while as chief trial counsel Dees drew $258,048 and as general counsel Levine drew $138,100, with these salaries set by the SPLC board of directors. In describing its program, the SPLC informed the IRS that it was "educating the general public, public officials, teachers, students and law enforcement agencies and officers with respect to issues of hate and intolerance and promoting tolerance of differences through the schools."

30. SPLC Web site; *Mighty Times: The Legacy of Rosa Parks* and *Mighty Times: The Children's March* (Hudson and Houston Productions, 2004).

31. Morris Dees, "Wall of Tolerance National Campaign for Tolerance" (invitational letter), 10 November 2005, in possession of author. Names can be typed into the database that will appear on the wall without making a contribution to the law center (SPLC Web site).

32. Supplemental teaching tolerance materials include the pamphlets *Ten Ways to Fight Hate: A Community Response Guide* and *101 Tools for Tolerance* as well as the student kit "Mix It Up at Lunch Day," a strategy to desegregate lunchrooms. In 2004, the SPLC sent the kit to more than sixty schools that requested the program. The September 2006 *SPLC Report* explained that the center created its endowment in 1974 out of the fear that "the day will come when nonprofit groups will no longer be able to afford to garner support through the mail." It listed the endowment at $164 million and elsewhere identified some people who through "tribute gifts" or planned giving called "Partners for the Future" had helped increase the endowment, which Dees claimed had reached $175 million (Dees, interview).

PART III

Consuming the South

Foodways and the Performance of Southern Culture

Southern Eats

John Shelton Reed

Some anthropologists and the odd historian aside, it's only recently that the academy has begun to take the study of foodways seriously. Fifteen years ago or so, a couple of accomplished food scholars proposed to my university that they teach an undergraduate honors course on the subject, which they were willing to do *without pay.* The general response was along the lines of "You can't be serious." But they were very serious indeed. They eventually got the course offered on a trial basis, and it was immediately oversubscribed, with some of our very best students eager to write the sort of research papers that university teachers dream about their students writing. Now this course is taught every year, still oversubscribed, and my university is congratulating itself on having been on the cutting edge.

That course caught a wave that has now washed up all sorts of interesting flotsam, including the three chapters that follow. Scholars have begun to see the usefulness of the fact that you are what you eat, as everyone is fond of saying. (Googling that assertion in late 2006 produced nearly 1.5 million hits.) And it is equally true and perhaps more interesting (though less often remarked: about eight hundred hits on this one) that you eat what you are—or, at any rate, what you think you are or what you want to be. The study of the acquisition, preparation, and consumption of food opens windows into many larger psychological and societal questions.

Anthony J. Stanonis provides a penetrating historical look at how southern foodways have reflected and reinforced the patriarchal and racist assumptions of the dominant class of white southerners and persuades me that they certainly have done that. But there is another side to that story, I think.

The South's political history, like those of most peoples, has been largely a sorry chronicle of division, conflict, oppression, and exploitation, but the region's cultural history has been more often a matter of borrowing, sharing, swapping, and mutual influence—across racial lines. As W. J. Cash wrote, in the South "Negro entered into white man as profoundly as white man entered into Negro, subtly influencing every gesture, every word, every emotion and idea, every attitude."[1] Perhaps today that can go without saying, but when he wrote it in 1940, it was far from the conventional wisdom.

Only in our music might this blending be as evident as it is in what southerners eat. The banjo, for example—an African instrument that hardly any African Americans play these days—is at the core of bluegrass, maybe the "whitest" music there is, while the European guitar accompanies America's "blackest" music, the blues. But we can still speak of "black" and "white" music—in fact, we have to. There is no similar consensus on whether one can speak of black and white food, and I for one don't think we can. The table is one place—it may be *the* one place—where the cliché "It's not about race, it's about class" actually holds true.

I have yet to encounter convincing evidence of any significant differences between the cuisines of blacks and whites of similar incomes and education. "Soul food," for example, celebrated in the 1970s as the essence of negritude, looks suspiciously like the food of southern poor whites, who have also generally eaten low on the hog. Things don't get more soulful than South Side Chicago or Mississippi "gut parties," to eat chitlins and hog maw—but my friend Jerry Leith Mills fondly recalls a North Carolina "chitlin function" attended entirely by white boys of the species *good old*.

When this subject was discussed at a recent meeting of the Southern Foodways Alliance, someone brought up chicken country captain as an example of a "white" southern dish that has absolutely no African American roots or constituency, and it's true that this curried chicken concoction seems to have gone directly from Bengal to the upper-class tables of eighteenth-century Charleston (or Savannah—there's a dispute here). Today it is still eaten mostly by the country-club set, but I will bet that some members of the South's rapidly growing black business and professional class have given it a try. The last time I inquired, something like one *Southern Living* reader in eight was African American. And you could even argue that it is, in a way, part of their heritage. After all, who cooked it in eighteenth-century Charleston?

No, in the South blacks and whites have historically eaten at separate tables, but insofar as their means allowed, they ate the same things, a splendid creole blend of African, European, and Native American. And these days, when blacks and whites come together in fellowship, as they do (albeit all too rarely), food usually seems to be involved.

Carolyn de la Peña's fascinating history of Krispy Kreme—well, for starters, it makes me hungry. (As Roy Blount Jr. has observed, hot

Krispy Kremes "are to other doughnuts what angels are to people.")[2] It also provokes me to reflect on the many southern things that have ceased to be southern, not because southerners gave them up but because we exported them so successfully. Coca-Cola was an early example, going from a regional thirst-quencher to a symbol of American civilization, then—as the opponents of "coca-colonization" feared it would—teaching the world to sing in more than a hundred languages. Holiday Inn and Wal-Mart have followed the same path. NASCAR, country music, and the Southern Baptist Convention may be doing the same, and until its recent financial troubles (eclipsed, to be sure, by those of Enron, WorldCom, and the Hospital Corporation of America—all southern enterprises), Krispy Kreme looked set to become America's if not the world's doughnut—they were for sale at Harrod's in London the last time I was there. This is not the model of a disappearing South that most people who have used that phrase had in mind.

Finally, there is Hon Fest. Frankly, it looks like fun to me—even if it is a guilty pleasure, now that I have read Mary Rizzo's persuasive essay about its erasure of black folks. Moreover, what are we to make of its mocking of working-class whites, however kindly intentioned? As a white southerner who far too late in the day was no stranger to burnt cork, I do not ask this self-righteously.

There is much (excuse the expression) food for thought in all three of these chapters. Each is a fine example of the sort of unexpected insight that an oblique angle on everyday life can provide. I will close with a couple of recent food-related observations of my own, left unanalyzed as an exercise for the reader.

My wife and I often eat lunch at a hole-in-the-wall "country buffet" place that offers fine black-eyed peas, turnip greens, and fried chicken—utterly typical, except that many of the construction-worker customers these days are Mexican and the Chinese owner-cook takes their orders in Spanish. And recently, when I went to a low-rent grocery in Mississippi to pick up some flour tortillas, I found some with a label that I read as "Ole Mexican Foods." I come from East Tennessee, where lots of things are "ole," so it took a minute before I realized that the word was, of course, *olé*. The fine print revealed that Olé is headquartered in suburban Atlanta, with branches in Texas, Florida, Kentucky, South Carolina, and North Carolina.

You want to talk about new southern cuisine? Keep your eye on Olé.

NOTES

1. W. J. Cash, *The Mind of the South* (New York: Vintage, 1941), 51.
2. "Southern Comfort," *New York Times Magazine*, 8 September 1996, 67.

Just Like Mammy Used to Make

Foodways in the Jim Crow South

Anthony J. Stanonis

Novelist Walker Percy offered a curious interpretation of why his adopted city of New Orleans experienced relative calm in 1968 while racial upheaval caused the skylines of other American urban centers to disappear behind plumes of smoke. Writing for *Harper's Magazine,* Percy declared, "I attach more than passing significance to the circumstance that a man who stops for a bite in Birmingham or Detroit or Queens, spends as little time eating as possible and comes out feeling poisoned, evil-tempered, and generally ill-disposed toward his fellowman; and that the same man can go around the corner in New Orleans, take his family and spend two hours with his bouillabaisse or crawfish bisque (which took two days to fix)." The leisurely consumption and enjoyment of food in the Louisiana city, in Percy's view, somehow kept a lid on racial tensions: "It is probably no accident that it was in Atlanta, which has many civic virtues but very bad food, that a dyspeptic restaurateur took out after Negroes with an ax handle and was elected Governor by a million Georgians ulcerated by years of Rotary luncheons." The ugly confrontation between Lester Maddox and black civil rights advocates who sought entry into Maddox's Pickrick restaurant shortly after passage of the Civil Rights Act symbolized for Percy the connections linking consumerism, food, and racial custom. Indeed, in the city supposedly too busy to hate, a defiant Maddox chose to close the Pickrick rather than integrate his establishment. Maddox capitalized on the publicity by briefly converting the site into a tourist attraction. His souvenir stand sold more than ten thousand pick handles imprinted with the words "Pickrick drumsticks," a celebration of the wooden weapons used by Maddox's supporters to intimidate those attempting to desegregate the restaurant.[1]

Percy's comments say a mouthful about race relations and foodways in the United States. New Orleans, of course, was no oasis of social harmony, as the violent school desegregation protests there in the early

1960s demonstrate. But Percy's observations should not be dismissed as mere hyperbole. Though he may have exaggerated the racial peace within the Crescent City, Percy nevertheless offers a key insight into southern culture under Jim Crow. New Orleans shared in a regional history that witnessed the propagation of culinary-defined social customs through the expanding twentieth-century consumer market and tourist trade. White southerners ingested far more than food when they or their guests sat down at a table. Their diet, eating practices, restaurants, and cookbooks often conveyed messages that affirmed the racial and patriarchal status quo of the Jim Crow regime.[2]

Given the close relationship between the "ways people think about food and sex," as historian Hasia Diner has noted, white southerners' fixation with food should not seem surprising, especially in light of their anxiety regarding miscegenation. Despite the recognized role of food as an "agent of memory," scholars have largely ignored how white southerners have played with their cuisine. The few works that have so far explored the region's foodways, such as the popular *Cornbread Nation* series, tend to overemphasize food's ability to unite southerners across racial lines. John T. Edge, director of the Southern Foodways Alliance, has written that items such as fried chicken and doughnuts "are democratic foods that conjure our collective childhood and call to mind the question once posed by a Chinese philosopher: 'What is patriotism, but nostalgia for the foods of our youth?'" This may be so. But what does my nostalgia as a man born in Louisiana during the 1970s mean when I fondly remember breakfasts with my parents at the (eventually) controversial Sambo's restaurant chain? And how will the patriotic young Texan of today remember his experiences at Johnny Reb's Dixie Café in Hearne, an eatery known to host gatherings of the Southern Independence Party. Sambo's and Johnny Reb's Dixie Café represent a not-yet-forgotten southern past linked to foodways. Indeed, the categorization of food as "southern" has long sublimated blackness within the region. In 1931, black social commentator Horace Mann Bond stressed the dominant white culture's denial of blacks' regional identity: "In the South the white man is the Southerner, the Negro—well, a Negro." This cognitive trick permitted white southerners to recognize black influences on regional culinary custom without jeopardizing white supremacy.[3]

Cooking Dixie

The mass production of consumer goods and the rise of mass tourism sparked by the automobile revolutionized traditional modes of living in the South. Housewives discovered that store-bought soap, canned vegetables, and other goods readily available at expanding grocery store chains such as Piggly Wiggly eliminated much of the work that previously absorbed their time. The spread of electricity across the region after the First World War likewise opened kitchens to products such as blenders, electric ranges, and refrigerators. Motor vehicles made markets more accessible. Women therefore found more time and more ingredients with which to experiment with meals.[4]

Empowering white women in the kitchen required reinforcing their superiority over black servants. Only under the watchful eye of white authority could blacks be permitted to labor in spotless modern kitchens packed with brand-name goods and appliances. Opinion held that white supervision was necessary for the efficient operation of the kitchen, given blacks' wasteful tendencies. Edna Ferber captured white angst in her popular novel, *Showboat* (1926). The character Parthy Ann Hawks intrudes into the southern riverboat's galley, where she is shocked by the wastefulness of the "somewhat savage" black cook and his assistants. Ferber grants none of them a name, making the workers interchangeable with the thousands of black kitchen helpers spread across the country. Insulted by Hawks's comment that she had never seen "a filthier hole" than the ship's kitchen, the head cook reaches as quick as a "panther" with "one great black paw into the pan of parings, straightened, and threw the mass, wet and slimy as it was, full at her." His violent action, of course, leads to the cook's dismissal. Fears about the cleanliness of black bodies influenced white perceptions as well. Melton McLaurin, as a youth in North Carolina during the mid-twentieth century, believed that black saliva transmitted "black germs" that threatened to inflict whites with "unspeakable diseases, diseases from the tropics, Congo illnesses." Referring to his black playmate, McLaurin commented that the boy's saliva carried his "black essence, an essence that degraded me and made me, like him, less human."[5]

Cookbooks guided white women through the modernization process. Equally significant, cookbooks asserted white women's racial superiority over black helpers, who had long been praised for their cooking talents. *Southern Ruralist,* an Atlanta-based magazine, compiled recipes from readers into a book, *Favorite Southern Recipes* (1912). Targeting "Southern farm women," the cover depicts a white housewife gleefully mixing batter in a bowl while a bug-eyed mammy complete with kerchief has her hands raised in amazement. The racial message was clear. The cookbook made the white housewife as skilled as (if not more skilled than) her black domestic servant. Popular trademarks, such as Aunt Jemima, likewise played on the perception of blacks as excellent kitchen help even while easy-to-prepare packaged goods assisted whites in reducing their dependence on black cooks. In the opinion of Henrietta Stanley Dull in *Southern Cooking* (1928), the reason for bolstering white women's

Whites often justified Jim Crow by arguing that blacks were both dirty and disease ridden. This mid-twentieth-century postcard demonstrates white concerns with maintaining cleanliness in a kitchen worked by a black domestic servant. (From author's collection)

culinary skills in the face of black competition was clear: "The woman is the heart of the home, and the kitchen is the heart of the house." White women needed to assert their superiority lest blacks dominate the domestic space. The Burpee Can Sealer Company sponsored the publication of Florence Roberts's *Dixie Meals* (1934), a book of recipes and etiquette for the "young and inexperienced housekeeper" that Roberts dedicated to her granddaughters: "Your place in life I do not know, / But you must learn yourself, the maid to show." A skilled white housewife needed to claim greater knowledge than her black servants in regard to food preparation and service.[6]

White southerners had good reason to express anxiety about their black kitchen help. Blacks' status as kitchen servants displayed the racial hierarchy but put at risk whites' reputation as hosts and even their lives. During the days of slavery, whites feared the possibility that their enslaved cooks would poison meals.[7] Although such anxieties seemed to ease after emancipation, whites still confronted blacks who used their culinary skills as a weapon against their employers. Aletha Vaughn resented the way whites denied servants like her the "best food"—vegetables, beef, and chicken—and instead offered cheaper bologna or banana sandwiches dressed with mayonnaise. One white housewife went so far as to label with an X any food off-limits to her black workers. Vaughn complained, "A lot of the time I felt like spitting in their food, but I didn't. I would just go on and say: 'Well, they'll get theirs. This is their heaven, I suppose.'"[8] Other domestic servants showed far less restraint. The practice of poisoning lingered. In 1964, for example, Vera Mae Bromell of South Carolina was found guilty of putting poison in the orange juice served with her employer's breakfast.[9] But kitchen revolts frequently took less deadly forms. In *A Wake for the Living,* Andrew Lytle recalled the relationship between Elizabeth Buntin and her black servant, Frank. Lytle remarked, "I was told that, if he liked you, he would see that you ate well. If he disliked you, he would ruin the dishes." A well-timed kitchen coup could seriously embarrass a white family, not only by damaging their reputation for hospitality but also by suggesting that they failed to maintain social order. In one instance during the 1930s, Frank rebelled against conservative club women who visited the Buntin household: "Once Elizabeth had her garden club or the Junior League out from Nashville for lunch. . . . Apparently Frank didn't care for either club, and the meal was so bad and the hostess so embarrassed that she went into the kitchen and, mincing no words, said, 'Get out of there, you little black son-of-a-bitch and don't come back.'" Frank's actions forced Elizabeth to abandon propriety by penetrating the kitchen and assuming the patriarchal role of household head, a point made both by her firing of Frank and her unladylike cursing. The subversive actions allowed Frank to assert himself under a racial system that denied blacks the power directly to confront whites. Elizabeth well understood the need quickly to quash such an attempt. Racial supremacy trumped womanly etiquette.[10]

Cookbooks downplayed rebelliousness in the kitchen by defending blacks' loyalty to their white employers and by emphasizing blacks' ignorance. In *The Savannah Cook Book* (1933), Harriet Ross Colquitt described the reticence of black domestics who hesitated to surrender recipes that earned them respect from whites: "Getting directions from colored cooks is rather like trying to write down the music to the spirituals which they sing—for all good old-timers (and new-timers, too, for that matter) cook 'by ear.'" Blacks' reluctance to write down recipes suggested that they understood the power of their cooking skills under Jim Crow. The blacks interviewed by Colquitt were coy, "not only very bad on detail, with their vague suggestions of 'a little of dis and a little of dat'; but . . . extremely modest about their accomplishments . . . so they invariably add a few superfluous embellishments, by way of making them sound more imposing for the 'company.'" The cooks, dependent on their skills for employment, likely sought to sabotage Colquitt's efforts. They had little incentive to aid white housewives in one of the few spaces where blacks could command respect and a significant degree of agency. But Colquitt ignored the power play, instead turning to dialect to imply blacks' ignorance and emphasizing their modesty to defuse any concerns about their superior cooking skills. In contrast, in *Jesse's Book of Creole and Deep South Recipes* (1954), Edith Ballard Watts of Gulfport, Mississippi, recognized that the family servant, Jesse, "ruled our kitchen." Watts nevertheless made certain to reassure her readers that "Jesse is still with us, still simple, affable, and always courteous, and still the undisputed factotum of the family's separate, scattered kitchens whenever any one of the five children that Jesse helped to raise wants to put on the dog in a culinary way on some special occasion." Jesse remained happily on call.[11]

Illustrations were central to the racial message propagated by cookbooks hawking southern cuisine. The Montgomery, Alabama, Junior League issued *Southern Recipes* during the 1940s. The front cover depicts a mammy ringing a bell while two black children run toward her and the food she has prepared. The dedication page presents a sketch of the White House of the Confederacy. Racial humor permeates the text. The "Poultry and Game" section depicts a lanky black man with a duck under his left arm. With his right hand, the big-eyed, big-lipped figure shoots dice.[12] Ruth Berolzheimer's *The United States Regional Cook Book* (1947) provided the "woman who cooks" a compilation of noteworthy recipes separated by region. The section devoted to southern cooking mixed recipes with numerous illustrations of either elite gentlemen accompanied by young belles being served by well-dressed black servants or images of both races enjoying a leisurely life on the plantation.[13] As concern about black civil rights increased by midcentury, some cookbooks downplayed the racial imagery. Early editions of the famed *Gourmet's Guide to New Orleans* (first published in 1933) carried a cover illustration of a black man in a chef's costume holding a tray of steaming food. By the 1960s, the black figure was replaced with the face of a white man in a chef's hat. The man wore a pointed, waxed mustache, apparently an attempt to tie New Orleans cuisine closer to the French than to the city's blacks, who were beginning to voice their disgust with Jim Crow. The cookbook, however, continued to bear a foreword in which Dorothy Dix stated that New Orleans cuisine rested on "what an old colored cook once described as the 'ingrejuns' necessary to good cooking." A mix of French, Spanish, New England, and Virginia influences, the New Orleans flavor described by Dix was "finally glorified by the touch of the old Negro mammies who boasted that they had only to pass their hands over a pot to give it a flavor that would make your mouth water." Though a black figure no longer symbolically served readers the best recipes found in the port city, the magical touch of black hands remained.[14]

But cookbooks constituted much more than guides to whitening the modern kitchen. These manuals also served as souvenirs of southern locales and the customs such locales represented. At the same time consumer products and appliances elbowed for kitchen space, Americans began to recognize automobile travel as a national rite. Distant places and cultures, especially those in the warm climes of the South, gained notice. Cookbooks with regional foci preserved the experience of a place for actual travelers and allowed potential travelers a voyeuristic journey into an exotic culture. The tantalizing, old-fashioned dishes of distant locales countered the sterility of modern kitchens, where, according to a mid-twentieth-century article by social commentator Harry Botsford, the "corners are rounded; the floor is tile; the walls are impervious to moisture; the lady of the house can stand in the middle of compact premises, stretch forth an arm and reach everything she needs for what she considers a good meal." Observers such as Botsford, who praised his "hopelessly old-fashioned" stove, condemned kitchens that had become as antiseptic "as a hospital operating room." The popularity of cookbooks featuring regional dishes apparently grew in part from a desire to maintain a connection to traditional foodways in a space where the "average housewife produces such abominable food in a trifle less than a jiffy." Cookbooks therefore served as guardians of long-standing social practices as well as promoters of culinary delights.[15]

Cookbooks made explicit their dual role as manuals for the modern kitchen and as culinary travelogues that converted countertops into distant places. Helen Woodward, describing the origins of *Two Hundred Years of Charleston Cooking* (1930), declared that the "cooking of Charleston, like the city itself, is like nothing else in the world." In contrast to the monotonous fare made in the household kitchen, Charlestonians saw cooking not as "a necessity but an art." Woodward presented the cookbook itself as a method for transcending time and space: "When I arrived in Charleston I was ill and rather wobbly. I came to love Charleston better than any place I had ever known in my life. And I wanted to send to a few people for whom I care some of this Charleston. But you cannot send away a place. Places you can describe and photograph, but you cannot share them." The solution proved simple. Woodward decided to apply her writing skills to the physical re-creation of place through food, thereby transporting not only sights but smell, taste, texture, and even sound to far-off homes. "As we sat idly one day in my sunny courtyard, it occurred to me that while places cannot be shared, food you can both describe and share," explained Woodward. But simply collecting recipes for publication failed to offer readers the standardization necessary to reproduce the dishes that had made Charleston famous. To ensure their suitability, the recipes were sent to Lettie Gay, who "tested and standardized" each dish "in the testing kitchen of the New York Herald-Tribune Institute." The resulting collection condensed centuries of culinary tradition into a form that allowed for the easy replication of authentic Charleston cuisine and the conversion of distant homes into ephemeral Charlestons.[16]

Travel, food, and modern homes went hand in hand. When Ed Corbin of the popular magazine *Better Homes and Gardens* visited Antoine's on a 1935 trip to New Orleans, he immediately sought a recipe for the publication's "Famous Foods from Famous Places" series. Rather than simply have the restaurant's proprietor, Roy Alciatore, write a brief description of the city and its culinary traditions, Corbin turned to Lyle Saxon, a Louisiana writer of nationally popular travel books about the state. Corbin explained that the magazine was "unusual in that the editorial content is confined entirely to subjects of home interest—namely, gardening, building, remodeling, selection and preparation and serving of food, child care and training, and interior decoration." Stating that the monthly publication, founded in 1922, had a paid circulation of more than 1.4 million by the mid-1930s, Corbin tempted Saxon by citing that the readership consisted of "people with better than average incomes, living in better than average homes which they own." In other words, these readers possessed the wealth to travel—and to buy travel books such as those authored by Saxon. The magazine may have focused on the modern home, but its inclusion of recipes from distant places revealed that re-creating travel experiences in the kitchen was important to Americans' pursuit of status as well as their sense of sophistication. Furthermore, the recipes tantalized readers by making them curious about the food prepared by Antoine's chefs. The likely result was to reproduce the experience of the Hilliard family from Kansas City when they "ate at Antoine's paying $4.00 for a $.50 meal—just because we had 'tourist' written on our faces." They too had read the boasts about New Orleans cuisine. So firm were the connections between food and travel that the Ford Motor Company began publishing its own collection of recipes from famous restaurants by the 1950s. The first publication sold more than 450,000 copies—"far more than anyone expected," according to William Kennedy, editor-in-chief for the company's publications division. When *The Second Ford Treasury of Favorite Recipes from Famous Eating Places* appeared in 1954, the dust jacket promised readers that whether "you go by automobile or in imagination, it takes you on a gourmet's tour of the United States."[17]

For white southerners, celebrating culinary tradition meant not only exploiting potential tourists and quelling potential racial rebellions hatched over pots and pans but also safeguarding the patriarchal structure of southern society. In her critique of southern patriarchy, writer Lillian Smith commented that cooking and gardening provided rare avenues in which women could channel their energies. She argued, "Whatever the hurt in our lives, there are these memories of food, and flowers, and of southern gardens, filled with our mothers' fantasies that had no other way to creep into life." Cookbooks, often authored by women, regularly targeted the region's mothers, wives, and daughters. One review of regional cookbooks explained southern white women's tendency to produce culinary guides: "Not too surprisingly, the South, with its many women's clubs and its tradition for good cooking and pride in family heirloom recipes, produces a disproportionately high number of fundraising cookbooks." By easing food preparation, these books lessened the anxiety of women who were expected to produce meals for their family on a daily basis. Lena Richard, a New Orleans caterer, authored the *New Orleans Cook Book* (1940) in response to the "constant and insistent demand for my recipes and menus by the housewives." Although her cooking school trained both sexes, Richard's cookbook targeted women. She explained that her purpose lay in putting "the culinary art within the reach of every housewife and homemaker."[18]

Kitchen work was so central to many women's lives that some women, such as Daisy Mae Stapleton of Tennessee, even described the husband-wife relationship in terms of a recipe. Her cookbook prescribed the proper way to prepare a man: "Like crabs and lobsters, husbands are cooked alive. They sometimes fly out of the kettle and so become burned and crusty on the edges, so it is wise to secure him in the kettle with a strong silken cord called comfort, as the one called duty is apt to be weak." Stapleton stressed that a "steady flame of love, warmth and cheerfulness" would make any man "very digestible, agreeing with you perfectly; and he will keep as long as you choose, unless you become careless and allow the home fires to grow cold." Couching her instructions in terms of a recipe, Stapleton neutralized women's power over men by limiting women's role to that of comforting, domestic companions who might manipulate but would never usurp the position of the male heads of household.[19]

Consuming White Southern Identity

White southerners argued throughout the twentieth century that Dixie fostered eating habits that contrasted with the flawed American society found outside the region. White southerners generally defended their traditional ways, including patriarchal and racial customs that grounded Jim Crow society. Food provided a powerful means of safeguarding white hegemony. Whereas cookbooks attempted to cushion the impact of modernity on the South by preserving the region's mores and permitting its re-creation in kitchens everywhere, white southerners also preserved eating practices, promoted brand names (and slang), and patronized restaurants that fortified their commitment to Jim Crow.

No meal was more important in this regard than the first meal of the day. Commenting on his home region, David Cohn remarked, "Few things are so illustrative of the leisureliness and spaciousness of Delta life [before the Second World War] as its old-fashioned breakfast." The Mississippi native lamented the decline of the white patriarchal household symbolized by the family gathered to eat a morning meal. Cohn continued, "In the days before Americans—including Deltans—had begun to take their food on the run like escaping convicts; before the omnipresence of tin cans, ready-to-serve frozen messes mass-produced by distant, anonymous corporations, and drugstores where men eat standing like horses amid a miscellany of hot-water bottles, packaged candy, and hair dyes; when eggs were a dime a dozen and the Diligent Housewife had not yet become the Domestic Engineer—in that dear, dead time, Deltans sat contentedly down to their old-fashioned breakfasts." Breakfast reflected a supposedly peaceful time of social order. The wife and children showed respect to the male head of household. Black servants, who assisted wives by cooking meals for the white middle- and upper-class families, worked hard but remained "cheerful" in their service. When time came to pick cotton, Cohn argued that even servants happily ventured into the fields since the task "was a welcome relief from the daily routine." The white patriarchy, according to Cohn and like-minded southerners, was reaffirmed each time a meal was served. White southerners cherished breakfast and fondly recalled the time as a moment of family union. Murry Falkner, brother of author William Faulkner, noted how he and his siblings "would charge into the dining room for breakfast, which was always an important meal for the whole family." Even those outside the South noted the cultural emphasis placed on breakfast in the region. In a 1919 *Atlantic Monthly* article on national eating habits, Richardson Wright observed that white southerners treated breakfast as a "great function." Breakfast was the most important meal of the day less for its nutritional value than for its daily, early morning affirmation of the social order.[20]

The celebration of southern white patriarchy through food took a particularly notable form at Pirateland, a theme park located on South Carolina's Grand Strand. Visitors during the mid-1960s could take a boat ride through a section of swamp intended to re-create the secluded haunts of Revolutionary War hero Francis Marion, the "Swamp Fox." The centerpiece of the attraction was the reenactment of the legendary "Sweet Potato Breakfast." Popularized in a sketch of John Blake White's 1836 painting that was placed on Confederate ten-dollar bills, the breakfast referred to an incident in which a British officer sent to confer with Marion about a prisoner exchange confronted a shocking scene of patriotic—and manly—sacrifice. Marion's men lived without tents. They used logs for chairs. And when Marion asked if his guest desired food, the officer, "wondering where the dining room could be, saw one of Marion's ragged soldiers approach him, carrying a piece of bark for a plate on which there were sweet potatoes, roasted at the campfire." The British officer, according to the legend reported by Pirateland promoters, subsequently resigned from the army after declaring that he could not fight "such brave and courteous men." The live re-creation in the 1960s of a scene depicted on an engraving made for the Confederacy about a Revolutionary War meal suggested a long regional history in which the dining experience invigorated white southern manhood. Without their wives or homes, the white men of the South could live off the land "with apparent relish." They were not dependent on their womenfolk or weakened by the feminizing influences sheltered within the domestic spaces Marion's soldiers defended.[21]

Eating habits and local terminology for foods marked southern cultures. For example, in Louisiana, Cajuns fostered group identity through crawfish. Consumers required skill to properly peel and eat the small crustacean to avoid the distasteful parts of the local delicacy. In the years after the Second World War, Florida greeted travelers to the state at welcome centers located on key highways. Hostesses distributed cups of orange juice, thus promoting a major agricultural product, introducing travelers to a beverage widely enjoyed by Floridians, and meeting tourists' expectations regarding southern hospitality. Neva Horne, a longtime hostess, remarked, "It's a way of life with us." In much of the South, breakfast selections in particular exposed foreigners within the community. Along the Mississippi Gulf Coast, residents such as Russell Quave called mullet by the local term, "Biloxi bacon," an item also celebrated in "a lot of the seafood restaurants in the city of Biloxi." Newspapers in the tourist town of Myrtle Beach, South Carolina, repeatedly used breakfast dishes to identify visitors. In one account from 1959, a writer for the paper recalled an encounter with three patrons of a local restaurant. He asked, "You have Florida license plates on your car but what part of New England are you originally from?" Stunned, the three tourists responded that they were from Rhode Island. When asked how he knew they were northerners, the newspaperman simply said that he had "a hunch." The hunch was one widely recognized by fellow southerners. "For breakfast they had soft boiled eggs and tea," explained the writer. Some ten years later, Larry Boulier reported that the "way of knowing whether or not a Canadian golfer has visited us before is to observe him when he is served breakfast. He will not make any comments when he is served grits."[22]

Acquainting local and outsider alike with southern racial and patriar-chal custom extended beyond eating rituals such as breakfast to affect the meaning of food items themselves. The best of southern cuisine became identified with the white culture of the region, even when such items were imported from black foodways. In 1951, a *Life* magazine article on the usefulness of okra gave little note of the importance blacks played in introducing the vegetable into the regional diet. The piece, addressing the "majority of Americans who never heard of okra," whimsically stated that the pod was not a "culinary item that children generally beg their mammies for." This did not mean that okra was not a "substantial food, the kind that sticks to your ribs, a valuable ingredient in some of the best stews a man ever ate." To affirm the value of the vegetable, the writers for *Life* associated okra with a hearty Confederate general—not Rob-ert E. Lee but rather the first national leader of the Ku Klux Klan: "What was good for Nathan Bedford Forrest ought to be good for lean and hun-gry Yankees." Okra was thus cast not only as a nutritious and palatable side dish but as one worthy of white dining rooms. The vegetable seemed especially good for invigorating boys and men rather than women.[23]

Throughout the region, race and foods became intertwined. Postcards, ads, board games, and other paraphernalia often showed blacks enjoy-ing greasy chicken and juicy watermelon, images that reinforced white assumptions about black inferiority. Foods eaten with the hands, fried chicken and watermelon depicted blacks as unable to grasp the codes of white civilization symbolized by table manners and properly used utensils. Furthermore, cultural historian Patricia Turner has argued that foods such as watermelon suggested that blacks' nutritional needs could be met by easy-to-raise crops or animals. Other foods were not only less palatable but also symbolic of the lowly status of blacks in the region. Chitterlings (hog intestines) supply one example. Whites regularly gained the assistance of blacks at hog-killing time by offering them this part of the animal. John Faulkner, another of William Faulkner's brothers, remembered, "All Negroes and some white people seem to love them." Despite a few whites' interest in chitterlings, Faulkner disavowed having ever tasted hog intestines and associated the smell with his town's segre-gated black neighborhood, where the "stench of chitterlings cooking in almost every house" hung in the air. Foul odors, as historian R. Marie Griffith has noted, reinforced whites' "disgust toward the supposed fetor of foreign bodies" by distinguishing the "'stink' of particular races or classes of people from the 'sweet' smells of one's own kind."[24]

Catfish also buttressed racial stereotypes. The fish was a bottom-feeder, a scavenger that prowled river and creek beds. Although rural south-erners of both races consumed catfish despite its strong musty flavor, many southerners preferred carp or bass until the controlled feeding of farm-raised catfish in the 1970s. Blacks, however, became particularly associated with the whiskered fish. Paul Laurence Dunbar celebrated black southerners' enjoyment of and respect for catfish in a poem, "Fishing": "Need n't wriggle, Mistah Catfish, case I got you jes' de same, / You been eatin', I'll be eatin', an' we needah ain't to blame." The personification of the catfish and the suggested guilt voiced by Dunbar's fisherman as he reels in his catch reveals just how strongly some blacks recognized the similarity between their lowly social status and the catfish's lowly status on the food chain. But southern whites held a less sympathetic viewpoint. In his novel *Porgy,* DuBose Heyward fictionalized Charleston's black ghetto known as Cabbage Row by substituting the name Catfish Row. George Gershwin's opera, *Porgy and Bess,* propelled the ghetto—and blacks' link to catfish—into the national consciousness. The stereotyped images of blacks as raucous, dysfunctional inhabitants of Catfish Row continued to serve as a touchstone for conceptions of black life late into the twentieth century. In a 1992 article for *Ebony,* Lerone Bennett lamented how books, television shows, and other media treated black characters as "archetypes . . . destined to play prefabricated roles in portable and prefabricated Catfish Rows." It is little wonder, then, that Elvis Presley sparked a revolt during a late-career concert in Norfolk, Virginia, when some of his black backup singers marched off-stage after he commented that they smelled like catfish.[25]

Studies of eating customs reveal the power of race in determining what families consumed at their dining tables. Stigmatizing foods supplied a means of affirming social order. In 1943, John Bennett explored food-ways along the Ohio River. The whites he interviewed identified musk-rats, yellow corn bread, wild game, and greens as "nigger food." Tony Larry Whitehead's 1984 study of foodways in North Carolina revealed similar concerns regarding food and race. Black families ate more pork products, though typically cheaper cuts, than white families. Whites consumed only high-end cuts of pork. Whites also prized beef as a symbol of status. Poor blacks and middle- and upper-class whites "referred to such pork products as neck bones, 'fatback,' feet, ears, and tails; chicken necks, feet, giblets, and backs; black-eyed peas, and dried beans as 'poor people's food.'" Middle- and upper-class blacks identified the same items as "black people's food." Poor whites, according to Whitehead, rarely used such polite terminology, preferring instead to classify such items as "nigger foods." Avoiding the foods listed by Whitehead served as a marker of racial pride and superiority for the whites he surveyed across the class spectrum.[26]

The watermelon possessed particular power to define racial divisions in the South. Some communities in the region, such as Bessemer, Alabama, reinforced white supremacy through public festivals involving watermelons.

Foods offered a means of reinforcing white stereotypes of blacks. Here, an early twentieth-century postcard links watermelons to stereotypes of black criminality. (From author's collection)

This late nineteenth-century promotional flier for Baltimore-based Nigger Head Oysters echoes a theme of white cannibalism of blacks common in white southern foodways. (From author's collection)

Labor Day celebrations in the steel mill town included what *Life* magazine called "watermelon scrambling." Citizens and visitors to Bessemer gathered on curbsides to watch children attempt to grab a watermelon from a pile in the center of a downtown street while the local fire department used fire hoses to hold them back. According to *Life*, the 1953 Labor Day festivities supplied "even more fun" for spectators. The magazine reported, "Four convicts from the city jail were entered in eight successive scrambles. They scrambled mightily . . . and the winners . . . were rewarded by having their sentences reduced." Although the captions made no mention of race, one photograph showed a white fireman bearing down on two black convicts with a powerful jet of water. A crowd of white onlookers stood in the background. Another photograph depicted two successful black convicts enjoying their watermelon—as well as their reduced sentences. Even late into the twentieth century, the watermelon could evoke powerful racial symbolism. During the 1980s, hundreds of white protesters harassed black marchers from Atlanta who traveled to Forsyth County to celebrate the life of Martin Luther King Jr. The whites barked, "Kill the niggers! Kill the niggers! Run the niggers back to the Atlanta watermelon field." To the suburban whites, Atlanta, with its black majority population, was not the leading metropolis of the South but instead a huge watermelon patch filled with uppity darkies whose activism merited death for trespassing beyond the bounds of a racial stereotype depicting blacks as contented melon munchers.[27]

Whereas some foods, like watermelon, carried implicit racial meanings easily evoked when white supremacy was threatened, other foods carried more overt messages about race. Florence King remembered that when she was a white child in the 1940s, the town's Woolworth store sold "Tar Babies," "little licorice candies shaped like black children." In this instance, a prominent national chain—whose segregated lunch counters would galvanize the sit-in movement of the 1960s—marketed a product that subtly buttressed the racial status quo by dehumanizing blacks. Many white southerners seized the opportunity afforded by the candy to add greater insult to blacks. "Everybody privately called them 'nigger babies,'" recalled King, "but my grandmother had taught me that using the word 'nigger' was one of those things no lady could do and still remain a lady." King recognized the contradictions raised by the social views of her "arch-segregationist" grandmother, the civility she encouraged, and black candies purchased to eat at the movies. Put simply, King believed that in the South, "it is much better to be known as a white cannibal than as white trash who uses words like 'nigger,' because to a Southerner it is faux pas, not sins, that matter in this world." Suggestions of cannibalism did not stop at candy. Even brand names played on the coloring of food to reinforce the racial hierarchy in which whites figuratively consumed blacks. In 1977, journalist William Raspberry remembered, "As a kid in the South, I used to see on the grocery shelves cans of 'Nigger Head' brand oysters. . . . The label carried the expected caricature of a black man." The dark oysters offered an opportunity for whites to gain sustenance by devouring symbolic blacks.[28]

Though most such references faded from the southern lexicon by the late twentieth century, the legacy of Jim Crow lingered. Some white southerners, including popular radio broadcasters such as Bill Huff of North Carolina, continued to use the phrase "nigger toes" to refer to Brazil nuts in the 1990s. Such phrases survived in part because they seemed devoid of racial meaning, functioning in some users' minds as solely the name of a food. Earline Spillers, a black teacher in Mississippi, recalled an incident involving a white substitute teacher who entered the school lounge and chuckled, "Guess what they're having for lunch? Nigger's toes." Spillers let the faux pas pass because the woman "did it *innocently.*"[29]

Symbolic cannibalism and marketing strategies, especially in regard to fried chicken, reveal much about the difference between race relations in the South and the rest of the nation. Maxon Graham, who operated the famed Coon Chicken Inn chain in Utah, Oregon, and Washington from the 1920s through the 1950s, emphasized the blackness of fried chicken. The restaurants were notable for the grotesque, winking black face topped by a bellboy cap that served as the chain's trademark. Graham placed the giant head at the entrances to his restaurants as a gimmick to attract children. The face seemed to devour patrons as they passed through the entrance. With few blacks living in the West, his version of racial cannibalism raised little concern. Conversely, Colonel Harland Sanders began his career operating a small restaurant in Corbin, Kentucky, that housed a pet crow named Jim Crow. When Sanders began franchising Kentucky Fried Chicken after the Second World War, he used his own face—the image of a white southern gentleman—to market a food often associated with blacks. His first franchisee competed against the Coon Chicken Inn in Salt Lake City. But Sanders's image suggested that fried chicken was a food for the genteel and white, a message that likely comforted the white southerners who served as the chain's initial customer base and the white Americans beyond the South who grew concerned with the consequences of integration. The company's association by name with a southern state threatened sales outside the region, however. Emphasizing the recipes of distinguished restaurants or even centuries-old urban centers, as cookbooks and magazines had initially done, was far different from a blanket attachment to Kentucky. Commenting in a 1966 issue of *Atlantic Monthly* on the emergence of Kentucky Fried Chicken as a publicly traded company, Charles Morton sneered, "I confess to a certain degree of regionalism, even of prejudice, in making this conjecture, but some of the very worst meals I have ever eaten were in the middle South, and the more Southern the dish was vaunted to be, the more discouraging it was in reality. I wonder, therefore, whether the Kentucky Fried Chicken Corporation might not score a great coup by firing the goateed man and his string tie, and moving its operation base and changing its name, becoming the Fried Chicken Corporation of Vermont." But company officials had little choice given that the fledgling chain depended on white southerners fearful of being politically and socially consumed by the black population long held under thumb. And southerners sensitive to northern liberalism would have had just as much trouble swallowing New England.[30]

Other major southern fried chicken chains echoed Sanders's racial message. Through the 1980s, Popeyes, which originated in New Orleans during the early 1970s, used as a trademark the famed spinach-chomping cartoon character noted for his defense of white America from the yellow hordes of Japan during the Second World War. North Carolina-based Bojangles, founded in 1977, evoked through its name images of the famed black dancer Bill "Bojangles" Robinson, whose joyful steps had suggested black contentment with Jim Crow. Such longing for a return to happy darkies reflected a white society weary of the social changes brought by the civil rights movement. Furthermore, both Popeyes and Bojangles served "Cajun" fried chicken. Selling spicy chicken as Cajun was more than an assertion of exoticism or a means of tapping into a culinary fad that swept the nation during the 1980s. Louisiana boosters during the early twentieth century presented the Cajuns, French settlers of south Louisiana, as a racially pure white people, much as scholars celebrated white Appalachian and Ozark mountaineers as pure-blooded Anglo-Saxons. Not surprisingly, the nineteenth-century presentation of Cajuns as inhabitants of central Louisiana's easily accessible prairies and woods, on which most Cajuns lived, gave way in the popular imagination to the view of Cajuns as isolated—indeed, racially sheltered—residents of the state's dense swamps. Even Church's failed to escape such concerns with race. As a chain particularly prominent in black neighborhoods, Church's faced unfounded though persistent rumors during the 1980s that the Ku Klux Klan owned the company, begun in San Antonio, Texas, in 1952. In a market in which its chief competitors emphasized whiteness and black docility, Church's less explicit racial advertising led many African Americans to interpret the silence as evidence of an insidious conspiracy orchestrated by the Klan to sterilize black men through drugged chicken.[31]

Even well after the 1960s conflict over civil rights had abated, restaurants continued to reflect a white culture not yet able to accept racial equality. White expectations pressured black waiters and cooks to adopt a submissive air. During an investigative tour of race relations in the South undertaken in the 1970s, black journalist Chet Fuller took a job at a Red Lobster in Anderson, South Carolina. The restaurant, part of a national chain, nevertheless operated within the parameters set by local custom. Fuller observed, "There were no blacks in positions of power. All the managers and assistant managers were white. Blacks were servers, waiters, cooks, kitchen helpers, or dishwashers." A racial hierarchy remained intact. Fuller noted that his lowly position as a busboy—he wore black pants, a white shirt, a white apron, and a black bowtie—spurred telling reactions from white and black customers. Fuller recorded how he interacted with black patrons: "My head automatically lowers itself—I guess in shame—whenever black people come into the restaurant. They look at me queerly. I can feel their eyes on me, but they turn their heads quickly when our eyes meet." As a menial laborer dressed in servile garb, Fuller provided a reminder of the long history of white social and economic repression of blacks. "I can tell from the uneasiness in the air whenever a black person enters that I am a burden to him, especially if he is in a party of whites," wrote Fuller. Conversely, white customers saw nothing unusual in Fuller's dress or position. He occupied a role that met white expectations of blacks in the South. Fuller explained, "The whites who visited the restaurant treated me differently. In fact, they didn't notice me at all. As far as they were concerned, I was as much a part of the décor as the fishing nets that hung from the ceiling, and the paintings on the walls." In the late 1980s, author V. S. Naipaul recalled the advice he received from a friend who warned that "in moments of street danger avoid eye contact." Southern blacks who served whites widely followed this rule. Naipaul particularly pointed out that the avoidance of eye contact was "practiced all the time by black waiters in Atlanta."[32]

Racial custom continued to segregate eating establishments across the South in the late twentieth century. Elsewhere during his journey, Fuller entered a small diner called Mama's Kitchen in Dawson, Georgia, only to realize that he was the sole black customer. A few minutes later, a "nervous black man" entered and placed a to-go order. Fuller noted, "It was clear that he didn't want to remain in the room one minute longer than he had to." While waiting, the black customer kept his eyes on Fuller. The journalist squirmed with discomfort. Fuller recalled, "He stared at me as if he were saying in his mind, 'Boy, what the fuck you doin' sittin' up in here 'mongst all these white folks? You crazy?'" In his 1992 study of the Mississippi Delta, Richard Schweid also noted the continued segregation of rural southern eateries. In Belzoni, Mississippi, blacks ate barbecue at Wimp's, whereas whites congregated at the Pig Stand.[33]

By the late twentieth century, the urge to recall the region's agrarian (and consequently white supremacist) past began to appear in subtle physical form at the region's interstate exits and tourist centers. Gone were the most blatant reminders of the Jim Crow South. Mammy's Shanty, an Atlanta restaurant widely popular with locals and tourists, disappeared from the cityscape in 1971.[34] Other businesses downplayed race by erasing offending imagery from their storefronts. Mammy's, a landmark diner in Myrtle Beach, retained its famous name but removed the image of a smiling mammy from above its entrance. New Orleans's famed Aunt Sally's praline shop likewise erased depictions of mammies from company products. Nostalgia for the past perpetuated white fantasies, however. The faux-country-store design of the Cracker Barrel Old Country Store restaurant chain, which first appeared in Lebanon, Tennessee, in 1969, celebrates an era when the South remained largely rural and isolated. The architecture also recalls a period when deference to white authority went unquestioned, a point magnified by the sale of Confederate flag bandanas and mammy dolls in the store portion of each restaurant through the 1980s. During the 1990s, the National Association for the Advancement of Colored People filed successful antidiscrimination lawsuits against the company.[35] Few have linked food, the southern past, race, and architecture more thoroughly than Maurice Bessinger. A leader in the failed fight to keep the Confederate flag flapping over the South Carolina Capitol, Bessinger, who resisted integration until ordered to do so by the U.S. Supreme Court in 1968, now uses his chain of barbecue eateries to celebrate the Confederacy. Rather than a country store motif, Bessinger packages his restaurants as rustic cabins, thereby remembering the white yeomanry of the southern frontier. Inside, the walls are lined with poems and prints honoring the Lost Cause. A small library of handouts, pamphlets, and books condemn the War of Northern Aggression and excuse the peculiar institution destroyed by that war.[36]

The Aftertaste of Jim Crow

Although sensitivity to civil rights has eased the concerns with patriarchy and white supremacy that once flavored southern recipes, the leftovers of Jim Crow culture continued to blend into descriptions of southern food in the last three decades of the twentieth century. A booklet of recipes published in 1980 was sold to tourists in the North Carolina mountains under the title Cookin' Yankees Ain't Et: Ol' Plantation and Mountain Recipes. The compilers included such treats as "Mammy's Baking Powder Biscuits," "Pickaninny Doughnuts," "Topsy's Nut Drop Cookies," and "Corned Beef Hash (General Lee's Favorite)." The booklet clearly promoted the linkage of racial imagery with southern foods, though the association appeared more as a marketing ploy—local color—than an assessment of whether the recipes came from black or white kitchens.

Maurice Bessinger of South Carolina models his barbecue restaurants (including this one, in Columbia, South Carolina, shown in 2006) on white yeoman cabins, complete with pro-Confederate literature and art inside as well as Confederate battle flags outside. (Photo by author)

Although the celebration of plantation fare lessened, hints of racial sentiment survived, as the popularity of Ernest Matthew Mickler's *White Trash Cooking* (1986) demonstrates. Mickler explained the difference between white trash cooking and soul food: "White Trash food is not as highly seasoned, except in the coastal areas of South Carolina, Georgia, and North Florida, and along the Gulf coasts of Alabama, Mississippi, Louisiana, and Texas." The segregation of black and poor white culinary traditions emphasized by Mickler dissipated in a long list of places where no difference existed. Mickler continued by stressing the supposedly better quality and range of poor white dishes even while noting the miscegenation of southern foodways: "It's also not as greasy and you don't cook it as long. Of course, there's no denying that Soul Food is a kissin' cousin. All the ingredients are just about the same. But White Trash food, as you'll see by and by, has a great deal more variety." Furthermore, the Junior League of Charleston, South Carolina, continued to reissue its widely popular cookbook from 1950. In twenty-nine printings accounting for more than seven hundred thousand copies by 1994, the cookbook scattered among the recipes sketches of African Americans along with Gullah phrases. But the Gullah phrases merely rehashed the southern cookbook cliché of using black dialect for humor. The section on salads, for example, began, "Salad? Da' w'en dey teck grass an' ting an' put fancy dress on um lukkuh gal gwine tuh chu'ch."[37]

The preservation of historic sites in the South, a practice long dominated by elite white women, continued to offer visitors a skewed remembrance of the past that made the racial caste system less visible, though not forgotten. During the 1970s, the women of the Pilgrimage Garden Club in Natchez offered the cookbook *Monuments and Menus* as a celebration of the Mississippi town's antebellum estates. Very few mentions of blacks and the drudgery of slave life appeared. Instead, recipes such as that for "Jeff Davis Pudding" were interspersed with pictures and descriptions of "fine mansions" preserved as "national shrines." A poem placed at the beginning of the recipe collection cast a romantic glow on the sites described therein. The verse, "At Natchez," supposedly captured the sentiment of tourists visiting the river town:

I had not known these things were so.
Unreal they'd peeped from out the page
Of romance of another age.
I had not dreamed that I might see
A lady fair with stately grace
Descend broad stairs, or slowly pace
Through vaulted hall to welcome me:
But now at Natchez—now I know.

The harsh day-to-day events of the plantation South were obscured, especially in regard to slavery. A Junior League cookbook published in Columbia, South Carolina, in 1984—with a run of ten thousand copies—argued, "The Southern approach [to entertaining] recalls wafting strains of soft music, scents of jasmine or wisteria floating in the wind and unobtrusive servants passing silver trays of centuries-old family receipts." The recollection may not have noted the race of the unobtrusive servants, but the call to replicate as closely as possible plantation grandeur carried a powerful if implicit message of racial division.[38]

When Martin Luther King Jr. spoke on the steps of the Lincoln Memorial in 1963, he looked to a future in which racism no longer embittered relations between whites and blacks. King proclaimed, "I have a dream that one day on the red hills of Georgia, sons of former slaves and sons of former slave-owners will be able to sit down together at the table of brotherhood." His vision has come closer into focus. Both blacks and whites can, with rare exception, freely enjoy the services of eateries throughout the South. Both races now generally feel comfortable sitting together in their private dining rooms. The cultural taboo against interracial dining has eroded. Yet the racial meanings identified with southern foodways linger. Though not as powerful as it was early in the twentieth century, the legacy of white supremacy continues to crash King's table of brotherhood.[39]

NOTES

1. Walker Percy, "New Orleans Mon Amour," *Harper's Magazine*, September 1968, 90; Bob Short, *Everything Is Pickrick: The Life of Lester Maddox* (Macon, Ga.: Mercer University Press, 1999), 53–66.

2. For information on the civil rights struggle in New Orleans, see Mary Lee Muller, "New Orleans Public School Desegregation," *Louisiana History* 17 (Winter 1976): 86–88; Adam Fairclough, *Race and Democracy: The Civil Rights Struggle in Louisiana, 1915–1972* (Athens: University of Georgia Press, 1995), 335–80.

3. Hasia Diner, *Hungering for America: Italian, Irish, and Jewish Foodways in the Age of Migration* (Cambridge: Harvard University Press, 2001), 3, 8; John T. Edge, *Fried Chicken: An American Story* (New York: Putnam, 2004), introduction; Horace Mann Bond, "A Negro Looks at His South," *Harper's Magazine*, June 1931, 98. Introducing *Corn Bread Nation 1*, John Egerton writes, "Food is so central to the South we all like—the Good South of conviviality and generosity and sweet communion" (*Corn Bread Nation 1: The Best of Southern Food Writing*, ed. John Egerton [Chapel Hill: University of North Carolina Press, 2002]), 1). For an examination of the relationship between food and nationalism, see James McWilliams, *A Revolution in Eating: How the Quest for Food Shaped America* (New York: Columbia University Press, 2005), 308–21. For a rare critical study of race and southern foodways, see Mary Titus, "'Groaning Tables' and 'Spit in the Kettles': Food and Race in the Nineteenth-Century South," *Southern Quarterly* 30 (Winter–Spring 1992): 13–19.

The Sambo's restaurant chain began in Santa Barbara, California, in 1957, taking its name from a merger of the co-owners' names (Sam Battistone and Newell Bohnett). Although national in reach, the chain was largely based in the Sunbelt, targeted retirees, and incorporated imagery from the children's book *Little Black Sambo* in its decor. Battistone was particularly prominent (and eventually infamous) in my hometown of New Orleans, where he was majority owner of the New Orleans Jazz, the National Basketball Association team that played in the city between 1974 and 1979. After the final season, Battistone, a Mormon, moved the team to Salt Lake City. While Sambo's was not unique to the South, the controversy over the chain reflects the power of local culture to reinterpret the meaning of images. The benign origins of the name and the company's representation of the book, written in 1899 by a Scottish woman and set in India, took on negative connotations in a nation with a white supremacist history that long labeled African Americans as lazy, ignorant Sambos. See "Age Is No Limit to Sambo's," *New York Times*, 20 November 1980; CNN.com, "Sambo's Revival Running into Hot Water," 28 January 1998, http://www.cnn.com/US/9801/28/sambo.revival (accessed 22 December 2007).

4. Jane Busch, "Cooking Competition: Technology on the Domestic Market

in the 1930s," *Technology and Culture* 24 (April 1983): 224–44; Jessamyn Neuhaus, *Manly Meals and Mom's Home Cooking: Cookbooks and Gender in Modern America* (Baltimore: Johns Hopkins University Press, 2003), 28–33, 40–41, 180–81.

5. Edna Ferber, *Showboat* (New York: Grosset and Dunlap, 1926), 30–31; Melton McLaurin, *Separate Pasts: Growing Up White in the Segregated South* (Athens: University of Georgia Press, 1987), 37–38.

6. *Favorite Southern Recipes* (Atlanta: Southern Ruralist, 1912), dedication page; Henrietta Stanley Dull, *Southern Cooking* (New York: Grosset and Dunlap, 1968), 3; Florence Roberts, *Dixie Meals* (Nashville: Parthenon, 1934), n.p.; Neuhaus, *Manly Meals*, 48–51. For insight into the meanings and identities conveyed by cookbooks, see Anne Bower, ed., *Recipes for Reading: Community Cookbooks, Stories, Histories* (Amherst: University of Massachusetts Press, 1997).

7. Titus, "'Groaning Tables,'" 13–19; Sharla Fett, *Working Cures: Healing, Health, and Power on Southern Slave Plantations* (Chapel Hill: University of North Carolina Press, 2002), 159–64; Mary Chesnut, *Mary Chesnut's Civil War*, ed. C. Vann Woodward (New Haven: Yale University Press, 1981), 218.

8. Susan Tucker, *Telling Memories among Southern Women: Domestic Workers and Their Employers in the Segregated South* (New York: Schocken, 1988), 207–8.

9. "Negro Maid Draws 4-Year Jail Term," *Myrtle Beach Sun News*, 12 March 1964.

10. Andrew Lytle, *A Wake for the Living* (1975; Nashville: Sanders, 1992), 261.

11. Harriet Ross Colquitt, *The Savannah Cook Book* (New York: Farrar and Rinehart, 1933), xv–xvi; Edith Ballard Watts, *Jesse's Book of Creole and Deep South Recipes* (New York: Weathervane, 1954), vii–viii.

12. *Southern Recipes* (Montgomery, Ala.: Montgomery Junior League, n.d.), 75.

13. Ruth Berolzheimer, ed., *The United States Regional Cook Book* (Chicago: Cuneo, 1947), 163, 165, 187, 217, 251.

14. Natalie Scott and Caroline Merrick Jones, *Gourmet's Guide to New Orleans*, 6th ed. (New Orleans: Scott and Jones, 1941), i; Caroline Merrick Jones, *Gourmet's Guide to New Orleans*, 16th ed. (New Orleans: Jones, 1960), vii.

15. Harry Botsford, "I Don't Like the Modern Kitchen," *American Mercury*, February 1955, 69; Neuhaus, *Manly Meals*, 37.

16. Blanche Rhett, Helen Woodward, and Lettie Gay, eds., *Two Hundred Years of Charleston Cooking* (1930; New York: Random House, 1934), ix, xi, xv. In regard to the issue of condensing distant places into small American kitchens, Ethel Renwick captured the role of cookbooks with her title, *A World of Good Cooking; or, How to Fit Five Continents into an American Kitchen* (New York: Simon and Schuster, 1962).

17. Ed Corbin to Lyle Saxon, 15 April 1935, Mr. and Mrs. Kenneth Hilliard to Lyle Saxon, 27 December 1932, Lyle Saxon Papers, Manuscripts Department, Howard-Tilton Memorial Library, Tulane University, New Orleans; Nancy Ken-

nedy, ed., *The Second Ford Treasury of Favorite Recipes from Famous Eating Places* (New York: Simon and Schuster, 1954), dust jacket, 7.

18. Lillian Smith, *Killers of the Dream* (1949; New York: Norton, 1978), 142; Mimi Sheraton, "Regional Cookbooks at Their Best," *New York Times,* 5 January 1977, 73; Lena Richard, *New Orleans Cook Book* (Boston: Houghton Mifflin, 1940), preface; Minrose Gwin, "Sweeping the Kitchen: Revelation and Revolution in Contemporary Southern Women's Writing," *Southern Quarterly* 30 (Winter–Spring 1992): 56–61; Patricia Gantt, "Taking the Cake: Power Politics in Southern Life and Fiction," in *Cooking Lessons: The Politics of Gender and Food,* ed. Sherrie Innes (Lanham, Md.: Rowman and Littlefield, 2001), 63–67, 72, 78, 80–82.

19. Daisy Mae Stapleton, *Daisy Mae's Favorite Recipes* (New York: Pageant, 1958), foreword.

20. David Cohn, *The Mississippi Delta and the World: The Memoirs of David L. Cohn,* ed. James Cobb (Baton Rouge: Louisiana State University Press, 1995), 76–77; Murry Falkner, *The Falkners of Mississippi: A Memoir* (Baton Rouge: Louisiana State University Press, 1967), 21; Richardson Wright, "Breakfasting as a Fine Art," *Atlantic Monthly,* November 1919, 662.

21. "Authentic Re-Creation of Revolutionary History Being Constructed at Pirateland," *Myrtle Beach Sun News,* 9 April 1964, 5. The famous incident is more popularly known as the Sweet Potato Dinner.

22. C. Paige Gutierrez, "The Social and Symbolic Uses of Ethnic/Regional Foodways: Cajuns and Crawfish in South Louisiana," in *Ethnic and Regional Foodways in the United States: The Performance of Group Identity,* ed. Linda Keller Brown and Kay Mussell (Knoxville: University of Tennessee Press, 1984), 175–78; "They Spread Sunshine with a Smile and Orange Juice," *Panama City News-Herald,* 21 April 1968, 7; Russell Quave, interview by R. Wayne Pyle, 18 March 1980, Center for Oral History and Cultural Heritage, University of Southern Mississippi, Hattiesburg; "Sun Spots," *Myrtle Beach Sun and the Ocean Beach News,* 1 July 1959, 2; "Crumbs from the Cracker Barrel," *Myrtle Beach Sun News,* 13 March 1969, 4.

23. "It Sticks to the Ribs," *Life,* 19 February 1951, 38.

24. Patricia Turner, *Ceramic Uncles and Celluloid Mammies: Black Images and Their Influence on Culture* (New York: Anchor, 1994), 15; John Faulkner, *My Brother Bill: An Affectionate Reminiscence* (New York: Trident, 1963), 51; R. Marie Griffith, *Born Again Bodies: Flesh and Spirit in American Christianity* (Berkeley: University of California Press, 2004), 128. For the role of the senses in reinforcing Jim Crow, see Mark Smith, *How Race Is Made: Slavery, Segregation, and the Senses* (Chapel Hill: University of North Carolina Press, 2006), 76–89.

25. Paul Laurence Dunbar, *Lyrics of Love and Laughter* (New York: Dodd, Mead, 1903), 30; Lerone Bennett, "The 10 Biggest Myths about the Black Family," *Ebony,* November 1992, 118; Peter Guralnick, *Careless Love: The Unmaking of Elvis Presley* (Boston: Little, Brown, 1999), 569–71. Although none of Elvis's backup singers, the Sweet Inspirations, in hindsight thought that he was using a racial slur against them, according to Guralnick, the reference came

during a "hostile" confrontation in which Elvis spoke words with an "ugly undertone" (*Careless Love*, 570).

26. John Bennett, "Food and Social Status in a Rural Society," *American Sociological Review* 8 (October 1943): 563; Tony Larry Whitehead, "Sociocultural Dynamics and Food Habits in a Southern Community," in *Food in the Social Order: Studies of Food and Festivities in Three American Communities*, ed. Mary Douglas (New York: Sage, 1984), 115–17; Mary Ann Wimsatt, "'Intellectual Repasts': The Changing Role of Food in Southern Literature," *Southern Quarterly* 30 (Winter–Spring 1992): 63–65, 67–68.

27. "A Hose Braved," *Life*, 28 September 1953, 30–31; V. S. Naipaul, *A Turn in the South* (New York: Knopf, 1989), 61.

28. Florence King, *Southern Ladies and Gentlemen* (1975; New York: St. Martin's, 1993), 11–12; William Raspberry, "Nothing Can Soften the Image of 'Sambo,'" *Washington Post*, 16 November 1977.

29. Cindi Andrews, "On Air: Alamance Talk Show a Hit," *Greensboro News and Record*, 21 October 1996; Earline Spillers, interview by Worth Long, 8 August 1999, Center for Oral History and Cultural Heritage, University of Southern Mississippi, Hattiesburg.

30. Scott Farrar, "The History of Coon Chicken Inn," Jim Crow Museum of Racist Memorabilia, Ferris State University, http://www.ferris.edu/jimcrow/links/chicken (accessed 31 January 2007); Harland Sanders, *Life as I Have Known It Has Been "Finger Lickin' Good"* (Carol Stream, Ill.: Creation House, 1974), 79, 91–95; Charles Morton, "What's New in Fried Chicken?" *Atlantic Monthly*, June 1966, 121.

31. "Cajun Riding New American Taste for Spicy Food; But Yuppie Craze Hasn't Scored Yet with Middle Market," *Adweek*, 16 December 1985; Michael James Forêt, "A Cookbook View of Cajun Culture," *Journal of Popular Culture* 23 (Summer 1989): 26–33; Anthony Stanonis, *Creating the Big Easy: New Orleans and the Emergence of Modern Tourism* (Athens: University of Georgia Press, 2006), 217–19; Patricia Turner, "Church's Fried Chicken and the Klan: A Rhetorical Analysis of Rumor in the Black Community," *Western Folklore* 46 (October 1984): 294–306.

32. Chet Fuller, *I Hear Them Calling My Name: A Journey through the New South* (Boston: Houghton Mifflin, 1981), 107–8; Naipaul, *Turn in the South*, 62.

33. Fuller, *I Hear Them Calling My Name*, 141; Richard Schweid, *Catfish and the Delta: Confederate Fish Farming in the Mississippi Delta* (Berkeley: Ten Speed, 1992), 29.

34. "Willie B. Borders, 85, Famed Restaurant Cook," *Atlanta Journal-Constitution*, 6 March 2002.

35. "Restaurant Protesters Acquitted in DeKalb," *Atlanta Journal-Constitution*, 3 April 1992.

36. "What Do You Mean, Chicken Supreme?" *Economist*, 13 January 2001.

37. Louise and Bil Dwyer, eds., *Cookin' Yankees Ain't Et: Ol' Plantation and Mountain Recipes* (Highlands, N.C.: Merry Mountaineers, 1980), 5, 10, 13, 36; Ernest Matthew Mickler, *White Trash Cooking* (East Haven, Conn.: Jar-

gon Society, 1986), 3; *Charleston Receipts* (Charleston, S.C.: Junior League of Charleston, 1994), 209. For more on the controversial *White Trash Cooking*, see John T. Edge, "*White Trash Cooking*: Twenty Years Later," *Southern Quarterly* 44 (Winter 2007): 88–94. The Junior League of Charleston accused Mickler of lifting twenty-three recipes "almost verbatim" from *Charleston Receipts*.

38. *Monument and Menus* (Dallas, Tex.: Williamson, 1972), 7–8, 42; *Putting on the Grits* (Columbia, S.C.: Junior League of Columbia, 1984), 6.

39. Martin Luther King Jr., "I Have a Dream," in *A Testament of Hope: The Essential Writings of Martin Luther King Jr.*, ed. James Melvin Washington (San Francisco: Harper and Row, 1986), 219.

Mechanized Southern Comfort

Touring the Technological South at Krispy Kreme

Carolyn de la Peña

These doughnuts touch people to the core of their being.
—Lincoln Spoor, Krispy Kreme owner

Few things in southern culture inspire as much passion as the Krispy Kreme doughnut. The first evening I arrived in Thomson, Georgia, for the conference that inspired this anthology, my fellow participants (all southerners) discerned that I was a Yankee writing about Krispy Kreme who had never eaten a Krispy Kreme *in* the American South. They rejected my California-based claim to doughnut expertise. The following evening, one of them drove me sixty miles round trip to Augusta so that I could sample a "real" Krispy Kreme hot off the line. The dozen glazed we brought back to the conference hotel inspired a lengthy session of Krispy Kreme story trading: everyone, it seemed, had some particular affinity for these objects that transcended the rational.

This essay considers the particular passion for Krispy Kreme doughnuts in the South. Relying on corporate marketing materials, design and architecture plans, consumer letters, corporate histories, and southern historiography, I argue that Krispy Kreme doughnuts have achieved their iconic status because they have been, since their inception, clearly connected with visible means of production. This is not to ignore the particular taste of the doughnut or the myriad social contexts in which customers enjoy the sugary treats. It is also not to minimize the fact that visible machines for food production are not unique to the South. They are, in fact, an entrenched artifact of the post-1945 fast-food landscape in the United States that stretched from the McDonalds chain born on the West Coast to the White Castles of the American heartland to the Piggly Wiggly emporiums scattered across the Southeast. Yet there is something unique about Krispy Kreme. Visitors to my hometown, Riverside, California, rarely travel as tourists to the original San Bernardino McDonalds to taste the "real" Big Mac. And White Castle hamburgers, while frequently noted by their fans as having a particularly pleasing miniaturized size, do not come home by the dozens when people return from visits to their home states. Most Californians would agree that any McDonalds is as good as the next; many White Castle fans head to their local grocery's freezer section to satisfy a craving for the regional specialty. As for Krispy Kreme, however, southerners frequently argue that the taste is connected to the place. Krispy Kreme's store design has been more important in shaping its consumer experience than has been the case at other fast-food environments. Unlike McDonalds or White Castle, Krispy Kreme spends little on direct-to-consumer advertising and marketing. Instead, Krispy Kreme stores are themselves the marketed messages. The company has long relied nearly exclusively on coupon distribution, fund-raising discounts, and publicized store openings to promote its product; all of these approaches bring consumers directly into the stores.[1] My mandatory trip to the Augusta store makes sense in this context. People cannot merely taste Krispy Kreme: they need to experience it.

E. P. Thompson has argued that food should be understood not as a solid material for consumption but rather as a process within which every point offers "radiating complexities."[2] Thompson's analysis concerns the dynamics of a working-class food revolt, yet his metaphor remains useful in considering how the act of eating engages an individual with the social processes embedded in production, labor, and consumption. We can easily think of food exclusively as a taste or unit of energy dissemination, yet when we eat we also ingest—literally—the cultural practices of food production. Our decision, then, to eat or not to eat is not driven by an abstracted neutral preference of texture, taste, or environment. It is based on our willingness to embrace particular people, practices, and places and to reject others. In this essay, I argue that Krispy Kreme doughnuts have radiated a particular set of cultural complexities about the place of machines in the South. By analyzing the consumer experience of Krispy Kreme from its inception in 1937 to its transsouthern turn of the 1990s, paying particular attention to the visible mechanization of Krispy Kreme stores and product, I argue that the doughnut has attained its cult status as much because of its environment as of its taste. Since the 1930s, Krispy Kreme has embedded intimate visual access to complex machines within its consumer experience. This approach has been particularly advantageous for a product native to a region that has, since the postbellum period, actively sought to realize particular industrial dreams. This essay considers three periods in Krispy Kreme's development: the company's inception and initial growth as a labor-driven factory between 1937 and 1958, the chain's redesign and expansion as a labor-free mechanized system between 1958 and 1973, and its reconfiguration into a retail-oriented doughnut theater from the late 1980s until the present.

Krispy Kreme's interior design has allowed consumers to experience distinct relationships with machines. In the 1930s, as the South faced deep ambivalence about the cost of industrial progress, the store interiors presented a balance of old-fashioned hand labor and innovative mechanized production techniques. During the 1950s and 1960s, this balance shifted with the removal of visible labor. The change enabled consumers to experience doughnut purchasing as both an act of personal pleasure and a civic responsibility. It also allowed consumers to synchronize their appetites to the rhythm of efficient machines. In the late 1980s, a self-conscious attempt to create doughnut theater transformed production machines into performers and relegated laborers and customers to the role of tenders and viewers, resulting in the disruption of the original relationship crafted between consumers and machines and likely contributing to Krispy Kreme's financial difficulties at the dawn of the twenty-first century. As the company's recent hardships suggest, the craving for Krispy Kreme has long been fueled by consumers' desire for a pleasurable doughnut and a pleasurable relationship with machines.

A Hole in the Wall: Krispy Kreme and the Promise of Southern Industry, 1937–1958

Krispy Kreme is a curious southern tradition. Unlike biscuits or black-eyed peas, doughnuts claim no lengthy lineage in the South. Doughnuts, or *fast nacht kuchen*, were introduced by German immigrants to Pennsylvania and, with the exception of the French beignets of New Orleans, appear to have made few inroads in the South prior to 1937.[3] In spite of the region's lack of doughnut tradition, several food practices accommodated the snack's successful transplantation. First, food is essential to southerners' sense of place, tradition, and memory.[4] The performance of ritual events and festivals depends on food: hoppin' John, collard greens, fried okra, cornbread, and stewed tomatoes, for example, mark New Year's for many southerners. The region was therefore well suited for a food that evoked a sense of place and could be connected with significant events. Second, many southerners possess a prominent sweet tooth. According to historian John Egerton, "Southerners of every class and calling have coveted sweets since the Virginia colony was in its prime."[5] This desire intensified after the commercial production of baking powder and baking soda in the 1880s, making sweets cheaper to make and purchase. For a century, baked goods have been frequent indulgences for most classes of southerners and an expected component of a hospitable southern meal. Third, the ubiquitous craft of biscuit making inclined southerners to become connoisseurs of yeast-based sweets, skilled in judging minute distinctions in ingredient ratios, oven temperature, and makers' skills. And finally, fried foods such as hush puppies (cornbread balls fried in fish grease) regularly appeared in daily diets, thus easing acceptance for a food item that is primarily a sweet fried ball of potato and flour.

When Vernon Rudolph arrived in Winston-Salem, North Carolina, in 1937 at the age of twenty-two, he had every reason to believe that southerners would eat doughnuts. Rudolph and his uncle had purchased a store and recipe from New Orleans chef Joe LeBeau in 1933 and begun a small family wholesale business with locations in Nashville, Atlanta, and Charleston, West Virginia. The family also purchased a small doughnut shop in Paducah, Kentucky, not far from Vernon's birthplace in Marshall County. Four years later, Rudolph stretched his entrepreneurial wings, setting out in his Pontiac with two hundred dollars and some doughnut-making equipment. According to company lore, he found himself in Peoria, Illinois, perplexed about what town would be best for doughnut making. The answer came while looking at a package of Camel cigarettes. "A town with a company producing a nationally advertised product has to be a good bet," he purportedly said before driving to Winston-Salem to open his first Krispy Kreme.[6]

For Rudolph, Winston-Salem was a pragmatic choice. He could assume that a working-class town famed for rolling Camel cigarettes would have plenty of prospective doughnut customers with secure incomes even during the Great Depression. His decision to promote his product by giving away free samples in the evening further suggests that the industrial labor pool influenced his decision: many Winston-Salem residents had their first taste of his product after a day's work in the tobacco mills. Yet Rudolph was from the beginning interested in doughnut-producing machinery, so his choice of location also suggests that he saw an opportunity to pursue his unique product in a region closely affiliated with industrial success.[7]

Historians tend to focus on the northern states when telling the story of American industrialization. Mill work in Pennsylvania in the 1850s, stockyard labor in late nineteenth-century Chicago, early twentieth-century immigrant labor in New York City—these are the stories used to detail the frenetic pace of industrial expansion in American urban centers and industrial life's social and cultural impact on workers. Within these narratives, it is easy to overlook the Piedmont area of North Carolina, where Charlotte and Winston-Salem stood among the South's fastest-growing cities between 1880 and 1910.[8] Winston-Salem emerged as a model city of southern industrial progress, one of the few to live up to the halcyon dreams of southern industrial promoters after Reconstruction.

In the wake of the Civil War, many southerners saw industrialization as a way to deal with racial problems and achieve economic independence from the North.[9] Capitalists, legislators, and members of the popular press reached a consensus, agreeing that industrial development could ensure progress and decrease the region's reliance on the North as a provider of finished goods. As the *Greensboro Patriot* explained to readers in 1883, the "next census" would show that "counties living on one crop carried only to the first stage are stagnant and lifeless—the land worn out and the population gone to more congenial climes. . . . [A]griculture, manufacturers, mining, and commerce must unite to make a state prosperous."[10] For many southerners, under the right set of early twentieth-century circumstances, technology could create boomtowns across the region. Turning a rural hamlet into a profitable urban center seemed to require only efficient machines and a bit of imagination. Furniture, cigar, cigarette, flour, iron, and steel factories were among the most common investments, their future profits touted to potential investors in expensive brochures that detailed the riches that would befall any man able to tap existing mineral resources and/or lay the rail connections to deliver manufactured goods to a nation of waiting consumers. Most of these industrial investment schemes failed, yet even the spectacular failures barely eased the fever. In 1890, George Thomas, trying to justify his reluctance to invest in a new industrial town, asked incredulously, "Do you think they can make a city out of every village in the south?"[11]

Although actual industrial investment did not pay off for most small-town southerners, the era created a visible prioritization of technology. Large cities such as Montgomery, Alabama, led the nation in investments in electrification and transportation technology. Factories emerged in towns small and large, in many cases because civic boosters hoped to create another Birmingham, Alabama, a city that had risen from ruin in the depression-plagued 1870s to become the "dreamed of southern industrial city" by 1910.[12] According to historian Edward Ayers, "hopeful capitalists built twenty-five blast furnaces" in the Birmingham vicinity alone between 1885 and 1892, with many of these facilities located "in remote places."[13] As a result, many southerners came to equate proximity to urbanity with success, current or pending; life on the farm could appear retrograde in comparison, though in actuality little differentiated the quality of life in city and hinterland.[14] This sense of progress and activity was embedded in the assessments of industrial sites of rural southerners such as Arthur Hudson, who recalled childhood trips into town on "frosty" Mississippi mornings during which he "smell[ed] the exciting train smoke."[15] Southern "technological exuberance" also showed up in the popular press, as evidenced by one Arkansas reporter's choice of metaphor to explain his town's sluggish rate of growth: "A great many business men, even in towns the size of Harrison[,] are content with being nickel-in-the-slot machines when they might be electric motors."[16]

In Winston-Salem, Rudolph found a place that lived up to expecta-tions. Forty-five miles away lay Greensboro, a town that in the early 1880s established new factories that converted raw materials into fin-ished goods. By the 1890s, Greensboro had become the home of North Carolina Steel and Iron and its newly prosperous investors. "I do not believe there is any possibility of failure," said one citizen regarding Greensboro industries. "It is like reading the tales in Arabian Nights, for-tunes are made so easily."[17] Rudolph tapped the similar optimism about opportunities in Winston-Salem. The affiliation between Krispy Kreme and Winston-Salem had several benefits. First, the city assured Rudolph that his business would have plenty of industrial employees and industry leaders as customers. Second, the location suggested that Krispy Kreme itself would become associated with an economically successful part of the region, a valuable asset for a man with an eye toward expansion.

The third asset was a consumer base likely to take note of his ma-chines. When Rudolph opened his first Krispy Kreme shop downtown, he sold wholesale only. According to company records, he began market-ing doughnuts to the public only after people smelled them cooking and knocked on the door. To meet demand, Rudolph installed a window in the wall through which customers not only purchased doughnuts but also saw directly into the production area, where Rudolph's equipment created uniform doughnuts. Whether Rudolph thought it was important for customers to see his doughnut machines or whether opening the win-dow onto the production process was simply the most efficient means for direct sales remains unclear. Nevertheless, between 1937 and 1958, Rudolph opened roughly thirty shops across twelve states in the South-east; all were designed with windows providing easy visual access to the production floor. According to training materials, Rudolph's employees received instructions to "cut [doughnuts] directly inside the front plate glass window" "to attract attention."[18]

Furthermore, when customers lined up for an original Krispy Kreme, they participated in an experience expressly constructed as a factory tour. Rudolph publicized store openings with flyers distributed to neighboring residents asking them to visit the "Most Modern Retail Doughnut Shop in the South" to see its "Modern, Wide Open Kitchen." By character-izing the stores as factories and offering tours, Rudolph may have been attempting to assure prospective customers of food purity. Food com-panies had long provided production tours to ensure cleanliness after the impure practices of processing and canning companies came to light with the passage of the 1906 pure food and drug laws.[19] However, little about the store design during this period suggested a factory, particularly given consumers' familiarity (much of it resulting from firsthand experi-ence) with factories and mills or with the pseudofactories of "progress" represented frequently at exhibitions, such as General Motors's highly publicized Futurama at the 1939 New York World's Fair.[20]

Records suggest that Rudolph and other franchise owners considered the stores industrial spaces. According to Scott Livengood, a former Krispy Kreme chief executive officer, company officials referred to stores as "plants" well into the 1970s.[21] Customers likely viewed store interiors as hybrids, spaces that combined technological innovation and old-fashioned craftsmanship. Once inside the store, customers observed a combination of mechanized and traditional labor: employees operated automated mixing and frying equipment alongside bakers who blended mixes, rolled dough, and cut doughnuts by hand. By the late 1940s, the main spectacle became the Ring King Junior, Rudolph's newly patented device capable of producing up to seventy-five dozen doughnuts an hour by fully automating the extruding and frying process.[22] Even this machine, as attention-drawing as its continuous frying process could be, was dwarfed by its operators, who constantly monitored the mix and ensured the removal of doughnuts from the lower baskets to the upper cooling trays.

Customers likely enjoyed the Krispy Kreme "factory" expressly because the shops did not look like factories. A consumer environment that allowed people to watch and eat, a process at once efficient and hospitable, modern and artisanal, appealed to people in a region where pundits had long argued over whether industry and modernity invited an era of progress or destroyed the nostalgic traditions of rural southern life. Many southerners heard such cultural debates, exemplified by Robert Winston's comment that the growing urban center of Durham, North Carolina, was "sucking the very life-blood from the slow, old-fashioned towns nearby." And with the erosion of small towns and "slow, old-fashioned" habits came the erosion of what made the South unique. Ambivalence thus permeated the modernization process: while boosters welcomed growth and profit, others lamented the loss of tradition and place that industry represented. As Ayers has diagnosed, "The growing southern cities were not so much signs of urban opportunity as of rural sickness."[23]

Krispy Kreme's ability to balance the agricultural with the industrial and the factory with pleasure carried particular appeal during the 1930s. The Agrarians, a vociferous if small group of intellectuals loosely affiliated with Vanderbilt University, published I'll Take My Stand (1930), a collective anti-industry manifesto. These academics argued that in their haste to reenter the Union, southerners had cast aside entrenched southern values in a "rush to industrialize." The Agrarians and many other observers believed that only the South's agrarian roots could preserve a tranquil, spiritually focused life that would rescue the nation from its reckless march toward industrial progress and social disintegration. But

The Most Modern Retail Doughnut Shop in the South

18 Delicious Varieties to Choose from!

"Made Light and Krispy the Krispy Kreme way"

● ———————— ●

★ **Glazed** ★ **Jelly Filled** ★ **Cream Filled**
★ **Cinnamon Twists**
★ **Cake Doughnuts with Chocolate**
★ **Vanilla and Maple Icing** ★ **Peanuts**
★ **Cocoanut** ★ **Glazed** ★ **Sugared**
★ **Cinnamon and Other Combinations**

● ———————— ●

See them made continuously in
our Modern, Wide Open Kitchen

● ———————— ●

ACRES OF FREE PARKING

RISPY KREME Doughnut Co.

A Krispy Kreme advertisement, circa 1950, inviting customers to see doughnuts made "continuously in our Modern, Wide Open Kitchen." (Krispy Kreme Doughnut Corporation Records, circa 1937–97, #594, Box 7, Folder 7, Archives Center, National Museum of American History, Behring Center, Smithsonian Institution, Washington, D.C.)

Employees combine hand and machine labor at a Birmingham, Alabama, Krispy Kreme in 1958. (Krispy Kreme Doughnut Corporation Records, circa 1937–97, #594, Box 19, Folder 2, Archives Center, National Museum of American History, Behring Center, Smithsonian Institution, Washington, D.C.)

such verdicts could be reached only by individuals in positions of privilege who remained largely unaware of the difficulties of agricultural labor that had driven many people to industrial jobs.[24]

Southern mill workers may have arrived at the same verdict of "reckless" southern industrialization, albeit from a different evidentiary base. The overproduction of cotton during the 1920s depressed prices and heightened competition, economically ravaging the region. Between 1920 and 1930, the South's urban population increased by 25 percent as residents sought opportunities away from farms and mill towns. Yet low wages, lack of job security, stretch-outs, and layoffs meant that most people could not regard industrial employment as viable.[25] The onset of the Great Depression worsened conditions, resulting in strikes and high unemployment that revealed the precariousness of southern industrial dreams.

Customers who frequented Rudolph's Winston-Salem store may have been unaware of these broader issues when they came in search of doughnuts. Machine dreams and industrial volatility did not cause the success of Krispy Kreme, of course; rather, this dialectic produced a climate particularly well suited for the success of Krispy Kreme. LeBeau, the French chef from whom Rudolph's uncle purchased a store and doughnut recipe, floundered in New Orleans. The Rudolphs encountered similar difficulties after opening their shop in Paducah. Even Adolph Levitt, who created the automatic doughnut machine and promoted it heavily in his New York City store, enjoyed limited success. Only in the southern belt of textile and tobacco mill towns, beginning in Winston-Salem and stretching across the region, did machine-made doughnuts generate fevered demand. Krispy Kreme offered consumers tangible (and edible) evidence of the long-perpetuated and deferred promise that machines brought ease and comfort to southern life. Yet Rudolph's factory did not displace rural ways: handwork, batter mixing, and southern hospitality stayed very much a part of Krispy Kreme. In this sense, the doughnut embraced the city without displacing the village.

Circular Soldiers: Visible Machines and Synchronized Consumers, 1955–1973

Historian Terry E. Smith has argued that in the 1920s and 1930s, visual representations of modernity came to constitute a "regime of sense." Working across representations of industry, agriculture, cities, products, and consumers, Smith posits that the visual symbols of modernity provided by photographs, murals, and world's fair displays created a way of thinking about modernity for those who viewed them. Since that view validated the continued expansion of automated production, a regime of sense emerged that benefited the government and large corporations. To make this argument, Smith advocates active interpretations of the visual: a photograph or experienced environment not merely represents what he calls a "regime of truth" but becomes a "constructive constituent of [that] regime."[26] Here I consider the experience of consuming Krispy Kreme doughnuts from the late 1950s through the early 1970s as an intensely visual one—a mode of seeing the product that actively changed the meaning of consumers' experiences. An extensive redesign of both the physical space of the store and the means of doughnut production enabled Krispy Kreme to create a motorized performance that engaged participants in a carefully constructed relationship between consumer pleasure and mechanization. The new arrangement upended the previous balance between machines, hand labor, and consumers. Whereas consumers' previous visual experience suggested that machines properly complemented hand labor, the new design enhanced machines and nearly removed labor from view. The resulting environment emphasized the connection between machines and consumers. To understand this change and its support within a region of entrenched ambivalence about the place of industry in everyday life, this process must be considered a creation of both physical space and a "regime of sense." For southerners confronting a cultural modernity that arrived distinctly later than that of the North, Krispy Kreme's visible assembly line offered patrons an opportunity to partake in a practice that both signified progress and connected them intimately to the rhythms of machines.

Between the 1950s and the late 1960s, Krispy Kreme expanded its stores within and beyond its home region. Successful expansion brought significant profits, enabling Rudolph to improve his machine systems to craft a fully uniform doughnut. To this end, he gradually eliminated hand cutting from stores in the 1950s and replaced these employees with automatic cutting machines. He also centralized machine production facilities in a separate machine shop in Winston-Salem. There, engineers created the most advanced machines for doughnut production, including automatic proofing, cooking, glazing, and loading machines. Rudolph emerged in this period as more an engineer than doughnut maker: one employee remembered his boss's insistence on pursuing innovation even at the cost of profit and efficiency. In the mid-1960s, Rudolph installed a computerized batching system in store mix departments and refused to give up on the system even when its malfunctioning card-reading system necessitated frequent production stoppages.[27]

Customers experienced this march toward automation through a standardization of taste and an automated visual experience. The first change was slight, the second dramatic. Rudolph's desire to increase doughnut sales spurred his decision to pursue these standardizations. While the Krispy Kreme wholesale business remained a vital contributor to company profits, Rudolph increasingly saw the stores themselves as important sources of consumer desire and brand identification. With roughly thirty shops across six southeastern states and a growing base of loyal customers, he recognized the necessity of constructing stores easily identifiable from nearby interstates and of producing products that delivered a uniform taste across disparate localities. Here, however, I focus on another motivation: providing customers an unobstructed view of an intensely automated production process.

Krispy Kreme's mechanized redesign took two forms in the late 1950s and 1960s. The first can be seen in the Birmingham, Alabama, store built in 1959. Here customers experienced a retail space similar to earlier stores; the difference lies in the windows behind the cash register that allowed customers to see into a new, more automated production center. The design effectively separated retail from production and privileged the retail delivery of product over the wholesale production behind the back window. The view into the back production area captivated customers' attention, however. Over the next few years, Rudolph spearheaded efforts to redesign store interiors with the single goal of expanding this industrial view.

It is in many ways curious that southern consumers increased their consumption of Krispy Kremes after a renovation designed explicitly to render machines more prominent within the purchasing experience.[28] A partial explanation lies in the transnational, postwar attraction to all things industrial, a desire stoked by the National Association of Manufacturers (NAM) through promotional vehicles such as the popular public television series *Industry on Parade*. Narrated by the National Broadcasting Company's Arthur Lodge, the 13.5-minute episodes, part documentary and part propaganda, ran from 1950 through the mid-1960s. A typical episode featured four short segments on factory production in the United States, encouraging viewers to meditate on the importance of the free market, investment in business, and the symbiotic relationship between maximum machine production and a high American standard of living.[29] The series repeatedly featured American factory workers contentedly producing goods for consumers' material comfort. This circle of machine, labor, and consumption was best expressed by two NAM promotional materials: NAM's "Soldiers of Production" series, in which audiences in eleven cities in 1945 heard speakers stress the virtues of factory work, and *You and Machines*, a classroom instruction book that taught students that "better living comes from machines" and "better machines cost money." Within these materials, NAM sought to clearly establish placated, efficient labor and industrial investment as the core generators of material pleasure for consumers. The most important contribution consumers could make to the health of this system was to buy more items produced by better machines.[30]

Of course, neither *Industry on Parade* nor NAM's educational efforts caused southern consumers to crave Krispy Kreme doughnuts. Rather, these school-sanctioned messages of citizenship via industrial investment and home-experienced visual tropes of machines producing material pleasure and protecting democracy encouraged both northern and southern consumers to view machines in a positive light. Krispy Kreme's new interiors echoed the lesson. The *Industry on Parade* trope of machine presentation mirrored that of Krispy Kreme's new automated system. Each episode allowed customers to witness mechanized production, to see the product as an infinitely replicable, uniform entity, and to ingest visually the product and ideology at the end of the segment. In addition, *Industry on Parade* relied on food factories to make the pleasurable connection among machines, products, and consumers. Roughly one in five episodes featured some variation on the mechanized process of modern food production—oranges speeding along conveyor belts to become frozen juice, veggies and fruits efficiently compressed into "nutritious" foods for babies, tons of wheat pressed into packaged crackers, and flash-frozen green beans by the truckload. Each segment featured close-up shots of conveyor belts and production machines collaborating to produce dizzying rows of uniform products. Lodge rendered food heroic through rhetorical flair: oranges did not merely travel on conveyor belts, they were "as so many rush-hour subway riders battling for position"; cans of beans were not just seasoned with tomato sauce and sugar but rather comprised the comforts of "Grandma's recipe" made efficiently for the masses.[31]

Although *Industry on Parade* appeared across the nation to generally enthusiastic reviews, southern cities proved particularly receptive to Lodge's material. Commentators suggested that the series served not merely as good entertainment but also as an important educational tool. "We find this to be an excellent, informative show [and] wish there were more shows like it," reported the film director of WBTV in Charlotte and Greensboro, North Carolina, to the show's producers in 1952. Norfolk, Virginia, viewers purportedly considered the shows "very interesting," wrote one station manager in his program evaluation. In Huntington, West Virginia, the programs proved popular enough that one station manager sought to "make arrangements with the schools in this area to use the film in their weekly assemblies." A manager at the public broadcasting station in Richmond, Virginia, declared *Industry on Parade* "the finest [material] of its kind offered to television stations."[32] In the context of such enthusiasm, Krispy Kreme undertook its extensive renovations. A newspaper story on the opening of one of the new stores included a photo of doughnuts on a conveyor belt behind consumers in the retail area, captioned, with Lodge-like rhetorical flourish, as "circular soldiers marching off to market."[33]

In this environment, Krispy Kreme transformed its interior production view from one of homegrown mechanics to one of large-scale industrial science. According to a company brochure, the uniform redesign of all Krispy Kreme stores included "enhanced" viewing windows "to show conveyor belts moving fresh-made doughnuts past the eyes of hungry consumers."[34] Company newsletters reveal the concerted effort to improve consumer access to doughnut machines. In 1965 the Tuscaloosa, Alabama, shop installed plate-glass windows, "allowing customers to see activity in the production room." In 1963 the third Nashville, Tennessee, store opened with "a back wall with windows looking into the production area." Some stores opened additional areas to consumer inspection, such as the Fort Walton, Florida, store, where in 1959 customers observed the packaging room while purchasing doughnuts, an approach that the franchise owner believed increased business by allowing people to see "doughnuts packaged under sanitary and efficient conditions with a minimum of confusion."[35] Company architects and executives, according to internal documents, served as standard-bearers, bringing the message of visible production to the hundred stores across the South. "Possibly accent tile could be introduced to make the production area more interesting to the viewer," suggested a company executive to one store owner in the mid-1960s. Such a change would better "exploit the feature you have of seeing your products produced."[36]

By 1965, Krispy Kreme realized its ideal store design in the Ponce de Leon Avenue franchise in Atlanta. Archival photographs reveal a new seamlessness between the retail and production areas and a significant increase in the size and number of automated machines in use. To understand how this environment functioned as a regime of sense whereby consumers experienced a relationship to machines as beneficial, it is helpful to consider Krispy Kreme in this era as a three-stage process. The exterior rendered the interior transparent and fully visible from the parking lot and surrounding streetscape. Designed to attract attention from surrounding boulevards and highways, the store presented two primary symbols to alert drivers to Krispy Kreme: a large sign emblazoned with the standard crowned "KK" and a view that passed directly through the retail space and into the mechanized production area in the back of the building. After entering the store, customers found themselves invited to sit at a rectangular counter, where an all-female, primarily white staff accepted their orders. Customers seated at the counter could look out the windows onto the parking lots or, more likely, look behind the menu boards through the wide windows at the conveyor system carrying an endless stream of hot doughnuts. Customers who pressed their noses against the glass could glimpse the production area itself, a six-thousand-square-foot space where doughnuts whisked from machine to machine without, it seemed, the aid of human labor.[37] One company brochure aptly described the production facility as a "modern laboratory" where the "completely automated" process had "revolutionized the industry."[38] The uniforms of female attendants strengthened the signification of a high-tech space. Dressed in white shoes, dresses, and triangular caps, these women looked more like nurses than doughnut packagers. The expansive space, hygienic environment, and sparse white-coated machine attendants make *laboratory* a particularly effective descriptor. The production area appeared to be an environment where actual laboring bodies impeded rather than assisted in the production of goods. Over the next decade, most Krispy Kremes were redesigned with this same three-part formula, although stores frequently differed in the size and complexity of their automated machines, depending on the demand of their wholesale markets.

Taken as a regime of sense, Krispy Kreme's postwar redesign asserts that machines themselves should generate doughnuts. Human hands were necessary only in the final stages of the process, and then those hands were kept at bay by sanitary "sticks" used to catch doughnuts by the holes.[39] This marked a dramatic departure from previous Krispy Kreme interiors as well as a departure from the world of industrial progress promoted by the NAM. *Industry on Parade* relied on visual narratives of labor. As Lodge's voice explained the broader democratic significance of supporting industrial expansion, cameras featured men and women actively engaged in making and operating machines. Consumers' attraction to automated, labor-free doughnuts in the 1960s South merely echoed the attraction of labor-free production heralded primarily in the North during the 1930s. As Jeffrey Meikle and Joel Dinerstein have argued, the 1930s in general represented a time of popular machine aesthetics that privileged the pace and sound of the machine over the presence of its human operator or creator.[40] Literature, films, and world's fairs abound with examples of Americans equating the performance of the machine with progress. Some pundits warned against the dangers of the machine, particularly as it facilitated the regimentation of labor; nevertheless, outside of the South, consumers regularly celebrated machine aesthetics. The popularity of industrial photography, world's fair exhibits, and streamlined trains reveals an attraction to what Smith calls "an anatomy of the mechanical," or a particular presentation of machines as complex entities capable of performance if not agency.[41]

Southerners largely avoided embarking on celebrations of machines in the 1930s. Their own particular history of fostering volatile industrial economies and the prominence of anti-industrial public intellectuals encouraged a more ambivalent view of machines than contemporary northerners possessed, particularly in regard to questions of human labor. Perhaps in part as a result, Rudolph, in spite of his engineering abilities, opted to restrict mechanization to his Ring King Junior until well into the 1950s.[42] At the same time, the stark mechanization of the Ponce de Leon Avenue store affords an opportunity to ask why southern consumers displayed eagerness—arguably, even more eagerness than their northern peers who frequented the less visibly automated factories of McDonalds or White Castle—to purchase and ingest products of the technological laboratory.

Syncopation, or the lack thereof, provides a useful metaphor for the industrial experience of many southerners, especially after the Second World War. In his analysis of jazz music, Dinerstein argues that a "techno-

The new Krispy Kreme store design in the early 1970s at the store on Government Street in Mobile, Alabama. (Krispy Kreme Doughnut Corporation Records, circa 1937–97, #594, Box 19, Folder 2, Archives Center, National Museum of American History, Behring Center, Smithsonian Institution, Washington, D.C.)

dialogic" exists in American music whereby African American musicians worked, particularly in the 1920s and 1930s, to incorporate the sounds of machines into rhythms that could be experienced by the human body.[43] Duke Ellington's "Harlem Air Shaft," for example, used horns to render the sound of babies crying, windows breaking, and trains passing into melodies that became physical experiences for listeners. Music facilitated this syncopation of body and machine that consumers desired. Krispy Kreme accomplished much the same result.

Wartime industrial expansion, much of it fueled by federal dollars, produced profound growth in southern factory employment and a profound sense of dislocation and disorder on the part of many who experienced the boom.[44] The South, in the words of historian David Goldfield, "transformed itself into the epitome of the urbanized, postindustrial sunbelt," but the transformation may have represented too much, too fast. In Mississippi, income rose by 100 percent during the war years, yet without the accompanying infrastructural support, even secure income failed to guarantee housing or a viable mode of transportation to or from a factory job. In 1943 a *Washington Post* reporter toured the urbanizing South and encountered cities overflowing with war workers who lacked basic services, describing the situation in an article titled "Journey through Chaos." Continued government sponsorship of the military-industrial complex during the Cold War perpetuated southerners' growing pains.[45]

The Ponce de Leon Avenue store in Atlanta, circa 1965. (Krispy Kreme Doughnut Corporation Records, circa 1937–97, #594, Box 19, Folder 38, National Museum of American History, Behring Center, Smithsonian Institution, Washington, D.C.)

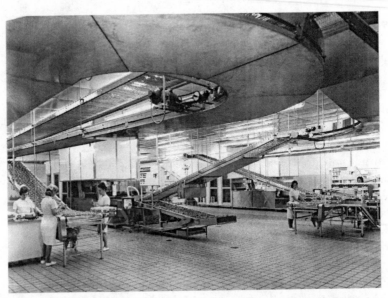

The back production area at Atlanta's Ponce de Leon Avenue Krispy Kreme, circa 1965. (Krispy Kreme Doughnut Corporation Records, circa 1937–97, #594, Box 19, Folder 38, National Museum of American History, Behring Center, Smithsonian Institution, Washington, D.C.)

Krispy Kreme represented the antithesis of a journey through chaos. Customers inextricably linked the visual pleasure of watching doughnuts precisely and efficiently produced with the sensual pleasure of consuming those produced doughnuts. From the vantage point of the early 1990s, Lisa McNary recounted her memories of her first experience with Krispy Kreme twenty-five years earlier. It was "the first shop I ever saw" that "mechanically showed the flipping of doughnuts into that pool of luscious icing." Wes Eisenberg of Jacksonville, Florida, recalled equally vivid memories of going to Krispy Kreme as a child and watching "the machines for the longest time" while his father, "mesmerized by the mechanics," stood nearby. Visiting an "original" store in the 1990s, Tim Boyer described what pleased him about the encounter in terms that could well have been written in the 1960s: there was, he declared, "something very special about following the doughnut's life cycle all the way to my mouth."[46]

Each account suggests Smith's description of the "anatomy of a machine." Here close exposure to automated machines and conveyor belts lent the machines some near-human attributes in consumers' minds. The arrangement achieved an immediacy between the machine and the consumer, a phenomenon all the more notable for the fact that stores positioned machines behind glass, well beyond consumers' reach. Krispy Kreme directly connected consumers and machines, in part precisely because of this distance. Watching the machines required one's attention—customers had to look through the window to follow the process. Looking away meant losing track of a doughnut. Searching for the process pulled consumers into the mechanized process and involved them in the creation of their doughnuts. The lack of apparent operators likely facilitated patrons' interest; customers may have stood in as proxies to ensure that doughnuts in fact reached the desired destination—the viewers' mouths.

Good Krispy Kremes were and are hot Krispy Kremes. To procure hot doughnuts, customers in the 1960s synchronized their desires to the rhythm of machines. Krispy Kreme officials waited until the late 1980s to schedule production times to coincide with retail demand. Previously, shops geared hot production toward wholesale customers, ensuring a system in which production times varied from store to store and customers remained uncertain regarding the availability of hot doughnuts. Since stores eyed wholesale markets, machines typically operated late into the evening and only irregularly during the day, depending on sales. When doughnuts were hot, a light would go on at the front of the store, alerting passersby (and potential customers). Stewart Deck recalled that as a child, he had enjoyed what he called "the whole experience" of seeing doughnuts made. Part of this experience was "standing in the parking lot, waiting in the car for the hot light to come on."[47] According to Scott Livengood, Deck was not alone—customers often waited for the production machines to run before entering the store. The pursuit of a Krispy Kreme frequently necessitated looking for doughnuts at times when consumers might not otherwise have desired them.[48]

Photographs from the Ponce de Leon Avenue store thus can be deceiving. If the "laboratory" is seen as a region devoid of workers, the space appears alienating and cold. Such a system seems far removed from the blended space where hand labor and machine technique combined to produce Rudolph's early products. The postwar Krispy Kreme certainly reveals a new machine aesthetic in the South that was encouraged by programs such as *Industry on Parade* that depicted progress in the form of "circular soldiers" and that resonated particularly in a region that had yet to experience industry without chaos. Nevertheless, consumers may not ultimately have experienced the interior as terribly different from that of the 1937 store, given the cultural context. Both enabled customers to establish a desired rhythm with machines. In the 1930s and 1940s, customers likely found balance in the production process; by the 1950s and 1960s, the customer-production relationship appears focused on the consumption process. The complexity of Krispy Kreme's machines drew in eyes, ears, and taste buds as consumers found themselves absorbed in the process without the distractions of machine operators. Whether through *Industry on Parade* messages or the workings of the machines themselves, customers had ample opportunity to learn that they had a part in the production process. *You and Industry* is an apt title for Krispy Kreme's regime of sense in the postwar era. By erasing labor and emphasizing machines, Krispy Kreme's physical space encouraged an intimate experience of industrial production that created pleasure. The exchange elevated customers' importance within the automated system and syncopated production and consumption needs between human and machine.

Doughnut Theater: Reading the Postindustrial Krispy Kreme, 1973–2006

In 1985, prospective Krispy Kreme employees received specific instructions about how to do their jobs the "Krispy Kreme Way." "As you look into the retail area and into the production area," explained an employee manual, *Becoming a Production Professional*, "you quickly see that windows allow our customers to watch us make their doughnuts. Krispy Kreme is on display and you, as the person who actually makes the doughnuts, are the star of our show." After employees learned to master the craft and performance of production, the brochure explained, they were invited to "take a bow."[49]

Shortly after Vernon Rudolph died in 1973, Beatrice Foods purchased Krispy Kreme. Beatrice introduced numerous changes to the products and space of Krispy Kreme, most notably by adding soups and sandwiches to the menu and changing the doughnut recipe. Between 1976 and 1988, Krispy Kreme halted its forty-year period of store expansion. In 1988, several franchise owners united to buy back the company. They followed their successful bid with a strategic expansion plan intended to increase profits and resurrect brand equity. The grand scheme emerged after the new owners concluded a series of focus-group discussions with loyal customers that sought to define more clearly Krispy Kreme's core attraction. The answer appeared in a set of general themes, including *wholesome, positive,* and *fun family times.* Each of these themes formed part of something the company called "the hot doughnut experience."[50]

Beginning in 1989, Krispy Kreme consciously set out to capitalize on this experience. The company adjusted the production times in existing stores to ensure that the doughnut machines ran at times of peak consumer demand. All franchise owners received instructions to "take [a] large block of time in the morning and evening and dedicate it to the retail customer and the hot doughnut experience."[51] Krispy Kreme became, in the words of corporate biographers, "a true retail company" by moving the focus from wholesale to in-store consumption. Since consumer research clearly showed that patrons visited Krispy Kreme because of the mechanized production system and the great-tasting doughnuts, the best strategy for the company's post-Beatrice revitalization appeared to be in retiring production processes that befit "a wholesaler that just happened to do some retail sales."[52]

Between the late 1980s and the late 1990s, Krispy Kreme expanded far beyond the South, opening high-profile stores in Las Vegas, Manhattan, and Los Angeles. Each of these new retail centers was designed as a "doughnut theater." Instead of occurring behind glass walls, removed from the retail area, doughnut production now moved into the retail space. Customers who entered theater stores confronted the conveyor system as they lined up to buy at the counter: they could not miss the constant stream of doughnuts flowing into the retail area, often making a semicircle out from and then back to the counter before heading back to be boxed or sold directly to waiting customers. To draw customers into the theater, stores illuminated the "Hot Now" light from 5:30 A.M. to 11:00 A.M. and 5:30 P.M. to 11:00 P.M. To ensure that customers realized that they were part of the show, many stores incorporated participatory elements, including the distribution of paper production hats to kids and occasional invitations for customers to come backstage to see the machines positioned out of sight.

According to Mac McAleer, a franchisee in Texas and former member of the board of directors, promoters of the reorganization sought a "multi-sensory" method of retailing that would cause customers to associate Krispy Kreme with fun times.[53] Customer letters to the company continued to emphasize the doughnut machine, so McAleer and Livengood decided to center the experience on production by moving the machines from behind the glass to a more interactive position. "One thing that we are very intentional about is making sure that the doughnut-making process is visible and that the Krispy Kreme experience is a multi-sensory experience," Livengood told readers of the company's official corporate biography, published in 2004. "There are certain elements of our brand that are captivating. Once in the store, we have our doughnut-making theater. We have that glass wall where you can see the entire doughnut-making process going on."[54]

This strategy has succeeded in many respects. Lines at store openings in Las Vegas and Los Angeles stretched around the buildings as customers eagerly awaited "Hot Doughnuts Now." The Manhattan store generated a literal feeding frenzy, with hour-long lines and extensive press coverage that included Nora Ephron declaring in the *New Yorker* that "the sight of all those doughnuts marching solemnly to their fate makes me proud to be an American."[55] Throughout the late 1990s, Krispy Kreme expansions provoked displays of consumer exuberance. Some of this phenomenon must be attributed to the company's savvy promotional techniques, which included sending dozens of free doughnuts to newspaper and television news agencies before openings as well as to television personalities who might mention the product on the air. However, such public enthusiasm also suggests that the theater appealed to Krispy Kreme buyers both beyond and within the South. The theater concept has proved successful as measured by expansion. By January 2007, the chain had expanded to 395 stores in forty states and had outlets in Canada, the United Kingdom, the Philippines, South Korea, Mexico, Japan, Hong Kong, Australia, Indonesia, and Kuwait.[56]

If Krispy Kreme's success has to some degree resulted from a regime of sense in which customers experience machines in ways they find pleasurable, these new theaters may tell us something about the place of machines, labor, and consumer pleasure in the early twenty-first century. The interior spaces of these retail environments leave little doubt that machines at Krispy Kreme have changed dramatically from the 1940s and 1960s. There is no hand labor here; there is not even a laboratory with scientific tenders. Employees are instructed that their primary responsibility is to help put on a show for consumers, a job description that can be followed only if employees do not need to pay attention to operate the machines. Customers no longer tour the Ring King Junior in the "factory" of the 1940s, look through the small windows of the 1950s, or watch the production process from their barstools as in the 1960s. Today, Krispy Kreme machines, with their curving conveyor belts, literally embrace customers, pushing out into the consumer space rather than pulling consumers into the production space. Consumers see the final moment of conveyed consumption and retail workers delivering the show. And the old serendipity required to connect consumers with hot doughnuts has disappeared; today, doughnuts are not "Hot Now" for only a few hours each day.

If doughnut theater is how Americans now want their Krispy Kreme, the current place of industry in everyday life helps us understand this preference. In the postindustrial era, when the promise of factory work has proven illusory for most Americans, we may indeed desire to experience Krispy Kreme machines as something other than mirrors of the factory experience. While the nostalgic photos of old southern Krispy Kreme stores hanging on the walls or on exterior murals continue to connect the store experience with mechanized labor and factory views, the production machines themselves tell a much different story. They are now scaled down, friendly, and even performative. At today's Krispy Kreme, even the machines work in customer service.

Several years ago, Livengood, the former Krispy Kreme executive, suggested that experiencing the store's new retail environments was like "standing on the ocean front and watching the tide come in." The key element in producing this analogous experience, he explained, was the conveyors, which offered "that same consistent, relaxing motion that is really positive to people who may or may not understand what is happening to them."[57] It is possible to make too much of such a statement; Livengood certainly is not suggesting that the company designs its facilities to hypnotize its consumers. Yet the description of the store as the ocean and the conveyor belts as the "tide com[ing] in" reflects a dramatic shift from the iconology of machines in earlier stores. In the 1930s and 1940s, customers experienced directly the combination of hand and machine labor involved in doughnut production and imagined themselves partaking of an agrarian factory floor. In the 1960s, a more automated environment facilitated a synchronicity between consumers and machines; the view may have been "mesmerizing," but consumers were spellbound by viewing the actual production process. Livengood's rhetoric suggests that technology now happens to rather than for consumers at Krispy Kreme. No longer participatory laboratories of innovation, stores since the 1990s have turned production machines into another element of the interior decor.[58]

Increasingly, however, evidence suggests that customers are finding something lacking at Krispy Kreme. Sales began to drop after 2000, a fact that some observers attributed to Krispy Kreme's rapid expansion. It might also be attributed to the hot doughnut machine. In 2001, after three years of research, the company introduced a dramatically different doughnut production technique in several stores. Requiring only one thousand square feet instead of the six thousand needed for a typical factory store, the new machine facilitated brand expansion in urban areas or smaller suburban markets where the cost of retail space was prohibitive or the customer base was limited. Doughnuts could not be made in such limited space, but they could be reheated. Premade doughnuts are brought into the store, often from a commissary or off-site factory production area not open for viewing. They are then placed into the machine, reheated, and then conveyed and glazed in front of retail customers. "I was amazed," commented one executive who experienced the system at a Charlotte store, "just amazed and proud. Every customer who came through picked up a hot doughnut, ate the doughnut, and was happy. They never noticed the piece of missing equipment, the fryer." "We've gone to great measures," he continued, "to make sure the experience is the same." The decline in sales, however, suggests otherwise.[59]

There are numerous possible reasons for Krispy Kreme's recent profit plunge. The chain's expansion may translate into too many stores making it too easy to get doughnuts. In time, demand may rise to meet supply. Or the decline in sales might stem from the fact that Krispy Kreme no longer delivers the same experience that built passionate connections to this product over its first half century. Krispy Kreme officials certainly understand that customers come for the machines. But in the rush to create a multisensory experience, they likely failed sufficiently to probe the ways in which consumers wanted to see the machines.

By crafting an experience that emphasizes performance over production, Krispy Kreme has departed from the formula Vernon Rudolph inadvertently created, a formula that succeeded precisely because customers wanted to know what was happening to them because of machines. This process was held together by an echoing effect whereby Krispy Kreme functioned not merely as a doughnut factory but rather as a factory closely connected to "real" factories, either in its self-conscious presentation or in its visible iconology. Today, discerning what a Krispy Kreme "factory" might mirror is difficult—as difficult as defining the postmodern South. Now that there are few factory jobs and the decline of viable unions to ensure fair industrial wages for those jobs that remain, Krispy Kreme can no longer easily be framed as one of many industrial processes in the landscape. Factory jobs failed to create viable "cities of every village," as southerners once hoped. And many cities that factories did foster, continue, along with their inhabitants, to struggle in the wake of out-sourcing and plant closures facilitated by cheaper land and cheaper labor in the global marketplace. Perhaps in this regard, people do understand what is happening to them at Krispy Kreme. Standing in the center of the retail theater, customers look into a mirror of our lowered industrial ex-pectations. As with increasingly packaged factory tours where consum-ers watch premade videos of industrial production before being routed quickly to the gift shop, we happily celebrate machine-made products. But such happiness depends on keeping a safe distance from the actual process of production, lest we ask where, by whom, and at what cost our goods are produced. Krispy Kreme once manufactured pleasure by visu-ally embedding consumers within the signifiers of their industrial dreams. For southerners raised in a culture long haunted by a sense of inferiority to northern industrial power, the pursuit of such dreams continues to make worthwhile an occasional nostalgic, if lengthy, road trip. But the current troubles faced by Krispy Kreme suggest that whether by attempt-ing to appeal to a national market or simply because of changes within the South itself, the store has lost much of its meaning, both in the chain's home region and among descendants of the southern diaspora of the twentieth century. Indeed, given fears of corporate outsourcing, the ma-chines central to the production of Krispy Kreme doughnuts might trig-ger more angst than comfort. Krispy Kreme's recent decline may simply result from overextension or the popularity of the Atkins diet. It may also be that our problem with the doughnut actually involves the view.

NOTES

1. Krispy Kreme spends roughly one hundred thousand dollars a year on ad-vertising and promotion. In 2004, it was the third-strongest brand after Tar-get and Apple, both of which spend "tens of millions of dollars" on advertise-ments and promotions (Kirk Kazanjian and Amy Joyner, *Making Dough: The Twelve Secret Ingredients of Krispy Kreme's Sweet Success* [Hoboken, N.J.: Wi-ley, 2004], 82).

2. E. P. Thompson, "The Moral Economy of the English Crowd in the Eigh-teenth Century," in *The Essential E. P. Thompson*, ed. Dorothy Thompson (New York: New Press, 2001), 321. I thank Amy Bentley for bringing this essay to my attention.

3. A. Monroe Aurand Jr., ed., *Cooking with the Pennsylvania Dutch* (Harris-burg, Pa.: Aurand, 1946), 7.

4. Southerners typically connect food experiences to particular memories. "When I think of home . . . I think of food like this," commented Natalie Grant of Alabama during a "southerners" feast for expatriates living in Manhattan (John Egerton, *Southern Food: At Home, on the Road, in History* [New York: Knopf, 1987], 2).

5. Ibid., 28.

6. Finding aid, Krispy Kreme Doughnut Corporation Records, circa 1937–1997, #594, Archives Center, Smithsonian National Museum of American History, Washington, D.C., http://americanhistory.si.edu/archives/d7594.htm (accessed 26 November 2007). See also Kazanjian and Joyner, *Making Dough*, xv.

7. Rudolph's decision to give away doughnuts in the evening suggests that Krispy Kreme doughnuts were not originally intended for breakfast. This may explain why there is little evidence of resistance to the product in spite of the fact that the southern breakfast was seen as an essential social and familial event and played an important role in the performance of patriarchy across classes into the twentieth century. For more information, see Anthony Stanonis's essay in this volume.

8. Edward Ayers, *The Promise of the New South: Life after Reconstruction* (New York: Oxford University Press, 1992), 322–24.

9. Followers of Booker T. Washington could see in industrial growth an opportunity for blacks and whites to achieve social coexistence rather than integration. With additional training in the trades and industrial labor, blacks would find valued employment and gradually move up the economic ladder, creating economic collaboration while protecting racial separation, a process Washington described as like "separate fingers on a hand of mutual progress" (ibid., 55).

10. Ibid.

11. Ibid., 62. For studies of southern attitudes toward industrialization, see David Carlton, *Mill and Town in South Carolina, 1880–1920* (Baton Rouge: Louisiana State University Press, 1982); Robert Dorman, *Revolt of the Provinces: The Regionalist Movement in America, 1920–1945* (Chapel Hill: University of North Carolina Press, 1993); Douglas Flamming, *Creating the Modern South: Millhands and Managers in Dalton, Georgia, 1884–1984* (Chapel Hill: University of North Carolina Press, 1992); Paul Gaston, *The New South Creed: A Study in Southern Mythmaking* (Baton Rouge: Louisiana State University Press, 1976). According to W. J. Cash, the late nineteenth-century South sought to build "more than a thousand mills" (*The Mind of the South* [1941; New York: Vintage, 1991], 192).

12. Ayers, *Promise of the New South*, 59.

13. Ibid. Such sentiments were supported by the reaction of one journalist in Greenville, Alabama, who, when streetcars arrived in 1892, predicted that "the next things will be electric lights, then will come factories, etc. let the good things come" (*Greenville Advocate*, 26 October 1892, qtd. in ibid., 72).

14. According to Ted Ownby, factory workers were "associated with consumption in the minds of all Southerners" in the late nineteenth century because the high wages and cash payment system in factories gave such workers more disposable income than rural workers (*American Dreams in Mississippi: Consumers, Poverty, and Culture, 1830–1998* [Chapel Hill: University of North Carolina Press, 1999], 85). For more information, see Joe Gray Taylor, *Eating, Drinking, and Visiting in the South: An Informal History* (Baton Rouge: Louisiana State University Press, 1982), 107. Some contradiction exists in the ways in which middle- and upper-class southerners viewed factory workers, particularly in the

nineteenth century. Factory workers may have been associated with higher wages than agricultural laborers during this period but were not generally afforded more respect than those who worked outside of the factory. According to Cash, there was "social contempt" for industrial workers by 1900, as is demonstrated by the common epithets of "factory rats" and "lint heads" to refer to cotton mill workers (*Mind of the South*, 201–2).

15. Arthur Palmer Hudson, "An Attala Boyhood," *Journal of Mississippi History* 4 (July 1942): 151, qtd. in Ayers, *Promise of the New South*, 59.

16. *Harrison Times*, 6 March 1897, qtd. in Ayers, *Promise of the New South*, 59. Cecilia Tichi argues that mechanical metaphors were commonly used during this era to describe the workings of the human body (*Shifting Gears: Technology, Literature, and Culture in Modernist America* [Chapel Hill: University of North Carolina Press, 1987]).

17. Ayers, *Promise of the New South*, 62.

18. Louise Skillman, "A Brief Outline of the History of Krispy Kreme," 1977, Krispy Kreme Records, Box 1, Folder 2. Rudolph opened his second shop in Charlotte, North Carolina, in 1938, and another in Charleston, West Virginia, in 1941. By 1946, he had incorporated the assets of other shops he converted into Krispy Kremes. By 1947 a "number" of new stores were licensed to franchisees. By 1952, Krispy Kreme had expanded to Tampa, Florida. Information on store openings taken from the timeline featured in Kazanjian and Joyner, *Making Dough*, 196–99.

19. Krispy Kreme advertisement, circa 1950, Krispy Kreme Records, Box 7, Folder 7. Prospective customers likely connected the offer to tour the factory with better known factory tours, such as that at Heinz, where, since the late nineteenth century, members of the consuming public saw for themselves that Heinz's ketchup was the product of clean young women in clean white aprons using hygienic funneling techniques. For more information, see Laura Shapiro, *Perfection Salad: Women and Cooking at the Turn of the Century* (New York: Modern Library, 2001).

20. The presentation of doughnut fryers in popular culture may have made customers more likely to associate doughnut machines than similarly simple machines with factories. In the Homer Price story "The Doughnuts," Robert McCloskey has his hero do battle with an overzealous Ring King look-alike in his uncle's diner (*Homer Price* [New York: Puffin, 1943], 50–68). Eddie Cantor's *Palmy Days* (1931) is set in a doughnut factory, where the machines provide the syncopation for the female dancers/operators. And the 1933–34 Chicago World's Fair featured an automatic doughnut fryer among its modern inventions.

21. Kazanjian and Joyner, *Making Dough*, 11.

22. Ibid., 103. Krispy Kreme did not develop the first automatic doughnut machine in the United States. Adolph Levitt built a machine in 1920 that he displayed in his Manhattan bakery window. By 1930, his success enabled him to open a large store at the corner of Forty-fifth and Broadway that featured his machines. It appears likely that Rudolph purchased a similar machine before developing his own Ring King Junior. According to Levitt's granddaughter, Levitt sold 128 of these machines—which bear a striking resemblance to the Ring

King—the first year. See Sally Levitt Steinberg, *The Donut Book* (New York: Knopf, 1987), 23.

23. Ayers, *Promise of the New South*, 63.

24. For information on the Agrarians, see *I'll Take My Stand: The South and the Agrarian Tradition* (1930; Baton Rouge: Louisiana State University Press, 1970), xxv–xxvi; Paul Conkin, *The Southern Agrarians* (Knoxville: University of Tennessee Press, 1988), 57–88; Dorman, *Revolt of the Provinces*, 105–44; Grace Elizabeth Hale, *Making Whiteness: The Culture of Segregation in the South, 1890–1940* (New York: Pantheon, 1998), 138–45. For contemporary perceptions of labor conditions in the 1920s and 1930s, see Cash, *Mind of the South*, 257–62, 271–72, 345.

25. A privileging of rural practices on the part of certain elites lent a nostalgic patina to traditional homespun ways of life. At the same time, those individuals who desired the goods produced by industry could be cast as dangerous colluders. Elvis Presley's mother, Gladys Smith, was considered a rebel in rural Mississippi in the 1920s and 1930s because she spent too much free time shopping and did so for pleasure. William Faulkner and Eudora Welty's novels from this period similarly reveal the tension caused by southerners who challenged the traditional restraint of rural values through their "frivolous" purchases of modern products. Welty's *Ponder Heart*, for example, characterizes the transgressive consumption of one female character by referencing her relationship to an industrial machine: "Bonnie Dee kept the washing machine on the front porch, just like any Peacock" (Ownby, *American Dreams*, 98–99, 147).

26. Terry E. Smith, *Making the Modern: Industry, Art, and Design in America* (Chicago: University of Chicago Press, 1993), 7.

27. Information on the company's automation can be found on the corporate Web site and in Charles Fishman, "The King of Kreme," *Fast Company* 28 (October 1999): 262.

28. It would be fruitful to research the ways in which the American Doughnut Manufacturers Association encouraged mechanization of its product after the Second World War. One ad produced by the association featured a serviceman in military uniform speaking with a white-collar executive while standing over an automated doughnut machine. The accompanying text, "So you want to go into the Doughnut Business," suggests that servicemen were a particular target for franchise ownership and that machines were viewed as important draws for this demographic. See Steinberg, *Donut Book*, 100.

29. *Industry on Parade* #119, *Industry on Parade* Film Collection, 1950–1960, #507, Archives Center, Smithsonian National Museum of American History, Washington, D.C. "In America," one segment begins, "we are likely to wake up to the music of a radio clock, arrive at work in a precision-built train or a mass-produced automobile, sit at a desk or stand at a machine in a centrally heated and air-conditioned building, come home to a delicious meal made with frozen foods, telephone friends and family anywhere in the country, enjoy an evening of television, and go to sleep in pajamas made of synthetic fabrics under an electric blanket." A brochure on the series published sometime in the mid- to late 1960s reports that "despite the fact that NAM ceased producing new programs for this

series at the beginning of 1960, re-issues are still being played one or more times a week over about 250 stations in this country, as well as the foreign and military outlets" (National Association of Manufacturers Records, 1895–1990, Hagley Museum and Library, Wilmington, Del.). Individuals have told me they remember seeing the series during their childhoods in the mid- to late 1960s.

30. Children were an especially captive audience for NAM's lessons. As early as 1945, the NAM had sent, by its estimate, study materials to more than one million children in three thousand schools across the country. Titles such as *You and Industry*, *What Makes Opportunity*, *American Dream*, and *About Machines* became school texts for a generation of young children eager to learn the ropes of postwar economic success. For information on this educational campaign, see Henry E. Abt, "Review of the Group Relations Department Activities and Recommendations for 1945," NAM Records, "Group Relations Review," 1944, Box 844; weekly report, 10, NAM Records, National Information Committee Administrative Files, Box 842; untitled report on advertising, November 8, 1942, NAM Records, Box 843, 1943 Folder; *You and Machines*, NAM Records, Series 16, Box 221, *You and Machines* Folder. For more information on the shift to consumer citizenship and NAM's role in this process, see Lizabeth Cohen, *A Consumer's Republic: The Politics of Mass Consumption in Postwar America* (New York: Vintage, 2003).

31. *Industry on Parade* #342, *Industry on Parade* Collection.

32. All evaluations were written between 1950 and 1952 and can be found in *Industry on Parade*, NAM Records, Series 1, Box 158.

33. Henry Lamb, "Doughnuts Cover USA," *Forsyth Suburbanite Progress*, Krispy Kreme Records, Box 14, Folder 5.

34. Franchise Manual—Recommendation on Updates, Krispy Kreme Records, Box 12, Folder 13.

35. *Krispy Kreme Newsletter*, November 1963, March 1965, Krispy Kreme Records, Box 14, Folder 2.

36. "Franchise Review and Recommendation," 23, ca. 1965, Krispy Kreme Records, Box 12, Folder 13.

37. Photographs of the Savannah, Georgia, store from 1968 offer an excellent look at the sorts of views afforded to customers in the retail area. Retail windows look directly onto the conveyor system and the beginning of the automated production area (Krispy Kreme Records, Box 19, Folder 44).

38. One photograph in the Krispy Kreme archive features a group of white-collar businessmen examining a conveyor machine at the Ponce de Leon Avenue store in Atlanta in 1965. Their intent expressions as they study the machine (tended by a female packer) suggest that they found the system revolutionary and worth visiting (Krispy Kreme Records, Box 19, Folder 38).

39. Human hands still were responsible for mixing Krispy Kreme batter. These hands were typically black rather than the white ones featured in visible production areas. It is unclear from company records whether the company's retail environment was segregated in the 1960s. Newsletters and photographs suggest that very few blacks worked in the retail area. (One photograph from the early 1960s appears to feature a light-skinned black female employee.) Race may have

contributed to the decision to move mixing out of customer view in the 1960s; photographs showing "mixing" employees from the 1940s overwhelmingly feature whites, yet by the 1960s, this department appears to have been predominantly black. According to historian Anthony Stanonis's essay in this volume, food has long functioned for southerners as a means for conveying "messages that affirmed the racial and patriarchal status quo." Krispy Kreme's 1960s redesign occurred squarely within the civil rights area, when blacks resisted whites' longstanding separation of dining facilities on the grounds that blacks, as Stanonis explains, lacked "cleanliness." In light of such tensions, the act of moving the mixing room out of view should be understood as an act of rendering black labor invisible. The act may have allowed customers to understand the "expertise" of doughnut production as emerging entirely from white male engineers and white female attendants rather than the cooperative process of black hand labor and white mechanized systems.

40. See, for example, Jeffrey Meikle, *Twentieth Century Limited: Industrial Design in America, 1925–1939* (Philadelphia: Temple University Press, 1979), 199, 207; Joel Dinerstein, *Swinging the Machine: Modernity, Technology, and African American Culture between the World Wars* (Amherst: University of Massachusetts Press, 2003), 141–48.

41. See Smith, *Making the Modern*, 147. Crowds packed into Norman Bel Geddes's Futurama at the 1939 New York World's Fair to place themselves on conveyor belts to "ride" by visions of future progress produced by machines and mechanized systems.

42. Trade show photographs reveal that well into the 1960s, Krispy Kreme used the Ring King Junior fryer rather than conveyor systems when presenting at local industrial events. See, for example, photographs from trade shows in Atlanta (1951) and St. Louis (1958). In 1951 no machine was visible; by 1958, only the Ring King Junior was on display (Krispy Kreme Records, Box 23, Folder 20).

43. See Dinerstein, *Swinging the Machine*, 126.

44. Southern cities had grown by 36 percent in the 1940s, leading the nation in urban growth, much of it spurred by government investment in military centers (David Goldfield, *Promised Land: The South since 1945* [Arlington Heights, Ill.: Davidson, 1987], 21–39).

45. Ibid., 8–9.

46. Lisa McNary to Krispy Kreme, November 12, 1996, Krispy Kreme Records, Box 15, Folder 10; Wes Eisenberg to Krispy Kreme, February 25, 1997, Krispy Kreme Records, Box 6, Folder 10; Tim Boyer to Krispy Kreme, November 12, 1996, Krispy Kreme Records, Box 6, Folder 13.

47. Kazanjian and Joyner, *Making Dough*, 180.

48. "Krispy Kreme Doughnuts," in *Uncommon Practice: People Who Deliver a Great Brand Experience*, ed. Andy Milligan and Shaun Smith (New York: Financial Times Prentice Hall, 2002), 83.

49. *Becoming a Production Professional Using 150 Equipment*, 3, ca. 1985, Krispy Kreme Records, Box 6, Folder 3.

50. Kazanjian and Joyner, *Making Dough*, xvii, 9–11.

51. Ibid., 11.

52. Ibid.

53. McAleer qtd. in Kazanjian and Joyner, *Making Dough*, 10.

54. Ibid., 12.

55. Nora Ephron, "Sugar Babies," *New Yorker*, February 1997, 31–32. See also Roy Blount Jr., "Southern Comfort," *New York Times Magazine*, 8 September 1996, 67.

56. "Krispy Kreme Donuts Inc. KKD (NYSE)," http://stocks.us/reuters.com/stocks/fulldescription.asp?symbol=KKD (accessed 22 December 2007).

57. Livengood qtd. in Kazanjian and Joyner, *Making Dough*, 12.

58. Evidence suggests that the visual presentation of machines has, in fact, become more important than the use of machines to efficiently produce doughnuts. In 2004 Krispy Kreme stock plunged when reports revealed that they had miscounted expenditures as revenue. Several articles appeared documenting the company's questionable accounting practice of recording the money acquired from the purchase of production machinery by new franchisees as profit for the company as a whole. That amount, roughly $770,000 by 2004, which should have appeared as a liability against the parent corporation, was instead appearing as a gain. Interpreted one way, the machines had then become far more profitable products than even the doughnuts. By developing costly "performative" machines and insisting that all franchisees purchase that equipment from the company, Krispy Kreme guaranteed a profit each time they opened a store even before baking a single doughnut. The brand had become so caught up in the experience of its machines—or what they interpreted to be the experience of its machines—that they overextended franchises financially to produce a doughnut experience rather than a doughnut (Rick Brooks and Mark Maremont, "Sticky Situation: Ovens Are Cooling at Krispy Kreme as Woes Multiply," *Wall Street Journal*, 3 September 2004).

59. Kazanjian and Joyner, *Making Dough*, 111.

The Café Hon

Working-Class White Femininity and Commodified Nostalgia in Postindustrial Baltimore

Mary Rizzo

Baltimore is where Regular Joes live and make something other than
money, offering the visiting Washingtonian a glimpse of what America
must be like. —Steve Twomey, *Washington Post,* 23 October 1997

Hair *is* politics in Baltimore. —John Waters, filmmaker
and Baltimore native

In Baltimore native John Waters's 2004 movie, *A Dirty Shame,* an upscale white couple moves from Washington, D.C., to a working-class
Baltimore neighborhood. The couple, hailed as gentrifiers in an early
scene that shows them refinishing the front of their newly purchased row
house, gushes to their mostly uninterested neighbors that they love Baltimore because "it's a real city of diversity." Yet the film shows few people
of color, suggesting that the diversity being lauded is within the category
of whiteness itself. For the liberal D.C. couple, Baltimore's quaintness
derives from the "Regular Joes" who live there and from their lack of cultural capital. As sociologist Pierre Bourdieu argues, cultural knowledge
and taste are indexes of class position and important tools in the creation
and maintenance of social hierarchies. The Baltimore natives, with their
supposed strange tastes in clothes and hairstyles and, in this particular
film, alleged odd sexual predilections, provide a fascinating Other to
middle-class gentrifiers looking to add some mild spice to their lives.[1]

While Waters's film is fiction, the issues it addresses—gentrification,
whiteness, and cultural capital—have fundamentally shaped contemporary Baltimore, particularly in Hampden, a neighborhood located
northwest of downtown. A working-class area since the early nineteenth
century, Hampden suffered a severe downturn in the 1970s and 1980s
as a consequence of the closing of the factories that employed most of its

residents. Since the 1990s, however, it has undergone intense gentrification and an economic renaissance. According to a 2005 *Baltimore Sun* article by Jamie Smith Hopkins, between 1999 and 2004, the average sale price of a Hampden row house more than doubled. The centerpiece of Hampden's revitalization is Thirty-sixth Street, known to locals simply as the Avenue. As a marker of a changing neighborhood, the Avenue is a schizophrenic mix of the past and present, blue collar and white collar. The discount Hampden Bargain Center stands near an upscale boutique filled with trendy vintage clothing. A pawn shop abuts a store selling high-priced skateboards. The residents reflect the same dynamic; at times the Avenue is an uneasy mix of hip shoppers and longtime working-class occupants.

The Café Hon, owned by Denise Whiting, is the epicenter of this paradoxical neighborhood. Roundly credited with galvanizing the wave of gentrification that Hampden currently enjoys, Whiting's café opened in April 1992, serving upscale diner food in an atmosphere designed to evoke the late 1950s and early 1960s. Repeatedly recycled in popular film, television, and fashion, this era supposedly represents a time of American innocence and prosperity. This is true too at the Café Hon, where the decor and menu work synergistically to evoke nostalgia for a time when Hampden's residents worked at the same factories and felt comfortable in a neighborhood populated by people more alike than different. Most importantly, the Café Hon localizes this cultural nostalgia by focusing on a city icon: the white working-class Baltimore "Hon." As a recent commentator explained, the Hon is a "middle-aged woman with her hair done up in a teased beehive, wearing cat's-eye glasses, leopard-print stretch pants and high-heeled sandals, accompanied by the ever-present scent of Aqua Net hairspray." With her dated clothing and accessories, the hyperfeminine Hon embodies the era the café revives. In addition to her unmistakable style, her most recognizable attributes are her strong-mindedness and desire to nurture others. When a Hon asks, "How ya doin' hon?" she actually means it.[2]

Yet the Café Hon expresses all this with smirking irony that is central to its success. After all, it is hardly the only faux-1950s diner in existence. The use of the Hon as the café's icon fosters an atmosphere of playfulness and whimsy directly tied to the restaurant's geographical location, making the eatery a tourist destination. There is no better place to experience this playfulness than at the café's annual Hon Fest. In 1994, the café began sponsoring a street festival with a quasi-beauty contest to crown the "Best Hon." While traditional beauty pageants test participants on how seamlessly they fit middle-class models of proper femininity, the Best Hon contest asks women to approximate an outrageously anti-middle-class femininity rooted in working-class southern

Michelle Perkins-Pfeffer
and Susan Hodges dressed
as Hons for Hon Fest 2005.
(Photo by author)

culture. Winners receive such prizes as a case of Aqua Net hairspray and a leopard print toilet seat cover. While the first Hon Fest attracted a small crowd, the event has grown into a several-block-long street festival with numerous activities, including Spam bowling, the Hon Run, a fashion show, and the Lil' Hon and Miss Honette contests. Approximately twenty thousand people attended the 2004 Hon Fest. The festival undoubtedly is an economic boon to both the Café Hon and the surrounding neighborhood, drawing tourists from across Maryland and nearby states. Nevertheless, Whiting claims that its overriding goal is to "honor and appreciate the working women of Baltimore."[3]

Yet in honoring and appreciating the "working women" of Baltimore, Hon Fest commodifies nostalgia for an imagined past of racial and class homogeneity through connections with a nurturing feminine figure. In this essay, I examine Hon Fest as a means of understanding the links among tourism, commodification, and white working-class femininity in the South. Today, tourism ranks among the top three economic sectors in every former Confederate state. Although Abraham Lincoln averted the secession of slaveholding Maryland by establishing de facto martial law, marketing the past to attract tourists has been equally important in the economic redevelopment of this border state.

This "heritage tourism" often focuses on a distant past, such as at Colonial Williamsburg or Civil War battlefields. However, in the face of deindustrialization, Baltimore has commodified its industrial past for tourists. As Baltimore's white working-class population has decreased, a concomitant fascination with its culture has arisen. For its mainly middle-class and professional participants, many of whom are the sons and daughters of people who joined the white flight to the suburbs during the 1960s and 1970s, Hon Fest offers a momentary escape from their real lives into a nostalgic fantasy that can perhaps be best understood through anthropologist Renato Rosaldo's term, *imperialist nostalgia*. As Rosaldo writes, "Curiously enough, agents of colonialism . . . often display nostalgia for the colonized culture as it was 'traditionally.' . . . The peculiarity of this yearning, of course, is that agents of colonialism long for the very forms of life they intentionally altered or destroyed."[4]

By focusing on a white working-class feminine icon, the Hon erases the city's minority working-class residents both now and in the past. Hampden and similar neighborhoods across the city were hotbeds of racial tension in the twentieth century, as white working-class residents, feeling powerless against government efforts to integrate schools and ensure fair housing practices, used intimidation and violence to maintain the racial status quo. As in much of the South, Baltimore's women were both active participants in segregationist efforts and symbols of what was imperiled by integration. The Hon is a souvenir of this era. To the people attending or participating in Hon Fest, the Hon simply represents fun—a kitschy reminder of the past. But her role as a symbol of Hampden suggests something deeper. While today Baltimore is a racially diverse city struggling to survive in a postindustrial economy, Hon Fest offers tourists and gentrifiers the opportunity momentarily to take on the identity of the white working-class Hon and immerse themselves in a romanticized past where community rested on a bedrock of racial and class homogeneity. As John Waters has commented, "Hair *is* politics in Baltimore."[5]

Race and Class in Hampden: Making the Hon

Founded in 1729, Baltimore by the early nineteenth century was well on its way to becoming an industrial center overwhelmingly populated by the working class. The 1830 census showed that half of the city's population labored as mechanics or tradespeople in skilled or semiskilled craft work, while fewer than 1,000 professionals lived within the city of 80,620 inhabitants. During the 1830s, investors converted gristmills, located in the neighborhoods of Hampden and Woodberry, to the production of cotton duck, a kind of sailcloth, to tap the booming shipping industry based in the Inner Harbor. Baltimore quickly became the country's leading manufacturer of cotton duck, and the cotton mills employed Hampden residents into the 1970s.[6]

As in New England, Baltimore's cotton mill owners established company villages in which the mill companies had a large measure of influence over their employees' social lives. Mill workers were overwhelmingly rural white southerners from nearby states. As historian D. Randall Beirne argues, this in-migration fundamentally affected Hampden's character: "For almost a hundred years this Anglo-Saxon, rural American culture has been dominant in these communities and produced the atmosphere of a rural town within the larger urban atmosphere of Baltimore City." More than other neighborhoods, Hampden continued to be known for its insularity as a result of both the mill companies and location. Roughly triangular in shape, Hampden is bordered by Druid Hill Park on one side. The campus of Johns Hopkins University, founded in 1876, adjoins another side, while to the north wealthier suburbs act as an economic barrier. As Hampden resident and teacher Margaret Doyle noted in 1979, "Hampden . . . was pretty much a closed community for many years."[7]

While Hampden remained a closed community, the complexion of the rest of Baltimore rapidly changed. The city's population swelled with English, Irish, and German immigrants during the nineteenth century. Later, Italians and eastern Europeans also arrived in large numbers. These groups tended to cluster by ethnicity and religion in a widening arc from the oldest part of the city near the harbor outward toward the mill villages. With the 1864 adoption of a state constitution that abolished slavery, Baltimore also became home to a large number of southern blacks. Conflicts arose in the late nineteenth century as white and black laborers vied for industrial and skilled craft jobs, such as caulking ships, a job that Frederick Douglass once held. At the same time, the city expanded geographically through the development of mass transportation. Distant suburbs such as Hampden became more accessible to the downtown center. As blacks sought new housing opportunities, the city government passed a 1913 ordinance that mandated residential segregation, thereby establishing black ghettos. With its combination of an industrial economy, racial and ethnic diversity, southern heritage, and Jim Crow practices, Baltimore existed uneasily on the borderlands between the North and South. The tensions between white ethnic and black workers during the middle of the nineteenth century remained palpable into the late twentieth century.

The issues that stoked the fires between these groups—work, education, and housing—were not particular to Baltimore. As Sherry H. Olson argues, Baltimore became increasingly tied to global economies when its corporations began to be controlled from outside the state, making the city especially vulnerable to market fluctuations. When the world economy faltered, so did Baltimore. The Great Depression proved particularly disastrous, but the upswing spurred by defense spending during the Second World War lifted the city out of the economic doldrums. With guaranteed work, Hampden's residents thrived. Baltimore companies, especially the cotton mills, even began to advertise for additional laborers, drawing workers from nearby southern states. Many came from Appalachia— in particular, Virginia, North Carolina, and West Virginia. Employers specifically targeted rural whites with experience in southern textile mills. The migration, which also included a sizable number of blacks, caused Baltimore's population to balloon from 859,000 in 1940 to 1,250,000 by late 1942. In 1979, Baltimore native Nora Frederick discussed the changes the Second World War brought to the Hampden mills: "They said something about, they'd think about bringing German . . . prisoners of war into the mill. Oh my golly, that's all we needed. . . . We all had somebody in the service . . . and we didn't want any prisoners of war in there, so then the colored people started coming in." Before the war, native white Baltimoreans, especially union members, denigrated southerners of both races as a result of their willingness to accept extremely low wages. However, when the mills hired blacks, locals' animosities shifted away from white southerners, setting the stage for intense racial conflicts, as exhibited by the 1943 Western Electric strike.[8]

In accordance with federal fair employment orders, Western Electric hired seventeen hundred black workers and promoted one black woman to a supervisory position. The company also desegregated its restrooms. In response, a group of white women workers walked out. Although women had sparked the strike, male laborers intensified the protest by forming picket lines encircling the plant. With this action, the male strikers showed that their masculinity was defined in part by the ability to protect female members of the white community. As Doyle noted, "The boys from Hampden would fight the boys from Woodberry. Or they'd fight the boys from Talmayco. . . . The scraping and fighting was part of the code. . . . It was an old-fashion code, which I had noticed maybe as part of the southern inheritance, that it was rather chivalrous." While this code shows the construction of gender roles in Baltimore's white working-class population, it did not mean that women abandoned the public sphere. For example, in the 1970s, when the city planned to bus students to schools to force integration, women led the opposition. Betty Deacon, a leader of the antibusing group, thought that "women naturally became more involved in community issues faster than men."[9]

For the women of Hampden, the middle-class ideal of a stay-at-home wife and mother was rarely a reality. Instead, Hampden's women began to work outside the home while still quite young, inculcating a sense of self-sufficiency and a willingness to fight for their rights. Mary Frederick recalled that she left one textile mill and found employment in another because "I didn't care for the job that I had up there then because it was below my *dignity*. I had come down from eighty dollars a week down to about fifty dollars a week." Instead of remaining at a job that devalued her labor, she quit and found one that appealed to both her self-esteem and her pocketbook. While these women reacted to deeply felt slights, they did not view the strict sexual division of labor within the mills, which was based on "natural" differences, with any disdain. Just as the men of the neighborhood matured with a code of honor that made protecting women and home a high ideal, the women of the neighborhood grew up willing to fight for themselves and especially their community. At the same time, they remained feminine enough to let their men protect them, qualities incorporated into the iconic Baltimore Hon.[10]

Even more than work, housing was a racial issue in Baltimore. As Spencer Rich noted in a 1989 *Washington Post* article, Baltimore was one of nine "hypersegregated" U.S. cities, with blacks "tightly packed" into certain neighborhoods. This hypersegregation resulted from the long-standing racial customs of white power brokers. Baltimore maintained clear racial boundaries even after the courts ruled Jim Crow laws unconstitutional. Shrewd profiteers practiced blockbusting, the "intentional action of a real estate operative to settle an African American household in an all-white neighborhood for the purpose of provoking white flight in order to make excessive profits by buying low from those who fled and selling high to those who sought access to new housing opportunities." The fear of lowered property values served as an effective method of encouraging whites to sell their houses. In a period of ten years, for example, the area known as Edmondson Village changed from a predominantly white to a predominantly black neighborhood. In response, black activists, led by the National Association for the Advancement of Colored People (Baltimore, the home of Thurgood Marshall, had one of the most active branches in the country) fought such divisive trends. While these efforts certainly aided Baltimore's African American population, black activism increased the sense among working-class whites that blacks sought special favors from the government and strove to encroach on neighborhoods that had been built over decades.[11]

This was particularly true in Hampden, a neighborhood that remained 90 percent white in the midst of a city with a majority black population. Through the late nineteenth and twentieth centuries, ethnic and religious associations helped members purchase houses, creating tight-knit neighborhoods where extended families lived within blocks of each other, much like the original mill villages. When owners died or wanted to sell, they often did so through private networks of family and friends, maintaining this homogeneity. As Lisa Leff reported in a June 1987 *Washington Post* article, the vacancy rate for housing in Hampden stood at only 4 percent, demonstrating the population's stability and thereby allowing residents to see themselves as a community distinct from the rest of Baltimore.

While members of a community often share a geographical space, they are further connected, according to historian W. Edward Orser, by a "broad consensus regarding morality and values" that forms "the basis for a common identity." In addition to a mutual racial, ethnic, and religious heritage, Hampdenites shared similar social values and attitudes that they felt distinguished them from others, especially African Americans. In a series of oral histories completed in 1979 as part of the Baltimore Neighborhood Heritage Project, Hampden residents reminisced about what made their neighborhood unique in the golden years of the mid-twentieth century. A sense of harmony, neighborliness, and a commitment to hard work pervades much of their discussion. Loice Foreman recalled that in Hampden, "everybody was neighbors," suggesting that people treated each other with mutual respect. However, "neighbors were all alike," suggesting that geographical proximity was not enough to define a true "neighbor." While neighborly aid could be counted on, individual effort mattered most. As Myrtle Talbott summarized, "Back then people didn't get any help, they helped themselves, unlike now." While Talbott failed to elaborate, she likely referred to the federal government's aid programs and especially Lyndon Johnson's Great Society.[12]

As Michael Kazin and others argue, members of the white ethnic working class felt increasingly ignored by the federal government during the 1970s. Their anger focused on liberal do-gooders who, from working-class whites' perspective, gave handouts to the undeserving. Hampdenites did not see race as the most critical issue. In oral history after oral history, the interviewees distance themselves from notions of prejudice. These Hampdenites, like other white working-class ethnics of the era, used the language of culture and values to explain their resistance to desegregation and government largesse. Luther Butler, a longtime Hampden resident active in local politics, noted that "the further back we go, the more people had more respect for anybody who kept themselves neatly attired and had good job, had good money and they acted real nice." In his eyes, dress, occupation, and behavior marked a proper identity. When the interviewer specifically asked Butler about racial tensions in Hampden, Butler continued to apply the language of culture and values, even in describing the Ku Klux Klan's activities in the neighborhood: "First let me clear up something about the Klan. There were over 870 members here and one thing you hear all kinds of tales, you hear all kinds of things. First you think, some guy on the horse with a whip, whipping on the darkies and stuff like that. That's a lot of hogwash." Butler elaborated, "The Klan in Hampden was definitely out for rapists, child abusers, and wife abusers, and that's all. That is all. They would naturally work them over and then tar and feather and tie them to a cross tie and push them down Jones Falls. Now, we got colored people here, my God! . . . Some of these people I have known here since I was kids [sic]. . . . They respected us and we respected them." Butler argued that the Klan did not terrorize blacks but simply enforced social codes, especially the protection of innocent white femininity. In this way, Butler voiced traditional notions of southern masculinity bound by codes of honor and protectiveness. Violence against geographical and racial outsiders was "natural" and merely the means by which a nice neighborhood remained that way. However, Butler acknowledged that race played an important role in the neighborhood by referring to individual black families who had lived in Hampden for generations. But because whites believed these few families accepted the code ("they respected us"), whites acquiesced to a small black presence ("we respected them"). This relationship had limits, however. When a nonwhite family moved to Hampden in the late 1960s, local whites threatened to burn the blacks' house unless they left. While Butler criticized the threat of arson as excessive, he argued, "I guess my answer would be like this: you have a flat tire, what do you do? You fix it. OK. If your generator is going up, you fix it. Right. Well, if that is the only way to get them out. But try the easy method because nobody wants to get hurt, but if that doesn't work, do what is necessary."[13]

How Ya Doin' Hon? Style and Nostalgia in Postindustrial Baltimore

Deindustrialization in the 1970s only intensified the racial conflicts bubbling in Baltimore. By 1973, the mills that had supported the blue-collar residents of Hampden had closed. Working-class whites who could afford to do so fled the city. Between 1950 and 2000, Baltimore's population declined from almost 950,000 to 650,000. Hampden and other such neighborhoods became battlegrounds, places where frustrations about economic decline erupted in violence against outsiders, especially blacks. In the mid-1960s, George "Bunny" Brooks, one of the first African American store owners in Hampden, had his windows repeatedly broken. Two decades later, Hampden whites harassed a black family that moved to the neighborhood as well as black students bused to its schools. These incidents contributed to Hampden's reputation as a dangerous place for African Americans.

While the majority of Hampden residents denounced violence, they also argued that because of their neighborhood's history, the area retained a distinct culture and community. The 2000 census showed that Hampden remained 93.5 percent white, though it had experienced a dramatic increase in its black population, which rose from 45 in 1990 to 203 in 2000—a jump of 351.1 percent. The continuing racial imbalance reveals a persistent divide between Baltimore's black and white populations that is only exacerbated by the popular memorializing of the Hon. As Janine Bradley, the former head of the Hampden Village Main Street Association, told me when I asked her whether the Hon still existed, "Baltimore is 60 percent black, and they're not Hons."[14]

Hampden's downturn was reversed in the 1990s by an influx of young, educated professionals (often artists, writers, graphic designers, and others in creative fields), many of them the children of white working-class parents who had fled Baltimore for the suburbs. Longtime Hampden resident Jean Hare "can't understand people that made a lot of money and didn't move out of Hampden. . . . I think now that people are looking for a feeling that might relate to something historical, Hampden might be interesting to some people who aren't forced by their economic situation into living there. . . . It was like living with fins on Cadillacs. I mean right now, who wants them?"[15] These new residents, drawn by low real estate prices and their parents' memories of Hampden as a tightly knit community, began to fundamentally shift the class identity of the neighborhood. At this time, the Café Hon started utilizing the Hon as a public symbol of the neighborhood and its past, both to draw new residents and to attract tourists looking for a bit of Charm City's well-known quirkiness.

In this way, Hampden followed the municipal government's plan to encourage gentrification and tourism as the cure for the city's economic woes. The "Baltimore City Economic Growth Strategy" argues that Baltimore should try to draw residents who are "students, singles, young couples, and empty nesters [who] are gravitating to urban centers to be near amenities, diverse populations, and jobs." These imaginary residents, interested most in culture and amenities, tend to be professionals or preprofessionals, not the working class of the city's past or the undereducated, service-industry laborers of its present. Drawn by inexpensive rents, public events such as Hon Fest, and cultural representations such as Waters's films, these new residents and tourists displace the remaining blue-collar residents, supposedly the source of the romanticized local culture and sense of community they seek, a process like the imperialist nostalgia that Rosaldo describes. Jeanne, a contestant at three Hon Fests, put it this way: "Baltimore is a big city, but it's not that big. It has neighborhoods, and there's a closeness that you know everyone. Some of that's changed now with the yuppies moving into all the row houses. That family aspect, the generation-after-generation aspect, is fading a little bit." As the old residents (and reminders of the lived past) are priced out of the neighborhood or die, the new residents and tourists can construct the Hon as a kitschy symbol of the working-class women of the 1950s and 1960s whose style and personality fuel her appeal and who is revived with an abundance of irony and playfulness.[16]

As this process of class turnover occurs, differences in cultural capital between the been-heres and the gentrifying come-heres have set the stage for conflict. I conducted ethnographic research at Hon Fest in 2002, 2005, 2006, and 2007. At each event, I spoke with Hon Fest attendees and residents about Hampden, Hon Fest, and gentrification. Every year, interviewees agreed that Hampden was in the midst of a demographic shift from "old-timers" and "blue-collar people" to "yuppies" and "artistic-type people." Many people considered the change positive, as it had coincided with a decrease in crime and an increase in economic activity. However, my interviewees also noted that tensions existed between the groups, though the animosity had lessened substantially by 2006, probably because fewer long-term residents remained in the neighborhood.[17]

Social friction replaced old communal ties. Benn's experience is exemplary. A newcomer to Hampden in 2002 and the owner of a bookstore, he described older residents who "resent" the new people "with weird haircuts, tattoos, and facial piercings walking up and down the street." In 2006, Leslie, who uses the Hon in her artwork and who lived in Hampden from 2000 to 2005, noted that when she first moved to the neighborhood, she experienced "some initial animosity towards the young professional people." However, these tensions abated as older residents found that they could sell their houses at a substantial profit. But young investors in Hampden homes created other fault lines as differing images of the neighborhood clashed, especially around the Café Hon.[18]

Steve, the owner of a hardware store that celebrated its twenty-seventh anniversary in 2002 and had been bought out by 2006, articulated a common sentiment that the café divided the neighborhood in half. In his view, two types of people lived in Hampden: those who dined at the Café Hon and "the locals [who] would still rather have a hamburger and French fries and a Coke rather than vichyssoise or whatever."[19]

The description of the food served at Café Hon is emblematic of the disparity in cultural capital and class difference between old and new Hampdenites. The Café Hon does not serve vichyssoise or any other kind of French cuisine. The menu centers on "typical" 1950s diner foods—meatloaf, chicken salad, chipped beef, and the like. If the café strives to serve such common American fare, why would some longtime residents feel strongly that the eatery is not for them? Prices provide a partial explanation. In 2002, the meatloaf sandwich at Café Hon cost $5.95 at lunch and $11.95 at dinner (which included salad, bread, the vegetable of the day, and mashed potatoes and gravy). At nearby Mike's Diner, a meatloaf sandwich cost $3.95.

Atmosphere further separates the two restaurants. The Café Hon does not merely serve food but uses it to create a tourist experience. As folklorist Lucy Long describes, "culinary tourism" is "the intentional, exploratory participation in the foodways of an other—participation including the consumption, preparation, and presentation of a food item, cuisine, meal system, or eating style considered to belong to a culinary system not one's own." This Otherness occurs along a variety of possible dimensions, including culture, region, time, religion, and—most important in the case of the Café Hon—social class.[20]

Long argues that white trash cookbooks humorously express stereotypes of the uncivilized Other while also "address[ing] a somewhat morbid curiosity about groups considered outside the mainstream." The menu and decor of the Café Hon place the restaurant squarely in the realm of a working-class past where the hamburger, French fries, and Coke that Steve mentions were supposedly items of daily fare. The café strives to prove its authenticity as representative of this past by repeatedly describing its food as "homemade," emphasizing the difference between the café and mass-produced fast food. The Hon waitresses further add to the image of authenticity. As tourist Mary Foster described in an April 2005 *New Orleans Times-Picayune* article, "We were sitting in Café Hon, a faux 1950s diner near the Johns Hopkins main campus. 'You decided what you want, hon?' the waitress asked, breathing life into the appellation." Cultural representations consistently show women (whether as white suburban mothers or southern black mammies) using food to nurture others. In the context of Hon Fest, the white Hon embodies the feminine nurturer, happily offering her labor to serve others' needs. At the same time, the Hon's whiteness erases the fact that the majority of laborers in Baltimore are service industry workers of color.[21]

Menu additions such as the "Bean L. T. Sandwich," a panethnic combination of "hummus, lettuce and tomato on wheat toast with tortilla chips and salsa" meant to appeal to vegetarians and people wary of foods, like bacon, that have been labeled unhealthy, reflect a desire to woo Hampden newcomers. While the menu constructs authenticity by wrapping food in local culture, the café's decor converts the restaurant into a place of pleasure that emphasizes a nostalgic relationship with a fantasy past. In 2002, visitors to the café were greeted by a life-size statue of Elvis Presley swiveling his hips as well as an injudicious display of plastic pink flamingoes (in homage, no doubt, to John Waters's film of the same name). Both Presley and the flamingoes pointed to the late

1950s and early 1960s as the moment memorialized by the restaurant. More importantly, they also represented a working-class style defined by excess, from Presley's gold lame suit to the flamingo's neon color. By 2005, Elvis had left the building, replaced by a refurbished diner counter, large mirrors, and signs proclaiming "Jello Pudding," "Homemade Pie," and "Hot Fudge Sundaes." For tourists interested in a souvenir of their Café Hon experience, a large merchandise area near the front door offered feather boas, beehive wigs, and mugs with the Café Hon logo. As a "staged experience," the Café Hon constructs itself as both an authentic blue-collar diner and a realm of pleasure and fantasy rooted in nostalgia.

The nostalgia that Whiting evokes with the decor and food is a commodification of the 1950s and 1960s for the upwardly mobile residents discussed in the "Baltimore Economic Growth Strategy." As Janine Bradley noted, when "gentrification comes, some of [the Hon culture] is disappearing." Ironically, only with gentrification and the loss of that Hon culture could the image of the Hon draw "artistic-type people" to the neighborhood. As Rosaldo explains, "Much of imperialist nostalgia's force resides in its association with (indeed, its disguise as) more genuinely innocent tender recollections of what is at once an earlier epoch and a previous phase of life." Many of the longtime, working-class residents of Hampden critique the changes in their neighborhood and potentially make the new residents uncomfortable. Drawn to the neighborhood by a distinctive working-class culture that they help to displace, the new residents freely appropriate this culture in its absence, fondly misremembering an "innocent" earlier epoch that was, in actuality, a time of intense racial conflict.[22]

The tensions between the been-heres and come-heres notwithstanding, the idea of community draws young adults to settle in Hampden. Dante, whom I interviewed in 2006, felt that young professionals came to the neighborhood because it represented a type of community absent in outer-ring suburbs. Former Best Hon Heidi recalled stories about a neighbor who sat on her stoop so much that she wore a dent into the stone, suggesting that a unique public culture had long existed in Hampden. Waters has done more than anyone to perpetuate the image of Baltimore as charmingly quirky, populated by offbeat characters who rally around their community. Waters's 1998 film, *Pecker,* set and filmed in Hampden, centers on the rise to fame of amateur photographer Pecker, who captures the eccentricities of his neighbors and family members with a winning naïveté and compassion. Unlike the ironic artists and art dealers who swooped down on Baltimore after *Pecker*'s success, the celluloid Hampden is a place where people truly connect with each other. The "Baltimore Economic Growth Strategy" converted these popular images into public policy: "The quality of Baltimore's built environment, including . . . its tight knit neighborhoods[,] give it a special character, that creatively utilized, can shape the world's view of Baltimore."[23]

Today, Hon Fest creates a sense of community through the shared class position and cultural attitudes of its participants and its carnivalesque qualities, which at times cut across Baltimore's historic racial divide. People of color increasingly attend Hon Fest, a remarkable turnaround considering the neighborhood's reputation as hostile toward nonwhites. Pamela, an African American woman and lifelong Baltimore resident, attended her third Hon Fest in 2006. As she put it, Hon Fest celebrates the 1950s and 1960s because "it was fun and it was nice back then, wasn't a lot of crime and crazy things going on." However, she acknowledged that controversy surrounded the term *Hon*. She noted that for blacks, "years ago it was a negative thing" because "black people went into the stores and somebody would say, you know, 'Oh hi, Hon.' You know? They took it the wrong way." Pamela interpreted whites' application of *Hon* to blacks as a subtle effort to condescend or be disrespectful to black customers as a means of maintaining neighborhood boundaries. But in Pamela's view, the term has lost any negative connotations. In fact, her granddaughter entered the Lil' Hon contest, suggesting the malleability of the Hon image even with regard to race. Pamela and her granddaughter simply consider Hon Fest carnivalesque fun.

As Mikhail Bakhtin argues, a lack of distinction between performers and spectators defines carnival, inverting social hierarchies and creating a free space with liberatory potential. While the Best Hon contest distinguishes between performers and spectators, a large percentage of the women who attend Hon Fest—even those who are not competing—dress as Hons. Others utilize this atmosphere of freedom in a variety of ways, from men dressing as Hons to members of other subcultures, like punks and Goths, comfortably displaying their style affiliations on the street. Strangers routinely compliment each other on their attire and pose for photos. The communal nature of the event allows strangers safely to interact, but only because they share cultural capital and class status, which is expressed most clearly through the use of style.[24]

For some attendees, Hon style provides a connection to women's history, but for most the attire is exaggerated into caricature. Many of the new residents of Hampden are the professional children of former working-class residents. A number of the women who entered the Best Hon competition connected the Hon with close female relatives. Susan, crowned Best Hon in 2006, saw her win as a tribute to her mother, who supported her young family through a variety of jobs after Susan's father died. In this way, some of the contestants use Hon Fest to strengthen ties to the history of working-class women's lives.[25]

According to feminist historians, working-class women have long used fashion and style to create distinctive cultures. For example, some early twentieth-century immigrant women spent significant percentages of their salaries on mass-produced clothing and hairpieces. Not simply fashion victims, these women demonstrated a new American identity through commodities that connoted modernity. While such actions suggested a desire to emulate the upper classes, these women engaged in more than mimicry. Working-class women purchased dresses, cosmetics, and other consumer items to create their own styles differentiated from haute couture by bright colors and showy embellishments.[26]

For working-class women after the Second World War, the abundance of mass-produced consumer goods coupled with the era's affluence allowed for the further development of a class-inflected style. Fashion historian Angela Partington argues that the development of cheaply manufactured and durable artificial fibers during the 1950s meant that natural fibers became associated with a higher social class. She explains that "the new synthetics became a sign of working-classness, because to working-class women quantity, disposability, colour, and 'easycare' became a priority while craftsmanship and 'naturalness' did not." While designers tried to instruct working-class women on the rules of restraint and good taste in dress and furnishings, these women, like their immigrant predecessors, chose flash and dazzle as well as practicality. Wearing faux jewelry, donning fake furs, and carefully constructing beehive hairdos represented economic access to consumer goods and the cultivation of a femininity based on display and beauty. This process was especially evident among southerners. As Lee Smith, a former model from Tidewater Virginia, explained, "Little hair means lady. . . . [B]ig hair says working class, rural or small town. . . . [B]ig hair generally means big heart. . . . [T]he largeness of southern beauty is a part of the largeness of southern life in general."[27]

Middle-class women deemed the postwar period's working-class female style to be tacky, overdone, and excessive. The gap between the middle- and working-class meanings of style informs the costumes worn by Hon Fest participants. Celebrants re-create social hierarchies of taste and culture through the use of irony. A joke I heard a number of times at Hon Fest underscored this interplay. After complimenting a woman on her Hon costume, the festivalgoer asked what she had done to prepare for the event. The Hon invariably feigned surprise and confusion, saying something like, "Get ready? This is how I always look." After a moment, everyone would laugh, demonstrating the recognition of the joke—a woman dressed in outrageously colored clothing and a beehive hairdo obviously was putting on an act. As one Best Hon contestant explained, "For yuppies like me, this is kitsch."[28]

To ensure that Hon contestants are recognized as different from "real" Hons, participants exaggerate style elements. Hons wear a variety of clothing associated with the 1950s and 1960s, from shirtwaist dresses to housecoats, preferably made from artificial fibers. Some Hons dress glamorously, while others approximate daily wear. In either case, middle-class sensibilities find the aggregated look tacky. The ubiquitous beehive hairdos, cat's-eye glasses, and heavy application of cosmetics provide the only common denominators of the Hon look. Otherwise, the women are dressed chaotically, mixing feather boas and leopard print with plastic pearls, a housecoat, and hair curlers. These nonnatural, mass-produced items supplied the raw materials for a postwar feminine working-class style viewed by its wearers as actually beautiful. At Hon Fest, however, such fashion signals tackiness or kitsch.

By combining so many disparate elements, these outfits verge on stylistic dissonance. Anyone wearing a housecoat, curlers, and pearls on the street demonstrates a disregard for or ignorance of middle-class sensibilities regarding proper public appearance. While Hon Fest participants swear to firsthand knowledge of real Baltimorean women who dressed this way during the 1950s and 1960s, the Hon is an exaggeration for comic effect. As Jeanne noted, "The image of the Hon at the contest is a bit overdone. The true Hon would have one or two accessories." Some contestants acknowledge this artificiality by creatively updating the Hon. Women have entered the Best Hon contest as the "Techno Hon," the "Hippie Hon" and the "Hawaiian Hon," combinations that make little cultural sense except as evidence of the postmodern desire for pastiche. However, this reimagining of the Hon only goes so far—I did not see one woman of color enter the Best Hon competition in 2002, 2005, 2006, or 2007, though they have attended the festival in Hon regalia.

Because the Hon is overdetermined by her style elements, it is possible to dress like a Hon while utilizing only tangential reference points and one key element, such as the beehive, leopard print, or feather boa. For example, a group of women at Hon Fest 2005 attended wearing oversized sunglasses and feather boas while carrying large furry bags. While only slightly related to the Hon, these items allowed the women to merge into the realm of play that Hon Fest permits. Their choice of costume suggests the event's real intent: to allow middle-class women a brief escape from their lives by appropriating a kitschy vision of white working-class female culture. As longtime Hampden resident Steve said in 2002 when asked what he thought of Hon Fest, "I think it's wonderful. . . . It's Halloween, right?"[29]

Like Halloween, women dressing for Hon Fest maintain an ironic distance, a camp aesthetic that allows them to reaffirm their middle-class identity vis-à-vis the tacky Hon. This process works in much the same

Three Hons at Hon Fest 2005. The woman in the middle won Best Hon 2003, while her daughter, at left, won Best Hon 2004. (Photo by author)

Ornaments sold at
Hon Fest 2005.
(Photo by author)

way that drag does. The drag queen who overemphasizes the markers of femininity draws attention to himself as a drag queen, not a "real" woman, thereby producing much less social anxiety than a cross-dresser who goes undetected. As the Café Hon's Web site notes, "You know you love to dress up with big hair Hon!" Dressing up (or in this case, dressing down in terms of class) signals a movement into play and fantasy as well as the eventual return to normalcy. For such play to be enjoyable, people who dress up must adopt identities different from their own and, more importantly, be recognizable as such. Best Hon 2002 contestant Genie told me in our interview that she considered herself working class as a consequence of her family background, though she possessed a college education and worked as a schoolteacher. However, when asked about Hon style, she clearly showed her distance. She described visiting a nearby beauty salon for a haircut: "I told them not to spray it, not to do it, and they did it, and it was so embarrassing I went home and took a shower to get it out. It's like, 'Oh, my god,' people really wear their hair [like this] every day. . . . And they say it's beautiful." While Genie shares a similar background with the Hon, she clearly maintains a different relationship with style and taste that allows her to offer a negative judgment of the Hon look.

Susan, Best Hon 2006, also described herself as from a working-class background, though she currently is working toward a graduate degree in library science. While she connected herself to her mother's working-class culture, she noted that her mother tried to stop her from speaking in the Baltimore dialect known locally as Bawlmer, which her mother felt would prevent her from achieving a middle-class lifestyle. At one point, Susan apologized, "I'm sorry I'm not talking like a Hon right now." Switching seamlessly to Bawlmer, she explained, "That's my education." Today Susan slips as easily into the dialect as into curlers and a beehive, but neither is a part of her day-to-day world. Some participants, like Susan, become involved in Hon Fest as a way to connect, albeit whimsically, with an exaggerated version of the past; for many others, however, it is the distance between reality and the masquerade that makes Hon Fest pleasurable. The celebration annually reiterates (and the Café Hon continually reinforces) the cultural capital of the participants through their difference from the Hon as an object of nostalgia.[30]

The nostalgic embrace of the Hon spurs consumption. The white working-class female body becomes first an icon and then a commodity as style indicators such as feather boas and beehive wigs are sold in the café. On the street, local artists sell ornaments that commodify the Hon herself. Leslie, one of these artists, began putting phrases in Bawlmerese on her pieces. "I felt a little bit uncomfortable because the people in this neighborhood talk like that, and I felt like I was kind of making fun of them." When asked to explain why such actions would be seen as making fun, she could not clarify her concern, instead repeating that people "just talk like that." Mimicry of working-class Bawlmer by a professional artist verged on parody. But artists and other vendors genuinely hope that their work serves both as a loving tribute and as a souvenir for tourists who desire to own something that represents Baltimore's former working-class culture.[31]

The commodification of Baltimore's industrial past and working-class culture for tourists has been an important part of the city's growth strategy. Baltimore's largest tourism project has been the redevelopment of the Inner Harbor, formerly a site for shipping and shipbuilding. Beginning in the 1970s, the city, in a public-private partnership, re-created the Inner Harbor as a dining and shopping mecca that includes a convention center, hotel, and various cultural institutions, such as the National Aquarium. While the revitalization of formerly abandoned buildings boosts the urban economy, how the Inner Harbor gained tourist value further contextualizes the popularity of the Café Hon and its festival. Part of a global trend toward industrial heritage tourism, former sites of industrial production are converted into either historical curiosities or sites for conspicuous consumption. The former Baltimore Gas and Electric Company became two entertainment areas called the Power Plant and Power Plant Live that house restaurants, bars, and a large Barnes and Noble bookstore. A similar commodification of class and promotion of consumption lies at the heart of Hon Fest. Jeanne argued that "if you go in a place such as Café Hon, it's pretending to be Hampden . . . under the guise of 'Let's capitalize on the Hon.' It's not the same. . . . You're not going to be waited on by the true grandma Hon." And although Hampden celebrates local business owners (80 percent of whom, according to Denise Whiting, are women), Budweiser sponsored Hon Fest 2006.

As David Harvey writes, "Projects concerning what we want our cities to be are . . . projects concerning human possibilities, who we want, or, perhaps more pertinently, who we do not want to become." Hon Fest is just such a project. As a commemoration of Hampden during the 1950s and 1960s, the festival recalls a time when this neighborhood harbored a tight-knit community where residents knew and cared for each other. However, rather than being based on racial or ethnic homogeneity, the festival is based on participants' shared middle-class status and cultural capital, which coheres around the Hon.

As the Hon's working-class culture faded as a result of the closing of the mills and more recently the settling of young professionals in Hampden, she became increasingly disconnected from any real historical context and emerged as a living symbol of the neighborhood. White and working class, the Hon is, as Susan said, the "embodiment of a strong woman." At the same time, she is a natural nurturer, placing her family's and neighbors' needs ahead of her own. The mainly middle-class women who dress as Hons for the event do so for the pleasure inherent in playing with their identity. Each Hon Fest allows them to escape their daily lives and delve into a different class status and femininity as part of a nostalgic fantasy. For some participants, dressing as a Hon is a means of paying tribute to female relatives who were real Hons. Nonetheless, the camp aesthetic that accompanies Hon Fest differentiates the participants from the working-class culture the event officially celebrates. To the majority of its attendees, Hon Fest is nothing more than a carnival that irreverently revives the past. Yet the romanticization of this past obscures the policing of racial boundaries that maintained this primarily white working-class neighborhood through much of its history. Today, of course, many people of color attend Hon Fest, a positive change in a neighborhood known for being dangerous to nonwhites. They mingle with the other participants, tourists, and new residents. All these groups together giggle at the costumes, pose for photos, and perhaps buy souvenirs of their Hon Fest experience. In this way, Hon Fest creates a community, albeit one that is based on a commodified nostalgia for the white, nurturing Hon.[32]

NOTES

1. Pierre Bourdieu, *Distinction: A Social Critique of the Judgment of Taste* (Cambridge: Harvard University Press, 1984).

2. Jeff Brown, "Hiya Hon," *AAA World*, May–June 2005, 16. Indeed, the fact that the café's waitstaff is almost entirely female and all-white suggests an elision between the Hon image and the real servers, making it seem that the work taking place in the restaurant is not work at all. Instead, the fantasy image of the Hon as a constantly upbeat white working-class woman obscures the waitresses' real labor.

3. "Hon Happenings," http://www.cafehon.com/honhappenings.htm (accessed 1 August 2005).

4. Renato Rosaldo, *Culture and Truth: The Remaking of Social Analysis* (Boston: Beacon, 1989), 69. On tourism in the South, see Richard D. Starnes, ed., *Southern Journeys: Tourism, History, and Culture in the Modern South* (Tuscaloosa: University of Alabama Press, 2003), 1.

5. Director's commentary for *Hairspray*, DVD, directed by John Waters (1988; New Line Home Video, 2002).

6. Sherry H. Olson, *Baltimore: The Building of an American City* (Baltimore: Johns Hopkins University Press, 1980), 90; http://www.census.gov/population/documentation/twps0027/tab06.txt (accessed 25 August 2007); Charles Belfoure, "Village Changes, but Keeps Its Spirit," *Baltimore Sun*, 18 April 1999.

7. D. Randall Beirne, "Hampden," in *North Baltimore: From Estate to Development*, ed. Karen Lewand (Baltimore: Baltimore City Department of Planning

and the University of Baltimore, 1989), 67; Margaret Doyle, interview by Susan Hawes, 16 August 1979, Baltimore Neighborhood Heritage Project, Langsdale Library, University of Baltimore.

8. Kenneth D. Durr, *Behind the Backlash: White Working-Class Politics in Baltimore, 1940–1980* (Chapel Hill: University of North Carolina Press, 2003), 16; Nora and Mary Frederick, interview by Susan Hawes, 10 July 1979, Baltimore Neighborhood Heritage Project, Langsdale Library, University of Baltimore.

9. On Western Electric strike, see Olson, *Baltimore,* 365; Deacon qtd. in Durr, *Behind the Backlash,* 173–74.

10. For an excellent discussion of gender in southern cotton mills, see Jacquelyn Dowd Hall, James Leloudis, Robert Korstad, Mary Murphy, Lu Ann Jones, and Christopher B. Daly, *Like a Family: The Making of a Southern Cotton Mill World* (Chapel Hill: University of North Carolina Press, 1987), 67–72.

11. W. Edward Orser, *Blockbusting in Baltimore: The Edmondson Village Story* (Lexington: University Press of Kentucky, 1994), 4.

12. Orser, *Blockbusting in Baltimore,* 12; Loice Foreman, interview by Susan Hawes, 26 June 1979, Baltimore Neighborhood Heritage Project, Langsdale Library, University of Baltimore; Myrtle Talbott, interview by Susan Hawes, 19 June 1979, Baltimore Neighborhood Heritage Project, Langsdale Library, University of Baltimore.

13. Luther Butler, interview by Susan Hawes, 3 August 1979, transcript, Baltimore Neighborhood Heritage Project, Langsdale Library, University of Baltimore. On populism and working-class politics after World War II, see Michael Kazin, *The Populist Persuasion: An American History* (Ithaca: Cornell University Press, 1998). The use of culture rather than race to justify segregation is explored in Jack E. Davis, *Race against Time: Culture and Separation in Natchez since 1930* (Baton Rouge: Louisiana State University Press, 2001), 3.

14. http://www.ci.baltimore.md.us/government/planning/census/censusnews1 .pdf (accessed 1 August 2005); Lisa Leff, "Melee Bares Race Unrest in Baltimore Neighborhood," *Washington Post,* 1 June 1987; Janine Bradley, interview by author, Baltimore, 14 June 2002. George Brooks describes the racism he encountered in Baltimore in Michael Anft, "Uneasy Street: Can Old Hampden Coexist with the New Avenue?" *Baltimore City Paper,* 25 February 1998. For more on violence against African Americans in Baltimore, see Paul W. Valentine, "2 Maryland Whites Admit to Stoning Blacks' Home," *Washington Post,* 28 November 1988.

15. Jean Hare, interview by Susan Hawes, 24 May 1979, Baltimore Neighborhood Heritage Project, Langsdale Library, University of Baltimore.

16. "Baltimore City Economic Growth Strategy," http://www.ci.baltimore.md .us/images/EconGrowthStrategy.pdf (accessed 1 August 2005); Jeanne, interview by author, Baltimore, 23 June 2006.

17. My use of "been-heres" and "come-heres" derives from Daphne Spain, "Been-heres versus Come-heres: Negotiating Conflicting Community Identities," *APA Journal* 59 (1993): 156–71. The terms *long-term* or *longtime residents* refer to people who lived in Hampden prior to its economic redevelopment, which began in the early 1990s.

18. Benn, interview by author, Baltimore, 8 August 2002; Leslie, interview by author, Baltimore, 10 June 2006.

19. Steve, interview by author, Baltimore, 7 June 2002.

20. Lucy Long, "Culinary Tourism: A Folkloristic Perspective on Eating and Otherness," in *Culinary Tourism*, ed. Lucy Long (Lexington: University Press of Kentucky, 2004), 21.

21. Ibid., 31.

22. Bradley, interview; Rosaldo, *Culture and Truth*, 70.

23. Dante, interview by author, Baltimore, 10 June 2006; Heidi, interview by author, Baltimore, 10 June 2006; "Baltimore City Economic Growth Strategy."

24. Pamela, interview by author, Baltimore, 10 June 2006; Mikhail Bakhtin, "Carnival and the Carnivalesque," in *Cultural Theory and Popular Culture: A Reader*, ed. John Storey (Athens: University of Georgia Press, 1998), 250.

25. Susan, interview by author, Baltimore, 10 June 2006.

26. For more on working-class women's use of style, see Kathy Peiss, *Cheap Amusements: Working Women and Leisure in Turn-of-the-Century New York* (Philadelphia: Temple University Press, 1986); Elizabeth Lapovsky Kennedy and Madeline Davis, eds., *Boots of Leather, Slippers of Gold: The History of a Lesbian Community* (New York: Penguin, 1994); Leslie Feinberg, *Stone Butch Blues* (Ithaca: Firebrand, 1993).

27. Angela Partington, "Popular Fashion and Working-class Affluence," in *Chic Thrills: A Fashion Reader*, ed. Juliet Ash and Elizabeth Wilson (Berkeley: University of California Press, 1993), 151; Lee Smith, "Inside the Beehive," *Allure*, September 2002, 156. On designers and working-class women's taste, see Shelly Nickles, "More Is Better: Mass Consumption, Gender, and Class Identity in Postwar America," *American Quarterly* 54 (December 2002): 581–622.

28. Margie, interview by author, Baltimore, 8 June 2002.

29. Steve, interview.

30. "Hon Happenings"; Genie, interview by author, Baltimore, 8 June 2002; Susan, interview by author, Baltimore, 10 June 2006.

31. Leslie, interview.

32. David Harvey, *Spaces of Hope* (Berkeley: University of California Press, 2000), 159.

Contributors

W. Fitzhugh Brundage is William B. Umstead Professor of History at the University of North Carolina at Chapel Hill. He is the author of *The Southern Past: A Clash of Race and Memory* (2005) and editor of *Where These Memories Grow: History, Memory, and Regional Identity in the American South* (2000), among numerous other works.

Karen L. Cox is an associate professor of history and the director of public history at the University of North Carolina at Charlotte. She is the author of *Dixie's Daughters: The United Daughters of the Confederacy and the Preservation of Confederate Culture* (2003) and is currently writing a book on the South in American popular culture.

Carolyn de la Peña is an associate professor and director of the Program in American Studies at the University of California at Davis, where she also directs the Davis Humanities Institute. She is the author of *The Body Electric: How Strange Machines Built the Modern American* (2003) and is currently working on a cultural history of artificial sweeteners in the United States. She teaches courses on technology, material culture, and foodways.

Glenn T. Eskew is an associate professor of history at Georgia State University. He is author of *But for Birmingham: The Local and National Movements in the Civil Rights Struggle* (1997) and editor of *Labor in the Modern South* (2001) as well as numerous other works.

John M. Giggie is an assistant professor of history at the University of Alabama. He is author of *After Redemption: Jim Crow and the Transformation of African American Religion in the Delta* (2007) and editor of *Faith in the Market: Religion and Urban Commercial Culture* (2002).

Patrick Huber is an associate professor of history at the Missouri University of Science and Technology in Rolla and is the author of *Linthead Stomp: Southern Textile Workers and the Creation of Hillbilly Music, 1922–1942* (2008) and coauthor of *The 1920s: American Popular Culture through History* (2004).

His research focuses primarily on prewar hillbilly and blues music, southern working-class culture, and racial violence.

Aaron K. Ketchell teaches history at the Barstow School in Kansas City, Missouri. He is author of *Holy Hills of the Ozarks: Religion and Tourism in Branson, Missouri* (2007).

Nicole King is a lecturer in the Department of American Studies at the University of Maryland, Baltimore County. She is also a doctoral candidate at the University of Maryland at College Park, where she is completing a dissertation on tourism and identity in modern South Carolina.

Ted Ownby is a professor of history and southern studies at the University of Mississippi. He is author of *American Dreams in Mississippi: Consumers, Poverty, and Culture, 1830–1998* (1999) and *Subduing Satan: Religion, Recreation, and Manhood in the Rural South, 1865–1920* (1990) and is the editor of collections on southern manners and race relations.

Eric W. Plaag is an independent historian in South Carolina who specializes in historic preservation and the material culture of the South. His current research focuses on the photography of historic southern structures and landmarks. His recent publications include essays in *Slavery and Abolition* and *New York History*.

John Shelton Reed is William Rand Kenan Jr. Professor Emeritus of Sociology at the University of North Carolina at Chapel Hill. His numerous works include *Minding the South* (2003), *My Tears Spoiled My Aim and Other Reflections on Southern Culture* (1993), and *Whistling Dixie: Dispatches from the South* (1990). He is also the coauthor of *1001 Things Everyone Should Know about the South* (1996).

Mary Rizzo works in public history and museum education in New Jersey, where she also teaches at the College of New Jersey in the Women's and Gender Studies Program and the history department. Her research interests include public history, class identity, and food studies. Her work has appeared most recently in *Eating in Eden: Food and Utopia in America* (2006).

Anthony J. Stanonis is a lecturer in modern U.S. history at Queen's University Belfast. He is author of *Creating the Big Easy: New Orleans and the Emergence of Modern Tourism, 1918–1945* (2006).

Index

Clark, Roy, 121
class, 98, 168n2, 179, 207, 227,
264–83
Clinton, William J., 75, 133, 188
Cobb, B. J., 101
Coca-Cola, 207
Coffin, William Sloane, 180
Cohn, David, 217
Cole, James, 157
Cole, Robert, 181
Coles, Robert, 187
Collins, Fred, 160
Colonial Williamsburg, 91–92, 187,
267
Colored Industrial Institute, 104
Colored Methodist Episcopal Church,
101
Colquitt, Harriet Ross, 212
Confederate flag, 94, 161, 171n56,
172n69, 180, 226
Confederateland, U.S.A., 155, 158–59
consumerism, 208, 235, 245, 254,
281
Cook, Bruce, 133
Cook, Mary, 108
cookbooks, 134, 210–16, 227–28,
275
Cookeville, Tenn., 69
Coon Chicken Inn, 223
Corbin, Ed, 215
Corbin, Ky., 223
cotton, 94, 179, 217
Cracker Barrel Old Country Store,
226
Curry, Glenda, 189, 191

Daniel, Pete, 152
Davis, Jefferson, 79
Dawson, Ga., 225
de la Peña, Carolyn, 206
Deacon, Betty, 269
Decatur, Ala., 180
Deck, Stewart, 251
Dees, Morris, 93, 178–86, 193–96,
199n19

Deliverance, 76, 124
Delpar, Helen, 161
Deming, Clarence, 111
Democratic Party, 91, 150, 152, 159
desegregation, 208–9
Dexter Avenue King Memorial Baptist
Church, 177, 178, 183, 193
Dillon, James, 151
Dillon, S.C., 70
Dillon County, S.C., 91, 150–61
Dillon Herald, 155, 157, 158, 159
Diner, Hasia, 209
Dinerstein, Joel, 248–49
Disney World, 191
Disneyland, 187
Dix, Dorothy, 213
Dixiecrats, 153
Douglass, Frederick, 103, 268
Douglass, S. D., 111
Doyle, Margaret, 269
Dukes of Hazzard, 69
Dull, Henrietta Stanley, 210–11
Dunbar, Paul Laurence, 220
Durham, N.C., 240
Durr, Virginia Foster, 182

Ebony, 220
Ebsen, Buddy, 132
Edgar, Walter, 152, 155, 157
Edge, John T., 209
Edmund Pettus Bridge, 187
Egerton, John, 236
Eisenberg, Wes, 251
Eisenhower, Dwight, 71, 156
Eisner, Michael, 199n19
Ellington, Duke, 249
Emancipation Proclamation, 103–4,
211
Ephron, Nora, 254
Eskew, Glen, 92
Eureka Springs, Ark., 142
Eyes on the Prize, 184, 187, 195

Faces in the Water, 194
Falkner, Murry, 217

Schafer, Wilhelmina, 151
Seaton, Bruce, 134–35
Second World War, 71, 89, 150, 223, 269, 278
segregation, 96, 157, 179
Selma, Ala., 179, 187
Shanks, S. C., 105–6
Short, Dewey, 128–29
Siegelman, Don, 191
sight, 244, 246–47, 252, 254, 263n58
Silber, Nina, 78–79
Silver Dollar City, 121, 132, 134
Sixteenth Street Baptist Church, 179
slavery, 92, 100, 166, 211, 266, 268
Smith, Lillian, 215–16
Smith, Terry E., 243, 251
Sombrero Tower, 148, 161, 166
South Carolina: Dillon, 70; Hamer, 154; Little Rock, 151, 153, 157; Myrtle Beach, 217–18, 226. *See also* Charleston, S.C.
South Carolina State College, 158
South Carolina Supreme Court, 160
South of the Border, 70, 90, 91–92, 148–68. *See also* Pedro; Sombrero Tower
Southeast Baptist District Association of the Arkansas Delta, 100–101
Southern Baptist Convention, 207
Southern Christian Leadership Conference, 198n11
Southern Foodways Alliance, 206, 209
Southern Independence Party, 209
Southern Literary Messenger, 86n42
Southern Living, 206
Southern Poverty Law Center, 179, 180–88, 193–96
Southwestern Christian Advocate, 101, 102, 103, 104, 108
Spillers, Earline, 223
Springfield, Mo., 126, 127, 137
Spurlock, Pearl, 120, 122
Stanonis, Anthony, 205, 262n39
states' rights, 80, 153

States' Rights Democratic Party, 153

Tabuchi, Shoji, 140–41
Talbott, Myrtle, 271
taste, 252, 253
Tax Reform Act (1976), 177
Teaching Tolerance, 186–87, 194, 195–96
Tennessee: Cookeville, 69; Memphis, 175; Nashville, 69, 237
Tennessee Valley Authority, 124
textile mills, 237, 242, 268, 269, 270
Thompson, E. P., 89, 235
Thomson, Ga., 234
Thurmond, J. Strom, 153, 155
Tillman, Katherine Davis, 108
Till-Mobley, Mamie, 191
tourism: association of, with shops, 70, 74; and civil rights movement, 92, 187, 193; and the culinary, 214–15, 217–18, 275; and heritage, 178, 187–88, 196, 199n19, 267, 282
trickster, 122–23, 126, 134, 143
Troy, Ala., 189
Troy State University, 188, 191, 193
truck stops, 70, 148
Tuan, Yi-Fu, 162
Turner, Patricia, 219
Turner, Victor, 122
Tuscaloosa, Ala., 246

Ulrich, Laurel Thatcher, 10
U.S. National Parks Service, 176, 187
U.S. Patent Office, 70
U.S. Supreme Court, 153, 156, 226

Voting Rights Act (1964), 187

Wall of Tolerance, 193–94, 195–96
Wallace, George, 183
Wal-Mart, 134, 207
Washington, Booker T., 90, 99, 258n9
Washington Post, 161, 249, 270